STRATEGIES, TIPS, AND ACTIVITIES FOR THE EFFECTIVE BAND DIRECTOR

Strategies, Tips, and Activities for the Effective Band Director: Targeting Student Engagement and Comprehension is a resourceful collection of highly effective teaching strategies, solutions, and activities for band directors. Chapters are aligned to cover common topics, presenting several practical lesson ideas for each topic. In most cases, each pedagogical suggestion is supported by excerpts from standard concert band literature. Topics covered include:

- score study shortcuts;
- curriculum development;
- percussion section management;
- group and individual intonation;
- effective rehearsal strategies;
- and much more!

This collection of specific concepts, ideas, and reproducible pedagogical methods—not unlike short lesson plans—can be used easily and immediately. Ideal for band directors of students at all levels, *Strategies, Tips, and Activities for the Effective Band Director* is the product of more than three decades of experience, presenting innovative approaches, as well as strategies that have been borrowed, revised, and adapted from scores of successful teachers and clinicians.

Robin Linaberry is the retired Director of Bands at Maine-Endwell Senior High School in Endwell, NY, and has held adjunct conducting/teaching positions at Binghamton University, Ithaca College, and SUNY Broome Community College.

STRATEGIES, TIPS, AND ACTIVITIES FOR THE EFFECTIVE BAND DIRECTOR

Targeting Student Engagement and Comprehension

Robin Linaberry

Routledge
Taylor & Francis Group
NEW YORK AND LONDON

First published 2021
by Routledge
605 Third Avenue, New York, NY 10158

and by Routledge
2 Park Square, Milton Park, Abingdon, Oxon, OX14 4RN

Routledge is an imprint of the Taylor & Francis Group, an informa business

© 2021 Taylor & Francis

The right of Robin Linaberry to be identified as author of this work has been asserted by him in accordance with sections 77 and 78 of the Copyright, Designs and Patents Act 1988.

All rights reserved. No part of this book may be reprinted or reproduced or utilized in any form or by any electronic, mechanical, or other means, now known or hereafter invented, including photocopying and recording, or in any information storage or retrieval system, without permission in writing from the publishers.

Trademark notice: Product or corporate names may be trademarks or registered trademarks, and are used only for identification and explanation without intent to infringe.

Library of Congress Cataloging-in-Publication Data
Names: Linaberry, Robin, author.
Title: Strategies, tips, and activities for the effective band director : targeting student engagement and comprehension / Robin Linaberry.
Description: New York : Routledge, 2021. | Includes bibliographical references and index.
Identifiers: LCCN 2020046947 (print) | LCCN 2020046948 (ebook) | ISBN 9780367472191 (hardback) | ISBN 9780367472184 (paperback) | ISBN 9781003034193 (ebook)
Subjects: LCSH: Bands (Music)—Instruction and study.
Classification: LCC MT733 .L55 2021 (print) | LCC MT733 (ebook) | DDC 784.092—dc23
LC record available at https://lccn.loc.gov/2020046947
LC ebook record available at https://lccn.loc.gov/2020046948

ISBN: 978-0-367-47219-1 (hbk)
ISBN: 978-0-367-47218-4 (pbk)
ISBN: 978-1-003-03419-3 (ebk)

Typeset in Sabon
by Apex CoVantage, LLC

Access the companion website: www.robinlinaberrymusic.com

CONTENTS

Detailed Contents — vii
List of Figures and Musical Examples — xi
List of Resources — xiv
Preface — xvi
Acknowledgments — xx

1 Introduction: The "Why" of This Book — 1

2 Score Study — 5

3 Warm-Ups and More — 33

4 On the Sound: Tone Quality, Blend, Dynamics, Ensemble Balance, and Articulations — 57

5 Intonation and Tuning — 77

6 Rhythm, Meter, and Tempo — 97

7 Percussion — 128

8 In the Rehearsal — 149

9 The "Intangibles" — 174

10 Wrap-Up — 188

11 The School Marching Band Program — 202
  CHRISTIAN CARICHNER

12 Conducting the School Jazz Ensemble — 214
  DANIEL FABRICIUS

About the Contributors — 231
Index — 233

DETAILED CONTENTS

List of Figures and Musical Examples   xi
List of Resources   xiv
Preface   xvi
Acknowledgments   xx

1 Introduction: The "Why" of This Book   1
On the Foundation of the Band Director's Education 1
On the Relevance of Visual Problems, Processing Disorders, and More: What We Know from Other Classrooms 2
The Band Director as Alchemist: Turning Our Observations into Action 2
How This Book Can Help You 3
How This Book Can Help Your Students 3
How and Why to Proceed 4

2 Score Study   5
Introduction 5
Section 1: "Conventional Wisdom" Reviewed 5
Section 2: Tools-of-the-Trade 6
Section 3: Efficiency Strategies for Personal Study 7
Section 4: The Score vs. the Parts 25
Section 5: The Score at the Root of the Curriculum 27
Concluding Thoughts 32

3 Warm-Ups and More   33
Introduction: The Nature of Warm-Ups 33
A Concise Overview of Some Warm-Up Categories 33
Section 1: More Ideas on the Circle of 4ths 36
Section 2: To Keep the Percussion Section Active 40
Section 3: Some Scale Games 41
Section 4: Chorales from the Band's Literature 44
Section 5: Exercises Based on Important Rhythms 47
Section 6: Exercises to Teach by Rote 49
Section 7: Additional Strategies 52
Concluding Notes about Warm-Ups and Chorales 55

4 On the Sound: Tone Quality, Blend, Dynamics, Ensemble Balance, and Articulations   57
Introduction 57
Section 1: Building the Concept of Tone 57
Section 2: Blend in the Ensemble 62
Section 3: Dynamics and Balance in the Ensemble 64
Section 4: Articulation in the Ensemble 68
Section 5: Conclusion and Springboard 75

5 Intonation and Tuning   77
Introduction: Using the Tuner 77
Section 1: Hearing Intonation 77
Section 2: Teaching Intonation—Individuals and Smaller Groups 78
Section 3: Teaching Intonation in the Full Band 82
Section 4: Even More Strategies to Improve Intonation 91
Conclusion: Final Thoughts about Intonation in Your Teaching 95

6 Rhythm, Meter, and Tempo   97
Introduction 97
Section 1: Building the Concept of Pulse for Rhythm 97
Section 2: Rhythm in the Ensemble—Exercises, Strategies, and Games 99
Section 3: A Buffet of Quick-Fix Strategies 122
In Conclusion 126

7 Percussion   128
Introduction 128
Section 1: From the Podium—The Director's Duties and Influence 129
Section 2: In the Bandroom—The Students' Environment 136
Section 3: In Lessons and Sectionals 140
Section 4: More from the Podium—Rehearsals and Performances 143
Final Words About Extra Obligations of the "Non-percussionist" Director 146

8 In the Rehearsal   149
Section 1: From the Podium 149
Section 2: More on the Rehearsal Environment 150
Section 3: General Rehearsal Methods—The Big Picture 152
Section 4: Rehearsal Strategies 155
  Part 1: Student-Centered Learning 155
  Part 2: The Director's Style, Delivery, and Choices 158
  Part 3: Discovering Errors and Determining a Response 161
  Part 4: Games and Diversions 170
Section 5: Additional Quick-Fix Tips 172
Final Words About "The Rehearsal" 173

9 The "Intangibles"   174
Introduction 174
Section 1: On Principles of Artistry, Phrasing, and Interpretation 174
Section 2: Making Logical Connections to Speech and Reading 176
Section 3: Additional Instructional Pathways to Musical Artistry 179

DETAILED CONTENTS

Section 4: Tying It All Together 183
Section 5: The Power of the It-Factor 185

10 Wrap-Up — 188
Section 1: Curriculum Matters 188
Section 2: Organization Matters 192
Section 3: Leadership Matters 194
Section 4: Competition Matters 195
Section 5: Other Matters 197
Section 6: Your Influence Matters 199

11 The School Marching Band Program — 202
CHRISTIAN CARICHNER

Development of a New Marching Program 202
Substitutions and Mini-Recruiting 203
Assembling a Show as a One-Person Team 203
Quick-Fix Strategies 205
Managing the Other Elements of a Marching Band Program 208

12 Conducting the School Jazz Ensemble — 214
DANIEL FABRICIUS

Jazz Ensemble Instrumentation 214
Literature Selection 215
Performance and Rehearsal Setups 216
Understanding Jazz Styles 217
Common "Rhythmic Grooves" Found in Jazz 220
Teaching Jazz Improvisation to Soloists 220
Jazz Ensemble Rehearsal Strategies 221
The Role of Each Jazz Ensemble Player 224
Secrets of the Rhythm Section 226
The Role of the Conductor 230

About the Contributors — 231
Index — 233

FIGURES AND MUSICAL EXAMPLES

1.1	Some pedagogical pathways	3
2.1	16-measure rest during 10-measure groupings	8
2.2	Rest-groupings above staff	8
2.3	*Centurion*—page turn problem	9
2.4	System dividers with separation penciled in	9
2.5	*Epinicion* by John Paulson, score p. 5	10
2.6	*Epinicion* by John Paulson, partial m. 27	11
2.7	*Voodoo* by Dan Bukvich, score p. 4	12
2.8	*Havendance* by David Holsinger, score p. 6 (partial)	13
2.9	*Via La Acadia* by Kristen Gilbert	14
2.10	Page 1 of Grainger's "blind eye score" for *Marching Song of Democracy*	15
2.11	Overture to *Colas Breugnon* by Kabalevsky/Hunsberger, Reh. #9	16
2.12	Overture to *Colas Breugnon* including the accompaniment parts	16
2.13	*Jubilation* by Kristen Gilbert	17
2.14	*Sedona* by Steven Reineke, mm. 20–22	18
2.15	*Declaration* Overture by Claude T. Smith	19
2.16	*Emperata* Overture by Claude T. Smith: fugue subject entrances aligned	20
2.17	Markings for repeating figures	21
2.18	*Spitfire!* by Gary Gilroy, alto sax mm. 139–143	22
2.19	*Spitfire!* by Gary Gilroy, selected instruments, mm. 138–145	23
2.20	Blueprint of a musical form	24
2.21	Examples of notation abbreviations	26
2.22	*A Yorkshire Overture* by Phillip Sparke, flute part p. 2	27
2.23	*River of Life* by Steven Reineke: examples of augmentation/diminution	29
2.24	*Fate of the Gods* by Steven Reineke: an enjoyable passage as motivation to practice	31
2.25	*Eternal Father, Strong to Save* by Claude T. Smith: technical challenges	31
3.1	Jamey Aebersold's "Cycle of Fourths" graphic	37
3.2	Ed Lisk's "Circle of 4ths" graphic	38
3.3	"Circle of Keys" graphic, from "Key Sequences: Warm-Ups for Band"	38
3.4	Partial scale figures	39
3.5	Partial scale figures	39
3.6	Full scale figure	39
3.7	Scales in canon during the warm-up: two versions	42
3.8	An expanding scale figure	43
3.9	A rhythmic "build-a-scale" setting	44
3.10	The rhythmic scale setting also supports other meters	44
3.11	Rhythmic augmentation to create a Chorale	45
3.12	*Spartan Proclamation* (Linaberry)	46
3.13	*Spartan Proclamation* transformed to a Chorale	47
3.14	Examples of structures created to support a specific meter (7/8)	48
3.15	Looping a targeted rhythmic figure using a scale	48

3.16	A specific exercise created to support *Armenian Dances Pt. 1*	48
3.17	A specific unison figure designed to support "Cool"	49
3.18	Call-and-response to gradually assemble a problematic figure	49
3.19	Instant Chorale: Solfege method	50
3.20	Curwen hand signals for duets	51
3.21	Targeted warm-up example	51
3.22	Using hocket techniques in a warm-up design	52
3.23	*Klangfarben chords* in 4-part assignments (suggestions)	53
3.24	*Klangfarbenmelodie* on a simple scale (ideas)	54
3.25	Review: three scales from the Circle to hear parallel vertical chords	55
3.26	Using two key signatures on the same notated music	55
4.1	SATB pyramid	58
4.2	Ed Lisk's *Circle of 4ths* graphic	58
4.3	*Crescendo* marking with "flare"	65
4.4	Arrival–departure chart v1	67
4.5	Arrival–departure chart, v2 for conducting motions	67
4.6	Frequently misunderstood articulation markings	70
4.7	Articulations: we hear … let's try …	70
4.8	Articulation track: envelope graph	73
4.9	Pictorial comparison of common articulations	74
5.1	Scale with a single-pitch drone	79
5.2	Pattern for tuning over a perfect 5th drone	79
5.3	Scales and arpeggios over a perfect 5th drone	80
5.4	Flute with drone: "Three Blind Mice"	80
5.5	D major scale to tune trumpet 3rd valve slide	80
5.6	F major scale to tune the trombonist's upper F	81
5.7	A sustained tonic as a tuning target	81
5.8	Sustaining a target for a "problem" pitch	81
5.9	Using a piano to spot-check a problem pitch	82
5.10	Unisons and octaves to tune during a scale-in-canon	86
5.11	The "Remington"	86
5.12	A "math equation" strategy: maj–min–dim–maj	87
5.13	Create a chord from an ensemble scale	87
5.14	Tuning by reduction	90
5.15	Intonation map graphic example	93
5.16	Tuning arrow markings for out-of-tune pitches	94
5.17	Alternate fingering choices based on the harmonic series	95
6.1	Speak while walking in steady pulse: subdivisions	99
6.2	Counting game with subdivision	99
6.3	Fill in the missing subdivisions	100
6.4	Subdivisions with sound and silence	101
6.5	Subdivided Fill and bopping	101
6.6	Basic bopping exercise for rhythm	102
6.7	Adding sustain to the bopping technique	103
6.8	Dotted quarter–eighth note for clapping	104
6.9	Dotted quarter–eighth clapping chart	104
6.10	A rhythmic "chunking" process	106
6.11	Pairing correct with incorrect	106
6.12	Fill the gaps	107
6.13	Remove the tie	107
6.14	Deconstruct to reconstruct	108
6.15	One rhythm, many locations	109
6.16	Syncopated figure in altered locations	112

FIGURES AND MUSICAL EXAMPLES

6.17	Extended syncopations: two notated versions	113
6.18	Written rhythm and sounded approximation	113
6.19	Move the rhythm to correct its precision	114
6.20	Notation for counting systems debriefed	115
6.21	Syllables and "lyrics" in rhythmic counting	115
6.22	Rhythmic "homonyms"	117
6.23	The "compound" rhythm tree	119
6.24	Pictorial meter signature	119
6.25	Rhythmic homonyms: simple to compound	120
6.26	Note direction notation pictures	121
6.27	Three layers of a rhythm	122
6.28	Counting, ticks, and marks: *Lights Out* by Alex Shapiro	123
6.29	Composite rhythm strategy: *Fanfare Ritmico* by Jennifer Higdon	124
6.30	Adding sounds to help with offbeats	126
7.1	Sample part-assignments chart excerpt	135
7.2	Excerpt from "Rudiments Inventory"	143
8.1	To keep organized planning notes during the rehearsal	162
8.2	*Dakota Fanfare* by Erik Morales	163
8.3	Modifications examples: *October Colors*	164
8.4	Modifications part 1: *Fate of the Gods*, clarinet	165
8.5	Modifications part 2: *Eternal Father, Strong To Save*, bassoon	165
8.6	Chart: play–rest overlapping	167
9.1	Chart: making musical connections to speech, writing, and reading	177
9.2	Chorale line without markings	179
9.3	Chorale line with expressive markings added	180
11.1	Subdivision of the foot-shape	207
11.2	Band, horns are Up!	208
12.1	Swing style example	217
12.2	Jazz rhythm rules: examples	218
12.3	Common "cliché" rhythms in swing	219
12.4	Jazz effects	219
12.5	Jazz ensemble warm-up: long tones	222
12.6	Jazz ensemble warm-up: three-note melody in swing style	223

RESOURCES

The following documents can be accessed via the companion website:
www.robinlinaberrymusic.com

Chapter 2

RW2.1 Vocabulary and skills lists: a guidesheet for repertoire

Chapter 3

RW3.1 Linaberry's Circle of Keys document
RW3.2 Widely programmed chorales, ballads and other lyrical compositions
RW3.3 Well-known works with beautiful lyrical sections

Chapter 5

RW5.1 Detailed description of tuning (electric bass) via harmonics
RW5.2 "Tuning by the Numbers"
RW5.3 Randomness strategies for tuning

Chapter 7

RW7.1 Percussion assignments, part I: preparatory work by the director
RW7.2 "Students' Self-Analysis"
RW7.3 "Percussionists' Track—Setting up the Lessons"
RW7.4 "Percussion Assignments—1st Task—September"
RW7.5 "Self-Assignment Guidelines"
RW7.6 Percussion assignments worksheet
RW7.7 For a sample "Master Percussion Assignments Chart"
RW7.8 "Personal Folder Assignments Guide"
RW7.9 "Bandroom Hacks and Shortcuts"
RW7.10 "Percussion List for Trips"
RW7.11 Section responsibilities chart
RW7.12 "Percussion 21"
RW7.13 Rudiments inventory

Chapter 8

RW8.1 Sample listing of band officer positions
RW8.2 Goals-based sectionals guide
RW8.3 Help-sheet for ensemble instrumentalists
RW8.4 An organizer/study guide

RW8.5   Listening guide for specific repertoire
RW8.6   Listening guide for guest performers
RW8.7   The great dartboard challenge

Chapter 9

RW9.1   Scripted lesson plan for "I Thought You Would Drive Your Car To Chicago"
RW9.2   List of suggested pieces for prism concerts

Chapter 10

RW10.1   Discussion of the Watkins-Farnum performance scale
RW10.2   Personalized goals sheets
RW10.3   PACE information
RW10.4   Sample rubrics and grading policy documents
RW10.5   Equipment/Responsibilities list for trips
RW10.6   Repair Self-Assessment Form
RW10.7   100 personalized lesson reminders in under two minutes
RW10.8   Sample "Officer Positions" document
RW10.9   "The Great Exchange"
RW10.10 Rubric Samples and Audition Sheets
         A "quick and easy" scoresheet
         A standard basic rubric for instrumental music
         A weighted scoresheet
         An innovative rubric allowing effective comparison when students have self-selected music at different levels of difficulty
RW10.11 Honors credit prototype
RW10.12 "Quotes on Music Education"
RW10.13 Sample band handbook

PREFACE

I enjoyed my undergraduate experience immensely. I paid careful attention to outstanding teachers, worked hard, seized every opportunity, and managed to stay at the top of my class. I entered the work force, eager and well prepared (I thought) to make a change in the world. I'd still like to think I did quite well. And then started a long series of career-shaping events:

- I accompanied my students to their All-State experiences, where I listened to a group of total strangers transform into a cohesive artistic marvel.
- I joined the local "band directors" band, and played under an eloquent volunteer conductor who could signal a cutoff, say exactly what was necessary—no more, no less—and restart the band for us all to hear our very obvious improvements.
- I played as a contracted local musician in *The Ice Capades*, *Ringling Brothers/Barnum and Bailey Circus*, and other traveling groups; each time, the director would lead a single one-hour rehearsal, and yet the group would be fully prepared for a run of thirteen shows, each lasting 140 minutes of almost non-stop playing.

The common denominator in every outstanding experience was the effectiveness of the director. A group's collective excellence was made possible through the guiding influence of a special individual—*and I noticed*. Each observation inspired me to learn more, so I began to collect and imitate those successful strategies. Specifically, I watched guest conductors and clinicians with a keener eye. I adapted methods to suit my needs, and—because some activities seem to yield results more easily—I was further inspired to create more of my own. I soon found a niche, I suppose—I was fortunate to work often as the guest conductor, feeling both the stress and joy of using those strategies to help students toward a great performance when time is short. Certain time-bound experiences (honor bands, summer programs, band camps, and the like) share a compressed version of the daily challenge of teaching through disruptions; that is, *the performance is coming, and the clock is ticking*.

The goal of this project, quite simply, is to share strategies with others. Experienced band directors usually develop pedagogical processes to meet all situations, in time. And we eventually discover preferences, finding that one way of presenting a lesson is more effective than other strategies. We all become better—and our students therefore have a better experience—when we know just what to do in those problematic teaching situations where a "solution" can be very elusive:

- How can I study the scores well enough to be an effective conductor? *I'm too busy!*
- How *exactly* do I teach students to be better in tune? *Most of these players don't seem to hear the faulty intonation at all.*
- Is there a way to teach my large band to deliver an emotional interpretation? *These students are pretty good, technically, but they sure don't show much artistry on their own.*
- How can I keep *everyone* engaged? *Some students in the band are virtuosos, ready for the recital stage, while others can barely remember the fingerings for basic notes.*
- And, "Good Lord, what do I do with those drummers?!!"

PREFACE

To answer these questions and hundreds like them, turn to this collection of specific concepts, ideas, and reproducible pedagogical strategies—sometimes like mini lesson plans—that can be used easily and immediately without further training. Many of these ideas are innovations of my own creation, while others have been borrowed, revised, and adapted from scores of successful teachers and clinicians observed over many years. But *all* of them can be highly effective to solve teaching problems and meet rehearsal goals.

The material included here represents a functional library of what I've found to be the most efficient teaching strategies, as well as those that have been the most well received by students. I offer this collection based on a longstanding personal observation: my own best-ever experiences at clinics and conferences have been those which provide me with exciting ideas, resources, and pedagogical techniques that I can immediately use to improve my own teaching. Or, "I can't wait to try that on Monday!"

Before discussing the organization, layout, and special features, you should know what is in your hands. *Is this the right book for you?*

This book is *not* . . .

- . . . "complete." That's not an indictment, however. It's just important to know this is not an all-encompassing stand-alone textbook for instrumental music education. This book is not focused on big-picture issues like budget, recruitment, working with administration, fundraising, and the like (although you'll find some pertinent materials). Nor does it address orchestra, modern band, or mariachi topics. I'll make plenty of references to other resources that offer greater depth on topics this book is not designed to address.
- . . . an edited reprint of others' opinions or essays. Those are wonderful reads, for sure, but are often a bit scattered in a less cohesive approach. This book puts its suggested processes and activities into groups, located in named chapters; if you need help building your group's steady pulse, there's a collection for that purpose.
- . . . tailored for beginner or early intermediate band instruction. Most of the great beginner books are designed to pair the "process" with the material. While I may firmly believe that teachers will find great ideas in this book for *every* level, I admit it's primarily designed to guide junior high, high school, college, and adult band directors.
- . . . a pedagogical sourcebook for each instrument, separately. There are no fingering charts within. While there *are* plenty of suggestions for the various woodwind, brass, and percussion instruments, other sources are better if your goal is to learning to teach bassoon.

Instead, let's examine the many ways this book will help you, now and into the latter years of your career.

This book *is* . . .

- . . . a great supplement to any chosen all-encompassing instrumental textbook.
- . . . conceived as a sourcebook of strategies, tips, and activities for the practicing band director, as the title suggests. The book addresses the topics most commonly encountered during the course of rehearsals and classes, including even "intangibles" like phrasing, emphasis, and interpretation. Teachers can choose which of the many included strategies will best match the situational need.
- . . . organized for *function*. With a quick view of the contents, you should notice that the layout easily transports you to chapters and topics addressing your needs. That systematic approach should help minimize the time you'll need to find (or re-visit) preferred material.
- . . . unusual in its special focus. Each chapter is conceived specifically to help teachers and students, rather than as a unit leading to a test. For example, the "score study" chapter bypasses typical form and analysis topics; instead, it highlights ways to use the score to design efficient teaching procedures.

PREFACE

- ... vetted and trustworthy. These are strategies that *work*. The materials here have stood the test of time; they've proven effective, and will continue to offer success. They are not trendy, nor are these activities strictly tied to technology. While blogs and online groups have become very fast sources of answers, this book arrives with extensive scrutiny by experienced, knowledgeable, and successful music educators.
- ... especially accommodating of the reader's *time constraints*. It is equally comfortable whether read in a single cover-to-cover session or as a series of 5-minute 'quick-fix' searches to specific problems.
- ... a *head start*. On the date I am writing this, we are entering the fifth month of a pandemic "standstill." Whenever schools resume, there will surely be considerable differences to band rehearsals, collegiate "lab school" practicums, and, of course, student-teaching. Much of the material in this book will help by simulating, or perhaps even replacing some of the lost or abbreviated experiences.
- ... a way to fill a noticeable void in collegiate study. Undergraduate programs simply do not have time to offer this experience-based material. Meanwhile, many graduate students transition immediately into Master's programs before entering the workforce. Therefore, even in the "advanced" courses, outstanding students will have missed the practical application of their textbook work. They frequently still need practical suggestions for how to engage and motivate their students, and specifically how to maximize the improvement of their bands. No textbook can replace the advantages garnered solely through experience—and yet here is a book that essentially puts "experience" into a large collection of manageable gift-wrapped packages.

And finally, this book is like a music education "buffet." Some of the material will be extremely palatable, while some of the recipes perhaps aren't on your diet. But these strategies aren't meant to replace your creativity, hard work, academic study or your inspired spontaneity. *Not at all*. Educators should enjoy the opportunity to take whatever they choose from this extensive spread.

On its Organization, Features, and Supplements

In its conception, this project was planned to be a personal notebook for my own teaching, mostly as a diary of sorts, listing descriptions of strategies when I found them to be particularly effective. My fear was that I would begin to forget some of my own best discoveries as I aged. My layout at that point was as much alphabetical as anything else, just to help me navigate the search through my own notes—articulation, balance, intonation, and so on. When I decided this would be a printed book, I needed a more logical presentation.

My decision was based in part on the opinions offered by early helpful expert reviewers. The final layout keeps the material organized, but in an order designed to align with the way it would be needed by, and encountered during, a standard rehearsal.

1. A very brief *introduction* further clarifies "why strategies are necessary."
2. *Score study* takes a less traditional view of score study, instead emphasizing an order that allows conductors to move from the initial music selection to "conducting the band effectively," as quickly as possible. It exposes pitfalls, and suggests unusual steps for ultimate efficiency. Further, it uncovers ways to utilize excerpts from the score in the design of warm-ups and further rehearsal processes.
3. The chapter on *warm-ups* (often the "bell-ringer" to the rehearsal session) reveals those connections to the score, but also attempts to be quite comprehensive, allowing the director to support imperative performance skills while avoiding mundaneness.
4. During the warm-up, directors will surely emphasize the "number one" obligation of any band, concentrating *on the sound*. This chapter addresses the ensemble's tone quality by first referencing its components, with strategic exercises designed to improve the beauty of the sound, for individuals and for the ensemble as a whole.
5. Good *intonation and tuning* is imperative of course, but cannot happen until after the warm-up, and is perhaps valueless until the tone quality is beautiful.

PREFACE

6. *Rhythm–Meter–Tempo* is necessarily one of the longer chapters. These topics lead the hierarchy of skills that "must be correct," but also there are inherent problems beyond performing a rhythm correctly: musicians must *read* rhythms, and should deliver them with fluency. This chapter alone offers well over one hundred bulleted ideas, processes, and functional rehearsal strategies to refine all aspects of the ensemble's rhythm.
7. *Percussion* is perhaps the most important poorly understood topic for a band director; while teaching percussion is a multi-faceted problem in itself, directors must be comfortable with a remarkable number of organizational and managerial tasks required if the percussionists are to excel. Suggestions are thoroughly detailed here.
8. The true focus of this book lies *in the rehearsal*, where the most effective directors will utilize an enormous collection of creative strategies to keep band members engaged.
9. *The intangibles* is a special chapter offering fun and unusual processes to support the notion that "artistry" *can* be taught.
10. Then we try to *wrap-up* with a brief look at just a few more of the vast number of topics important to the effectiveness of the band director's work.
11. The first of two auxiliary chapters, on *marching bands* (contributed by Christian Carichner), is a crash course on field shows, marching techniques, parading, and other aspects of marching within the band program.
12. Its sister chapter, on *jazz bands* (penned by Daniel Fabricius), offers expert information on instrumentation, literature selection, performance/rehearsal tips, and a variety of other information that will be invaluable, especially to directors who feel less confident teaching jazz.

You'll find a large number of charts, images, and musical examples throughout to illustrate topics from the text. I chose many of the musical examples to represent "standard repertoire" because I felt the pieces will more likely be available on readers' current library shelves. However, I also want to encourage readers to consider *diversity* in their literature selection. Try not to be forever bound by others' opinions; outstanding work is being produced by an ever-changing generation of gifted composers.

In addition, turn to the resources website to find dozens of sample full-length documents, including rubrics, policy templates, graphics, guides, games, and more. Most of these samples may be edited and adapted to your specific needs, and I remain committed to adding to this collection. Readers are invited to contact me to add to this growing collection of helpful resources. Of particular interest will be the "Bandroom Hacks and Shortcuts" file, which I believe will make every director's life just a bit easier.

A special note to university methods instructors: although you surely will already have a list of your most preferred strategies, this book will offer you the same flexibility of choice that it will provide to your students, and it can maximize the impact of your course(s) by providing hundreds of additional options within a manageable length and format. You'll encounter advice you've heard elsewhere, and perhaps some of these strategies are among your own favorites, but this book synthesizes numerous great examples into one location, which may be very helpful to your students.

Finally, with a great and growing collection of tools in our instructor's toolkit, and tricks in our magician's hat, if we're lucky enough to somehow keep the band experience enjoyable and inspirational for the students, I believe it's possible for readers to become like "magicians" of music education. The impact goes on, long after the end of the "trick." But we differ from magicians in that we don't conceal anything from our audience. All the secrets are revealed. Moreover, we work as a team with our students to share every aspect of this joyful endeavor with them. The real difference between m*agi*c and mu*si*c is, well, *us*.

Robin Linaberry
Owego, NY
July, 2020

ACKNOWLEDGMENTS

To Patricia Linaberry—my wife, best friend, and lifelong inspiration. I appreciate your exemplary love, patience, guidance, insights, and character beyond words. From you, I've learned everything that's important. I love you.

To Whitney Soltis and Chris Linaberry—for providing me with daily reminders that fatherhood is better than any other role. (But, thanks to Mckenna Rose Linaberry, grandfatherhood is looking great!)

To my mom, Phyllis—for giving me the first step and guiding every one after that.

To Michael L. Lurenz—for the tireless assistance with insightful editing, and for the gift of friendship.

To the *Influencers*, who all provided an important spark: Stephen P. McEuen, Donald A. Stanley, Dr. Mark Fonder, Edward Lisk, Arthur Carichner, and Dr. Elizabeth Peterson.

To the contributing authors, Christian Carichner (Iowa State University) and Daniel Fabricius (Binghamton University)—your expertise fills a special spot in this text and for your students.

To Kristen Gilbert, composer, and Craig Wagaman, graphic artist—for their kind and generous help with musical examples and image conversion.

To the team of anonymous reviewers—unknown specialists who guided this project expertly.

To the volunteer readers who generously gave time and outstanding suggestions leading to a host of improvements in this book: Kevin Bill, Kristen Gilbert, Tony Godoy, Gregory Harris, Jacquelin Kovacs, Jennifer Pham, Kristina Ruffo, Joel Smales, Collin Smith, Dr. Jay Stoltzfus, Lindsey Williams, Jessica Williamson, and David Yusko.

To the colleagues who influenced me daily, and to those who attended workshops and told me, "you should put this stuff in a book"—thank you (or, it's your fault!).

To the thousands of students and dozens of student teachers across the last four decades—for you, and with your help, this text proves that teachers matter.

And finally, to the Routledge staff, I owe my sincere gratitude for this opportunity, and for their guidance, insights, expertise, and especially patience with me throughout this extensive project. For these extraordinary professionals, somehow "thank you" seems not quite enough: Constance Ditzel, senior editor; Peter Sheehy, senior editorial assistant; Mhairi Bennett, production editorial manager; and Catherine Scarratt, production editor.

1

INTRODUCTION
The "Why" of This Book

On the Foundation of the Band Director's Education

The undergraduate conducting class often focuses on physical gestures, and on score study tasks necessary to guide the conductor's planning. Some courses include a "rehearsal techniques" component. But, to practice rehearsal techniques in the context of a college course, one must recognize that the ensemble is made up of peers in a music school. These are not adolescents in a fifth period rehearsal of a typical school band.

Of course, it's all a matter of time at the college level. Even for courses spanning two semesters, the syllabi will be filled with basic patterns in various meters, right- and left-hand functions, score tasks (e.g. reading, transposition, analysis, marking), repertoire study, and textbook readings. Then, we need hefty doses of "live practice" to apply cueing, interpretive movements, etc. ad infinitum. We learn to conduct the band, but perhaps not to *lead the band members* toward specific improvements. And in the brief span of four short years, we certainly cannot learn all that will be required to direct a successful, vibrant band program. We exit the undergraduate degree largely unprepared for the challenges ahead.

That's a generalization, of course.

But imagine how vital fault detection is to the successful music teacher. In most conducting courses, the identification of errors is not a tested objective—that competence was left for earlier aural skills classes. Perhaps this generalizes again, but to illustrate an important point: some imperative "band director" skills are beyond the scope of the four-year degree, and must be refined independently.

For example, error detection, though critically important, is but one small entry in the list of skills needing attention. Just ponder for a moment the kinds of skills demonstrated by the most successful band directors. Your list probably includes . . .

. . . understanding the score well enough to discover the technical issues facing each performer.
. . . a strong aural concept of what the band *should* sound like.
. . . the creativity to design warm-ups and rehearsal activities to sculpt the band's sound into the desired model.
. . . an acute awareness of balance, blend, and intonation concerns and, most importantly, a functional set of strategies designed to *improve* those issues.
. . . a command of rhythm, tempo, and style, and especially the skills to *teach* those topics, including the required reading skills.
. . . thorough knowledge of the performance techniques and inherent problems facing every section of the band's instrumentation, with special appreciation for the percussion section.
. . . a masterful control of instructional methods, from the choice of "perfectly effective strategies, perfectly timed," to the management of magnetic pacing that maintains students' attentiveness.
. . . effective communication, both verbal and otherwise.
. . . a recognizable poise—an "executive presence"—that draws the band members toward total engagement in the process.
. . . an astute cause-and-effect awareness of *all* components of the band's environment (the curriculum, grading/policies, organization, calendar, bandroom culture, and more), making every decision based on how the choice affects the band.

INTRODUCTION: THE "WHY" OF THIS BOOK

As readers can imagine, these are among many important skills that cannot be totally polished by a degree program alone. Sure, some gifted individuals seem to have more of these skills and aptitudes "built in." For others, it may be more difficult to reach fluency. But, for every reader, these are skills that will improve in time, with experience as a teacher.

So, reread the previous list. Add your entries to it. Now, contemplate *why* you feel those skills are important. It is likely that you have observed highly effective teachers/conductors who demonstrate skills from your list. You probably made notes (even just mental recollections) of specific strategies or phrases the conductors used. Those best-practice techniques used by your favorite influential teachers will do much to shape your own persona as a teacher.

But how do we build a working knowledge, learning to apply the best-practices for the best benefit of our students?

On the Relevance of Visual Problems, Processing Disorders, and More: What We Know from Other Classrooms

A child who is near-sighted (or far-sighted, or who has astigmatism) will do much better in life's activities with corrective lenses. Now he wears glasses and—voilá!—he has 20:20 vision! Of course, we know it's not always that simple. For a host of other visual problems and medical conditions of the eye, not to mention processing issues, the best remedies cannot be determined with an eye-chart exam. Fortunately, the medical profession has developed treatments.

Similarly, there's no prescription, like educational "contact lenses," that can ensure academic success for all students equally. Classroom teachers recognize the multitude of visual and neurological processing disorders. Then, they work carefully to design accommodations, personalized to address each student's unique needs and learning styles. The individualized approach is a powerful way to boost confidence, motivation, self-esteem, and overall success for each student.

Instrumental music teachers sometimes become very proficient with the right-or-wrong aspects of music (e.g. rhythms, fingerings, notes, articulations, markings), while forgetting that our students may also have learning deficiencies. Frustrations may result, not just for the students, but the directors as well because "The students just don't get it!" If we look more deeply, examining each student as an individual, we can then personalize the instruction to benefit the entire ensemble. Our problem, of course, is that the group may be very large; personalized accommodations, though warranted, are not always practical.

The Band Director as Alchemist: Turning Our Observations into Action

In terms of visual skills, we readily accept that some of our peers (our intellectual equals) may see "optical illusions" entirely differently than we do. In music instruction, we should consider that our students may have similar *auditory* difficulties, or at least "'differences." A year prior to this writing, a popular but divisive online question asked, "Is the voice saying 'Yanny' or 'Laurel'?" So, in our bands, what if our students simply hear things differently than we do? The visual and processing difficulties described previously are usually diagnosed before we ever meet our band students. Also, most of the processing and behavior conditions that could affect students' band activities have been documented. But for our work to be the most effective, we must recognize that some people just perceive sounds differently, and that musical cognition happens at different rates for all learners. This principle alone is enough reason for teachers to collect and utilize *several* effective strategies to teach each concept and musical skill. The student who still misunderstands after one or more teaching attempts will eventually find *something* that turns the lightbulb on.

So the critical questions for the band director remain, "How can I help *all* students, regardless of their aptitude, to learn the same concepts and achieve the same skills? And how can I inspire them *all* to work to the best of their abilities?"

We know that people learn in many ways. A person may think of him/herself primarily as a *visual learner* (or *auditory, verbal, physical, logical,* or some other less-recognized style). But no student is solely a single type of learner. Each person works best through a unique mixture of learning styles and, further, the students' learning styles tend to evolve and develop over time. The most effective way to reach the largest cross-section of students, therefore, might be with a *varied approach compiling an assortment of strategies.*

2

INTRODUCTION: THE "WHY" OF THIS BOOK

Figure 1.1 Some pedagogical pathways

How This Book Can Help You

Hopefully this is the reason you've elected to read these words: *a motivated and creative band director can never have too many educational strategies*. We share ideas with colleagues. We observe, borrow, and adapt from exceptional conductors, teachers, and clinicians. We read, practice, listen, and attend professional development sessions, always searching for more and better ways to teach music to our students. And even when we've amassed a great collection of methods, we will always benefit from additional ideas.

Readers may view this book much like a collection of *notes* scribed to detail effective teaching strategies, compiled after observing hundreds of teachers and conductors. Hopefully these strategies will spark new ideas to augment your own creativity. Adopt the content as your own, or just *adapt it* for your own style.

If you're already a seasoned teacher, this book will still offer you a generous collection of refreshing ideas. But if you're reading it in the earliest stages of your career, be advised: you'll be more successful, more efficient, and likely even more respected if you're *prepared*. In this case, "prepared" refers to something far beyond your collegiate coursework, or your musical performance skills—beyond what you learned during student-teaching or orientation sessions offered by your employer. Those elements are essential to your preparedness of course, but this reference is more akin to the "nature versus nurture" debate: be prepared to nurture your students' music experience not just with your instructional strategies, but also with the entire immersive atmosphere.

How This Book Can Help Your Students

Two easy questions can be catalysts for you to understand the influence your choices will have on the success of your students and your entire program:

1. What are your main goals for the program and for individual students?
2. Are your goals supported by everything you do, say, write, and design?

3

And an ethical follow-up question, of course, is: "How will I help each student develop a love of music along the way?"

How and Why to Proceed

At least some of our most effective work lies in *making the mundane less mundane*. According to neuroscientist David Eagleman, "Brains are in the business of gathering information and steering behavior appropriately. It doesn't matter whether consciousness is involved in the decision making. And most of the time, it's not."[1] We need to help students (and ourselves, for that matter) develop good habits. And to become firmly rooted, those habits require frequent repetition over time. Therefore, we should work to "disguise" tedious tasks by layering and embedding them in other more engaging activities.

An old proverb tells us, "The best time to plant a tree was twenty years ago. The second best time is today." So, start now to fill (or refill, or top off) your ever-growing instructional toolkit, starting with the following chapter, "Score Study," as you keep this philosophy in mind:

♮ If it works, keep it and use it.
♮ If it doesn't work, toss it and find something else.
♮ But if it *could* work with revisions, then the teacher is obligated to adapt.

Note

1 David Eagleman, *Incognito: The Secret Lives of the Brain* (New York: Vintage Books, a division of Random House, Inc., 2011), 5.

2

SCORE STUDY

Introduction

This chapter is dedicated to a less traditional view of score study. We have access elsewhere to thousands of pages of outstanding material by renowned contributors. Beyond our own classes, clinics, and observations, we can also refer to recordings, YouTube, and a growing library of detailed analyses of pieces we'll conduct.

Our obligations as band conductors/teachers are too numerous to list here; readers with even a single year of experience know that tasks and looming deadlines can keep us from doing the most thorough score study. Therefore, this material focuses more on the job of the *teacher*, rather than that of the *conductor*. Teachers can easily get bogged down with time-consuming harmonic analysis; while that is patently important, it's less essential than knowing how to help our players, and how to *lead* the ensemble through a piece, from beginning to end.

So, the emphasis here remains on strategies and time-saving activities in the category of score study and, consequently, rehearsal preparation. Again, let these suggestions represent only a jumping-off point to spur your further ideas.

Section 1: "Conventional Wisdom" Reviewed

- This ages-old advice is always a beacon:
    - Know the score so you can *look*—performers will look back.
    - Know the score so you can *listen*—listening clarifies your observations and guides your decisions.
    - Know the score so you can *interpret*—the best artistic product is possible only through an unbroken two-way stream of communication between the ensemble and its director. A face buried in the score disrupts that relationship.

- *Learn scores in multiple strategic sessions.* Design a checklist to organize your study sessions. Like a "hierarchy" of critical issues, list what you'll hope to learn with each new look. The first inspection might be a basic page-turning discovery mission for the simplest details, including general appearance, instrumentation, and labeling. Notice the road-map issues like page-turns and D.S. locations. This first look will also confirm that no pages are missing. Your list may include the following, in no special order, and more:

    - Rehearsal numbers/letters; measure numbers; movement-names.
    - An overview of form (a complete knowledge of form isn't necessary to start rehearsals), including main sections, transitions, modulations, and meter-changes.
    - Terms, tempo indicators, dynamics, fermatas, and other symbolic markings.
    - Meters and groupings, especially those influencing the conducting gestures.
    - Important cues and other details requiring the conductor's attention. Look especially for new entrances; players will appreciate your help after long rests.
    - "Teacher prep" concerns such as problem passages, alternate fingerings, trills, rhythmic challenges, solos, and other exposed parts.

- Phrases and phrase-lengths (to begin interpretive choices).
- Harmonic analysis (this can be ongoing; an incomplete analysis doesn't always hinder early rehearsals).
- Compositional techniques (detailed more in the following).
- Begin your score-marking decisions, although the study might never be complete!

- *Learn something from recordings.* Listen to several recordings. From multiple versions, you'll hear as many interpretations. You can compare as you begin to synthesize your own unique version, always staying true to the composer's intentions and stylistic traditions. You'll notice that some recordings are decidedly *not* outstanding. Flawed performances often help teachers by highlighting passages that will prove difficult.
- *Be a picture of the music.* Our best work requires that we *look like* the music in the score. To paraphrase Erich Leinsdorf from his *The Composer's Advocate*, the score is not the music.[1] Viewing the score as a blueprint—just a symbolic representation of *how to perform* the sound—we know that music itself only exists when we create it, which requires *modeling* from the teacher/conductor.
- *A strategy to develop your conducting as a "delivery" of the score.* Widely used by conducting teachers, this process became the author's perennial favorite for helping student-teachers. Compose a short pitchless passage having some of the common conducting challenges (i.e. meter-changes, interesting rhythms, anacruses, dynamic/tempo changes, fermatas). Practice conducting gestures that efficiently convey every marking. Then, engage a volunteer to clap or chant the unseen passage. Record the effort; the playback will reveal how closely the sound matches the notation. Frequent practice will support your band's performance through inspired, artistic conducting motions that *look like* the music.[2]

Section 2: Tools-of-the-Trade

- Score-marking conundrums:
  - *Don't over-mark the score.* While markings may be needed, there's also a limit. The more markings we add, the *less* likely we'll see and respond to them all.
  - *Let your score-markings be flexible.* They may even be temporary—to reflect changing needs of the ensemble, as well as your evolving interpretative ideas. You'll transform as a conductor; leave room for change when revisiting "known" scores.
- With these principles in mind, here are some recommended score-marking tools:
  - *Highlighter tape.* Apply and write on colored tape, which is removable without permanently affecting the score ("Finally, the 2nd trombones can make the entrance without my cue!").
  - *Paperclips, removable adhesive file-folder labels, Post-It® products.* With a wide variety of available options, these quick tools solve many problems:
    - identify groups of instruments (i.e. efficient visual shortcuts to melody, countermelody, accompaniment, bassline groups);
    - bind pages together when the ensemble needs a "cut," or when skipping movements;
    - bookmark locations for quick reference to a specific page; this efficient method protects scores from dog-eared pages;
    - pencil in plans and reflections exactly where needed; choose a larger sticky-note for a mini-plan or a checklist of rehearsal processes for the next session;
    - aid with page-turn problems (i.e. Coda or a D.S. sign on a distant page).
  - *A review of the obvious.* Remember that the best "score study" tools are at your disposal during the teaching sessions: a metronome, record-playback equipment, keyboard, pencils, notepad, manuscript paper, form diagrams, and other supportive documents/research.

Section 3: Efficiency Strategies for Personal Study

Knowledge gained through detailed traditional score study really has no shortcuts. However, some methods allow the busy teacher to reach a level of knowledge more quickly. This section offers specific strategies, putting one goal above others: these suggestions target time-saving efficiency. Many will still qualify as score-markings, meant to simplify the visual aspect of your study. Ultimately, these may improve your podium-time as well. TIP: While you may be conducting pieces from the library where you work, consider purchasing personal copies; your study, and markings, can then stay with you for life.

- *Full vs. condensed scores: The value of each.* For almost every purpose, a *full* score outperforms its *condensed* counterpart. The full score offers detailed information, with a view of every part, nearly always in the correct transposition. Many instrument-specific problems become "invisible" on the condensed score, where we might miss opportunities for helpful instruction regarding technical challenges and, thus, educational opportunities are lost.

    The full score is the "winner" in terms of some additional advantages:

    - it shows notation in correct octaves for each instrument, helpful for rehearsal decisions and feedback (e.g. for tuning problems, alternate fingerings);
    - the full score elucidates specific technical demands for each part, needed to design our instruction;
    - the full score clearly reveals best when an entrance-cue may be needed;
    - every percussion part is shown on the full score; this detail is crucial during rehearsals.

    Nonetheless, a band director might occasionally prefer a condensed score for the following reasons:

    - *concert-key simplicity.* No transposition is needed; realization at the piano is straightforward. It is remarkably quicker to identify vertical harmonies and non-harmonic tones from a concert-pitch score.
    - *ease of study.* The condensed format streamlines analysis of form, melody/harmony, use of motives, and more.
    - *brevity.* There are fewer page-turns, with more music on each page. Some conductors prefer to "Teach from the full score, but then conduct performances from the condensed score."
    - *educational advantages.* Condensed scores may simplify conversations with less-experienced musicians, whether in lessons, Music Theory class, or as a reference during mentoring.
    - *self-development strategies.* Condensed scores can help advance your own training, while double-checking your analysis. For example, from the full score, reduce a vertical structure to its basic closed position. Then, check your accuracy using the condensed score's already-reduced setting. TIP: Try alternating between full and condensed scores while you rehearse a passage. Then, close your eyes and conduct the passage once again. You may find that the acuity of your hearing differs with each pass, sometimes depending on the degree to which your visual senses contribute.
    - *adjudication options.* When viewing the condensed score, festival adjudicators often find it easier to comment on the band's overall sound (tuning, balance, artistic interpretation, and more) without distractions. However, choose the full score if you prefer to receive judges' specific commentary on instrumental technique, parts-balance in each section, percussion execution and other details.

- *Add and/or revise the rehearsal landmarks.* Rehearsal letters and numbers are usually aligned to the form. But not always. Compositions sometimes print rehearsal landmarks in convenience-groups, often of ten measures each. As the conductor, revising your students' parts with numbers at the start of a new phrase or section can yield greater efficiency in the rehearsals. The following are just some of the many reasons to alter rehearsal markers:

SCORE STUDY

- We frequently start a rehearsal-sequence at the beginning of a phrase, which won't align with the printed groups-of-ten numbering—*we lose time trying to describe the start-location to the ensemble.* "Letter J" is so much quicker.
- When asking band members to "count with me, 1–2–3–4–5 measures before 240," there will surely be players who miss the instruction, or who count incorrectly—*we lose time collecting lost players.*
- Even during rests, printed parts can be a source of conflict when the musician's aural phrase-length awareness isn't supported by the appearance of the page. For example, when an "easy" 16-measure rest is broken into parts by pre-printed rehearsal marks—*we may lose outstanding musicians from unnecessary counting errors* (see Figures 2.1 and 2.2).

Figure 2.1 The difficulty of counting a 16-measure rest when the rehearsal numbers use 10-measure groupings.

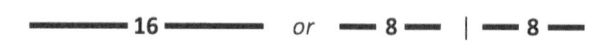

Figure 2.2 In this case, encourage players to revise the rests-grouping, and pencil it into the margin just above/below the staff as illustrated here.

Consider these common strategies for revising printed rehearsal markers:

- Pencil in all measure numbers. An instruction of, "let's begin at measure 242" becomes very easy.
- Pencil a new measure-number at the beginning of each line. This is a fast way to start the numbering process, and students can check each other for accuracy. After this start, additional numbers are completed later.
- For scores where, for example, "Letter B" begins a very long section, pencil in additional markers like B-1, B-2.
- For scores using only measure numbers, add rehearsal letters at key locations.

• *Markings for misaligned scores.* Our visual left-to-right tracking may become disoriented by alignment issues. Add marks as needed (e.g. draw a line across the open-page margin).
• *Page-turn markings.* If an important cue will be needed on the first measure of a new page, write the cue (or other important information) in the margin just before the page-turn. In the following score (Figure 2.3), notice that entire staves are missing (clarinets, tuba) until an entrance after long rests, where players may need your help. Add notes or markings as needed.
• *Special markings for special scores.* Scores sometimes have features that can contribute to visual confusion. Just a few common issues are detailed in the following.

Composers sometimes eliminate unnecessary staves to leave room for several staff-groups on the same page, each taking less vertical space. These staff groups are often separated only with double-slashes // (system dividers, separators). The separators are easily missed in crowded scores; choose a marking to assist your vision. Try adding a pencil marking to highlight the separation (Figure 2.4).

8

Figure 2.3 Centurion (Kristen Gilbert), mm. 11–19. Used with permission.

Figure 2.4 System dividers with separation penciled in.

An examination of the original full score to H. Owen Reed's masterwork *La Fiesta Mexicana* will show frequent instances of tightly squeezed print. Without adding pencil marks to separate staff-groups, Reed's score can provoke visual problems for the conductor.

Figure 2.5 shows the curved line penciled between the system-dividers; it provides increased visual ability to separate the staves.

Figure 2.5 Epinicion by John Paulson, score p. 5. Excerpts from "Epinicion" (B392) by John Paulson © 1975 Neil A. Kjos Music Company, San Diego, California. International copyright secured. All rights reserved. Reprinted with permission 2020.

Scores occasionally present challenges because of special notational procedures or unique features. Some use non-traditional symbols or aleatoric elements; others lack a meter signature entirely, relying instead on time-based text instructions for each motif or "event." Example: "Play and repeat this melodic fragment for twenty seconds, and then move to the next figure." Be prepared to add notes to clarify your conducting duties. Figure 2.6 shows repeated patterns, special notation symbols and conflicting tempo markings.

Figure 2.6 Epinicion (John Paulson), partial m. 27. Excerpts from "Epinicion" (B392) by John Paulson © 1975 Neil A. Kjos Music Company, San Diego, California. International copyright secured. All rights reserved. Reprinted with permission 2020.

Most non-traditional compositions include a key or chart to define their notational procedures. Still, the conductor may benefit from inventive markings to simplify the complications. Figure 2.7 uses primarily traditional notation mixed with the composer's own graphic symbols, but in an open-score format with ample white space.

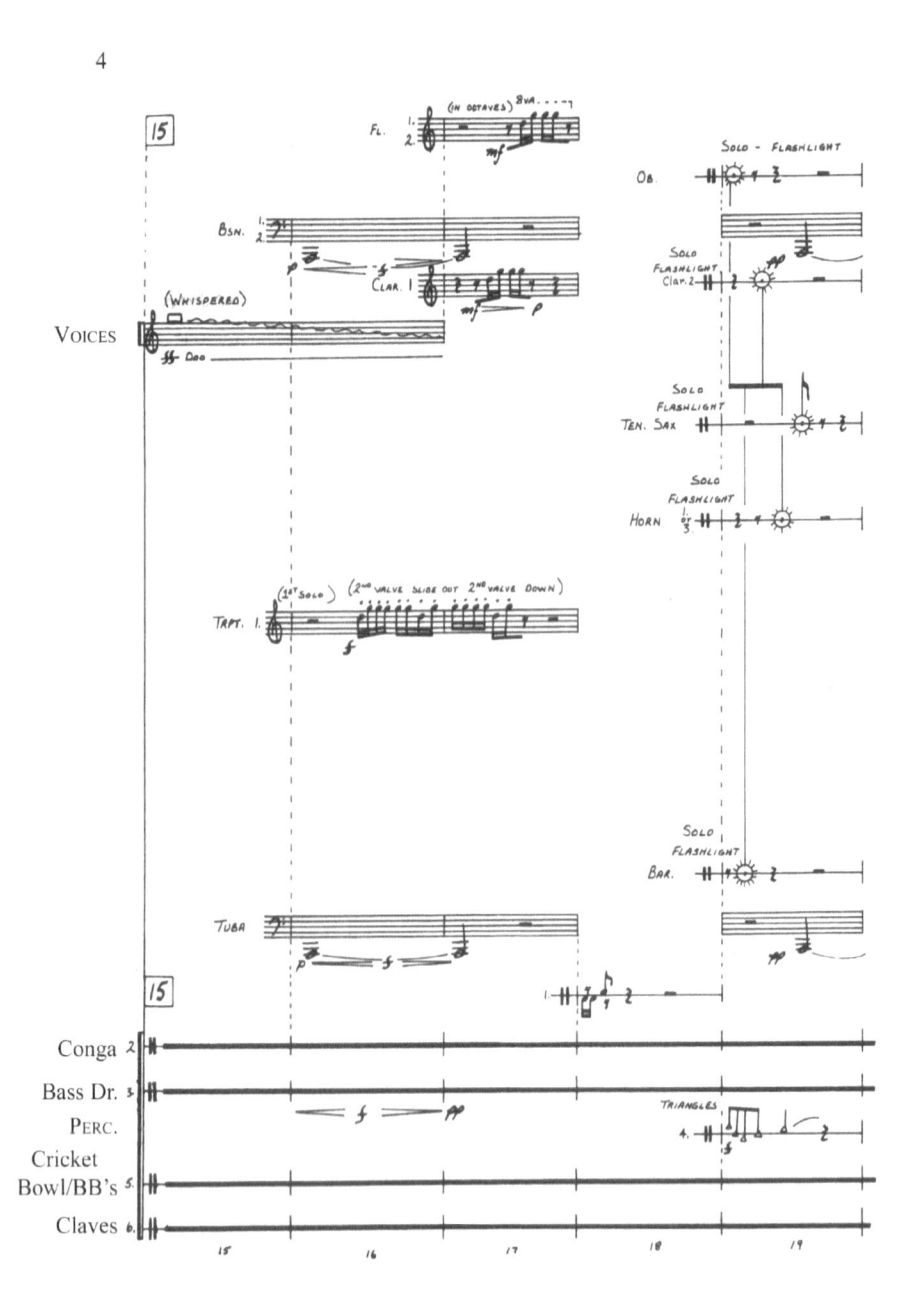

Figure 2.7 *Voodoo* (Dan Bukvich), score p. 4. Copyright assigned 1993 to Wingert-Jones Music Publications Inc., Kansas City, MO 64137. Used with permission.

Notice that measures, or even entire staves, are missing. This "cutaway" scoring practice can appear confusing at first; supplement the page with temporary labels or other innovative markings. We work as conductors to convey both verbal and gestural details to the performers succinctly and with the utmost clarity.

- *A special note about percussion markings.* It will prove very valuable to mark the names of instruments, or even students assigned to parts, into the score near percussion notation. Scores do not

SCORE STUDY

standardize the appearance and labeling of percussion. You'll appreciate your own markings to clarify instruments and players' names, when and where you need them.

- *Meter-change markings.* While the band probably won't fall apart from a poorly delivered dynamics gesture, a conductor who misses just *one* meter-change can cause an irreparable collapse. Compounding the difficulty, it is easy to overlook meter markings, especially when there are frequent changes. These standard suggestions can solve the more common problems:

    ▪ Superimpose large-size numbers to highlight meter-changes (Figure 2.8).

Figure 2.8 Havendance (David Holsinger) score, partial p. 6. Used with permission.

- Add pictorial assistance to clarify your conducting gestures. This practice is especially helpful for asymmetric groupings (Figure 2.9).

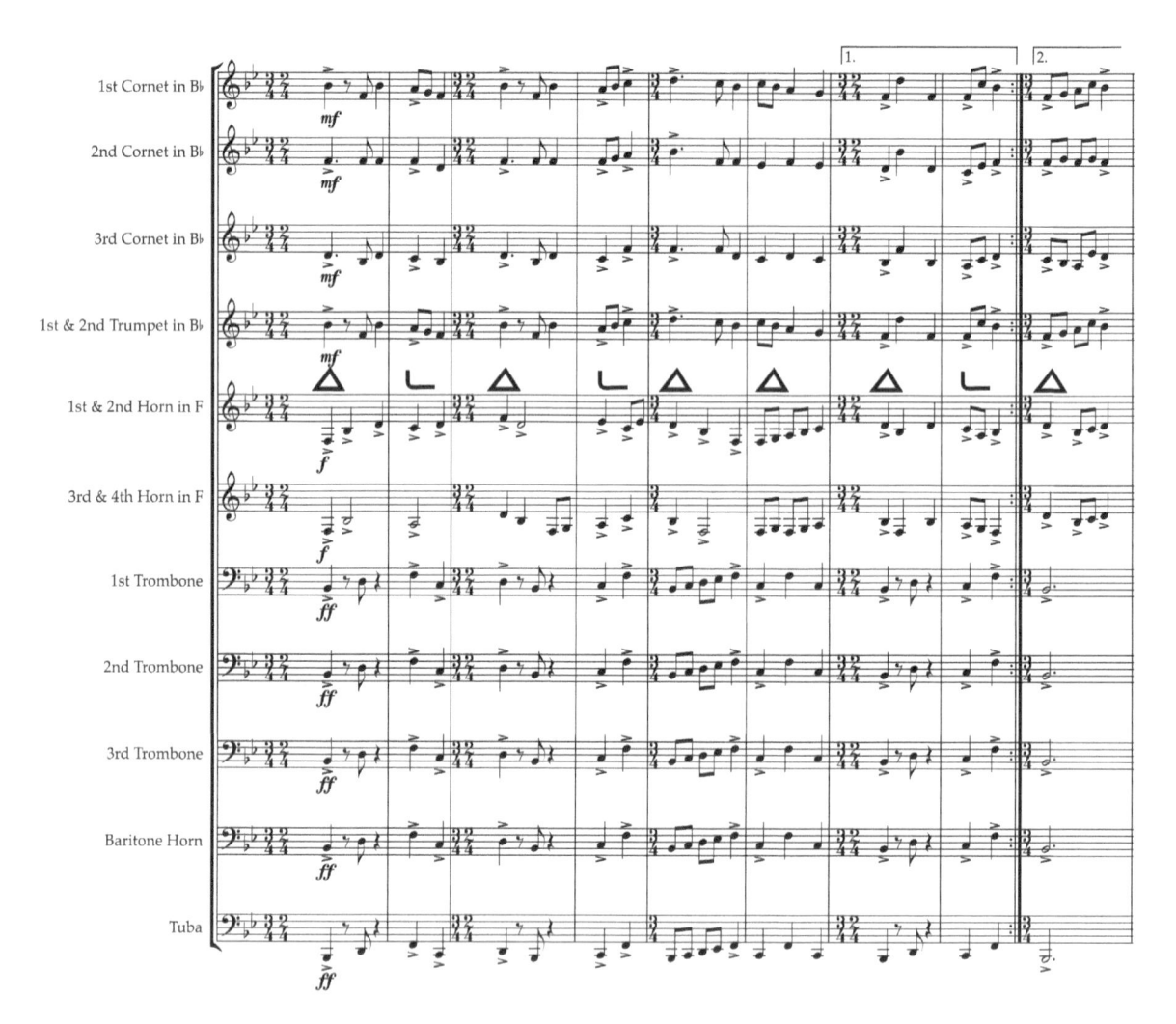

Figure 2.9 *Via La Acadia* (Kristen Gilbert). Used with permission.

- Create a simple blueprint for your conducting. Conductors can sometimes be overwhelmed by the stress of multiple cues and fast-paced meter-changes. Write your blueprint into the space above, below, or between staves. Or, like Percy Grainger sometimes did, draw a picture on a shopping bag!

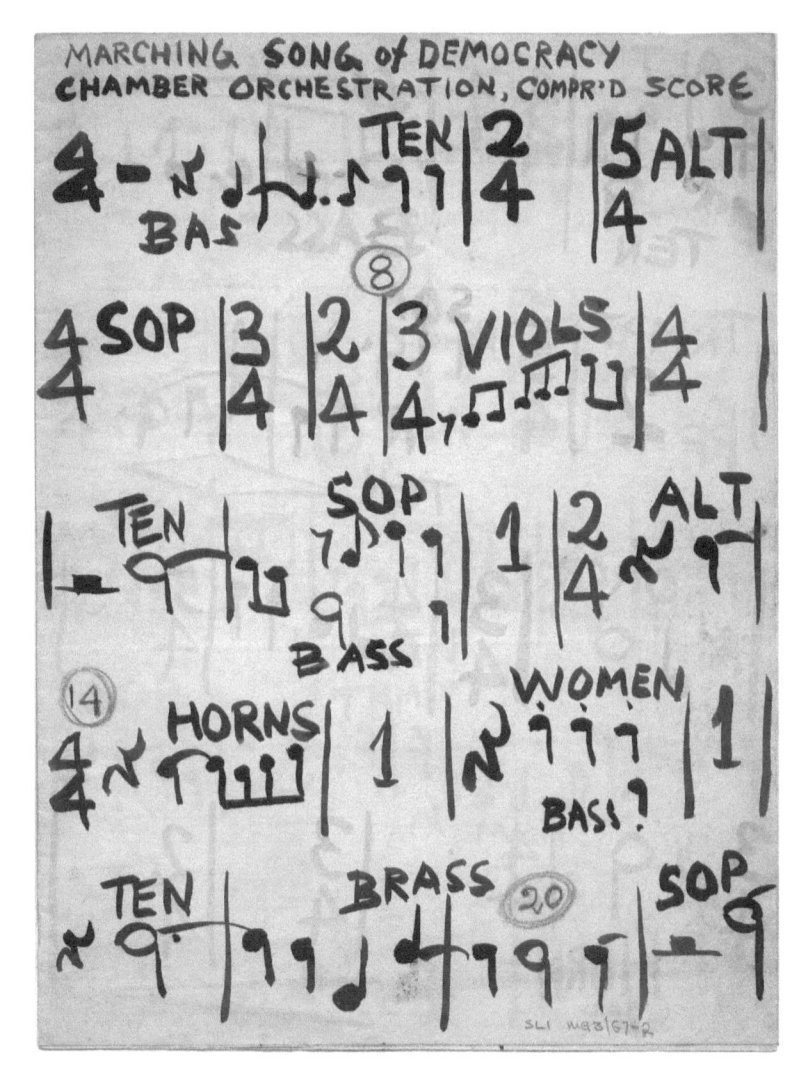

Figure 2.10 Used with permission: Page 1 of Percy Grainger's conductor's score for *Marching Song of Democracy*. No date. SLI MG3/57-2. Grainger Museum collection, University of Melbourne.

- *Write the number of measures in sections/phrases.* Most conductors can exude tremendous poise during standard time signatures without meter-changes, and especially in phrases of predictable 4- or 8-measure lengths. However, irregular phrase-lengths alone can disrupt the conductor's fluency even with no other significant challenges. And when combined with odd meters, meter-changes, and numerous cues, the irregular phrase-lengths can exacerbate problems.

  The conductor's principal obligation is sometimes simply to *keep going*, and of course—like other professionals—to "do no harm." A modest strategy is to identify the length of a phrase or excerpt, and then merely conduct that number of measures. As needed, write the number of measures in margins, or invent any graphic display to help maintain control. This kind of subtle visual "blueprint" can give us confidence to look away from the score, thus keeping eye-contact for the entire phrase. For example, because the Overture to *Colas Breugnon* is played "in one" at a brisk *Presto*, the printed notation of these odd-length phrases can confuse the players and conductor alike. Try adding brackets (or any graphic) to identify each phrase. A conductor could come to the conclusion shown in Figure 2.11 by examining the melody. But with further study, including the accompaniment parts, the same excerpt might indicate an alternative phrase-length design (Figure 2.12). Note how the accompaniment drives this conductor's choices differently.

Figure 2.11 Overture to *Colas Breugnon* by Dmitri Kabalevsky. Copyright © 1937 (renewed) by G. Schirmer, Inc. International copyright secured. All rights reserved. Used by permission.

Figure 2.12 Overture to *Colas Breugnon* by Dmitri Kabalevsky, including the accompaniment parts.

These comparative phrase diagrams are not to suggest that one is "correct" or even better than another. Rather, the illustration indicates that adding *markings* can dramatically improve conductors' confidence in complicated excerpts.

SCORE STUDY

- *The surprising challenge of asymmetric phrases.* Phrase structure can cause musical instability, even in compositions at a technically easier level. Bands will shape any phrase more securely when the conductor *looks like* the phrase, clearly modeling its beginning, peaks, ending, and style. Even in music with an easier appearance, score-markings may still help avoid uncomfortable errors. An iconic example occurs in the Overture to *Candide*, well known to a vast population of listeners. Several of its themes might trip the conductor because of phrase structure. One important excerpt—measures 47–61 in Walter Beeler's arrangement—is fifteen measures long, with a clever rhythmic twist in the twelfth bar. If distracted, the conductor risks missing the "big" prep, and the ensemble may crash on its *fortissimo* repeat. But these odd phrase-lengths are found in many compositions. Study scores for phrase-lengths and their implications on your conducting. The most successful conductor gives clear, stylistic cues to indicate new phrases; markings will improve the conductor's confidence to do so. Considering the challenges related to unexpected phrase-length, imagine the gesture needed to indicate the repeat in Figure 2.13.

Figure 2.13 Jubilation (Kristen Gilbert). Used with permission.

- *Scan scores vertically for rhythmic similarities.* Perhaps self-explanatory, this visual skill develops with practice. With a glance, we can sort the orchestration into groups based solely on rhythmic appearance. It's not necessary to do a harmonic analysis at this point, nor to solfege or otherwise practice the lines. Rather, this focus is to efficiently identify various components in the texture, and then use those groups in rehearsal processes. In Figure 2.14, with just a quick vertical scan, we can see that rhythms at measures 20–22 identify these groups:

  ✔ Melody—Fl, Ob, Cl, Tpt, Mall. 1.
  ✔ Bassline—St. Bs., Tuba, Euph.
  ✔ Rhythmic Chords—Trbs, supplemented by Perc.
  ✔ Countermelody/Descant —Horns, Alto Saxes.

SCORE STUDY

Figure 2.14 Sedona by Steven Reineke. © Birch Island Music Press. Used with permission.

- *Find lines for simultaneous rehearsal.* While studying a composition's form, search specifically for excerpts that could be combined to save rehearsal time. Figures 2.15 and 2.16 illustrate this basic concept (expanded later in Chapter 8). In Figure 2.15 the main theme is presented first by trumpets alone. It is then repeated in unison by a majority of players at rehearsal letter "A." This discovery allows directors to rehearse both groups at once, engaging a larger number of students while working on desired concepts concurrently.

Figure 2.15 Declaration Overture (Claude T. Smith). © Claude T. Smith Publications, Inc. Used with permission.

Figure 2.16 shows how several fugue subject entrances can be realigned to occupy the same space. With fugues, notice that combining a subject with its answer usually creates a line of parallel fourths/fifths which, in turn, can help ensembles develop better tuning (see Chapter 5).

Fugue SUBJECT entrances

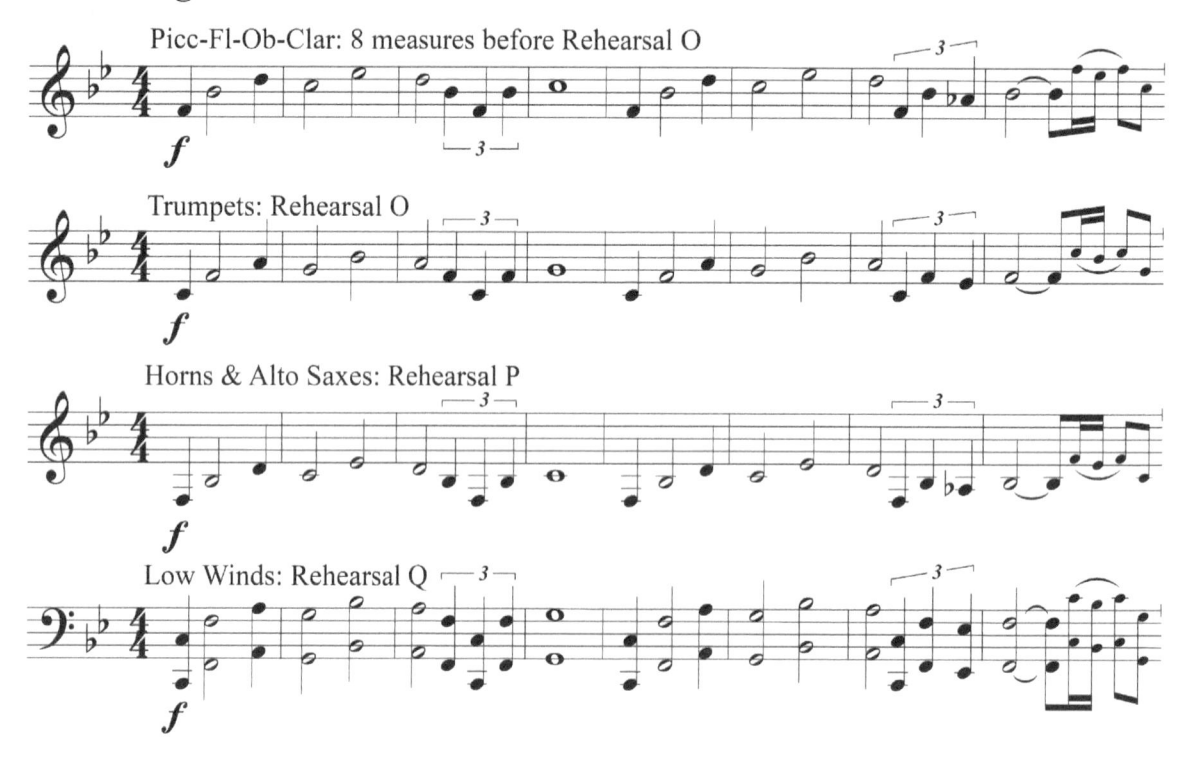

Figure 2.16 Emperata Overture (Claude T. Smith). © Claude T. Smith Publications, Inc. Used with permission.

With fugues, this same strategy works with countersubjects and sometimes with other contrapuntal lines and fragments.

Your study may sometimes reveal that the best simultaneous-rehearsal excerpts will include non-pitched percussion motifs. A shining example is found in *Incantation and Dance*, where John Barnes Chance uses a prominent non-pitched percussion excerpt to unveil the rhythmic aspects of the most important "melodic" motifs, long before their pitched versions are heard. For example:

- The rhythm of a claves solo becomes a figure later played by timpani and low voices.
- The rhythms introduced by a tambourine solo and a temple blocks solo, respectively, will later become well-known motifs by which this masterwork is identified.

- *Find (and use) patterns and repetitive ideas.* From an early age, instrumentalists can discover a marvelous relevance in their practicing: "If I practice a scale or other rudimental pattern, I can play it better whenever it appears in my music. And for each composition, when I learn a difficult passage, the same passage might show up later in the same piece." Through targeted score study, the clever teacher locates repeating patterns, along with reused passages, and will then utilize them in lessons.
- *Avoid getting lost in repeating patterns.* Performers can get lost while counting repeated figures for an extended time. The problem happens with ostinati and melodic fragments, but it is notoriously difficult in accompanimental and offbeat figures. Invent markings to help (Figure 2.17). Sometimes the best question is simply, "How many times will I play that figure?"

The common one-bar repeat symbol makes it easy to find & follow the repeated figure:

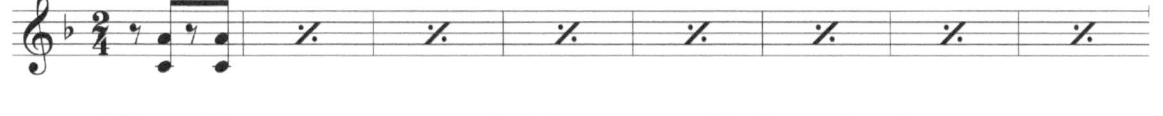

With or without measure-repeat symbols, however, *pencil in the number-of-repeats*:

When the repeated figure is longer, 2- and 4-measure repeat *symbols* **may still help:**

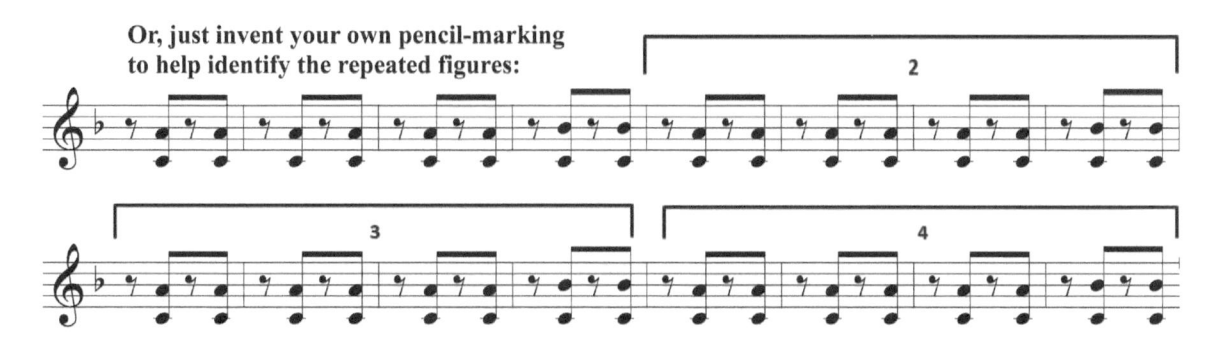

Or, just invent your own pencil-marking to help identify the repeated figures:

Figure 2.17 Examples of markings for repeating figures.

Sometimes the most helpful observation is simply that the pattern changes "here." But students may not be able to make that discovery independently. Use your score study to identify pattern-changes; then, develop instructional decisions to help the ensemble. A prominent example comes again from the Overture to *Candide* (Bernstein/arr. Beeler). In measures 231–238, the cut-time melody is laid atop an accompaniment built on a clever hemiola pattern. The melody outlines a clear 8-measure phrase, but the patterned accompaniment must make a clever "stutter step" to realign itself with the melody at the ninth measure (239).

Such patterns can be very elusive. Once found, however, these figures present exciting new instructional options for the director. Many of your discoveries help toward developing plans for the rehearsals. Whether you uncover the hidden treasures through painstaking score study, or simply by serendipity, the additional benefits are yours: you too are revitalized by the joy of learning, and you become a better conductor in the process.

- *Find and use ostinato figures.* As with other patterns, ostinati can be used to motivate performers and drive the instruction. An important example is the Chaconne theme from the First Suite in E-flat by Gustav Holst. This 14-note masterpiece repeats a full sixteen times during the movement, eventually covering all sections of the band. These repetitions and a famous inversion are easily revealed. But the theme is also fragmented, and its intervallic make-up is referenced and quoted throughout the second and third movements as well. Theoretical and instructional advice is easily found for Holst.

To apply this process to your band's lesser-known repertoire, look also for shorter and easily missed ostinati. Find these, and you'll view some of the composer's significant building blocks, which can then be shared during instructional sessions. In Figure 2.18, because the ostinato is five beats long, its usage in 4/4 meter causes each repetition to begin on a different beat of the measure. Thus, there are four statements across *five* measures of time.

Figure 2.18 Spitfire! (Gary Gilroy), alto sax 1, mm. 139–143. © 2008 Wingert-Jones Publications. Used with permission.

That the ostinato misaligns with the meter is interesting and may engage students in the process. But the composer's manipulation of the ostinato is *functional* to your teaching and conducting. This ostinato is scored with offset entrances much like a one-measure canon to create a chaotic-sounding mosaic of chirps (see Figure 2.19). The conductor's rehearsal strategy can remove the chaos, unifying the students' control of the figure. For example:

1. All instruments rehearse the passage simultaneously (describe that clarinets will begin at measure 138, alto 1 at 139, and so on). Playing the figure in unison gives students confidence and allows the teacher to provide unifying feedback (articulation, style, etc.).
2. Return to the passage as written, giving simple downbeat cues to assist each new entrance. Describe that students should play the passage as written.

Beyond patterns, repetitive figures, and ostinati, look carefully for all other recognizable figures (e.g. fragments, quotations, inversions, augmentations, diminutions, hemiolas). These discoveries will supplement the rest of your score study, providing further resources for the rehearsals and lessons.

- *Labels to assist with harmonic analysis.* With more experienced musicians, conductors can ask to hear "Anyone who has the third of this F major chord." But novice players require more specific instructions. Analyze a vertical structure, and add subtle labels to the score, using your own preferred method to visually identify the root, third, fifth, and any added or non-harmonic tones. Here are three labeling options among many others:
  ○ Pencil a number by each pitch (1, 3, or 5 for simple triads, adding 7, 9 where applicable); perhaps circle any non-harmonic tones.
  ○ Affix a sticky-note to the page, with each group clearly written on it: "The ROOT is played by _____; the FIFTH is played by _____; the THIRD is played by _____."
  ○ Use several colors of removable highlighter tape, or mark lightly with colored pencils (e.g. using blue for roots, red for fifths, yellow for thirds).

Figure 2.19 Spitfire! (Gary Gilroy), selected instrument parts, mm. 138–145. © 2008 Wingert-Jones Publications. Used with permission.

- *Sketch a simple form blueprint.* The various steps of score-examination suggested thus far probably won't provide a full analysis of the form. But with observations you've made after multiple passes through the score (see page 5), you'll already have some good ideas about form. Assemble those ideas into a basic blueprint, which you can improve over time. Figure 2.20 provides basic stylized example.

SCORE STUDY

"Spinning Wheel" by Blood, Sweat and Tears

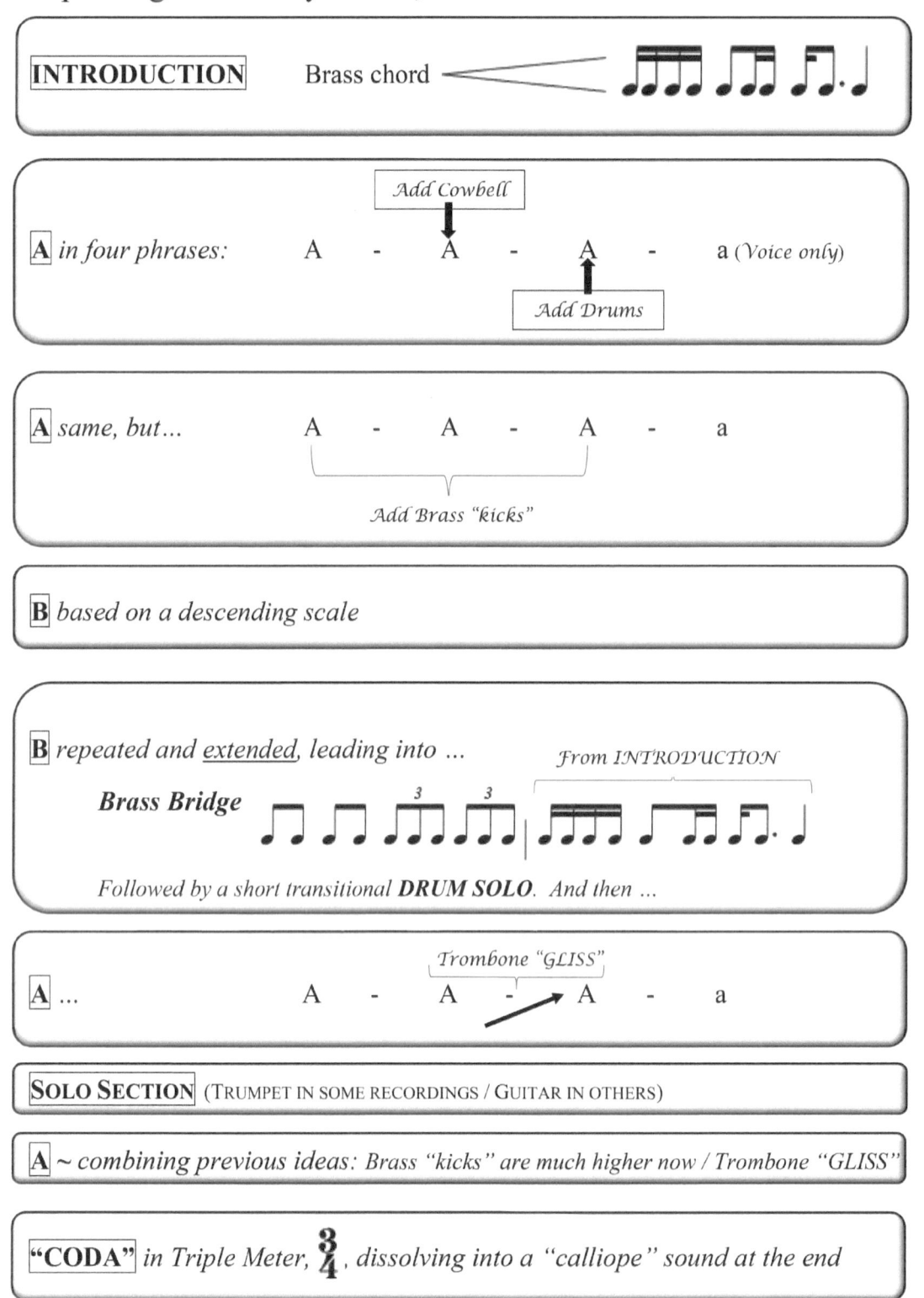

INTRODUCTION — Brass chord ⟨ ♪♪♪♪ ♪♪♪ ♪♪♪.♩

A *in four phrases:*   A — A — A — a *(Voice only)*
(Add Cowbell above third A; Add Drums above third A)

A *same, but...*   A — A — A — a
Add Brass "kicks"

B *based on a descending scale*

B *repeated and <u>extended</u>, leading into ...*   *From INTRODUCTION*
Brass Bridge   ♩ ♪♩ ♩³♩ ♩³♩ | ♪♪♪♪ ♪♪♪ ♪♪♪.♩
Followed by a short transitional **DRUM SOLO**. *And then ...*

A *...*   A — A —→ A — a
Trombone "GLISS"

SOLO SECTION (TRUMPET IN SOME RECORDINGS / GUITAR IN OTHERS)

A *~ combining previous ideas: Brass "kicks" are much higher now / Trombone "GLISS"*

"CODA" *in Triple Meter,* **3/4***, dissolving into a "calliope" sound at the end*

Figure 2.20 Blueprint of a musical form.

24

This form-chart was created for a pop song rather than a band composition, and the task was based on listening only; no score study was involved. That might seem almost irrelevant to this book, but it is included because students can benefit from this type of exercise, both with their band music and with personal listening. And they can learn by applying this skill, even if their own graphic shorthand method makes sense only to them (remember Grainger?). Listening for form is a rather advanced skill, so this endeavor—creating a "picture" of the form—will be another excellent component in your students' comprehensive musicianship.

Consider two efficient shortcuts to create a conductor's blueprint for a band piece:

- Choose the condensed score. The shorter, non-transposed view minimizes time needed to discover formal sections and thematic content throughout.
- Repurpose a part, writing important details in its whitespace. By choosing a "lead" part (1st Flute, Trumpet, Clarinet or Alto Sax), many of the themes, and therefore an outline of formal sections, can already be seen on the part.

- *Two final words on "shortcuts for your personal study"*

    - Errors often remain in a published version. So, save personal time by searching for pre-existing errata lists correcting your repertoire.
    - More serious problems arise when errors are found in parts but not the score: players may not recognize errors independently. Therefore, stay vigilant as the conductor, always assuming the *possibility* that parts have undisclosed errors. In teaching and rehearsals, consider both possibilities: player error and printer/publisher error.

Section 4: The Score vs. the Parts

Score study in undergraduate school often becomes a function of other classes. We use scores for harmonic analysis tasks, transposition, and more in Music Theory classes, while using scores to learn about composers and repertoire from each stylistic period in music history classes. Published scores are models of traditional music notation rules and procedures. However, when students transition to their professional teaching roles, the study must include examining the parts as well as the score. This short section explores a few of the reasons it is imperative to examine the *instrument parts* as an important component of the score study process.

- *Page-turns*. Instrumental parts may require a page-turn during an excerpt, a fact that may remain unknown to the conductor. Without viewing parts, the teacher will be left to wonder, "Why did the entire flute section just stop playing for two measures?!"
- *Mixed sets*. While this is a serious oversight, it can happen: players may be viewing different versions of the same piece, especially where schools own several adaptations of a march or pop title. Confirm that everyone has the same version, rather than misfiled parts from different arrangements.
- *Marches and other works with written repeats*. Although less common, be aware of this possibility: sometimes a score uses repeats and endings while the parts have no repeated section. *Be on guard for these discrepancies between the score and parts*. The parts might be printed with two 16-bar strains entirely spelled out into thirty-two measures while, from the score, a conductor observes a single repeated strain, which might have two rehearsal letters/numbers attached to it. Instructions like "Play the repeat section, but take the second ending" will lead to confusion.

SCORE STUDY

- *Notation problems.* A player's notation may differ from what is shown on the score. From the podium, the conductor cannot distinguish whether a player has a performance technique problem, or simply misunderstands the notation or an interpretive concept. The following are among the more common problems:
    - Measure-repeat signs, or especially 2-measure repeat signs—inexperienced players often mistake a 2-measure repeat for "repeat the measure twice."
    - The abbreviation for repeated alternations of two notes (as in a tremolo) or abbreviations for repeated patterns might be unfamiliar to players (Figure 2.21).

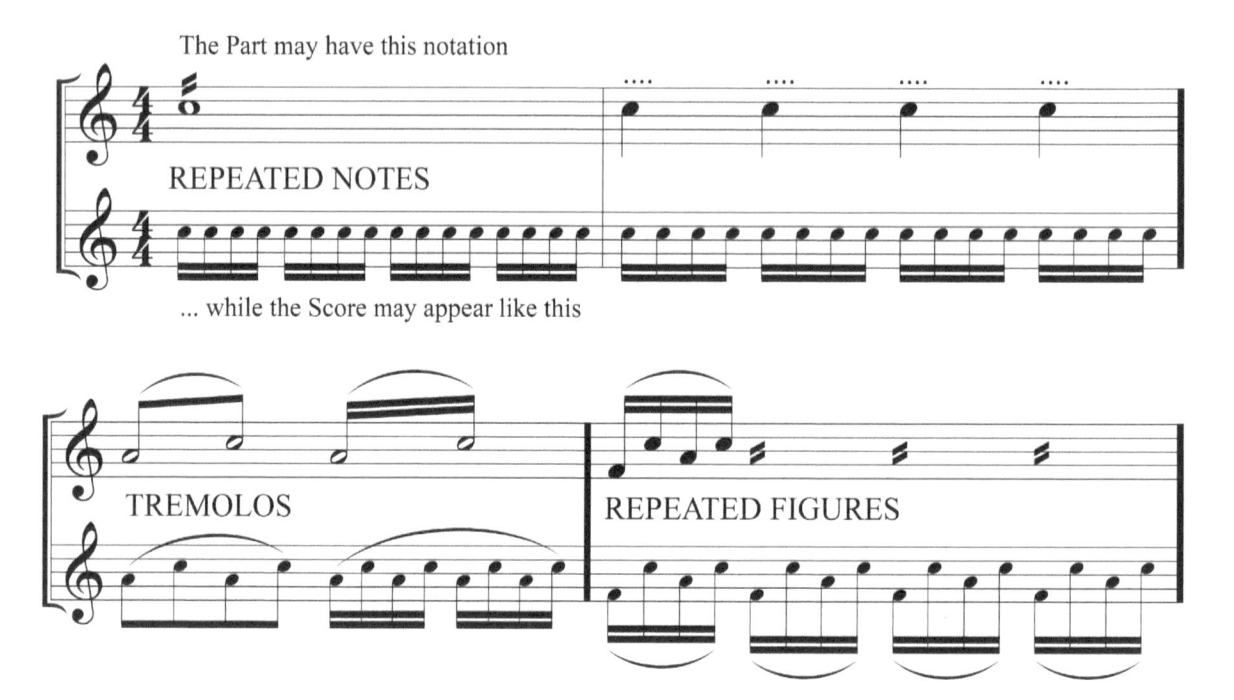

Figure 2.21 Examples of notation abbreviations which might have different appearances on the part and the score.

- Terms like *8va, 8vb, coll., alta, basso, loco,* and others might show up on a performer's printed part, but not in the score. Scan the parts; pencil significant differences onto the score.
- Here's just one specific example of a visual challenge in a part that will go unnoticed in the score: the flute/piccolo part from *A Yorkshire Overture* (Phillip Sparke) changes from unison to divisi on the single staff, but then to separate divisi parts notated on different staves. After measure 98, the two-staff system returns to notation on a single staff (Figure 2.22). However, the spacing between all staves (single and divisi pairs) is quite tight, and the change isn't immediately clear to players. In this excerpt, it is easy for students to get lost, while the conductor might misunderstand their difficulties.

Figure 2.22 A Yorkshire Overture (Phillip Sparke), flute part, page 2. Studio Music (a division of Salvation Army Trading Company). Used by permission.

- *Percussion part-assignments.* Percussion assignments are more easily determined using *parts* (see Chapter 7 for detailed suggestions). For now, please accept this good advice: view the parts to understand who is able to play what at any given time. Percussion assignments made using the score alone will be time-consuming at best, and the work could have errors and oversights.
- *Percussion incompleteness.* While not generally a concern with full scores, condensed scores often eliminate significant portions of the percussion notation. Because percussionists may require the conductor's cueing and guidance to be fully successful, pencil selected percussion entrances and figures onto condensed scores.
- *Percussion difficulties.* Reading from their parts, percussionists may experience problems that go undetected when the conductor views only the score. Examine the parts to discover visual challenges, spatial/equipment limitations, timpani tuning problems, and more. Tip: Leave the podium during rehearsals, visiting the percussion section to view their parts; anything missed during your study sessions will become apparent by seeing their perspective.

Section 5: The Score at the Root of the Curriculum

The use of baseline assessments is recommended in bands, just as it is prevalent in other academic disciplines. By determining students' skills and deficiencies, we can design more helpful plans, personalized for each student's needs.

We can use our repertoire to support the entire curriculum of technique, vocabulary, artistry, comprehensive musicianship concepts, and more. The director enjoys creative autonomy to extract curricular ideas directly from the music. The following brief suggestions may spark further ideas about using score study to link the repertoire directly to the remaining curriculum:

- *Create vocabulary and/or skills-lists selected from each piece.* It's unwise to assume that band members know everything they'll encounter on their printed music. Therefore, create a guide to clarify terms, symbols, and notational procedures extracted from the repertoire. The project could be a student-expectation: "Find, define and be ready for a quiz covering any material on the page." Or prepare a fill-in-the-blanks template, assigned to individuals, groups, or even volunteers for the benefit of the whole band. Refer to the resources website (RW2.1) for downloadable examples.
- *Determine alternative strategies for delivering your curriculum beyond the traditional conducting/teaching models.* These brief references are limited to score-study. Keep in mind that strategies involving technology, the internet or other evolving trends risk becoming obsolete.
    - *Recording and listening.* While using recordings for score study, list any resources you discover that include a video aspect, especially recordings that offer virtual page-turning or a scroll-view of the score. These can be found on publishers' websites, YouTube, and composer's sites. In class, project the score on a large display to support students' ability to follow a printed score. That experience alone is often a motivating moment. TIP: Consider projecting your score so students can view *your* markings.
    - *Using score study to supplement instrumental lesson classes.* Record the student's excerpt; on playback, let the student view the score rather than the part. With guidance, the student can learn to perceive other lines in the texture. As a follow-up, teach the student to play from the score. Using that new skill, a student can create a "one person ensemble," that is, play and record the excerpt; on playback, the same student uses the score to create a duet by playing a different part.
    - *SmartMusic®.* While examining your scores, remember to search the SmartMusic library. SmartMusic offers a remarkable number of strategies to support a musician's growth and enjoyment: play along with the recording; enable/disable the metronome click; decrease tempo to help learn passages; create a *loop* to focus on specific difficulties; disable the "accompaniment" so the student is playing in unison with his own instrument part.
- *Search for structures related to basic musicianship and fundamental performance skills.* Each piece features its own set of fundamentals, rhythmic figures, articulation patterns, and other building blocks; use them to formulate portions of the lessons/rehearsal curriculum. For example, to support a composition in the key of D-flat major, it's germane to have the band play scales, scales-in-thirds, arpeggios, and harmonic cadences in that key and its relative minor. Tuning and balance exercises can be created for almost any excerpt of any piece.

    We can extract percussion figures from the piece to accompany those fundamentals, or we can direct percussionists to play rudiments. Make it a goal to find the most prevalent rudiments and percussion patterns as a part of the score study.
- *Additionally, we can find compositional techniques to help organize the teaching.* Through our own training and performance, we become acutely aware of composers' building blocks in pieces we hear and perform. Nonetheless, we sometimes overlook them in the literature we teach. But of course, these common compositional tools are used throughout all pieces in your band's repertoire. Many students seem to love discovering "hidden" information in their music. Much of it is easily found because it's often highlighted in the Composer's Notes section. Explore your score, searching specifically for obvious examples of compositional tools and techniques. Observe how the main material is used and developed. Remember to look for fragmentation, rhythmic diminution/augmentation, inversion, retrograde, and more. Band students can be gently guided toward an

improved understanding and enjoyment of their music when they can hear and see these compositional tools in action. The examples in Figure 2.23 will help students discover the composer's usage of augmentation/diminution techniques.

Figure 2.23 River of Life by Steven Reineke. © Birch Island Music Press. Used with permission.

Your study can uncover musical cryptograms, serialism, quotations from other compositions, and many more devices. These techniques are attention-getters for students, so share them with the band; the connections will supplement the basic rehearsal material to create a more fun and engaging experience. Schedule wisely, choosing when you'll offer the extra information. That is, sometimes we discuss supplementary information in the early rehearsals to help students understand what they're about to do, but we can also delay a discussion until later rehearsals, to help reinvigorate students' investment in the piece.

The following listening activity may help students learn to recognize the composer's tools/techniques:

1. Listen first to (or even perform) *The Fairest of the Fair* by John Phillip Sousa. With Sousa fresh in their ears . . .
2. . . . let the students immediately hear *Fantasy on a Theme by Sousa* (Andrew Boysen, Jr.; Neil A. Kjos Music) to make exciting aural discoveries about the composer's manipulation of original themes.

- *Find figures and techniques related to method-book work and instrument-specific skills.* When students discover their "study material" used in a band work, they more readily accept skill studies as a necessary step toward mastery of the repertoire. It often takes the director's guidance to illuminate those connections, so keep a list of the fundamentals found through your score study. For example, the percussion rudiments studied daily in method books are found easily throughout the band's repertoire. The *context* (using the rudiments in "real" music) often flips the student's motivational switch to the "ON" position.

With careful foraging, the strategic director can find opportunities in a score for all players to apply their special techniques. Band directors work hard to choose quality music for its overall value to the program, but too often we still overlook the long list of teaching moments buried in the scores. So, add some "checkoff" components to your score study:

☐ In the *horizontal* view we notice melody, compositional fragments, form, modulations, rhythmic elements, need-for-cueing, and much more. Now, examine instruments' lines from the perspective of the *player*; namely, if required to play this piece yourself, what difficulties would you encounter on each instrument? What practice/performance decisions would you make? We easily detect the technical demands on our own major instruments. Elevate your score study by focusing especially toward your least-comfortable secondary instruments: what strategies will you need to teach for students to succeed? For example:

  ○ When should flutists choose *Thumb B-flat* over the *1-and-1* fingering?
  ○ Where should clarinetists apply the chromatic fingerings, pinky-key choices, and resonant fingering alternates?

  Find those performance skills and you can link the band's repertoire to the students' individual studies.

☐ In the *vertical* view, we typically look for textures (thick vs. sparse; polyphonic features), and for the colors in the orchestration, while working to analyze harmonic structures. Now make careful observations about tuning pitfalls (especially related to fingering options) and the way parts interact with others. For example:

  ○ In a C major chord, the third is assigned as a trombone's upper E, a clarinet's low F♯ and alto saxophone's open C♯ and yet those instruments each have different intonation problems.
  ○ Also, a main theme from Leroy Anderson's holiday masterpiece *Sleigh Ride*—scored as a unison line for clarinets and saxophones—is known and loved by audiences who expect it to be performed flawlessly, but it provides a difficult technical challenge and problematic vertical tuning.

The goal of all this is simple to state, but difficult to achieve: study the score and parts carefully, but then *use* your discoveries to help students learn how their "boring" method-book exercises will lead to the excitement of success with their band performances. With attention to both the vertical and horizontal study, you discover concerns for each instrument. You view the score through the lens of the performer to discover technical problems, fingering options, tuning deficiencies, and other issues.

Now, look through the lens of the teacher—what will you do to help the performers? This question is especially important if you are the primary resource for students; your best work will be imperative unless every band member studies privately with a respected specialist. Notice there is no suggestion to "view the score through the lens of the conductor." It's easy to find wonderful-looking conductors who, at the same time, are only marginally effective as teachers and motivators.

These suggestions will surely require a lot of time, concentration, patience and perhaps extra research. However, the results are clearly worth the effort. Two relevant examples illustrate this point. Figure 2.24 shows how using an enjoyable passage can help to motivate students.

SCORE STUDY

The "hook" - Clarinet students seem to love this melody in a comfortable key with "easy" fingerings:

The follow-up motivation - Once attracted to the sound of an "addictive" melody at measure 60, students will be more easily encouraged to practice the techniques required after a modulation, when the same melody needs advanced over-the-break fingerings:

* Use Alternate B (right side-key)

Figure 2.24 Fate of the Gods by Steven Reineke. © Birch Island Music Press. Used with permission.

The bassoon pattern in Figure 2.25 offers a technical challenge, perhaps requiring intervention by the well-prepared teacher.

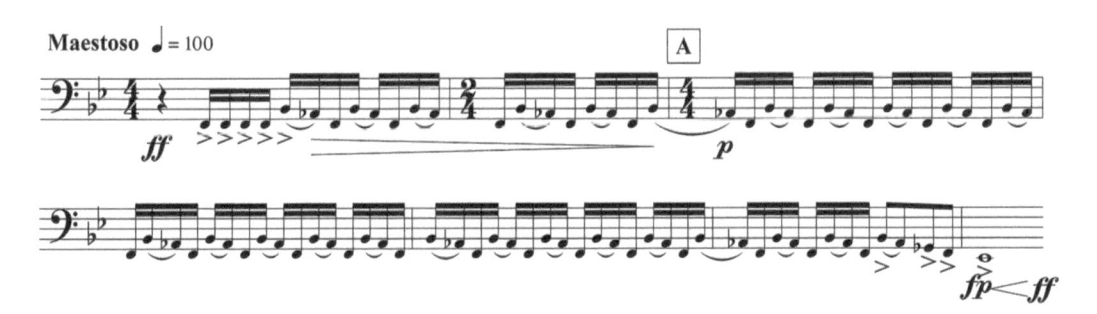

Figure 2.25 Eternal Father, Strong to Save by Claude T. Smith. © Claude T. Smith Publications, Inc. Used with permission.

- *Finally, a true "shortcut!"* Ask colleagues to examine your literature and give suggestions about specific problems in their instrument's part. For example, the most efficient way to help a student with the passage shown in Figure 2.25 is simply to ask a bassoon specialist. By asking for help, you can save an enormous amount of time. You'll also learn a lot, while building cooperative "bartering" relationships with colleagues.

Concluding Thoughts

As a teacher, you'll soon recognize the value of accumulating your study. By remembering what you've learned from every score, you can reverse the curricular direction. That is, start by listing skills you want to develop among your students. Then, as the later step, select repertoire to support the curriculum choices. For example, perhaps you want to share 12-tone compositional techniques with your students: *Tight Squeeze* by Alex Shapiro can introduce advanced compositional concepts to the band while engaging them with "an Afro-Cuban techno groove laced with a hint of big band jazz."[3] Or, while teaching jazz or music theory, perhaps you want to share an octatonic palette with your students: *Awakenings* by Kimberly Archer is there for you.

So, this brief chapter is surely not the "end" of the recommendations. Your work, as a teacher and as a conductor, will be guided by discoveries made during score study sessions. And your own continued immersion in repertoire can keep you refreshed.

Notes

1 Erich Leinsdorf, *The Composer's Advocate* (New Haven and London: Yale University Press, 1981), viii, 14, 203.
2 See Elizabeth A. H. Green, *The Modern Conductor* (Englewood Cliffs: Prentice-Hall, Inc., 1969), Appendix F, "Additional Practice Problems" (274–277) for a collection of notated exercises on this topic.
3 Alex Shapiro, email message to author, May 3, 2020.

3

WARM-UPS AND MORE

Introduction: The Nature of Warm-Ups

The beginning of a lesson is arguably the most valuable time during any class period. In many academic disciplines, teachers prepare "bell-ringers" to focus students' attention directly toward the day's concepts and objectives. In a band, students need to transition efficiently from their sometimes-chaotic arrival to reach a settled, productive rehearsal. Band musicians still require a mental and cognitive "warm-up," but our performers—and their instruments—also need a *physical* warm-up.

Directors typically mold warm-up experiences into a diet of long tones, scales, intervals, rhythmic figures, and especially chorales. But through inspired creativity, we can produce a wide variety of engaging supplements and variations. Convey the importance of the warm-up period consistently; that salesmanship can be effortless when the process is fresh rather than repetitive, and when the director's behavior clearly displays an unwavering belief in the purpose of the warm-up. Most importantly, students must easily notice the relationship of the warm-up to their band's improvement.

Use activities that help students become prepared for a productive session—physically, mentally, and conceptually. However, these important processes and exercises, while "routine," should never become mundane. Predictable repetition and drills often lead to a loss of students' attention or, worse, apathy and even resistance among some band members.

There are many outstanding warm-up books and ensemble development methods on the market; the author highly recommends *Sound Innovations for Concert Band: Ensemble Development* (Peter Boonshaft and Chris Bernotas), which offers nearly four hundred exercises targeting all facets of band performance. But if printed curricular materials aren't available, there are still many activities at the director's disposal.

This chapter offers strategies, concepts, and materials that are both functional and flexible, addressing a variety of objectives during the warm-up.

First, let's examine brief activities that can serve as supplements, even if a full warm-up plan is already in place. Directors could choose a rotating schedule, which can help ensure that students are exposed to multiple types of exercises. For instance, include "posture and breathing activities on Mondays and Wednesdays," "embouchure exercises and long-tone stability on Tuesdays," "technique and mechanics on Thursdays," "listening and pitch-awareness on Fridays," or a rotation aligned with a six- or eight-day cycle. The students will view these short processes, used briefly and in a rotation, as fun—even *entertaining*—exercises. It will be up to the director to reinforce the goals and seriousness of the work.

A Concise Overview of Some Warm-Up Categories

The warm-up period may evolve over time as the director gains experience, but many components of the warm-up will fall into general categories. Here is a broad view of those categories, accompanied by a few *reusable* activities. Whether using a printed warm-up, or a customized series of goal-oriented exercises, these categories will be important ingredients in developing students' skills.

Breathing

Breathing is the fuel for the playing vehicle. Breathing, with air-management, is fundamental to tone production, steady sustain, endurance, flexibility, range, intonation, phrasing, and, truly, almost all aspects of performance. It's also important to ensemble (the group's entrances, releases); by involving percussionists in your breathing exercises as well, you'll help to foster their rhythmic precision, listening skills, and awareness of phrasing. Some short full-ensemble breathing exercises include the following:

- *Building lung capacity and airway efficiency.* Using 16-count segments as an example . . .

    . . . Breathe in for 8 beats, out for 8
    . . . Inhale 6, exhale 10
    . . . In 4, out 12
    . . . In 2, out 14
    . . . In 1, out 15
    . . . "Breath-mark," out 16; repeat; repeat.

    This exercise trains students to take a deep, filling breath in the shortest possible time.

- *Variations*
    1. After describing the parameters, have students inhale *silently*, but exhale with a "*hiss*" (e.g. "sss," "shhh") to simulate the back-pressure found in many wind instruments. Try adding an articulation while exhaling. For example, "Tsss—Tsss—Tsss." Model for the students before beginning.
    2. Apply the hissing to a passage from the first rehearsal piece while you conduct; without playing, students will feel the relationship of their breathing to the phrasing and control of a passage.

- *Learning to "feel" deep breathing.* Standing and with instruments protected . . .

    . . . stay relaxed; bend at the waist until the torso is parallel to the floor.
    . . . inhale deeply until the 90-degree angle cannot be maintained.

    This exercise shows that filling the lungs involves the abdomen; the deep breath will feel "crowded," forcing the player to stand up a bit. Chest-only breathing will not be deep enough.

- *An ensemble game for breath control:*
    - Step 1. "Relax with instruments in play position. I'll conduct in 4/4. On beats 1–2–3, empty your lungs completely, and on beat 4 take a full breath."
    - Step 2. "Play Concert F as softly as you can control with good tone, but you must sustain one note on one breath."
    - Step 3. "When you run out of air, OR when your sound stops for any reason, stop playing."
    - Step 4. "Let's see how long you can last. Who will play the last sound in each Section?"

    Applying this exercise in other ways can double the benefits (i.e. sustain a chord from the repertoire to work concurrently on tone, intonation, balance and other beauty-based concepts).

It's important to *relax* during all breathing exercises.

Stretches, Posture, Physique, and More

Exercises in this category are easy to find and adapt, and they are fundamental to supporting our one true goal: to make a beautiful sound. Try this easy challenge to teach a lasting lesson very quickly. Richard Floyd calls this posture, "Sitting like you are about to stand."[1] The process might be described this way:

In a moment, I'm going to ask you all to stand up, but the goal is to make no sound—you must be completely *silent* when you move from sitting to standing... Now, sit back down and freeze in your start position.

This exercise provides the best posture for breathing and playing. Remind students about hand positions, and both the height and the placement of music stands.

Tone Development

Tone Quality is job #1: for musicians, the first goal is to produce a *beautiful characteristic sound*. Its maintenance and improvement will be an ongoing process for life (see Chapter 4 for details).

For individuals and ensembles alike, premium tone quality relies on at least the following components:

- An aural *concept*—musicians must recognize and emulate the best examples of Tone
- Well-developed fundamentals—"best tone" relies on a managed combination of posture, embouchure, breathing, and *listening/adjusting*. Remember to include percussionists in the development of tone.
- Quality equipment—equipment has an undeniable relationship to the sound a musician creates. Without access to the highest-quality instruments and equipment, consider lower-cost upgrades including professional mouthpieces, ligatures, reeds, head joints, and percussion sticks/mallets and heads, all of which can have positive benefits on a limited budget.

No band can produce a superior full-ensemble tone quality unless all players in the ensemble have outstanding individual tone, and unless the director "molds" the ensemble based on his/her own well-developed aural concept. Therefore, teachers should work carefully with individuals, stressing daily work on the development of tone quality. *Our Band will sound as beautiful as we can make it together—individually and collectively* (see Chapters 4 and 5 for ensemble-based tone exercises).

Singing, Clapping, Mouthpiece-Buzzing

These activities have a great place in the warm-up, as well as throughout rehearsals. The importance of *singing* can't be overstated. Clapping helps to teach and clarify rhythms, but can also be used selectively to accompany other activities. Brass players often buzz on the mouthpiece in their personal warm-ups, but buzzing can also help during full band sessions (e.g. brasses *buzz* while woodwinds *play* a scale).

Rhythm and the Internal Clock

Carefully chosen rhythmic elements in a steady metronomic pulse during the warm-up process can create a stabilizing support plan. Assign a specific rhythmic figure as the basis for the rest of the warm-up activity. Select a problematic rhythm, or a characteristic figure from the *style* of the composition to be rehearsed. Use the rhythm during the warm-up and then transfer its improved control immediately into the repertoire. Students without a good "internal clock" will have difficulty playing rhythms independently; the band's rhythmic warm-up activities provide excellent pulse support for them.

Articulations

The band's tone quality and overall *clarity* will be best if all players can produce various types of articulations proficiently. Unisons, chords, or scales, performed with articulations of your choice, can supplement most other warm-up procedures. Use as little tongue, jaw, and facial movement as possible. Make a brief recording and play it back for students to evaluate their sounds. Transfer the improved techniques and aural concepts directly into the excerpt. Tip: Although not truly in the "articulations" category, it's helpful to use rhythmic *breath-impulses* on long tones to further improve tone through diaphragmatic control.

Dynamic Control

Like almost any other warm-up exercise, the *crescendo–decrescendo* must be performed with a goal in mind, and that requires guidance from the director. Play a unison or chord throughout a *crescendo–decrescendo* sequence, working to maintain beautiful tone quality and stable intonation.

Scales

Just as scales form the basis of compositions, they also serve as a core element during warm-up procedures. For specific scale-based strategies applicable to the warm-up, see Section 1, "More Ideas on the Circle of 4ths" and Section 3 "Some Scale Games."

Intervals and Flexibility

Band musicians play diatonic and narrow intervals much more easily than the wider leaps. In general, the wider the interval, the greater the problem, especially for slurring and among brass players, flutists, and mallet percussionists. Including flexibility exercises in the warm-up encourages players to work on these types of exercises in their own individual practice. For the full band, the Remington exercise (see page 86) is a staple, and directors can choose *expanding scales* exercises, similar to those shown later.

Chorales

Chorales can improve a wealth of vital skills, and are imperative to the refinement of balance, blend, and tuning concepts. Students can improve listening skills by hearing their own role in the overall texture. Chorales support phrasing, note-grouping, musical line direction, and all other interpretive elements and artistic concepts. Through chorales, the director can continue to sculpt his/her concept of the band's tone and resonance. Because Chorales are critical to the concert band's sound, this book includes many chorale-based activities (see Section 4 "Chorales from the Band's literature").

Regardless of the activities and supplements chosen for your band's warm-up, be sure your design meets further goals: during the warm-up, the teacher can . . .

. . . establish classroom routines.
. . . reinforce behavioral expectations.
. . . impart information and communicate concepts to students, without the stress of being graded; this is especially good for students lacking confidence and/or skills.
. . . have a focused opportunity to *listen* and *observe*. Because you and your students are often working without as much printed notation, it's easier to keep your eyes and ears critically trained on both the process and the product:
   - Are the students participating as you expect?
   - Are they showing appropriate posture, embouchure, breathing techniques, and hand and body positions?
   - And most importantly, is the *sound* pure, resonant, and characteristic of the best band sound?

Although we surely can't address every *category* of musicianship in a single warm-up, it's helpful to keep these components in mind when designing the warm-up processes.

Section 1: More Ideas on the Circle of 4ths

"More ideas" starts by assuming that you've read Ed Lisk's work, and that you're aware of how integral the Circle of 4ths can be in band education. Starting with *The Creative Director: Alternative Rehearsal Techniques*,[2] Lisk's series of books teaches us that students can achieve more when provided with specific sequential steps leading toward well-defined goals. At the core of his methods we find the Circle

WARM-UPS AND MORE

of 4ths (with scales, of course) and "The Ruler of Time" for rhythmic awareness. One short paragraph cannot do justice to Lisk's brilliant pedagogical writings; band directors are encouraged to put *The Creative Director* series high on your reading list. Once your students can use the Circle, and when they have a basic understanding of music theory and key signatures, a multitude of activities become available to use during the warm-up process.

First, collect *graphics* of the Circle of 4ths (alternately, the Circle of 5ths or "Circle of Keys") and display the Circle in your band room. Lisk's books are a terrific resource, especially for their thorough pedagogical suggestions. Versions of the time-tested "old school" circle of keys graphic are easy to find; or, create your own.

Figure 3.1 is a fine example by renowned jazz performer and educator Jamey Aebersold, from his *Jazz Handbook*.

THE CIRCLE or CYCLE of FOURTHS

The "CIRCLE of FOURTHS" can also be called the "Circle of Fifths" or just "The Cycle." Practicing the scales, chords, and ideas in genaral via the cycle has been a common practice routine for jazz musicians and is highly recommended. It is a disciplined way of working through all twelve keys. Plus, many bass root movements to jazz and pop songs move through sections of the cycle.

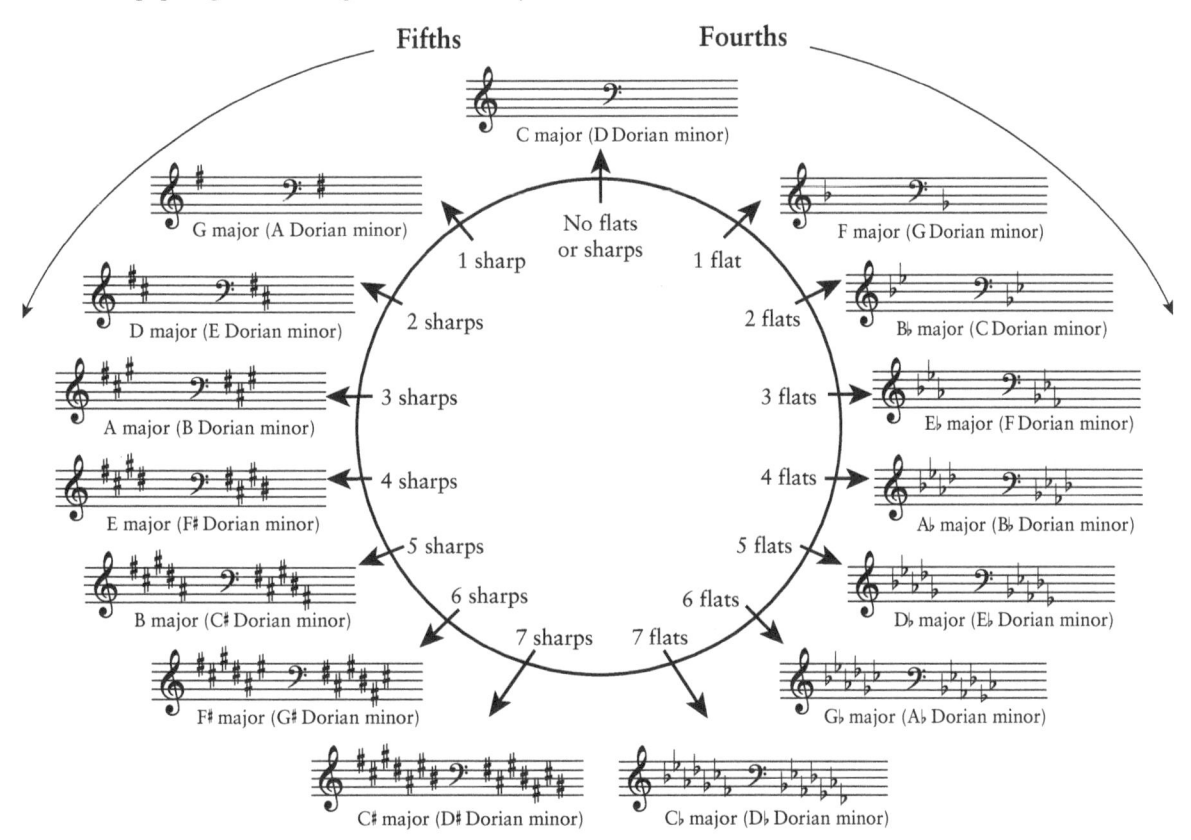

Figure 3.1 Jamey Aebersold's "Circle or Cycle of Fourths" graphic. Used with permission.

Next, learn to *use* the graphic in your lessons. You must be able to clearly explain the order of sharps/flats in key signatures, how the keys progress to one another, and the meaning of enharmonics. Ed Lisk's version, particularly when supplemented with the wealth of supportive text found in his books, takes care of that task for you (Figure 3.2).

Then expand on the usage of the Circle of Keys in your warm-ups by adding theory lessons to your procedures. Figure 3.3 shows the sequence of keys, along with the key signatures in *verbal* terms to

WARM-UPS AND MORE

Circle of 4ths

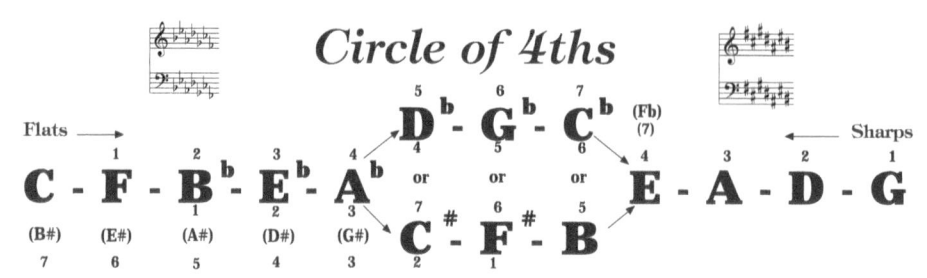

Flats →
1 2 3 4   5 6 7 (Fb)(7)   4 3 2 1 ← Sharps
C - F - B♭ - E♭ - A♭   D♭- G♭- C♭   or   E - A - D - G
(B#)(E#)(A#)(D#)(G#)   or   C#- F#- B
7 6 5 4 3   7 6# 5
                       2 1

The top number indicates the number of flats or sharps in that particular scale.
The bottom number indicates the correct order of flats or sharps.

Woodwind Choir

Group 1	Group 2	Group 3	Group 4
Piccolo	2nd Flute	3rd Clarinet	Bass Clarinet
Oboe	2nd Clarinet	Alto Clarinet	Bassoons
Eb Clarinet	2nd Alto Sax	Tenor Sax	Bari Sax
1st Flute			Contra Clarinets
1st Clarinet			
1st Alto Sax			

Brass Choir

Group 1	Group 2	Group 3	Group 4
1st Cornet	2nd Cornet	3rd Cornet	Baritone
1st Trumpet	2nd French Horn	2nd Trumpet	Euphonium
1st French Horn	2nd Trombone	3rd Trombone	Tuba
1st Trombone		3rd & 4th French Horn	
			String Bass

Percussion

Vibraphone (soft mallets)   Xylophone (soft mallets)   Marimba (soft mallets)   Tympani

© Copyright 1991 MEREDITH MUSIC PUBLICATIONS

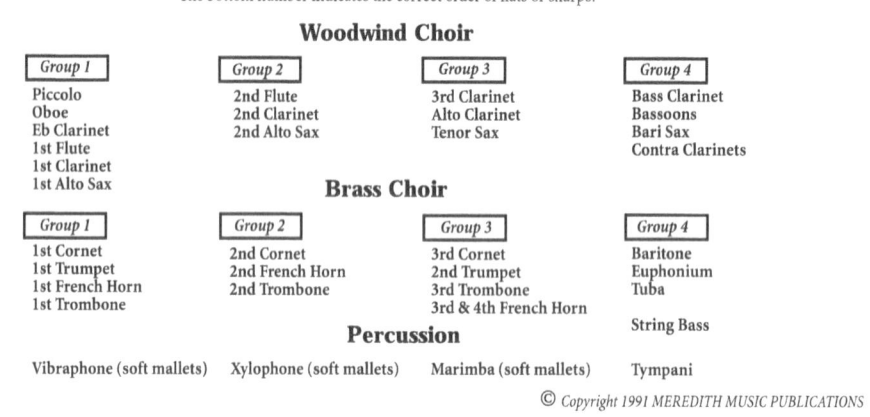

Figure 3.2 Ed Lisk's "Circle of 4ths" graphic. Used by permission, Meredith Music Publications.

Enharmonic Keys The "Circle of Keys", unwrapped ... *Enharmonic Keys*
=Db =Gb =Cb   =C# =F# =B

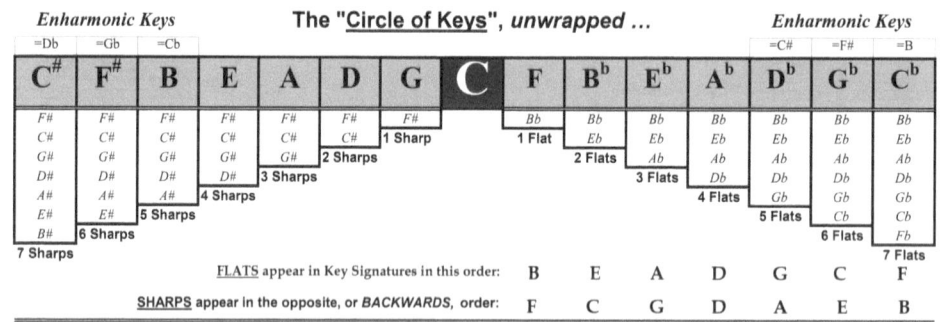

C#	F#	B	E	A	D	G	**C**	F	B♭	E♭	A♭	D♭	G♭	C♭
F#	F#	F#	F#	F#	F#	F#		B♭	B♭	B♭	B♭	B♭	B♭	B♭
C#	C#	C#	C#	C#	C#	1 Sharp		1 Flat	E♭	E♭	E♭	E♭	E♭	E♭
G#	G#	G#	G#	G#	2 Sharps				A♭	A♭	A♭	A♭	A♭	A♭
D#	D#	D#	D#	3 Sharps					2 Flats	D♭	D♭	D♭	D♭	D♭
A#	A#	A#	4 Sharps						3 Flats	G♭	G♭	G♭	G♭
E#	E#	5 Sharps								4 Flats	C♭	C♭	C♭
B#	6 Sharps										5 Flats	F♭	F♭
7 Sharps												6 Flats	7 Flats

FLATS appear in Key Signatures in this order: B   E   A   D   G   C   F

SHARPS appear in the opposite, or *BACKWARDS*, order: F   C   G   D   A   E   B

Figuring out the name of a Major Key when you can see the *Key Signature*:

1) For SHARP keys, *the last sharp in the Key Signature is Ti*. Go up 1/2 step to the very next line or space to find the name of the Major Key.
2) For FLAT keys, *the last flat in the Key Signature is Fa*. Count down four notes - "*Fa-Mi-Re-Do*" - to find the name of the Major Key.
   NOTE: Coincidentally, the *next-to-last flat* IS the name of the Major Key. This only works with Flat keys!!

Figuring out the Key Signature when you know the name of the *Key or Scale*:

1) First, determine if it's a SHARP Key or a FLAT Key. Notice that "F" is the only Flat key without a flat in its name!
2) Next, use the "Musical Alphabet" to create a basic scale before adding the Key. Example: "EFGABCDE"
3A) Now, if it's a Sharp key, remember that "the last sharp in the Key Signature is Ti". Add a sharp to the 7th note, or "Ti".
   Using the order of the sharps, simply keep adding sharps until you've reached the last sharp on "Ti". See above: E F# G# A B C# D# E
3B) If it's a Flat key, remember that "the last flat in the Key Signature is Fa". Add a flat to the 4th note, or "Fa".
   Using the order of the flats, simply keep adding flats until you've reached the last flat on "Fa". Using the key of Ab: Ab Bb C D♭ Eb F G Ab

Some guidelines for figuring out *Transpositions*:

"C" instruments play the "Concert" Key. If asked for "Concert Ab Major", simply play Ab Major.
"F" instruments play a Perfect 5th above Concert Key. **Subtract 1 b, or add 1 #: go 1 Key to the LEFT**, above. "Ab" becomes Eb.
"Bb" instruments play a whole-step above Concert Key. **Subtract 2 b's, or add 2 #'s: go 2 Keys to the LEFT**. "Ab" becomes Bb.
"Eb" instruments play a Major 6th above Concert Key. **Subtract 3 b's, or add 3 #'s: go 3 Keys to the LEFT**. "Ab" becomes F.

©2000 R. Linaberry

Figure 3.3 "Circle of Keys" graphic, from "Key Sequences: Warm-Ups for Band", R. Linaberry.

encourage students to "speak" the contents of each key. For example, "A-flat major has four flats: B♭, E♭, A♭, and D♭." Like other graphics, the enharmonics are clearly identified. However, by rolling this printed graphic into a *cylinder*, students can easily visualize the enharmonic keys as they occupy the same space. The cylinder version allows students to literally play "around the circle" of keys (see the Resources Website [**RW3.1**] for a printable copy).

During the warm-ups, have your best Circle of Keys *strategies* ready to go. After students know how to transpose a concert pitch to their instrument, some suggested Circle of Keys start-up strategies can include:

○ *Play around the circle.* Play unison whole notes starting with Concert C. After one measure, move to Concert F, then B♭, then E♭, and so on, making sure students know how to get through the enharmonic keys. Begin by using steady whole notes, but experiment with other note values, odd meters, relevant rhythms, articulation patterns, and more.

○ *Play partial scales in each key.* A partial-scale exercise can illustrate the 4th/5th relationships in the Circle, and can help players learn scales through *tetrachords*. Teach the students to play a small portion of the scale in each key; avoid notation by using verbal instruction, call-and-response, Curwen/Kodály hand signals or any other method. Finish each partial scale with a melodic cadence, leading the player's ear to the next key (Figures 3.4 and 3.5).

Figures 3.4 Partial scale figures, leading to the next key in the circle.

Figures 3.5 Partial scale figures, leading to the next key in the circle.

○ *Play each ascending/descending scale before moving to the next key.*

Figure 3.6 Full scale figure, leading to the next key in the circle.

○ *Play two adjacent keys simultaneously.* Divide the band to play chosen figures based on the sound of the open 4th/5th. By playing in two keys (e.g. Concert B♭ and F), students can work on any of the goals you've established, *plus* the band refines its awareness of beatless tuning (see Chapter 5) by playing parallel lines, always with a perfect interval sounding.

- *Build chords.* A main goal in any music education setting is to help students develop listening skills. This exercise teaches the sound of various chord qualities, and helps students improve them in their playing. To hear the minor triad, for example, assign three groups to play simultaneously in the keys of C, E♭, and G. Move around the circle as trained to hear other minor triads. TIP: Build triads, seventh chords, added-tone chords, quartal chords, or virtually any type of sonority with the Circle while also applying balance, blend, and tuning concepts.
- *Target specific chords from the repertoire.* Choose and analyze any problematic chord from a composition and reduce it to its basic root-position. Repeat the "build chords" exercise, playing around the Circle on the chosen chord quality. When the band arrives back at the original key, and is sustaining the chord with a beautiful sound, send players back to the chord as scored in the composition. Students should be urged to transfer the same beautiful sound from the closed-position exercise back to the wider scoring in the composition. TIP: Send players *gradually* (principal players first) from the Circle-sustain back to the targeted chord, stopping as needed to adjust the sound before adding other players.

Section 2: To Keep the Percussion Section Active

Percussion is an important topic, explored in greater detail later in Chapter 7. This section is limited to discussion of the band's warm-up, driven by this notion: if we don't involve percussionists in the warm-up, we're depriving them of an important musical and educational experience. Worse, inactivity can foster unwanted behaviors and apathy in the very backbone of our band. Mindful directors will engage percussionists throughout the entire experience, starting with the warm-up process.

Here are some easy ways to involve the percussion section in the band's warm-up:

- A default plan will provide activity, albeit at a basic level: use the percussion section as a timekeeper with a very simple steady pulse, or a basic rhythmic figure that can be conveyed easily by rote to fit the desired tempo and style. Caveat: while this process keeps students on task and uses some of their skills, it won't challenge them to advance their technique as much as other activities. Moreover, it won't help percussionists feel *important* or bring them joy about their band experience.
- During a scale or interval-based warm-up (like the Remington or a Circle of Keys strategy), the mallet instruments will already be playing. Assign a pulse or basic rhythmic figure to bass drum and crash cymbals, along with a rudiment or other chosen rhythm to the other battery instruments to engage the rest of the section. Display notation as needed.
- Using "Treasury of Scales" (or any chorales with pre-written percussion), give the percussion section your most careful attention. Offer detailed instructions and careful feedback designed specifically for percussion: help students to refine the balance, and their concept of rolls, dynamics, and phrasing. Expect a quality sound, and guide the students explicitly toward the goal.
- Superimpose a standard percussion warm-up exercise onto the winds' warm-up. For example, have *all* percussionists play a typical "eight on a hand" exercise.
- Similarly, a basic percussion ensemble or section warm-up etude can layer onto the winds' playing. A nice source is "Marching Percussion 101: Essential Drumline Warmups" (Brian S. Mason, Vic Firth).

- Mallet instruments and timpani can almost always participate using this simple strategy: give the mallet players a C part to read and assign the tonic note of the key for the timpani player to roll as a drone.
- During a Chorale, have the entire section play on *mallet instruments*: all students can play at least *one part* (Soprano, Alto, Tenor, Bass) on the mallet keyboard, while some can take two-, three-, or four-mallet roles. Roll the longer notes. Direct students to use their best balance/blend skills for a beautiful ensemble sound. Notate parts in advance if needed.
- Extract a short percussion excerpt from the band's repertoire. Loop a selected 2-, 4-, or 8-measure segment from the first piece to be rehearsed. Or, repeat a strain from a march.
- For wind warm-ups in logical phrase-lengths, separate those phrases with a piece of a percussion cadence, much like "trading fours" in jazz; for example, a 4-measure wind sequence (while percussionists keep basic time), followed by four measures of *resting* for winds while the percussionists play a chunk of their cadence.

If the budget allows, purchase a warm-up with the percussion section in mind. Some selected recommendations emphasizing percussion participation include:

- *Sound Innovations: Ensemble Development for Intermediate Concert Band* by Peter Boonshaft and Chris Bernotas (Alfred Music Publishing, 2012)
- *Symphonic Band Technique* by Tom C. Rhodes and Donald Bierschenk (Southern Music Company, 1986)
- *Technicises for Band* by Jim Probasco and Dan Meeks (Heritage Music Press, 2000)
- *The Artistry of Fundamentals for Band* by Frank Erickson (Alfred Music Publishing, 1992)
- *Symphonic Warm-Ups for Band* by Claude T. Smith (Hal Leonard, 1982)
- *Key Sequences for Band* by Robin Linaberry (PDF available from author, 2018)

Section 3: Some Scale Games

There's no dispute about the importance of scales, which serve as the bricks-and-mortar in the construction of almost all traditional compositions: students easily notice scales and scale-fragments throughout their band music. When students are accomplished at scales, they are likely to be equally accomplished at their instruments and the music they play. Besides the development of dexterity, coordination, and muscle-memory, students will also make great gains in sight-reading, control of ensemble timing, and knowledge of music theory. And, they'll probably do much better in their contests and auditions. Nevertheless, it can be notoriously difficult to motivate students to practice "boring" scales! We validate the importance of scales by making them the foundation of the band's warm-up process; and we can motivate students by occasionally including *fun* ways to play scales:

- *Scales in canon*. Major, minor, or otherwise, scales can be fashioned into canons. Those canons support basic scale development, but also serve as "instant chorales" and valuable listening exercises. Figure 3.7 ends on a long unison for listening; the *alternate version* may take a moment to describe to students, but it ends with a full triad in the tonic key. Experiment with part assignments for different sonorities, and use major, minor, and other scales.

Scale in Canon, ending on Unison

Scale in Canon, alternate version ending on Triad

Figure 3.7 Using scales in canon during the warm-up: two versions.

- *The expanding scale.* Known by other names, the expanding scale format is excellent as a *flexibility* exercise (Figure 3.8). At slower speeds, it also serves as a sequential method to learn new or "difficult" scales. Try it also with no conductor, allowing the ensemble to work on its precise rhythmic timing and "group pulse." By removing the scale-tones to leave only *intervals*, the exercise offers the same benefits gained by brass players from Arban studies.

Expanding Scale

Expanding *Intervals*

Figure 3.8 Expanding scale and expanding intervals to assist with scale-learning, flexibility, and steady pulse.

- *A rhythmic scale.* The scale format given in Figure 3.9 is excellent at any tempo. The "build-a-scale" method of adding new tones is helpful to students learning unfamiliar scales, and the rhythmic aspect assists with developing the group's steady pulse, clarity of articulations and overall precision. This works well without a conductor.

Figure 3.9 A rhythmic "build-a-scale" setting.

- *The rhythmic scale in other meters.* The rhythmic scale can also refine the group's pulse in other meters. We can also change the articulations (Figure 3.10).

Figure 3.10 The rhythmic scale also supports other meters.

- Once again, refer to Ed Lisk's *The Creative Director* series for further ideas about rhythmic activities with scales during the warm-up.
- *Note*—almost any scale warm-up has a default plan to accommodate students who haven't learned a scale, or who can't keep up at an advanced speed: those players can simply *sustain* a tonic unison, or a root–5th open drone.

Section 4: Chorales from the Band's Literature

- *The easy way #1.* Play a slow scale-in-canon in the key of the rehearsal piece.
- *The easy way #2.* Select a Chorale as a part of the concert repertoire. By programming a Chorale on a concert, it then becomes relevant and helpful to use it during the band's warm-up. As such, you're meeting both general and specific goals. *Any* chorale can allow you to work on tone and balance in addition to your favorite phrasing and interpretive concepts. But by choosing a specific Chorale from your performance repertoire, you achieve those important goals while also shaping the concert details. Use these moments to reinforce music-marking (penciling) processes. TIP: Chapter 7 offers strategies to engage the percussion section during chorales.

A list of widely programmed chorales, ballads, hymns, and other lyrical pieces can be found on the Resources Website [**RW3.2**].

WARM-UPS AND MORE

- *Many other types of compositions include Chorale excerpts.* Countless overtures and other pieces in A–B–A form offer extensive lyrical sections. Choose a lyrical excerpt to build your warm-up at the *beginning* of the rehearsal session. In addition, many multi-movement works include beautiful slow movements. The Resources Website has a list [**RW3.3**] of well-known works with beautiful lyrical sections.
- *"Instant Chorales" created on-the-spot from the repertoire.* There are some easy shortcuts to *create* chorales from almost any tonal piece, to use during the warm-up. Here are three of the most common strategies:

1. *Sustain* the first note of each measure. For example, to create a simple whole-note chorale, hold *Beat 1* of the first measure for four beats, then continue to Beat 1 of the second measure. This strategy exposes the basic chord progression for the excerpt, without any technical demands. This is a fine strategy for *marches*.
2. Play the excerpt *slowly*, and/or *augment the rhythms/meter.* For example, using *The Fairest of the Fair* (Sousa) (Figure 3.11) choose a very slow tempo and conduct in four (the eighth-note); ask the students to slur. "Now play this like a chorale."

"The Fairest of the Fair", John Phillip Sousa ~ Meas. 49-52, the Original version
March ♩ = 120

Read in 4/8 time, slowly and sustained to create a Chorale
Chorale ♪ = 60

Rhythms augmented > students can view the same sound in a more common Meter
Chorale ♩ = 60

Figure 3.11 Rhythmic augmentation to create a Chorale.

Note that in the second version of Figure 3.11 ($\frac{4}{8}$), students will follow conducting motions based on the eighth-notes in $\frac{4}{8}$ meter.

3. Play and *sustain* each "new" pitch. Much like sustaining "beat 1" of each measure, the strategy works for excerpts where vertical chord-changes are aligned. This is especially good for less-traditional or non-functional chord progressions, because the process affords the opportunity to isolate the chords. Students have time to hear, balance, and *tune* chords that are problematic in their original context (at a faster tempo, or with complex rhythms, or other technical distractors).

In its original tempo, the chord progression in the woodwind excerpt in Figure 3.12 can be challenging for students' ears.

Figure 3.12 Spartan Proclamation, excerpted from Linaberry.

But by creating a Chorale, the students can more easily hear (and *tune*) this non-traditional chord progression (Figure 3.13):

A♭ maj ~ C maj | E maj ~ A♭ maj | C ~ E | A♭ ~ C | (F)

As a bonus for students who might enjoy Music Theory in the context of band, in this specific chord progression (A♭–C | E–A♭ | C–E | A♭–C | F), students will see a special 3rds relationship. That is, each *third* becomes the root of the next chord.

Figure 3.13 Spartan Proclamation *excerpt transformed to a Chorale setting.*

Section 5: Exercises Based on Important Rhythms

While this process is self-explanatory (and therefore doesn't require extensive examples), it's remarkably relevant to your goals because you'll choose *specific* rhythms. By targeting problematic rhythmic passages, or even basic meters and "grooves," the warm-up concepts transfer smoothly into the composition you'll rehearse with the band. A simple checklist of options can guide you:

❏ *Books*. If the budget allows, put a rhythm book in each folder. Many notable "all-purpose" warm-up books have sections or chapters dedicated to rhythmic development. For a stand-alone rhythm book (which also supports sight-reading!), try *101 Rhythmic Rest Patterns* by Grover C. Yaus (Warner Bros, 1995). This collection of unison rhythmic exercises (arranged in progressive order) can work without a conductor, for more work on the band's group pulse.
❏ *Rhythm sheets*. Equip each folder with a rhythmic reference, especially one with rhythms grouped into categories (e.g. ties, dotted-eighth figures, syncopations, triplets).
❏ *Meters and "Grooves."* Create a relevant warm-up exercise to help refine a specific rhythm, meter or style (Figure 3.14). The rhythmic focus applied during the warm-up will then transfer directly into the composition.

These are only random suggestions, of course, meant to spark further creative ideas. Connect your own design strategically to the music your students are playing. Notation can help, but it may

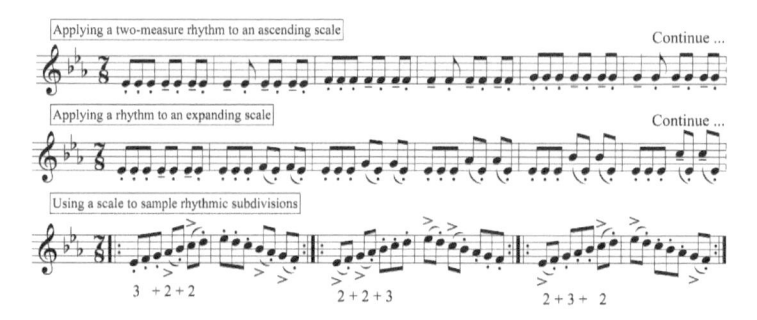

Figure 3.14 Examples of structures created to support a specific meter.

also limit students' ability to *listen*. Consider singing or playing a demonstration for students. Include careful instructions, whether verbal or *non-verbal*, to guide the students toward shaping the desired sound. Again, be conscious of the percussion section's engagement.

Specific rhythms from repertoire, looped. When small groups encounter a problematic rhythm, construct a warm-up exercise to engage *all students*. The target group receives the needed attention and feedback, but without the potential embarrassment of scrutiny by peers, which can be demoralizing. By engaging more students, this process also sustains better classroom management while reinforcing an important tenet of music education: "Listen carefully to what the other sections are doing, because their concepts and details will likely show up in your parts too." The following examples illustrate how this strategy can be applied to help your students' performance:

1. Trumpet students frequently misinterpret the rhythms in the *swing* section of Leroy Anderson's *Sleigh Ride* (Figure 3.15). Their accuracy can improve by asking the entire band to play the rhythm. Guide students with specific feedback about articulations, style and spacing. Then, send the trumpet section to their written parts while the remaining students play only the rhythm; even when some dissonances occur, students should be advised to listen to the *rhythmic* aspects of the performance.

Figure 3.15 Looping a targeted rhythmic figure using a scale.

2. To prepare for *Armenian Dances (Part 1)* by Alfred Reed at measure 87: display the rhythm in Figure 3.16 and assign "*sol*" to line 1, "*mi*" to line 2 and "*Do*" to line 3. Choose a scale; the actual excerpt is in A minor, but we'll start with C major. Begin by playing each line in unison to build rhythmic confidence while molding the group's style and articulations.

Figure 3.16 A specific design created to support *Armenian Dances*, mm. 87–88.

3. These rhythmic-support exercises can be expanded to become *pitched* unison exercises. The strategy in Figure 3.17 is included here under warm-ups, but it works just as well during the concentrated *rehearsal* portion of the period. Whether used as a warm-up or as a supportive activity during the class, this example shows how a full-band unison can reinforce the "Cool" rhythmic bassline in Bernstein's *West Side Story* (arr. Duthoit) at Rehearsal 18.

Figure 3.17 A specific unison design to support *West Side Story*, "Cool".

Section 6: Exercises to Teach by Rote

With clear and succinct details—conveyed verbally, or by singing or playing a demonstration—the teacher can convey a warm-up strategy *by rote*.

- *Call-and-response*. Jazz directors become comfortable with call-and-response as a common rehearsal tool. There are equally strong reasons for the concert band director to play (or sing!) figures that the students will then play back. Involve the percussion by starting a *groove* to accompany the activity. Try starting with single-pitch rhythms, 2–4 beats in length, asking the band to play it back immediately. Gradually lengthen the figures and add intervals of increasing width.

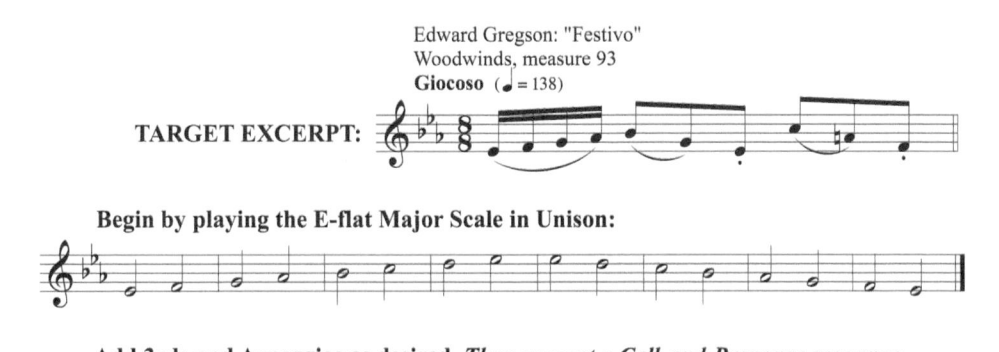

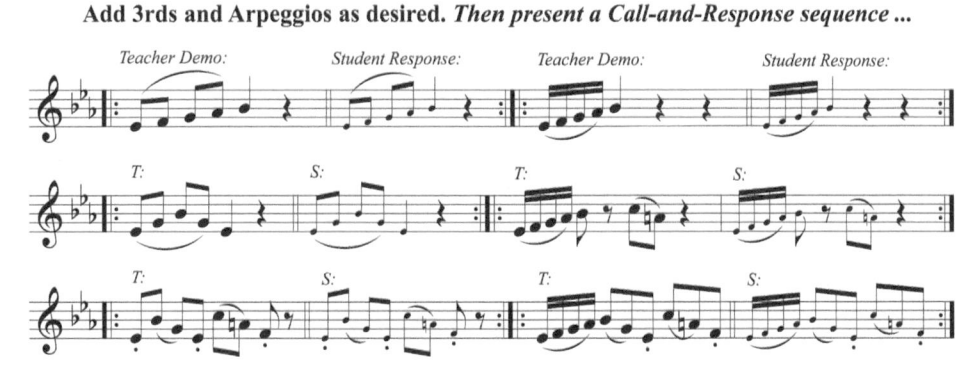

Figure 3.18 Call-and-response to gradually assemble a problematic figure. *Festivo* by Edward Gregson. Copyright ©1987 Novello & Co., Ltd. This arrangement copyright ©2020 Novello & Co., Ltd. International copyright secured all rights reserved. Reprinted by permission of Hal Leonard LLC.

WARM-UPS AND MORE

- *Fragments.* For an excellent practical variation, sing or play fragments of an important excerpt from the repertoire. Although this process requires some early practice for the teacher to present a logical lesson plan smoothly, it can focus the group toward gradually assembling a precise version of the goal figure. This strategy supports the "sound first, notation second" philosophy.
- *Scale-based figures.* These types of strategies are promoted by revered experts like Jamey Aebersold (*Jazz Handbook*; *How to Play Jazz & Improvise*), and Ed Lisk in his "Creative Director" series. Using the Circle of 4ths/5ths (or Cycle of Keys/Scales, as you choose):
    - "Hold the tonic note for 'X' beats, rest for 'X' then move to the next key."
    - "Play the first five notes of the scale up and down, then change keys."
    - "Play this rhythm" (model) "on Concert F, then move to B♭, E♭, etc."
    - "Play the scale from the root to the 9th, and back down. Rest for two beats and move to the next key."
    - Add your creative ideas; collect/adapt what you borrow from others.
- *Transposable figures.* Here are two creative strategies that are helpful to the development of students' total musicianship, *and* they tend to be fun as well. Numerous benefits will compensate for any extra time required to prepare and practice them:
    1. *Impromptu Chorales in any key.* In this case, teaching "by rote" is perhaps a misnomer. Teach students to use scale-degrees, indicated either by *numbers*, by *Solfege syllables*, or even by *Curwen/Kodály hand signs* to play (or sing!) a chord progression. Students can then perform from a display or, just as easily, they can perform a short melodic sequence from memory and then transpose immediately to any key.

        Try starting with a short unison line for the entire ensemble; then progress through duets, trios and beyond. *By rote*, you can ask small groups of students (e.g. SATB parts) to "memorize this: Do-Fa-Sol-Sol-Do. Now let's *play* it in the key of D-flat major." Figure 3.19 shows just one possibility of how to play and transpose a standard 4-part chorale without music notation.

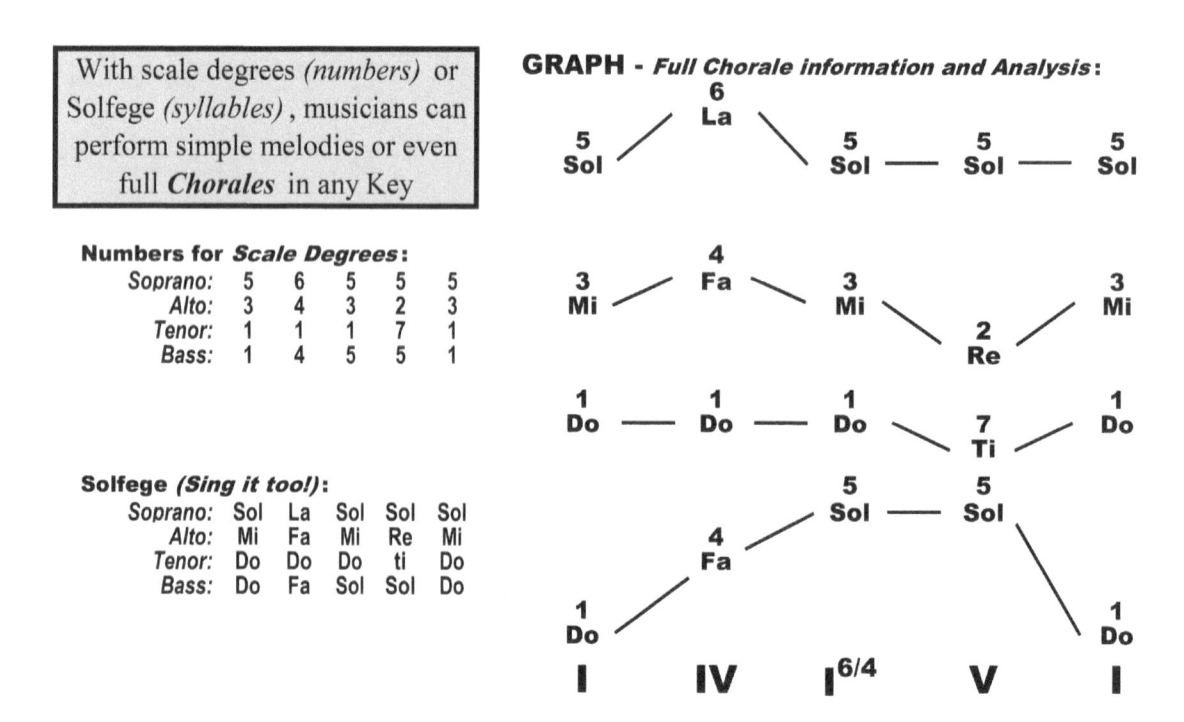

Figure 3.19 Chorale method based on Solfege syllables and scale-degree numbers.

2. *Duets (and even trios!) from hand signs.* Starting as early as possible, teach students to respond to your solfege hand signs. Begin with sustained tones, using predictable steps at first, rather than leaps. When students have developed confidence, you can communicate a range of creative exercises *non-verbally*. Then, when your own ambidexterity has developed, divide the ensemble into halves, each side following one of your hands to create a duet on the spot (Figure 3.20).

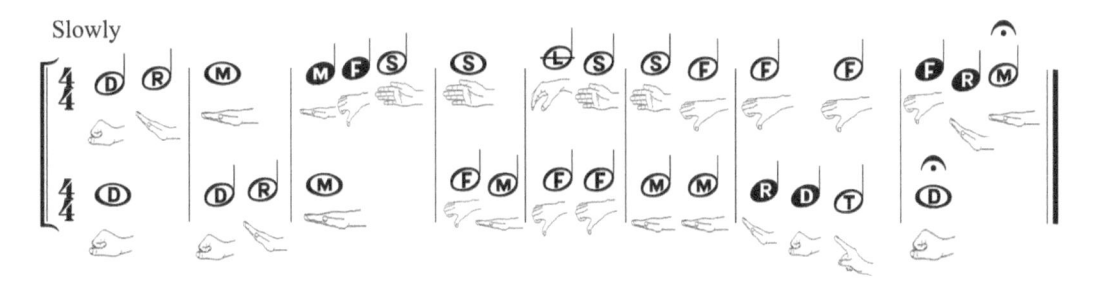

Figure 3.20 Hand signals for duets.

Tip: By adding a drone, either mechanically or by having bass voices sustain the note, you can create a trio: your hand-signals direct two pitches moving above the pedal-point tonic.

- *Creatively design warm-ups to address idiomatic skill-needs.* Figure 3.21 is constructed to support the octave-slurs helpful to flutes, the flexibilities important to brass players, and the scale technique so frequently required by the rest of the woodwinds. Continue to involve the percussionists with meaningful material as well.

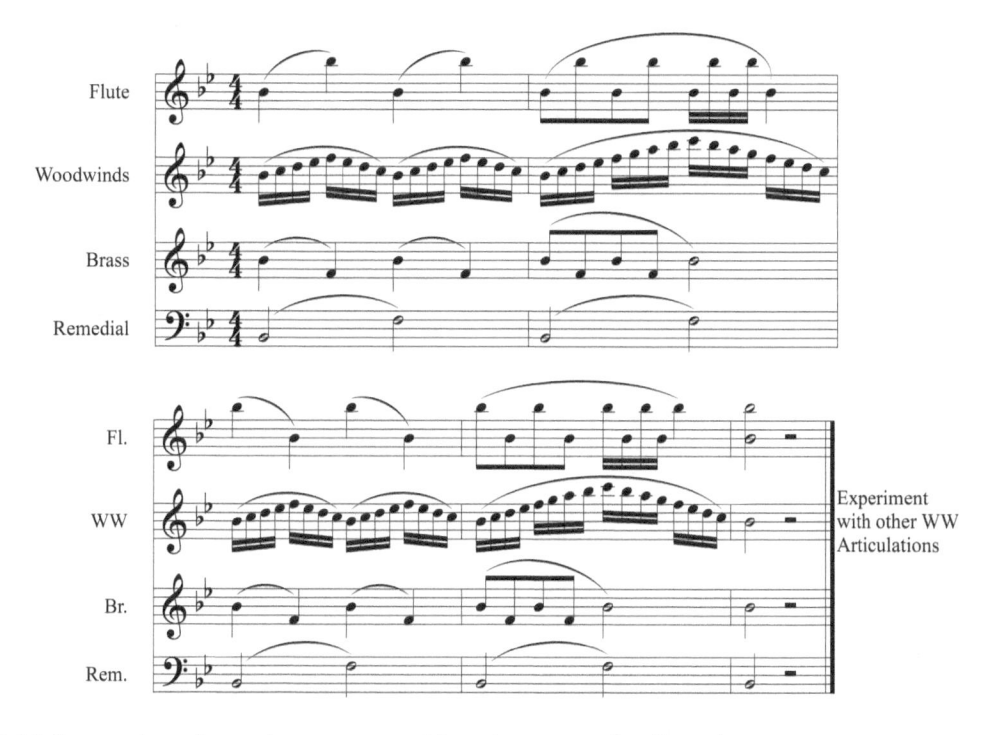

Figure 3.21 Structuring a focused warm-up to address instrument-family goals.

As director, you'll determine which instrument-specific goals you'd like to target. Then, design your own creative warm-up to meet those goals.

Section 7: Additional Strategies

- *Hockets and Pointillism in the Band Warm-Up.* Every player is critically important to the band. These suggested strategies will clearly convey that philosophy to our students, and the activities will be both enlightening and *fun* for the group. With these exercises, individuals do not perform the entire exercise; instead, each player is responsible for supplying individual, isolated notes, precisely placed, without which the full melody can't exist. Percussion ensemble players understand and accept this concept as the "norm"; we can use these activities to support wind players' rhythmic development.

  Notice that the sample exercises that follow are similar to the skills required to perform:

  ○ handbells
  ○ boomwhackers®
  ○ tonal marching bass drums
  ○ body-percussion.

  Even *jugglers* can perform exciting music if their rhythm is exact!

  The reason for making these connections is explicit: by using hockets/pointillism (or any general rhythmic games) during the band's warm-up procedures, we can help students develop their individual rhythmic responsibility, and the precision of the whole ensemble will improve.

  Figure 3.22 contains two examples to inspire your creativity. The first, a simple major scale, can easily be taught by rote; the second, a more complex hocket-setting of a common melody, would

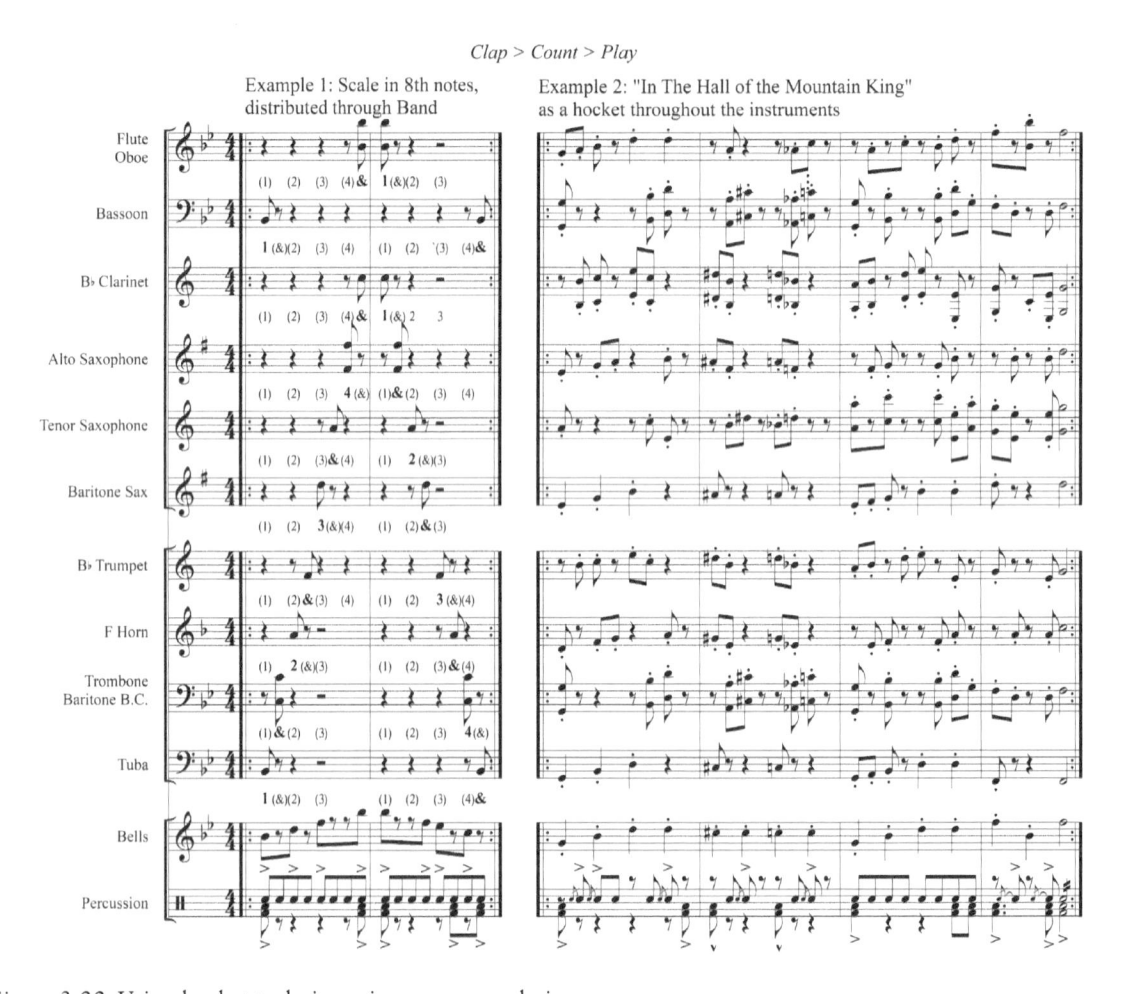

Figure 3.22 Using hocket techniques in a warm-up design.

require printed notation. Whether simple or complex, however, the benefits are the same, *and the students enjoy it.*

Two method books most notably fall into this category, and are *entertaining* for the students while they learn:

- *Technicises for Band (Putting the Pieces Together)* by Jim Probasco and Dan Meeks (Heritage Music Press, 2000)
- *Harmonized Rhythms for Concert Band* by Charles E. Forque & James Thornton (Neil A. Kjos Music Company, 1994).

Example #2 ("*In the Hall of the Mountain King*") in Figure 3.22 also provides a model of another compositional technique helpful during the warm-up. By designing exercises based on alternating *colors* and *textures*, we work further to refine Balance/Blend in the ensemble. *Klangfarbenmelodie* (translated to 'sound-color melody') exercises reinforce students' listening skills while continuing to support their rhythmic precision. When students use the Circle of Keys, only a few words will be required to begin a *klangfarbenmelodie* exercise with your band.

The musical example provided in Figure 3.23 requires very little verbal description for your students. Use a 4-part setting based on *Treasury of Scales* groups, Ed Lisk's well-organized groupings, "Upper/Lower Woodwinds and Upper/Lower Brass," or any creative design of your own to easily achieve a 4-part set of groups.

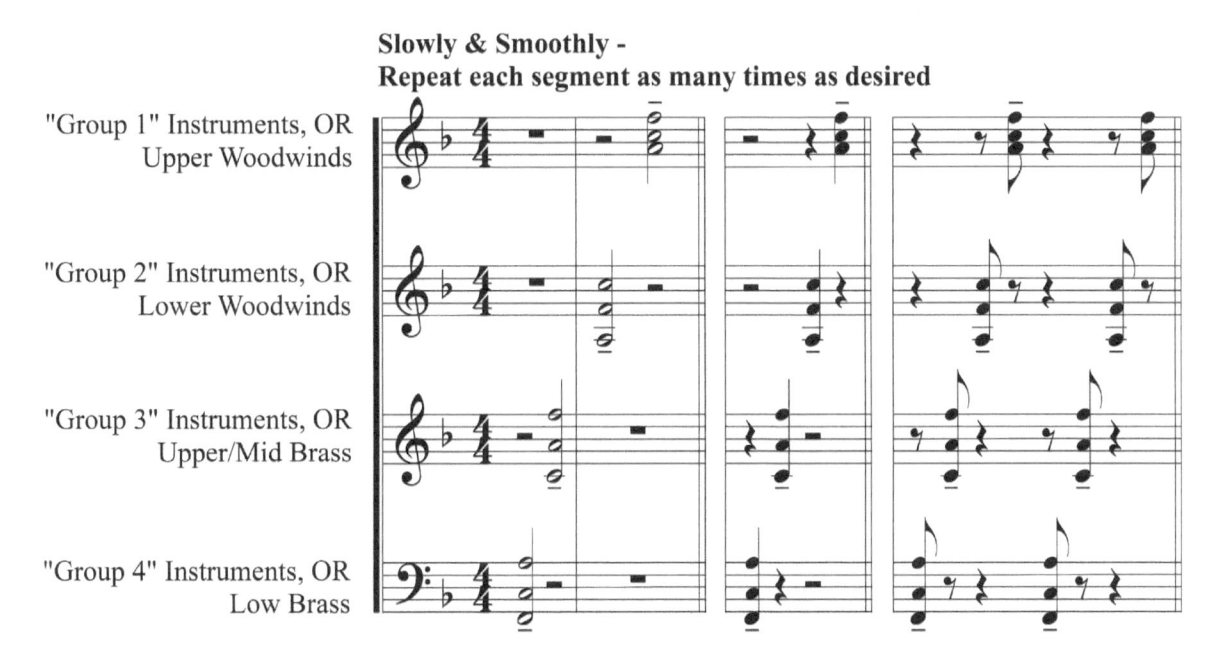

Figure 3.23 Klangfarben chords in 4-part assignments (suggestions).

Figure 3.24 is a more advanced exercise and would probably require written music notation, but it has the advantage of isolating instrument sounds. This will be an exceptional type of exercise to help students *blend* their timbre and *balance* their volume.

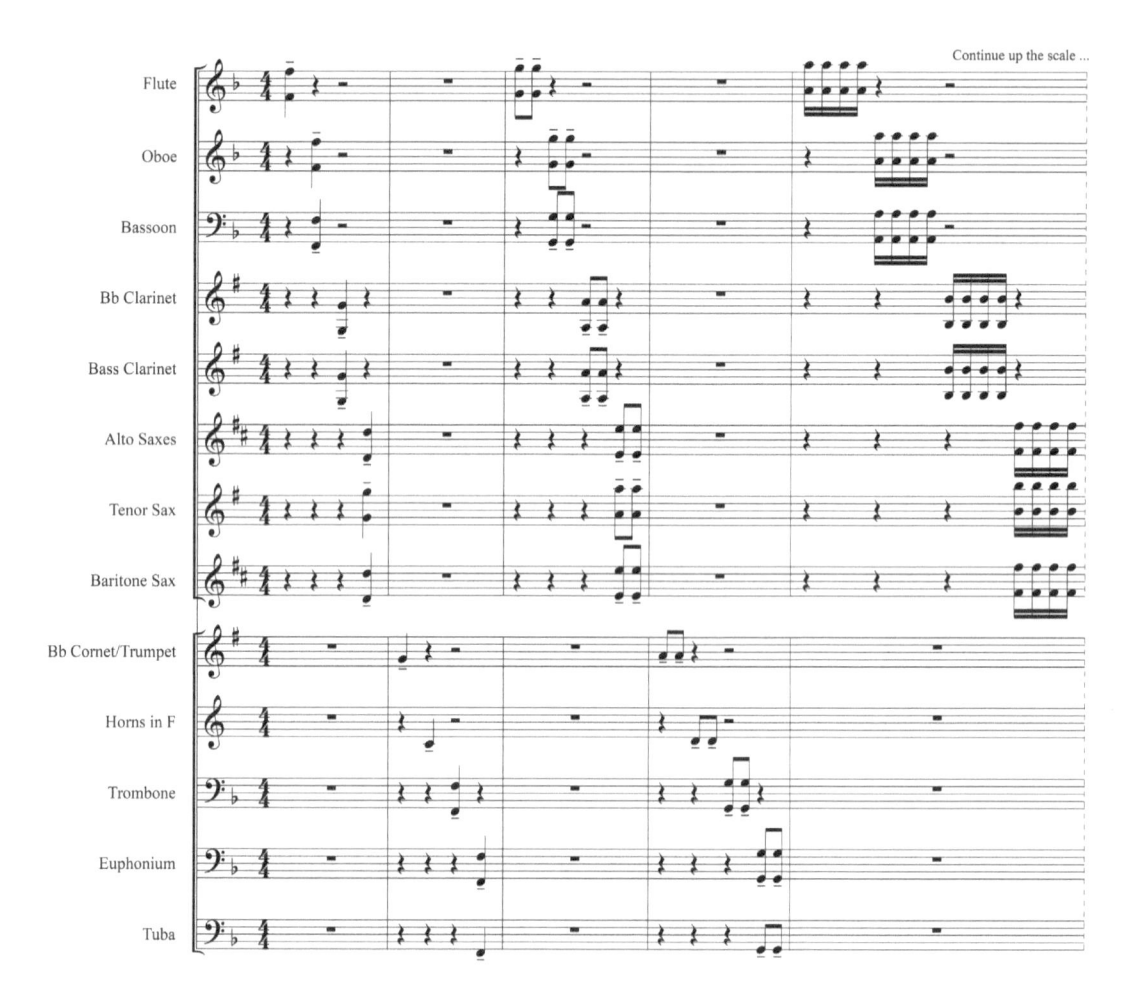

Figure 3.24 Klangfarbenmelodie on a simple scale (ideas).

Such exercises can be altered many ways and can be used in like-instrument classes as well; these will also support the group's improvement of internal pulse. Rather than limiting the color-matching to unison scales, try chords using a *Circle of Keys* approach.

- *Using IMSLP in the warm-up.* The International Music Score Library Project, with the mission of "sharing the world's public domain music," offers access to a vast collection of music. After a bit of a learning curve to navigate the website, you'll find access to a tremendous resource for chorales, sight-reading and full compositions.
- *Additional publications of note.* These include Collected Chorale Settings by David Maslanka (available from the composer's website at www.davidmaslanka.com, 2005) and *Function Chorales* by Stephen Melillo (www.stephenmelillo.com, 1980). More than just sets of chorales, these are wonderful teaching tools to support music theory, intonation, resonance, transposition, listening, student-creativity, and much more.
- *Combining scales/keys.* There are many gains available through performing *two* simultaneous scales.

We already know that we can get a series of parallel vertical chords (major, minor, etc.) by playing *three* scales at once. Figure 3.25 shows that by performing the B♭, D♭, and F *major* scales together, we can hear a series of *minor* chords on every tone (Figure 3.25).

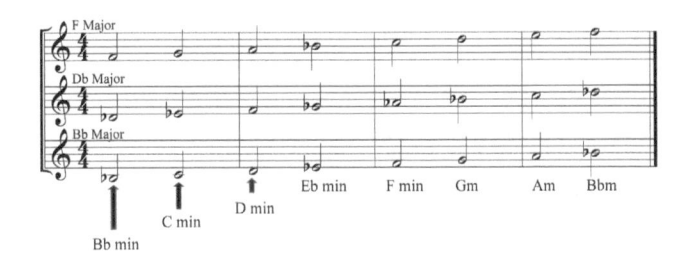

Figure 3.25 Review: three scales from the Circle to hear parallel vertical chords.

But the main benefit of producing an open 4th/5th interval is to assist with ensemble intonation. Students can improve their *beatless tuning* on open intervals by playing two scales a 4th or 5th apart (see Chapter 5).

- *Transposing for tone.* Bands typically just "sound better" in certain keys than in others. It's not the primary goal of this book to describe the reasons *why* a band playing in G-flat major sounds better than when the same band plays in an "easier" key of G major. For this specific suggestion, the goal will be to use transposition to transfer good tone and intonation into a new key. For example, start by playing a scale in a "less-enjoyable" band key. We'll choose D major, which requires other students to play E major (B♭ instruments), B major (E♭ instruments), and A major (F instruments). After playing the scale, ask the students to insert a new key signature (D-flat rather than D) in order to transpose the scale a half-step down. Get the best possible tone and intonation in one key, and then transfer that *sound* back to the original key (Figure 3.26).

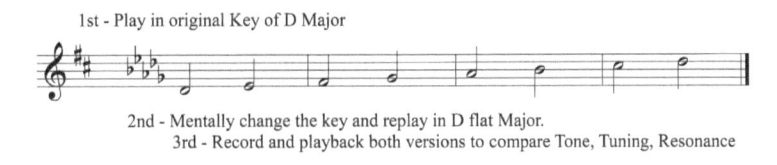

Figure 3.26 Using two key signatures on the same notated music.

Once the students know how to do this with scales, then you can use the process with *Chorales*. Choose a Chorale in A major and ask the band to play it in A-flat major instead. You may need to interject some rules so the students know how to address accidentals, but the results of this process will be worth your effort.

Concluding Notes about Warm-Ups and Chorales

Hopefully there will *never* be "final" thoughts about these topics! For now, the importance of this warm-ups section can be distilled down to a few key bullets:

- The Circle of Keys can serve as an unending source of opportunities: learn how to use it creatively.
- Fundamentals form the lowest rungs on the ladder to instrumentalists' success, and the warm-up process can support all kinds of fundamentals: remember that "fundamentals" include *listening* and *behavioral* skills as much as performance skills.
- The significant focus on Chorales in this section is by design: playing (and singing) Chorales may be the perfect vehicle to develop a band's overall sound, and to convey a vast collection of artistic, interpretive ideas. Use the previous suggestions only as a springboard toward many further designs.

- Do everything you can to keep percussionists involved and motivated.
- Be a role model every day: if the band members know that you believe in the importance of the warm-up, and that you are interested in (and appreciative of) their steps toward improvement during the warm-up, they'll "buy in." Your attitudes can lead them to become more engaged, more dedicated, and more able to recognize how the warm-up process is inextricably linked to their success.
- The warm-up process, like several other pedagogical categories for the band, offers infinite space for creativity by a strategic band director. Your work is not limited by a brief section of this one book. Be inventive.

Notes

1 Richard Floyd, *The Artistry of Teaching and Making Music* (Chicago: GIA Publications, Inc., 2015), 49.
2 Edward S. Lisk, *The Creative Director: Alternative Rehearsal Techniques* (Delray Beach, FL: Meredith Music Publications, 2000).

4

ON THE SOUND

Tone Quality, Blend, Dynamics, Ensemble Balance, and Articulations

Introduction

Beautiful tone quality is essential; it's a cornerstone in our understanding of many other elements of band education. "Band tone is of the utmost and primary importance because until we get what we call 'a good basic band tone' there isn't any point in going on to anything else."[1] An instrumentalist who can play faster than others—or higher, louder, more rhythmically precise, or with better articulations—will not be fully appreciated with poorly developed tone quality. The youngest and least-experienced listeners appreciate a lovely sound, and even non-musicians can discern good tone from bad. Tone is therefore "Job #1",—the first, last and most frequent responsibility of the performer.

The problem—for performers, but specifically for band directors—is that tone is a product of many influencing factors. Those components, along with blend and balance, will comprise the focus of this chapter. Refined tone is also arguably the greatest contributor to good intonation (see Chapter 5). It's easy to remember: at the heart of In*ton*ation is *ton*e. This chapter will be limited to strategies guiding the full ensemble toward improved wind-band tone.

Section 1: Building the Concept of Tone

An artist imagines the colors, shading, blending, points-of-focus, type of brush, and style of stroke, all before ever touching the paint or canvas. Similarly, the band director/teacher must conceive an 'auditory pre-vision' for the band—"what should it sound like?" Answering that question is paramount toward developing the group's sound. Musical tone quality is rooted first in the aural concept held by each individual performer, so personal tone-development work by every band member is key to the final ensemble success. But the linchpin to a full band's sound will be the director's concept of tone for the ensemble and, for such an elusive and intangible concept, a very wide variety of educational strategies will prove helpful.

A review of classic archetypes

In developing their unique concept of the band's best overall sound, contemporary band directors are often strongly influenced—even unconsciously—by one of the widely accepted standardized models of *tone*.

- W. Francis McBeth, in his seminal work, *Effective Performance of Band Music* (Southern Music Company, 1972), introduced us to the "Double Pyramid Balance System" (along with "The Pyramid Within the Section", and "The Christmas Tree Pyramid"). More importantly, McBeth offers procedural steps for how to utilize the system in exercises to develop *balance* and maintain it through dynamic changes.

  We've adopted this concept over the years to address *tone* because it does provide a "group version" of natural acoustics: the fundamental and its lower overtones are more prominent in the audible sound than the upper partials, which are less prominent as they ascend in the series. Generally, better band tone begins from more on the bass end, less on the treble end.

  In terms of ensemble tone quality, our most widely accepted sound results from this model, distilled in Figure 4.1 to a basic SATB pyramid.

ON THE SOUND

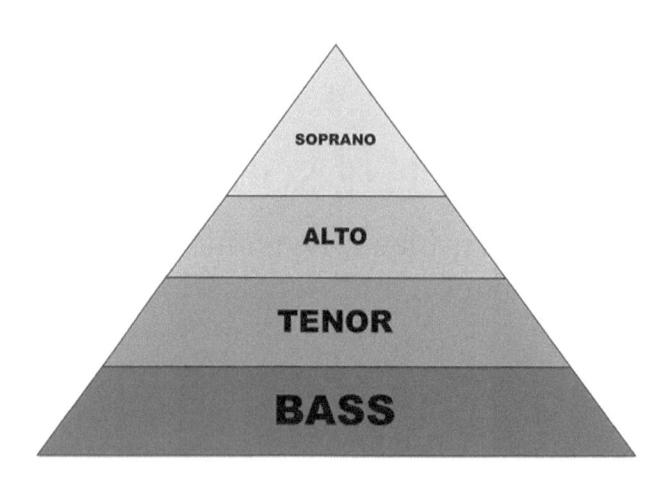

```
            SOPRANO
          ALTO
       TENOR
     BASS
```

Figure 4.1 SATB pyramid

Note: It will be important to be flexible with the application of the pyramid concept. Use it as a recipe for warm wind-band tone, but *not* as a maxim that "Tuba and baritone sax must always be loudest; trumpet 1, clarinet 1, flute 1 must always be softest." No. The actual *balance*, as we'll see later, will adjust to reflect the musical needs of the composer, the composition, the excerpt, the performance venue, and many variables within the group itself.

- With his groundbreaking resources in *The Creative Director* series, Ed Lisk further codifies the SATB groupings applied to the concert band sound. His brilliant systematic instructional approaches make use of his balance groupings (Figure 4.2).

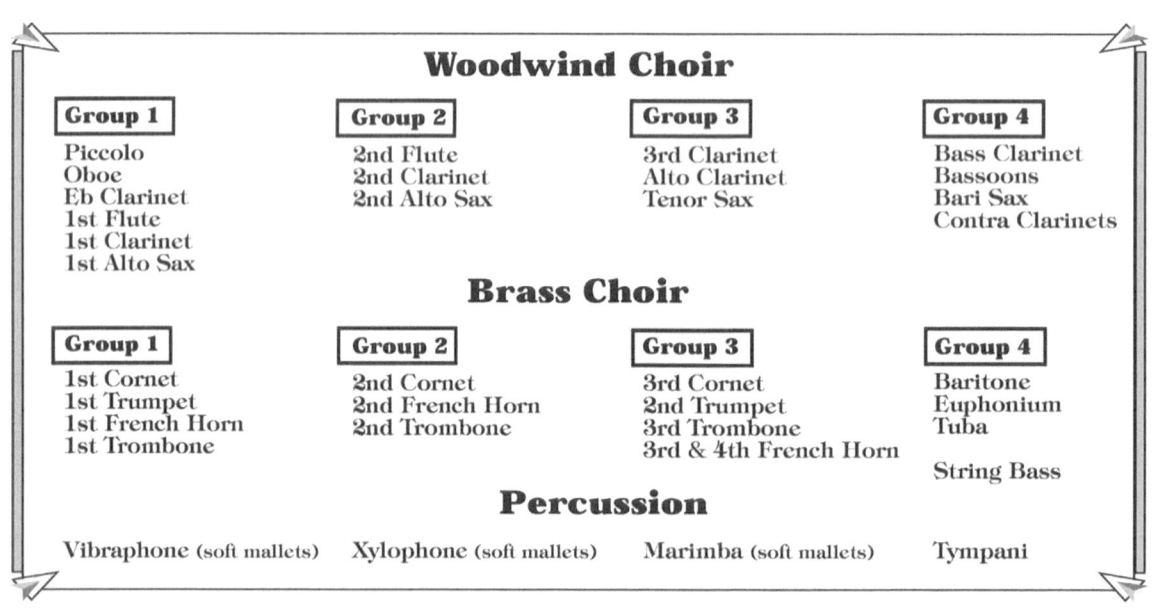

Woodwind Choir

Group 1	**Group 2**	**Group 3**	**Group 4**
Piccolo	2nd Flute	3rd Clarinet	Bass Clarinet
Oboe	2nd Clarinet	Alto Clarinet	Bassoons
Eb Clarinet	2nd Alto Sax	Tenor Sax	Bari Sax
1st Flute			Contra Clarinets
1st Clarinet			
1st Alto Sax			

Brass Choir

Group 1	**Group 2**	**Group 3**	**Group 4**
1st Cornet	2nd Cornet	3rd Cornet	Baritone
1st Trumpet	2nd French Horn	2nd Trumpet	Euphonium
1st French Horn	2nd Trombone	3rd Trombone	Tuba
1st Trombone		3rd & 4th French Horn	
			String Bass

Percussion

Vibraphone (soft mallets)   Xylophone (soft mallets)   Marimba (soft mallets)   Tympani

© Copyright 1991 MEREDITH MUSIC PUBLICATIONS

Figure 4.2 From Lisk's *Circle of 4ths* graphic. Used by permission, Meredith Music Publications.

These groups provide the basis for dozens of well-designed instructional procedures used to enhance and accelerate students' musical learning; the SATB approach remains the strongest acoustic model for rich, resonant ensemble tone quality. Band directors are encouraged to become familiar with the works of Lisk and McBeth.

- An additional principal element in the full-band tone model is also a precept of both balance and blend: no one player's sound should stick out above the rest of the group. A favorite analogy comes from Paula Thornton: "think of the ensemble sound as an envelope into which each musician had to completely fit his or her individual sound."[2]

With these accepted models to start our work, here is a suggested exercise to develop the SATB pyramid sound hrough *layering*. Hear only the bass layer performing as a *Soli*, offering feedback to refine its blend and tone. Then, add Group III, with a single instruction: "Hear each other clearly, but *hide* inside the sound of the previous group. We should feel that you're there, without overpowering the other group." Continue through other layers. Training for this full-group skill can begin with unisons, scales, and chorales, but students will transfer quickly to self-blending during repertoire passages; therefore, remember this process while rehearsing repertoire.

The Importance of Modeling

In band, as in their other endeavors, students will emulate role models. After observing performances and hearing *tone*, musicians then work to copy the model found to be the best. Provide your students with the best aural models as frequently as possible:

- Play recordings of the most outstanding wind bands as exemplars of *tone*.
- Bring guest ensembles to perform on-site for your students; the acoustics and room-resonance of live performances will far outshine what is heard from a recording played through speakers.
- Take students to hear a college band, a great community band, or a concert by a premier United States military band.

"Divide and Conquer" for Tone

Continue to supplement the full-band exemplars by influencing individual students. The brief suggested strategies below, whether used in small groups or full band settings, demonstrate the *Teacher's role* in helping individual students develop their timbral identity. Use these basic models to facilitate further creative ideas:

- Create the environment with tone as the goal:
  - Play highest-quality musical examples, either live or through speakers, as students enter/exit the room.
  - Display QR codes for students to link devices to great examples.
  - Experiment with various seating plans and room-alterations (reflectors, wall treatments, curtains, etc.), and *discuss* the effects of each.
- Perform high-quality demonstrations on your major instrument(s), including voice. Hearing one's teacher perform "live" is arguably the most influential and long-lasting experience to help develop a tonal target. Note: The director must be capable of producing a refined characteristic sound on the instrument.
- Perform a passage in comparative pairs, each time demonstrating how altering a fundamental skill can affect *tone quality*. Some options include:
  - Good posture/positioning vs. poor versions.
  - Desired vs. improper breathing and airstream management.
  - Correct vs. poorly formed embouchure.
  - Oral cavity effects (i.e. a lower tongue with "spacious" throat vs. a high tongue with "closed" throat).

- Equipment effects (i.e. premium/conditioned reed vs. old/chipped reed; student-model vs. upgraded mouthpiece/barrel).
  - Articulation effects of all kinds.
  - Adjustment effects (i.e. too much/too little vs. the correct amount of mouthpiece inserted; the advantage of playing on a tuned instrument compared to the "fight" when a performer's ear tries to play in tune while the instrument is too long/short).
  - Remember percussionists by comparing sticks and mallets, strokes and striking spot, good-vs-bad grips, etc.

- Share a demonstration we might call "Copy my Tone," where the teacher provides a sound that the students then imitate. The teacher plays various tone models, from warm-dark to bright-thin. From this type of exercise, students can assimilate all techniques for *adjusting* the tone quality, and can be guided comparatively toward choosing the darker, more resonant tone model.
- Use exemplary performers within the ensemble as models for others.
- Continue encouraging students to perform chamber music; like-instrument ensembles are especially helpful to the development of idiomatic blended tone.
- Build motivational incentives into your curriculum to encourage exposure to *good tone* models:
  - Host itinerant teachers and mentor performers.
  - Offer extra credit or merits to students who submit proof of attendance to selected events.
  - Continue to encourage private study, summer camps, and extra activity in church and community groups.

Components of Tone Quality Development

As we know, tone quality is a complex element, built from many components, all of which rely strongly on the musician's aural concept. Other important factors include posture, breathing, speed and steadiness of air, the embouchure (or stick/mallet selection and stroke), the player's physique, oral cavity factors, setup, quality of equipment, and much more. Several of these "building blocks" can be tangibly reinforced through strategic processes and activities, while some factors are not as easy for the teacher to control. Our focus remains on the development of the *full band*, but there will necessarily be some references to individuals' tone quality because, of course, better ingredients yield a better product.

If tone quality is a dish, its list of fundamental ingredients begins with *breathing*. Breathing, in turn, is inextricably linked to *posture* because support of the airstream is essential to producing full, characteristic tone quality on any wind instrument. Therefore, *breathing* and *posture* will be addressed first. Note that "breathing" is referenced here as a component of *tone quality* rather than of rhythmic precision or interpretive phrasing, which will be discussed in other chapters. While reading the suggestions for tone quality, and in creating your own activities, please remember to include percussionists; monitor the quality of their grip and stroke, and the choice of sticks/mallets, the quality of their equipment, and other factors.

Strategies, Tips and Activities for Breathing and Posture Development

Most students are adept at imitation, so we should never underestimate the power of demonstrations, role models and other influences. But we can encourage additional growth by taking advantage of students' many other modes of learning. Students also respond well to descriptive words, physical activities, analogies, metaphors, and graphic models. Provide inventive variety with your instruction. The following are some suggested breathing and posture exercises to spark others of your own creation.

Posture—though an incomplete list, these are some guideposts for addressing posture within the full band:

- Model and insist on a posture that allows players to move air in and out most easily with total control.
- Slouching affects the lungs, the diaphragm and intercostal muscles, therefore diminishing the efficiency of the entire breathing mechanism.

- Set the posture first: *bring the instrument to you; don't chase the instrument with your body.*
- A helpful group activity can be described this way: "In a moment, I'll ask you to stand up *silently*." That action alone requires students to move to an appropriate posture, with an erect torso and feet under the center of gravity.
- About posture, Richard Crain says "Place the head in its natural position so that the ceiling and the floor can be seen without having to move the head."[3]

Breathing—the following suggestions will function for full-band settings, but can help with individuals and small group lessons as well. Again, this listing is certainly not complete, but there is a more important caveat: musical breathing is a concept ripe for innumerable opinions. Readers will develop distinctive approaches over time. In the interim, these options will provide a starting repertoire for directors:

- "When I say so, everyone please inhale as quickly and *deeply* as possible . . . Go!" Invariably, we'll watch a sea of rising shoulders. Then, we can ask an easy follow-up question: "How many of you have lungs in your shoulders?" Discuss the appearance of efficient deep breathing. Note: the upper chest *does* expand, but we're trying to avoid stress and tension by keeping the shoulders relaxed.
- Review the "capacity-building" suggestion introduced in Chapter 3: "In for 8, out for 8; 6 in, 10 out," and so on. Finally, "*fill* to capacity in a single instant." Note: this exercise trains the body for a filling inhalation during a breath mark. An extension is to take two more "sips" of air at the fullest extent of the breath.
- Breathe in through the mouth, using a large unobstructed shape, as in the appearance of saying "hauw," "whoa," "hoe," or your favorite syllable
- Breathing should be relaxed, free from tension. Attempt to inhale in silence; extra sound indicates tension, inefficiency, or obstruction.
- To achieve "openness," use a short length of PVC or plastic/rubber tubing, or roll a sheet of clean paper into a ¾–1 inch cylinder. Insert it into the mouth for breathing. The device allows the player to *feel* unimpeded while breathing; it keeps the tongue down and eliminates obstruction. The feeling of this free inhale–exhale process will then transfer into playing. This experience needs to happen only *once* for the benefits to be felt, but it can also be practiced as a part of the routine.
- Exhale fluidly, immediately; do not stop the motion to hold the air in. Consider analogies like a pendulum or a golf swing to describe the breathing process, where the motion of the air is both smooth and constant.
- Practice taking breaths using the mouthpiece (headjoint, double-reed) alone. Without the full instrument, students can concentrate on posture and body control, learning to repeat the *feeling* of the efficient breathing process consistently.
- "*Pour* air into your lungs"—this metaphor is related to the prompt, "When you pour water into a glass, where does it go? Does it stay at the top? Or cling only to the sides? No, it fills from the bottom." In truth, air is a gas and not a liquid, so all areas will be filled at once; however, this is nonetheless an excellent motivator to help students feel the results of a deep, filling breath.
- "Get the guts out of the way"—this extends the previous metaphor, opening a discussion about what organs are above and below the diaphragm: "the heart and lungs are up here; rest of the organs are below the diaphragm." Demonstrate how proper posture allows the beltline and lower abdomen to expand, thus allowing the diaphragm to move with less obstruction.
- Ask students to place their flattened palms on their abdomen, fingertips pointing toward the center line, nearly touching each other. During a full breath, students will notice the abdomen expanding as the fingertips begin to separate.
- Breathing exercises for extra-musical purposes can affect the band's performance as well. Consider how the "mindfulness" and yoga breathing processes work to improve one's relaxation, focus and poise. Those traits undeniably contribute to the control required by exceptional performers.

- Analogies and "quick-fix" methods for breathing include:
  - Describe the speed of the airstream in mph terms (e.g. "it sounds like that phrase needs 50mph air, but yours is 20mph", or "to jump your bike from ramp-to-ramp, you wouldn't choose a slow speed").
  - Compare the relationship of the air column's speed to its "size" (e.g. especially for brass-players, "maybe we'll always use the same amount of air; the higher register is a faster-but-smaller airstream, while the lower register is slower-but-larger").
  - Can you hold a piece of paper to the wall with your airstream? (Note: this is more of a philosophy than a reality for most students. Avoid tension; try it with a single-ply square of toilet tissue.)
  - Seal the lips with soft skin from the hand or wrist; begin inhaling to create suction, then pull the hand away to fill the lungs instantly.
- Other imagery
  - Use a laser beam of air.
  - Imagine your air has a visible color; what speed and direction will you *see* during this passage?
  - Blow the type of air that will: fog a mirror; put out a distant candle.
  - When you inhale, imagine "pouring" sand into the shell of your body-cavity, envisioning each space from the tips of the toes to the top of the skull.
  - When you exhale, fill every nook and cranny inside your instrument with air—so much that the air needs to escape from every gap.
  - Yawn.
  - Temperature: warm vs. cool airstream

Additional Thoughts

- See Chapter 3 for additional full-band activities related to breathing.
- This section of our book addresses the physical aspects of breathing, with a focus on its value to tone quality. For the *musical* view of breathing, related to phrasing and artistry, see Chapters 8 and 9.
- The material presented previously, while helpful, is relatively superficial. For a thorough, strategic, and *fun* resource, consider *The Breathing Gym: Exercises to Improve Breath Control and Air Flow* by Sam Pilafian and Patrick Sheridan (Focus on Music, 2002).
- Find a nice section on breathing in *The Teaching of Instrumental Music* by Richard Colwell, Michael Hewitt, et al (Routledge, 2017) under "Diaphragm."
- Any breathing activity is deeply entwined with other factors (the student's size, age, ability, the excerpt, the instrument, etc.). Be flexible, personalizing the application of breathing processes.
- Most importantly, *all of your chosen exercises and activities should lead to the same goals*, which include developing at least these three skills:

  1. The ability to take a lung-filling breath in a very short amount of time, without muscular tension.
  2. The ability to sustain a beautiful long tone with an unwavering "straight-line" sound, characteristic of the ideal timbre for each instrument.
  3. The ability to control the tone during every portion of the exhalation, especially when the lungs are both nearly-filled and nearly-emptied.

- Note that relaxed breathing isn't innately problematic for every student.

Section 2: Blend in the Ensemble

Important: although Sections 2 and 3 are designed to offer numerous quick-fix tips and strategies, the current chapter has a more limited emphasis toward the *concept* of tone quality—and the components thereof—rather than the *applications*. With only a bit of overlap as required, a collection of more detailed rehearsal activities will be found in Chapter 8.

With a concept of *tone* in place, we and our ensembles can move more successfully into the application process. We can *sculpt* the ensemble's blend to a pleasant result, and transfer that beautiful sound into the performance repertoire, where we'll encounter a great variety of instances requiring balance and dynamic-control exercises.

Strategies, Tips and Activities for the Refinement of Blend, Balance and Dynamics

In this categorical subgroup, the hierarchy probably begins with *blend*. Unlike balance and dynamics, which must constantly shift to reflect the needs of the literature and performance space, our goals with ensemble blend are largely unchanged. In its most basic form, the primary goal is simply: "Don't stick out."

Most cases of "sticking out" can be traced to one (or more) of these three issues:

1. *Tone*—the student has an unmatched timbre, most noticed when *brighter* than that of neighbors
2. *Dynamics*—the student is too loud.
3. *Intonation*—the student is out of tune (Chapter 5).

Blend

This short collection of activities will focus primarily on students with unmatching tone quality. Specifically, these strategies provide a multi-pronged approach toward better blend by helping students learn to integrate their sounds into the band's tone. Any of these suggestions will yield positive results while you contemplate additional creative options.

- We can start with a simple instruction: "Don't stick out." Processes to support that goal include the following:
  - <u>Sing</u>! While students work to fit into the full ensemble tone, direct them through a series of vowel-changes to hear how tone is affected. Sample: while the band sings "ooo," a single student alters the vowel (without getting louder), perhaps to a bright "eee."
  - Repeat the exercise with instruments, playing the sustained sound while a volunteer alters the oral cavity shape to affect the tone. Use a smaller group (i.e. isolate a section or choose "seniors only") to clarify the listening experience.
  - Ask percussionists to play an excerpt, first separately in succession, and then together. *One* percussionist uses different sticks/mallets, or strikes a different play area on the instrument, to illustrate poorly matched tone.
- "I'll keep my eyes closed while listening to the band sustain the note. If I can hear you individually, I'll point to you." This role can be the province of the director but, for a more engaging rehearsal activity, allow a *student* to perform the listening task.
- Comparison is a proven effective strategy for music learning. A full-ensemble aural discernment process: "Use your best personal tone" and then, with a separate conductor's cue, "Use 'unfavorable' tone" while one or more students listen and comment on the result. Alternative instructions could include, "Use a big, fat, slow, warm airstream like the kind used to fog a mirror" followed by "now use a small, skinny, fast, cold airstream like you'd use to put out a distant candle." Or specifically for an incorrect ensemble tone, "raise your tongue and keep teeth close together."
- To fully understand blend, one must be aware that his/her own sound will become "part of" the overall sound. In a well-blended ensemble, each student may be somewhat invisible as an individual, but is an indispensable contributor to the total band's color. Direct students to "sound like the next-lower instrument"; thus, a clarinetist tries to be "inside the bass clarinet sound" while a horn player tries to "become part of the Trombone tone."

- As an extension of the previous exercise, ask sections to "sound like the next-lower Group." Use Lisk's Groups 1–2–3–4, or the SATB layers within McBeth's Double Pyramid system, or even with an instruction as simple as, "upper woodwinds, let the sound of the lower woodwinds wrap around yours."
- A script to paraphrase (a chocolate cake analogy): "When we bite into chocolate cake, what do we taste? Well chocolate cake, of course! We do *not* taste individual bites of flour, cocoa, egg, vanilla, and the other ingredients, but we know they're in there. We need our band to sound like cake, and not like piles of ingredients."
- Repurpose three important strategies (detailed elsewhere) to enhance the band's blend:
    - Utilize "Pass the Sound" ("F Around the Room"), giving verbal or visual/graphic feedback while the tone quality travels across the band (Chapter 3).
    - Use the "Playing in Trios" philosophy (Chapter 5) as a blend exercise; each student attempts to flawlessly match the tone of both immediate neighbors.
    - Adapt the additive "Tuning by the Numbers" strategy (Chapter 5), in this case not solely for intonation purposes, but applied for blend. For example, sustaining the last chord of a Chorale we'll start with tubas alone; every layer of entering instruments (numbered 1–8) added in succession should become part of the tuba sound. "Never sound louder than the layer just before you." Then, transfer this blended tone directly to a musical passage.

An important distinction—while *blend* represents the "chocolate cake" perspective of the band's overall sound, we use *balance* and *dynamics* to adjust the recipe further. We determine how much of each ingredient to include for our cake to be exactly the size, taste and density we seek.

The *blend* activities in the previous section promote our homogenized tonal model within the SATB pyramid. To continue with the chocolate cake metaphor, students may gain understanding by hearing the word *blend* used in its non-musical context: explain that all the cake's ingredients are blended together to create the smoothest possible batter for baking.

Note that not all compositions are meant to feature the lowest instruments, and passages occasionally require an entirely different sound. So, balance concepts are not carved in stone with a uniform agreement. Therefore, the homogenized sound—even if accepted as the "model"—must be altered often to accommodate the shifting needs of the performance. These alterations become the basis for the ensemble's balance, where the entire recipe is changed briefly. We purposefully increase the prominence of some sections and individuals, while decreasing others, all to reflect our interpretation of the composer's instructions in any given excerpt.

In the next section, remember that blend remains imperative to the band's best sound. But blend can also be viewed as a construct of players within their sections except for solo/soli passages, which demand further adjustments. Read about "The Christmas Tree Pyramid" (*Effective Performance of Band Literature*, McBeth) for additional information.

Section 3: Dynamics and Balance in the Ensemble

With blend as a prerequisite to beautiful wind band tone, the following suggestions offer engaging processes and helpful tips about dynamic changes and balance exercises. Again, this list is presented only as a catalyst toward readers' development of additional unique and hybrid strategies:

- Share a short visual lesson about dynamics, and then encourage students to follow up on their own: Play long tones, scales, arpeggios, and then excerpted passages with the goal of keeping a VU meter (also known as a decibel meter or sound level meter, many apps are available for free) *motionless*. Sound intensity is objectively measurable, of course, so students can view this process as an engaging challenge. Bonus: Students can *see* that their high-register playing, even unintentionally, is often louder.
- Employ a fun additional visual lesson: display a classroom noise monitor, which will evaluate the full band dynamic range. Some of these are colorful and very engaging for short-term usage,

ON THE SOUND

especially for younger students, but also may become a distraction over time. Elementary classroom teachers can offer valuable strategic advice.
- Describe *pp* as "the softest sound you can play with good tone", while *ff* is "the loudest sound you can play with good tone." *Tone* is the most important guiding principle.
- Teach with quantifiable labels which, compared with traditional letters, may be easier to conceptualize by younger students. Examples include the following:
    - Assign numbers 1–6 for dynamics, which can then be compared to *pp, p, mp, mf, f,* and *ff*: "Clarinets, please play at a level of '2' here."
    - Assign numbers 1–10, which will align to most volume controllers: "Low brass, can you *crescendo* from a '5' to an '8' in just one measure?"
    - Speak about percentages (0–100%) to align to other common measurement standards: "Saxes, please play that accompaniment figure about 50% softer."
    - Make an analogy using weights: "If you just played a '10-pound sound,' let's make it '25 pounds' instead."
    - We can even refer to density: For younger students, "that's a tiny cotton ball; we'll need to make it a huge marshmallow." And for older, "you're playing with pumice; can you give me polished marble instead?"
- Refine students' awareness with behavioral descriptors:
    - "When playing *pp–p* I strive to hear my neighbor better than I can hear myself."
    - "At *mp–mf*, we sound very equal."
    - "At *f–ff* I try to hear myself better than I can hear my neighbors."
- Train students to maintain a desired balance by actively controlling parameters of contrast during a dynamic change. The entire procedure must be monitored by the director, even when students are generally self-sufficient, but it yields the best results when three important parameters are sculpted by the conductor's ear:

1. The target *intensity*—although this is generally designated by the composer's dynamic marking, work on it in rehearsals to come to a group decision.
2. The target *timing*—the director can refine the sound with decisions like, "Low brass, let's arrive at the top of your *crescendo* by Beat 4, but trumpet I please don't peak until the beginning of the next measure."
3. The *shaping of the change* to that intensity—the director can draw a picture or provide an aural demonstration. For a graphic drawing, the written "hairpin" shape can be adjusted in many ways (Figure 4.3).

Figure 4.3 Crescendo marking with "flare."

McBeth presents these procedures in detail in his *Effective Performance of Band Literature,* in sections entitled "Solution I" and "Solution II."

- Redistribute students within a section:
    - The *divisi* design—revise the shape of the SATB pyramid by adding players to the lower end. For example: with *fifteen* clarinetists divided into parts I, II, and III, the former balance of 4, 5, and 6 may be altered to become 4, 4, and 7, or 3, 5, and 7.
    - The *assignments* design—put *leaders* in each divisi part after auditions. In many bands the best player sits first-chair, followed by all other players in decreasing-skill order; this common plan often yields grave weakness in the bottom parts.

- Reduce the number of players by *sharing*: when a section cannot be soft enough for the desired result, stand partners can split a passage; that is, "eight measures for each player," to thin the texture. In extreme cases, the director may have to intervene to cut further players. Keep self-esteem and good *salesmanship* in mind while communicating those expectations to the group.

To this point, the strategies suggested are mostly teacher-centered, but the ultimate music education strives for the student to be independent. Our best plans should therefore incorporate ways to engage students' individual listening and decision-making skills. More advanced student-centered dynamics activities could include these:

- Devise prompts that will lead your students toward a thought process like this: "I see the composer says *mp*, but I know my part is important because I have a chunk of the melody. I know I should play *mf* because I need to be heard." Try the following exercises as specific examples:
  - "We've talked about dynamics as numbers, '1' for the softest sounds and '10' for the loudest. Now, evaluate the passage we just played, and determine how important you think *your* role is, 1 for the least important and 10 for the most. Assign a matching dynamic level to your line, and let's perform it again with your own dynamic interpretation." Record and playback both versions for comparison. Richard Floyd offers a well-scripted version of this helpful activity in *The Artistry of Teaching and Making Music*.[4]
  - Give students several labels for musical lines in an excerpt from their literature (e.g. melody, bassline, countermelody, ostinato, accompaniment, ornamentation). The first step asks students to identify what role—what musical line—they play. Preparatory exercises are engaging, and helpful to check for understanding, like "Please play only if you have the countermelody." In this case, "If you have the melody please play it *f*, but if you have anything other than the melody your job is to support, not cover, so play a softer dynamic level. Let's see how you do." Again, record and playback the performance.
  - Craig Kirchoff describes a "Plus & Minus" plan.[5] Paraphrased, musicians should add "+" to the written dynamic marking when playing a primary line (melody), and "-" when playing a secondary line (accompaniment). Note: this plan helps to build a music-marking vocabulary so students can make quick dynamic adjustments for any reasons, including imbalance, ensemble size issues, or venue-based refinements.
  - An adaptation of the cake analogy addresses several decorative features (a candle, a few flowers and sparkles, and the frosting) on top of the most-important part: the cake itself. "And our percussionists and bassline players are like the cake pan, holding it all together." From here, it's easy to compare the importance of each group ("we'll get sick fast with too much of the frosting and flowers"), but then we allow students to make their own performance balance decisions.
- Teach a short lesson about dynamic adjustments for overlapping entrances. Choose a fugue, for example, or any other "layered entrance" passage. When each successive musical idea enters, the previous players *adjust* dynamics downward. This practice allows each layer of the texture to be heard with greater clarity, but the decision-making can be allocated to the students as they develop.
- Introduce a true student-centered "fix" for issues in dynamics and balance: allow students to self-evaluate, making productive adjustments from within.
  - With a sustained sound, the instruction can be as simple as "do your personal part to improve our sound." From your position on the podium, you will hear the band's output transform.
  - With a passage from the repertoire, use a succession of recording–playback comparisons. After each critical listening pass, prompt the students to make their own suggestions toward enhanced performance.
  - This short lesson plan offered by Bobby Adams is perfectly suited to helping students develop balance and dynamics awareness: "Have the band sustain a mid-range note. At random, point

ON THE SOUND

to one instrumental group and have them *crescendo* until it is much too loud, then *decrescendo* until it can't be heard, then bring it back to a more normal volume. You and the students will learn a lot doing this exercise. In time a particular sonority will become your sound."[6]

More Ensemble Tone Quality Suggestions

These additional rehearsal strategies will also promote better ensemble *tone* by training students to actively control blend, balance, and dynamics:

- To maintain a pleasant tone throughout the attack, body, and release of every sound, consider a concept we'll call "First in, last out," referring to the lowest instruments. In this principle, the low frequencies (tuba, bass clarinet, etc.) delicately anticipate the downbeat, while the upper instruments enter with a subtle delay. The opposite is true on the release, as the bass voices last slightly longer. When executed well, there will be no audible misalignment, but the tone quality sounds warmer from its beginning through its resonant release. A graphic representation of this concept might appear as shown in Figure 4.4.

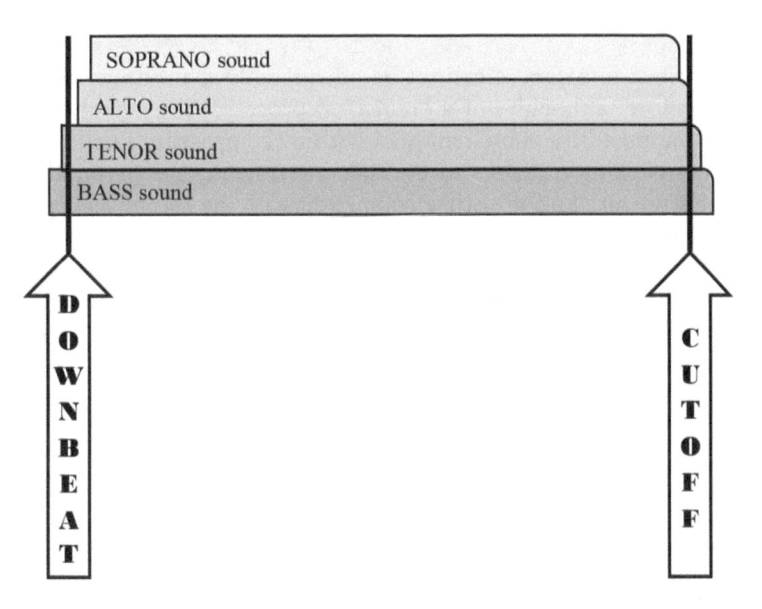

Figure 4.4 Arrival–departure chart v1.

The graphic in Figure 4.5 conceptualizes the timing of the SATB layers. The target start/release times are shown as dots on the "alignment" plane; we can see that, compared with the conductor's motions, the bass voices arrive ever-so-slightly early, while those same basses linger beyond the release. Again, the rhythmic imprecision should be too subtle to hear, but the tonal advantage is too helpful to overlook.

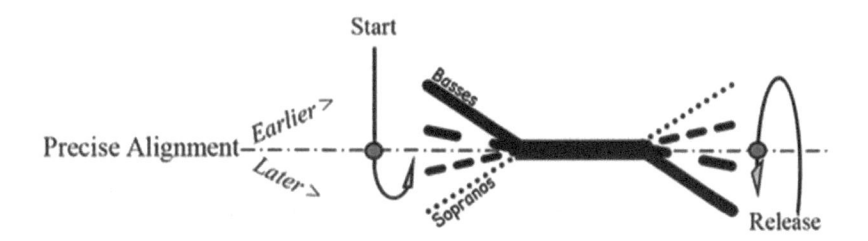

Figure 4.5 Arrival–departure chart, v2 for conducting motions.

- For an alternate view on this important tone-building concept, consider some relevant acoustic characteristics:
  - In some performance venues, the tuba might be twice as far from the front row of the audience as the piccolo.
  - The larger instruments simply retain the air column a little longer; the wave form can leave the piccolo immediately, while the tuba (with its 18 feet of tubing) requires several milliseconds for sound to leave the bell.
  - High and low frequencies behave differently with how they propagate, reflect, absorb, dissipate, and more.
  - Human hearing is most sensitive around the 2kHz range, which is especially good for the more common "melody" instruments in a band, but not so good for our band's bass instruments, which play much lower, topping out well below 1kHz.
- To further support the "last out" portion of the concept, think of the release in an orchestra: the larger the string instrument, the longer its resonance lasts when the bow is lifted. Since winds have no "continued vibration" when the air stops, we can create a more beautiful release by simulating the longer decay-time of the lower frequencies. We do that by releasing *slightly* later. Sally Wagner writes, "Think of it as *resonating down*."[7]

Keep in mind that serious imbalances cannot be adequately repaired by asking a small section to "just play louder." Therefore, although not a "rehearsal process," the overall development of a well-balanced instrumentation must be a consistent goal within the program's entire design. Be mindful of recruitment, retention, switching/transfers to another instrument, the pyramid within each section, distribution of skillful students, and all other components of the established program goals. While extremely important, these topics go beyond the scope of this book. *Instrumental Music Education* by Evan Feldman and Ari Contzius (Routledge, 2020) is an outstanding source of guidance.

It is worth noting that *balance* decisions—especially when students' assignments are redistributed—often have a success-rate highly reliant on the teacher's fair and unbiased policies, coupled with confident and charismatic communication. Be a careful and empathetic manager.

Section 4: Articulation in the Ensemble

An Articulation Preface

With limited rehearsal time available, it's not uncommon for articulation to be overlooked in the full-group setting. Warm-ups are often comprised of breathing, long-tones, singing, buzzing, flexibility slurs, scale-arpeggio figures, intonation, and Chorales. Exercises that *seem* to address articulation are more often targeted toward a rhythmic figure, or perhaps to develop speed or precision on a specific articulated passage. At the same time, articulation is undeniably a significant problem for many bands. Without command of the skills, the band may develop poor tone quality, uncontrolled dynamic effects, and rhythmic imprecision. Moreover, the quality of the overall performance also relies on the performers' uniform interpretation of an entire vocabulary of markings. We hope for the band to maintain its most beautiful tone quality through various articulations, all in the context of a specific style.

Therefore, it is important to address articulation during band instruction, and modeling is arguably the best tool for doing so. The director can incorporate a mixture of masterful recorded samples, singing, demonstrations, graphic visual models, and aural comparisons, always with ample specific feedback. But with so many variables across the array of instruments in the band—and even a wider variety of pedagogical opinions from professionals—the scope of this book will remain dedicated to the ensemble perspective of articulation.

A Concise Overview of Articulation

Most musical sounds have three parts: the sound's *start*, *sustain*, and *release*. Directors use other names, of course, so long as the students understand the references. We may use anything like "attack, sustain, release," "beginning, middle, end," or "head, body, tail." A preferred model refers to the "front end" and "back end" of the sound, because *attack* and *cut-off* may elicit harsher sounds than we desire. To best describe the complete sound, make careful reference to its *consonant* at the beginning, the *vowel* during the sustain, and the beautiful resonant release.

Some groups might respond well to direct, student-centered references like, "how does the sound begin?" Or, "what type of syllable should we use to start this sound?" The importance to the instruction is that the modeling and verbal references always stay relevant to the tone quality. Note a suggested baseline:

- With some exceptions, wind instruments will most often start a tone with a *consonant*, whether a harder /t/, softer /d/, or sometimes even a "nonexistent" consonant which often turns out to be /p/ as in "pooh." The action of the tongue during this consonant (the "front end") is a muscle skill requiring careful practice.
- The position of the tongue during the *vowel* (the sustain) has the greatest effect on how we perceive the overall tone quality.
- The best release ("back end") for wind instruments will require a relaxed, open throat along with unchanged posture and embouchure settings; the player avoids closing the throat or choking the air with the tongue.
- For percussion instruments, both the front-end and sustain are often affected equally by the player's stroke, the choice of sticks/mallets, and the playing area on the instrument itself (for more details, see Chapter 7).

For the most part, articulation problems will be absorbed when correct styling is achieved.[8]

And doing *anything* to target articulation during the full-band setting will send a message that the teacher believes in its importance—Occam's Razor.

Articulation Problems and Solutions

This list should provide strategic improvements for some of the frequent and pervasive articulation issues in bands:

- Light articulations, or too little attention to the *front end* by individuals in the band, can contribute to a generally unexciting sound. This band lacks clarity and dynamic contrast, and therefore has a limited ability to project emotion. While this is a serious problem, it should resolve itself gradually with attention to other issues during rehearsals.
- Extraneous motion in the articulation process often causes a raucous sound, with effects in many performance aspects beyond tone.
    - Work to minimize movement of the jaw, face, throat, tongue, and more.
    - Put small mirrors on music stands for students' self-evaluation.
    - Divide the band into player-viewer pairs. "Players, you'll tongue this easy passage with your best posture and as little movement as possible. Your partner shouldn't be able to see you move." For younger bands, we can create a sequential challenge to find a few prime candidates who might be willing to model their excellent posture/positioning for the full group.
- Band members don't recognize, or know how to interpret, the full list of common articulation markings.
    - Display a chart of common markings, and/or add it to the folders. Make it as complete as necessary for the band's age and experience-level. Consider extracting markings directly from the band's repertoire, leading to a cumulative listing for the entire year.
    - Design the warm-up and rehearsal exercises to address specific articulation markings.
    - Clarify any misunderstood markings; common examples include those shown in Figure 4.6.

ON THE SOUND

Figure 4.6 Frequently misunderstood articulation markings.

- Tonguing consecutive notes, the band frequently overemphasizes the notes in strong rhythmic spots, so other notes are lost.
    - A simple, direct instruction can work easily: "we're losing the second and fourth sixteenth-notes; can you give them more attention please?"
    - Modeling is very direct: "which sound do you like better?"
    - Use your preferred note-grouping strategy, or
    - Draw a graphic model: comparing a picture of the sound we hear now to a picture of the sound we want to hear (Figure 4.7)

Figure 4.7 Articulations: we hear ... let's try ...

- Staccato and other shorter markings are often "clipped" by wind players.
    - Redefine staccato; with cooperative participation of students, lean toward an interpretation of "spaced" or "separated" rather than simply "short."
    - Play staccato whole-notes, half-notes, and quarter-notes. With feedback and discussion, develop an idea about length, and the preferred back-end sound of each note. When the concept is refined, apply it to eighth-notes.
    - Record a series of beautiful staccato quarter-notes at a moderate tempo, and playback for listening. Then record staccato eighth-notes at the same tempo, but choose a slow 50% playback speed. Compare the back end of the notes of the two listening examples.
    - Consider this important reference to string instruments: whether it's a pizzicato or a bow-lift release, the string stays in motion during its brief decay, giving the listener a kind of aural afterglow. Because band instruments respond differently, we have to simulate the extra vibration; our attention to the "back end" allows the effect to be noticed. Apply the "first in, *last out*" concept as well.
    - Richard Floyd describes a beautiful analogy saying "Short notes are like basketballs." He notes that an underinflated ball may have the right appearance, but its responsiveness and especially its resonant ring will be lacking. "The air inside the basketball brings it to life. Similarly, the increased breath support inside short notes gives them beauty and resonance."[9]
- Legato articulations may yield a muddy sound. Moving pitches might be more exempt from problems, but the overall effect sounds more like a *tie* and less like a *slur*; in addition, vertical timing sounds sloppy and misaligned.
    - When executing softer legato consonants—especially in slower tempi—the players still must move tongues quickly; this minimizes disruption to the airstream. Then, the quick tongue motion must be precisely coordinated with fingering/slide movements.
    - To combat muddiness in a very large ensemble, consider altering the written articulation for a *portion* of the section. For example: "In all three trumpet parts, let's ask each 2nd chair player to lightly *tongue* notes instead of slurring," thus adding rhythmic "compressions" to the slurred line.

- Use an analogy for "denting" the airstream; an example is presented in "More Ideas on Modeling for Articulation."
- Many sources promote /d/ as the legato tongue consonant because it avoids fully cutting the airstream. This author prefers a special application for trombones. The "flipped" Spanish /r/ has its own tongue-position, which transfers well to trombone legato. The word for bull is *toro*; if spoken with its correct idiomatic accent, the /r/ has a special sound, which seems to be "*nearly*" /d/ and "*nearly*" /l/ in performance terms. It is effective because it dents the airstream rather than cutting it. A trombonist's legato line, therefore, might use "Doh-ro-ro-ro-ro-ro-ro."

• Marcato and other accented articulations can lead to a harsh sound. Specifically, bands frequently interpret the beginning of the accent with a very strong sound, but forget to retain beautiful tone after the consonant.

- After the accent, the tongue must return to its relaxed lower position, so the oral cavity can resonate a pleasant sustain. Slow-to-fast repetition in the rehearsal promotes the practice by offering less time on the consonant and more time on the vowel; with feedback, students can be guided to retain the desired tone in faster executions.
- Accented passages are more likely to create tension which, in turn, can cause harsh tone. Any of your favorite strategic processes used to promote relaxation can also be effective here.
- Play the passage without any accents; record and playback for comparison. Discuss the beauty and depth of the desired sound. Then put the accents back in, perhaps just player-by-player, constantly monitoring the evolution of the sound.
- Again in a larger ensemble, consider lessening the effect for a portion of the section. Example: "In all three Clarinet parts, let's ask the 1st chair player to use the written marking; all other players please lessen the accent."

• Many band students reach a critical articulation-speed threshold: "The music is too fast for me to single-tongue, but I can't double-tongue yet."

- Be aware that some students may not reach the required skill-level in time for a performance. Tolerance, motivation, and supportive encouragement will be important while considering a "Plan B" approach. Chapter 8 offers ideas about modifying literature for special circumstances.
- Important note: while every band may have some students in this category, having *several* indicates reconsidering literature selection.

• The articulations don't align with the movement of the fingers (slide).

- As above, see Chapter 8 for additional ideas.
- In severe cases, allow affected students to slur the passage, but *very softly* so as not to change the character of the music. The soft presence of the unarticulated line can still support the overall sound, and the feeling of success can boost self-esteem.

• Articulations are often the root of "apparent" rhythmic precision problems, especially in technical passages.

- Be wary. Identify the problem correctly before prescribing solutions. As a rehearsal exercise, try eliminating articulations—or allow students to select their own—to discover if the rhythm improves.
- Use a metronome or other audible pulse; utilize several other types of rehearsal processes to disqualify technique, youth, range or other factors as the source of the problems.

• Uncomfortable articulations can severely impact the *Style* of a performance.

- Modeling is the most direct solution. As in great jazz instruction, speak or sing the passage, substituting nonsense syllables or rhythmically similar words. Choose articulation sounds that are fluent, natural, comfortable, and effortless. Therefore, *language* itself is a great tool; see subsequent further suggestions.

- The band begins with a hesitant, "doo-WAAH" attack. The intensity of the tone is delayed when students articulate *before* having their airstream fully supported. For some bands, this is a ubiquitous problem during articulated passages.
    - Modeling is again a very effective solution.
    - Slow the passage and change to a connected Chorale without articulations. Build the desired tone together, and then gradually add articulations back to the passage while restoring its tempo to speed.
    - Meet with colleagues in feeder programs to immunize the program from this tonal defect.
- Low register is more difficult for articulation because, on many instruments, the embouchure and oral cavity must be more open. The tongue has a greater distance to travel for brasses, and lower wave forms are often slower to respond.
    - Discuss the need for a fast movement using the tip of the tongue only.
    - Insist on a well-formed embouchure and careful management of the airstream. Work together on an exercise to *anticipate* the ictus.
    - As a Plan B, severely affected students may play the passage an octave higher.

Some additional articulation problems are also prevalent, but the repair work will be more relevant to students in smaller groups. Just be vigilant in the full-band setting:

- Many wind musicians perform with tension and an elevated tongue position. Their thin tone quality may permeate the band, and their entrances are often harsh and unresponsive. In serious cases, the note is entirely incorrect: the oral cavity shape doesn't match the *register* of the target note, so the student produces a harmonic rather than the desired pitch.
- Some students don't tongue at all, or "throat-puff." Articulations are incorrect, and the *tone* can't be correct with superfluous sounds emanating from the throat. "Ooot, OOoo—ooot." Even if the group's tone quality isn't audibly affected, those students' stand partners will notice and can be distracted. With permission in the small group setting, record the student; a video is especially helpful to initiate the repair process.

More Ideas on Modeling for Articulation

As we know, students absorb information through all senses, and from a remarkably wide variety of influences. Some launchpad suggestions include the following:

- Use language to model articulations. We already practice our tongue movements and oral cavity shapes in the language we speak. Therefore, leading students to make connections through speech patterns is direct and intuitive. A well-delivered lesson is also more engaging than trying to explain a technique with typical detailed verbal instruction.
    - For example: "Aye yay-ee ih ih-oww uh Uhh" is fun to convert to, "Try playing it without the tongue." The students will immediately grasp the importance of correct and articulate usage of the consonants.
    - "Take a (take a, take a, take a) tool, and dig a (dig a, dig a, dig a) ditch" becomes a fun way to practice double-tonguing as "tuh-kuh-tuh-kuh tuh-kuh-tuh-kuh tooo" and "duh-guh-duh-guh duh-guh-duh-guh dooo."
    - Important note: capitalize on the students' native language. Students for whom English is a second language may be more successful when the exercise is customized for their fluent speech.
    - Use descriptive phrases to convey specific instructions: "Put a bigger 'T' on your 'Tah,'" "More tone, less tongue," "The listener doesn't like crunchy sandwiches; we need creamy peanut butter here," or "Be careful about the consonant on the front end of your note; don't turn our Tone into Foam."
    - Onomatopoeia can fill the void: express specific sounds using words like *tone*, *boom*, *din*, and *ta-da*!

ON THE SOUND

- Use commendable performances as models within the class. Just as we imitate, emulate and aspire, we also enjoy the feeling of accolades. Remember to highlight students and/or sections when their articulations are notably strong: "Oh, could you please play that again while we listen? That's *exactly* the articulation we want!"
- Use sound models as shared experiences:
    - If your brass section enters harshly on a legato passage, ask the clarinets to demonstrate a soft, subtle entrance.
    - A nice staccato sound is illustrated on xylophone or the upper end of marimba.
    - Melodic percussion offers a complete palette of articulations. We can demonstrate a gamut of sounds (easily and quickly) by mixing instruments and mallets.
- Use tangible physical activities to model articulation concepts:
    - "How fast can you tap sixteenth-notes with one hand on your thigh?" Students will easily see that a faster speed is possible by using less motion, from a closer distance, with poised relaxation.
    - Turn a faucet on to its full flow, and equate our airstream to the steady column of rushing water. With the convex side of a spoon, lightly tap the water to "dent" it; we can *see* a *legato* articulation. *Marcato* completely cuts the stream with a knife, which also shows a more energetic splash. *Staccato* demands a separation, as when a cup cuts through the stream, creating a visible gap in the flow. But the important part is that the water-pressure, like our air-support, stays constant.
    - Combine tactile senses with applicable musical skills through "whisper tonguing," or "wind patterning," well known in the teaching of Arnold Jacobs, Vince Cichowicz, and other masters. By blowing the steady airstream onto the hand, the student learns to *feel* all three parts of each tone (front-end, sustain, back-end) by playing the articulations. This exercise is performed only with the air—without a mouthpiece, instrument or buzzing—to train students to *feel* articulations, rhythm patterns in the focused stream of air.[10]
- Use student-centered activities, prompts, and well-designed questioning to promote critical thinking about articulation. For example:
    - Prompt students" personal decision-making with questions like, "Trumpets at Letter C, what syllable are you using? Horns and trombones, can you match that?"
    - Guide students' listening with questions like, "From your perspective, which section sounded late? Who had articulations that didn't match? Who sounded too short on the staccatos?"
- Use visual models to convey articulation concepts:
    - "Shape" the note envelope: model the start–middle–release with pantomime motions, conducting gestures, or a picture drawn in the classroom. Supplement the visual model digitally.
    - Use a signal graph display (the *track*) from a digital recording to demonstrate the appearance of the tone during and after the articulation. Help students to shape the performance with repeated attempts. Find a software program that offers good detail in the quality of the image (Figure 4.8).

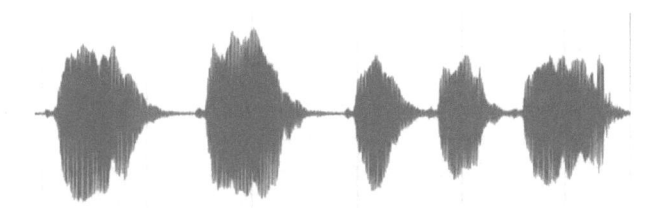

Figure 4.8 Articulation track: envelope graphs allow students to "see" their articulations.

ON THE SOUND

- Display graphics, or ask students to draw pictures, representing the envelope for each type of articulation. Follow by producing the sounds with the ensemble using the graphic as the blueprint. A basic example is shown in Figure 4.9.

Selected common Articulation Markings
Pictorial demonstrations

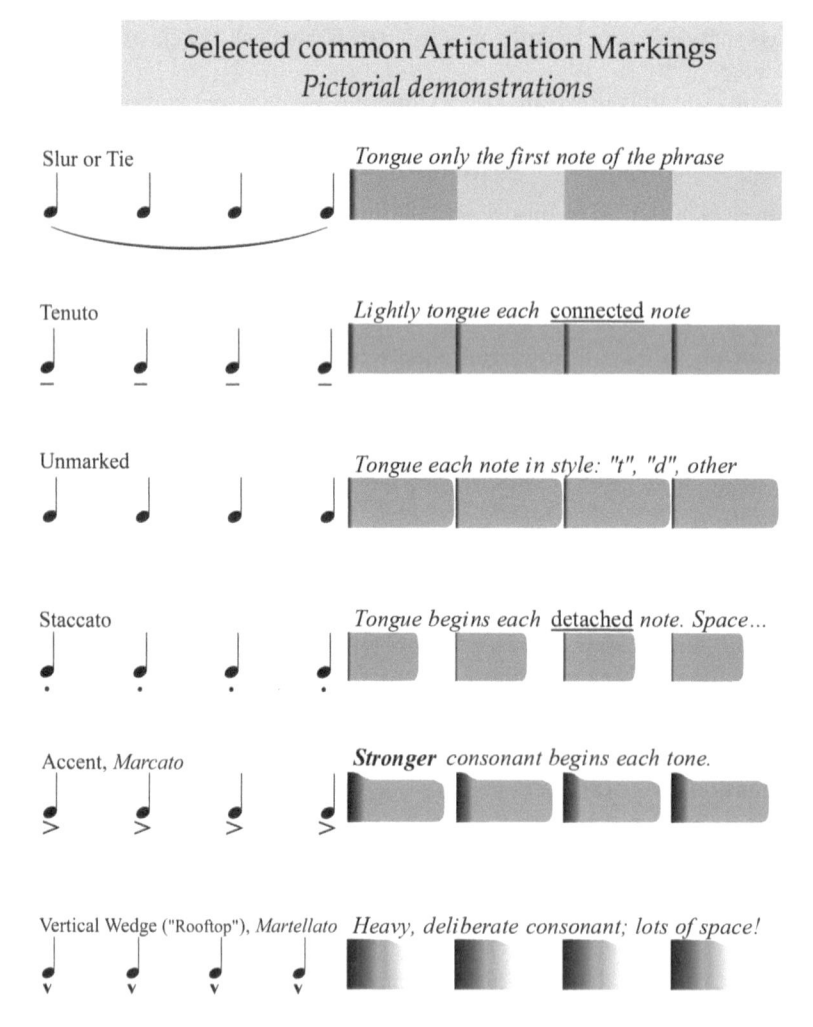

Slur or Tie — *Tongue only the first note of the phrase*

Tenuto — *Lightly tongue each <u>connected</u> note*

Unmarked — *Tongue each note in style: "t", "d", other*

Staccato — *Tongue begins each <u>detached</u> note. Space...*

Accent, *Marcato* — ***Stronger*** *consonant begins each tone.*

Vertical Wedge ("Rooftop"), *Martellato* — *Heavy, deliberate consonant; lots of space!*

Figure 4.9 Pictorial comparison of common articulations.

Final Words (for Now!) About Articulation

Articulation is inseparable from both rhythm and style. Imagine the effect of incorrect articulations if a band plays a Sousa march or a ragtime piece with muddied legato sounds, or a ballad punctuated by marcato accents. And as we've seen, articulation is a primary contributor to the band's overall tone. For the most mature performance, articulation must not interfere with tone.

In the best bands, therefore . . .

. . . every individual has the same unified approach to the *front end* and *back end* of notes.
. . . the sustain (body) of each note represents characteristic tone.
. . . each player has the knowledge and skillset to perform all markings, and does so by staying engaged in the interpretation process at all times.
. . . we're working consistently to develop a unified playing style among all players.

Section 5: Conclusion and Springboard

Bands may still lack a mature sound even with a blended, balanced, characteristic tone quality, and with control of the articulation skills for the front end of the note. The missing element for full maturity is often the connection of musical phrases (more fully addressed in Chapters 8 and 9). In the context of this chapter, encourage students to blow through the entire envelope of the note, paying careful attention to the back end. Younger students tend to rush, which includes leaning forward toward each new articulation. Work for a poised, full-bodied sustain.

Additional analogies and "quick-fix" methods for the band's *Overall Sound* include:

- Turn it upside-down: perform a short comparison with a full-band unison or chord. Alternate between the desired SATB balanced pyramid and its inversion. "Sopranos please play *ff*, altos *mf*, tenors *mp*, and basses *pp* . . . Let's hear that for a moment, and hopefully never again! . . . On cue, reverse the dynamics so we'll hear the *warm* tone we're trying to build."

    Demonstrate balance parameters with EQ controllers: while the band is listening to any recording, manipulate the bands of the equalizer, increase treble and decrease BASS. Compare to immature band tone and then, together, rebuild the favored sound. If possible, *display* the EQ controls.
- Regarding the SATB balance, try non-musical comparisons: "In a cheerleading or acrobatic pyramid, we never put the heaviest person on top" or "That sound is like a top-heavy building on sand; let's put our bottom-heavy building firmly on bedrock."
- On dynamic control for tone: "Never softer than, nor louder than . . . *beautiful*."
- On blending into the ensemble's tone: "We opened our can of beautiful blue paint, and we found some single drops of white lying right on top; let's stir them in," "Don't be the only thorn in our bouquet of roses," "You're neon-green in our rainbow," or "I was really looking forward to eating my big bowl of ice cream until I noticed just one tiny fly in it. Ugh." Follow with your own creative analogies.
- Richard Floyd describes the concept of "tasting" a note,[11] while in the *Musician's Toolkit* web series, David Starnes refers to the "Colors of Sound" (https://musicianstoolkit.com/home). Anytime a connection can focus students' performance to a desired result, the analogy is valid. Consider colors, temperatures, *fabrics,* textures, emotions, and more.
- Make a recording with front-located microphones using standard seating; make a second recording with the seating plan inverted (Grp 4 instruments in front, Grp 1 in back) and compare tone quality.
- Another cake-related reference may help: "A layer cake allows us to see, choose and taste separate parts of the cake individually; a marble cake uses the same components, but each bite contains a mixture of flavors."

Some aspects of a program's design, mostly within teachers' control, will also be helpful to the band's sound:

- Be specific on audition policies, both for acceptance (especially into select groups) and for seating placement within the group. Balance issues can be solved with careful structural management of the group.
- Augment weaker/smaller sections with pairing and substitution as deemed necessary.
- Redesign the seating plan as necessary for improved sound.
- Use clouds, reflectors or other acoustic room-tuning strategies; remember that the sounds behind the stage proscenium (especially low brass) may easily get lost up into the fly-space.
- During any ancillary exercise (a warm-up, a student-conductor, a short sequence of Sectionals) *move yourself* to alternate locations. Hear what the *students* hear, and what the *audience* will hear. Adjust as necessary.
- Finally, continue your reading, investigation, observation and ingenuity to mold the best possible sound from your band.

Full band long-tones, flexibility slurs, chorales and *crescendo–decrescendo* patterns are all essential components in tonal development. But those exercises—like the strategies presented in this chapter—do not have to consume a large amount of the rehearsal time. With a vigilant ear, and consistent use of feedback and modeling, the director can use every moment of the rehearsal to nudge the group consistently toward a premier *ensemble tone quality*.

Notes

1 Walter Beeler, "Improving the Sound of the Band." This version first appeared in the WASBE Newsletter, reorganized and edited by Mark Fonder, http://www.timreynish.com/conducting/conducting-articles/improving-the-sound.php.
2 Paula Thorner, "Your Students are Going to Reflect You," in *Rehearsing the High School Band*, ed. Stephen Meyer (Delray Beach FL: Meredith Music Publications, 2016), 81.
3 Richard Crain, "Developing Ensemble Quality in the Middle and High School Band," Midwest Clinic Handout, Dec. 20, 2007, https://www.midwestclinic.org/user_files_1/pdfs/clinicianmaterials/2007/richard_crain.pdf.
4 Richard Floyd, *The Artistry of Teaching and Making Music* (Chicago: GIA Publications, Inc., 2015), 133–135.
5 Craig Kirchoff, "The Plus and Minus System," in *The Conductor's Companion: 100 Rehearsal Techniques, Imaginative Ideas, Quotes, and Facts*, ed. Gary Stith (Delray Beach FL: Meredith Music Publications, 2017), 53.
6 Bobby Adams, *Music: From Skill to Art* (Chicago: GIA Publications, Inc., 2015), 41.
7 Sally Wagner, *The Pursuit of Excellence: A Band Director's Guide to Success* (Delray Beach, FL: Meredith Music Publications, 2016), 8.
8 Beeler/Fonder, "Improving the Sound of the Band."
9 Floyd, *The Artistry of Teaching and Making Music*, 89.
10 Elizabeth Peterson, "Sound Patterning and Wind Production," in *The Conductor's Companion*, ed. Stith, 81.
11 Floyd, *The Artistry of Teaching and Making Music*, 57.

5
INTONATION AND TUNING

Introduction: Using the Tuner

Previous chapters have suggested strategies guiding your ensemble's students toward becoming self-empowered, better listeners. This chapter explores in greater detail some engaging activities designed to harness those listening skills to improve our group's overall intonation.

The tuner is an outstanding tool for developing one's personal intonation, but with limitations. Recognize that tuning is relative, and intonation is a function of how we sound compared with pitches around us; the same "F" may require different tuning when it functions as the root or fifth, or as the third of a major triad. Therefore, musicians' best work is directed toward tuning with the ensemble, rather than by centering a tuner's display. Performing in tune requires a better tuner, namely "the well-trained ear." All strategies suggested here are directed toward helping to develop that ear-training.

Readers are encouraged to examine *Tuning for Wind Instruments: A Roadmap for Successful Intonation* by Shelley Jagow (Meredith Music, 2007) and *Instrumental Music Education* by Evan Feldman and Ari Contzius (Routledge, 2016, chapter 14). Feldman's *The Rehearsal Toolkit* (https://routledgetextbooks.com/textbooks/9781138921405/the-rehearsal-toolkit.php) provides a variety of recommended exercises.

Section 1: *Hearing* Intonation

Any ensemble's intonation is a product of how well its performers can identify and eliminate "beats"—those fluctuations between out-of-tune sounds. Therefore, the teacher's greatest effectiveness comes from helping students develop autonomy with tuning. Hearing the pulsating *beats* is an abstract skill, which for some is decidedly enigmatic: some students at first seem completely unaware of the sound of these beats. But this ability is arguably the most important ingredient in a student's intonation, and it can be enhanced more quickly when strategies are used. The following exercises are designed specifically to target students' independent ability to *recognize beats*.

Two processes to introduce the concept of beats and the beatless unison:

1. *View an autostereogram* (3D picture). This fun diversion confirms that tuning awareness isn't equally easy for everyone. Although some people locate the hidden image without any problem, for others it takes a concentrated effort. Try describing visual techniques (focus, depth-of-field) that can assist with the discovery. Yet, for some the image still remains hidden. Tɪᴘ: Prompt students with, "Please don't feel bad if you just can't see it. Do you notice that some people can see the hidden image easily, while others can't? The same is true for hearing beats in tuning. We are not all equally able to hear tuning discrepancies. Now let's train your ears to find the hidden information."
2. *Provide an illustration of beats using two sound-sources*. The tones could be provided by two skilled students but, for predictable precision, use tone-generators (handheld tuners or, better, two simultaneous online tone-generators). Sound two tones together, each at 440Hz. Gradually recalibrate *one* tone to 441, 442, 443, and so on. With each increment, students will hear the beats developing at 1-per-second ("Hey, that's the same as 60 on a metronome!"), 2-per-second, 3-per-second, respectively. Balance the volume carefully to optimize the beats. Then, decrease

the interval again until the two tones reconvene at 440Hz. At that instant, students will almost always understand and appreciate the beatless sound of a perfect unison. The objective of this demonstration: one of our most helpful musical skills is the ability to recognize beats and eliminate them as quickly as possible.

Four easy strategies to demonstrate in-tune and out-of-tune sounds:

1. Sound a stable pitch using a tone-generator, tuner, drone, or a superior student. With your own major instrument, match the pitch to demonstrate a perfect beatless unison. Lower your pitch slowly; beats develop slow to fast as you go further out of tune. Repeat the process, this time raising your pitch. Finish by settling on the tuned, beatless unison.
2. Sing a perfect unison with a tuner or tone-generator, using a syllable like "loo" to simulate a sine wave. As previously, alter your vocal pitch from tuned to sharp, then to flat, finally settling on the tuned beatless unison. Amplification may be helpful.
3. Demonstrate out-of-tuneness using two piano strings. Use a tuning hammer to carefully detune one string from a pair. Guide students to hear the changing speed of the pulsations (faster = more out-of-tune, and slower = better in-tune), and then restore the beatless unison.
4. Demonstrate tuning with harmonics, using the amplified strings of an electric guitar or bass. This process is a bit more complex, but its remarkable effectiveness is worth the preparation time. TIP: Place a snare drum (with loosely adjusted "wet" snares) next to the amplifier; the snares provide sympathetic vibration, making it easier for students to hear the beats. A detailed description is found on the Resources Website [RW5.1].

Section 2: *Teaching* Intonation—Individuals and Smaller Groups

Drones, for our purposes, are continuously sounding tones used as a point-of-reference for tuning. Well-designed drone exercises can help students develop techniques to improve both their auditory acuity and their resulting performance intonation. This section provides several brief strategies for tuning against a drone, with single-pitch drones as well as intervals (e.g. the perfect 5th).

Seven Introductory Skill-building Exercises Prior to Drone Activities

1. Start by reviewing in- and out-of-tune sounds, guiding students with prompts like, "Raise your hand at the instant you think I'm in tune; drop your hand again when I'm *out of tune*." Simple questions will promote helpful discussions (e.g. "*How do you know* when I'm in tune?").
2. Convince students that a tuner is a required musical equipment. Consider starting with free apps, but follow with efforts to get actual tuners to students.
3. Teach students how to use the tuner. We cannot assume that every player can use the tuner's functions competently. Consider training students—section leaders, perhaps—to serve as "tuner mentors."
4. Guide students toward playing stable, "straight-line" pitches: students hold any chosen pitch while watching the tuner, stabilizing its display. Whether in-tune or not, the goal here is to *steady* the pitch: the tuner's display is held motionless, without fluctuations.
5. Help students develop pitch-bending skills. Having learned to stabilize straight-line pitches, students should work to control the embouchure, jaw separation, tongue-height, airstream direction, and other subtleties. These manipulations can raise and lower pitches as needed for staying in tune. Guide students with activities like "Make the pitch flatter," or "Let's see if you can *raise* that pitch more than 5 cents." But students should know: pitch-bending to excess can have unfavorable effects on the tone quality.
6. With SmartMusic© or other digital programs, devise brief lessons employing the sound-matching functions. The program detects which pitch is being played ("B-flat") and sounds an in-tune version of the same note through the speakers; the student works to match the sounding pitch. Students can notice that the *beatless*, in-tune sound (aural) will also successfully center the tuner's display (visual). Use the record-playback feature to allow students to hear tuning as listeners, rather than as performers.

7. Use a "show-hide" toggle or simply hide the display, leaving only the *sound* of the reference pitch. The student attempts to match the sound by aural comparison. Finally, expose the display to reveal the student's pitch-matching accuracy.

Here's a critical caveat: *musicians who rely on only the visual display of a tuner are really not learning to play in tune*. It's helpful while tuning the "primary" pitch but, without an aural reference *and the listening skills to match*, a student's visual usage of the tuner does very little to help *performance tuning*.

Five Strategies for Band Members to Utilize Drones

1. *Apply pitch-bending skills to manipulate a unison against the drone.* Having worked with a tuner's visual display, the student then uses aural comparisons during pitch-bending. Later, during an ensemble or small-group lesson, it becomes natural to transfer pitch-bending to live sounds rather than drones. Students can then tune to the principal player. TIP: Engage additional students with guidance like, "Give your colleagues some feedback. When you hear beats, raise your hand; when beats disappear, drop your hand."
2. *Play a scale with a single-pitch drone.* This easy exercise in Figure 5.1 is a great initial step toward refined intonation. It works equally well with soloists over an electronic drone, with duets and small groups, and with the full ensemble. Give extra care to the perfect intervals where the intonation beats are most apparent:

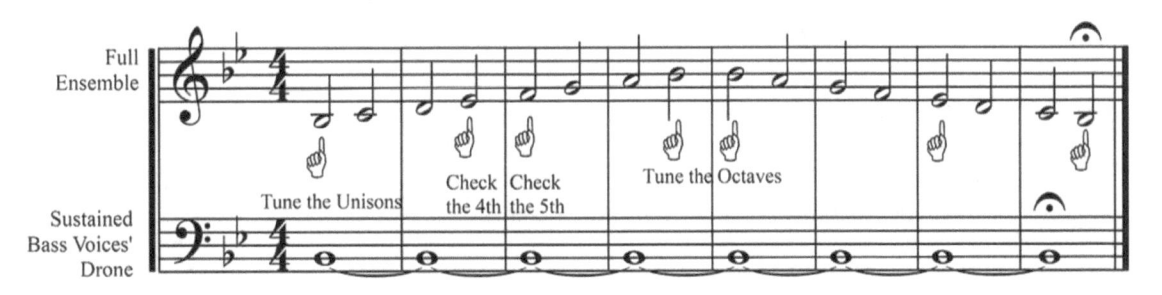

Figure 5.1 Playing a basic scale with a single-pitch drone.

With confidence on open intervals, this scale-process then leads students to improved tuning of other diatonic intervals. Work slowly, giving vigilant guidance while students work to adjust the 2nd, 3rd, 6th, and 7th. Note: this strategy also works well when the dominant is sustained. The first/last sound will therefore be a perfect 5th, with the band on the tonic and the drone on the dominant. Other strategies, like those that follow, take advantage of the sustained perfect 5th.
3. *Sound a perfect 5th drone: part 1.* The foundational work with 4ths and 5ths can be used to create a deeper understanding of performance intonation. Perform the short melodic figure exactly as written in Figure 5.2 to tune several scale-degrees by ear. Each note produces *two* intervals against the drone, rather than one.

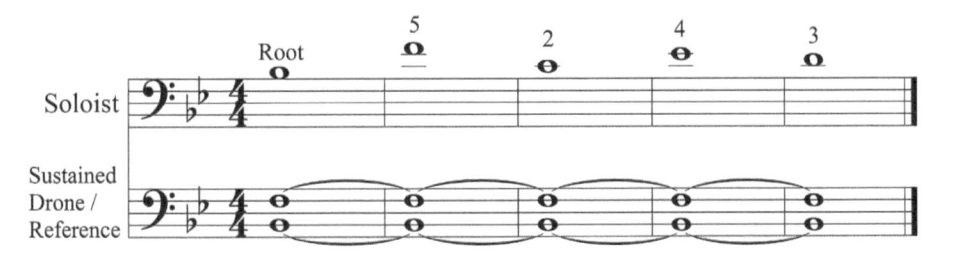

Figure 5.2 A pattern for tuning over a perfect 5th drone.

These five scale-degrees function exactly this way:

Do (Root) = Unison with the bottom; a 5th from the top of the drone
Sol (5) = Perfect 5th above the bottom; unison with the top
Re (2) = Major 2nd above *Do*; perfect 4th below *Sol*
Fa (4) = Perfect 4th above *Do*; major 2nd below *Sol*. It also helps students hear voice-leading as the line resolves to the final pitch
Mi (3) = This pitch completes the triad and provides the first step to helping students hear a *tempered* 3rd in a major chord.

TIP: To engage additional students, split the band in half; or, ask two advanced players to hold the drone pitches as a duet, or have a percussionist roll the open 5th on a marimba with soft mallets.

4. *Sound a perfect 5th drone: Part 2*. As shown in Figure 5.3. begin refinement of melodic tuning by playing standard scales and arpeggio exercises over drones, slowly. Especially during the arpeggio, pause to check accuracy of the 5th (raise it) and 3rd (lower it). TIP: this is also an engaging exercise for woodwind quintets, brass quintets and other chamber ensembles.

Figure 5.3 Scales and arpeggios over a perfect 5th drone.

5. *Use drones to repair instrument-specific intonation faults*. Be creative in designing more drone exercises to support students' intonation improvements.

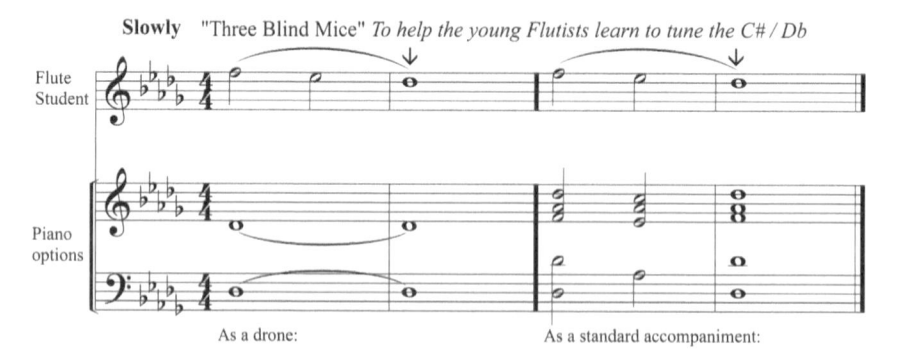

Figure 5.4 Flute with drone: "Three Blind Mice."

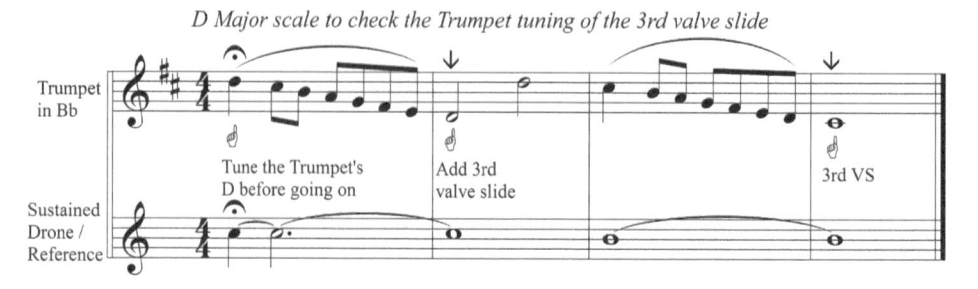

Figure 5.5 D major scale to tune trumpet 3rd valve slide.

INTONATION AND TUNING

Using an F Major scale to check the Trombonist's "bad" upper F

Figure 5.6 F major scale to tune the trombonist's upper F.

Five Activities Using Targets

The next strategies support the concept of *targets*, musically synonymous with "aiming" during visual activities like darts, archery, or even driving. A target provides an aural bull's eye, so the intonation adjustments work toward a specific goal. An analogy for our musical process is that we "set up targets" and then train students to accurately "aim" for better tuning.

In the following activities, playing partners will provide *targeting* activities for students. The most obvious method is for the teacher to sustain a note while the student aims for it, seeking a beatless unison. The target can be the tonic, or a note at a cadence, or really *any* flawed pitch selected from the melodic line.

1. *The tonic as the target.* After tuning together carefully, sustain a tonic while the student plays the melody. Approaching each occurrence of the tonic, the student should hear *and aim for* the target, as if it's a "homing signal." This technique also helps develop the sense of tonality. This first sustained tonic exercise in Figure 5.7 is a specific example of a drone; we've already seen how drones can help students learn to tune intervals.

Figure 5.7 A sustained tonic as a tuning target.

2. *Using any other scale degree as the target.* Targeting strategies are easily modified to focus on non-tonic pitches. Isolate and sustain a problematic pitch softly while the student plays. The student can hear and aim for the sustained target throughout the melodic playing. This strategy (Figure 5.8) supports the awareness of voice-leading and interval width. Tɪᴘ: For students who have not yet mapped their own tuning problems, expedite the process by selecting an inherently flawed pitch.

Sustaining a Target for a "problem" pitch (here, the Clarinetist's Throat A)

Figure 5.8 Sustaining a target for a "problem" pitch.

3. *Choosing a specific problem pitch as the target.* Using a tuned keyboard or your primary instrument, play the target note to "spot-check" its accuracy. Sound the pitch only when it arrives in the student's playing.

Figure 5.9 Using a piano to spot-check a problem pitch.

4. *Targeting with a tuner: sustained tones.* We've seen the advantage of a show–hide process using the display; this variation uses the tuner's *visual* function to improve specific notes, but also checks the student's tonality and awareness of horizontal tuning. Playing a brief excerpt, the student stops on the target pitch, adding a fermata to sustain the pitch "as heard by his musical ear." Continue holding it before glancing at the tuner. The teacher can participate by covering the tuner's display, revealing results only after the student comes to rest. Through repeated attempts, students begin to anticipate problems, and learn to pre-adjust for improved tuning. Over time, they improve their awareness of "problem notes."
5. *Targeting with a tuner: "flash tuning."* Having worked with sustained versions of problem notes, the students will learn to pre-adjust, based on what they've learned to anticipate. Next, add a strategy we could call flash-tuning. The student plays and releases a single note—"Play a staccato E-flat"—and views the results on the tuner display. With no time for pitch adjustments, the success relies on inner hearing (audiation) of the in-tune pitch before sounding it. Singing the pitch before playing it yields greater success. Tip: Students seem to view this as a game and—with its objective, measurable results—they'll repeat the challenge many times, enthusiastically.

Final Words About the Benefits of Aural Targeting

Through these easy-to-use activities, students are conditioned to improve tuning while playing, assuming the teacher gives immediate feedback. Moreover, these are very direct methods of revealing the problematic notes. Later, we'll examine the effectiveness of mapping each student's intonation tendencies with a personalized intonation chart. Targeting serves as a nice reminder while the student begins to memorize those personal "notes of concern." Tip: it can be comforting for students to hear that *all* players experience faulty intonation at times, but that advanced musicians have learned to fix the problem faster than others, with a highly trained ear and keen sensitivity to pitch discrepancies.

Remember that tuning is a complex skill, based on an accumulation of interrelated abilities, so these suggested exercises based on drones and targeting are components in a many-faceted approach.

Section 3: *Teaching* Intonation in the Full Band

Six Singing Activities to Improve Large-Ensemble Intonation

Singing helps in so many areas! In time, we'll all make this observation: band students who are also in chorus are generally better at tuning. They can also be more advanced with phrasing, tone-quality, sensitivity, interval accuracy, and more. It follows therefore that we should incorporate singing in band rehearsals. Here are some brief descriptions of activities relevant to intonation:

- When the tuning pitch is provided, have the students *hum* the pitch before playing.
- Isolate any note or chord (e.g. a composition's final note); direct students to play it, then *sing it* for tuning improvements, and return to playing.

INTONATION AND TUNING

- Use vocal exercises, altering specific vowels to demonstrate oral cavity changes, tongue positions, and airstream; discuss the effects on both intonation and tone. Then, alternate singing and playing to ingrain the comparisons.
- *Sing* a passage you've just played, especially if it's a chorale, using a neutral syllable or Solfege. To extend this exercise, use Solfege to transpose the passage to a different key.
- "Let's pause after that note. Now sing the *next* note" (allow time for the singing, followed by your feedback) "OK, now return to the instrument, audiate the next note, and aim for the center of that pitch. Breathe . . . play." This exercise helps improve intonation, while enhancing musicians' ability to hear intervals. TIP: This approach will improve brass players' accuracy.
- A singing strategy for use during tuning: for most band instruments, the Concert B♭ can be produced with just one hand. So, with a B♭ drone sounding:

    1. Students *hum* the pitch while plugging one ear with the free hand; the stopped ear naturally amplifies the sound of the voice.
    2. The student then *plays* the pitch on the instrument, still plugging one ear; the instrument's vibrations transfer through the teeth, jaw, and other bony structures.

        With this process, a musician can compare the vibration-oriented inner resonance to the external sounds being produced.

For more singing opportunities, see "A Solfege Strategy" (page 86).

There is no limit to the benefits of singing in the band rehearsal. Here, the discussion has been limited; Chapter 8 explores more about singing in our battery of effective band rehearsal strategies.

Strategic Playing *Activities to Improve Large-Ensemble Intonation*

- *Pitch-bending for ensembles.* Pitch-bending in the full band can help center the pitch. Leading the group with hand-signals or cues of your invention, do a short sequence of in-tune and out-of-tune unisons. However, remind students to "*Always* produce your best personal tone." After bending up and down, settle on a unison and let the band *sustain*. When students are focused and listening, a simple long unison can yield almost magical improvements.
- *Mouthpiece-buzzing to help brass players improve intonation.* When carefully monitored, mouthpiece buzzing can help center the brass players' tuning while also refining tone quality.

    1. Introduce buzzing in small groups to build comfort and acceptance; your guidance will help students rise above the potential for giggling when brass-player friends buzz.
    2. Have brass players buzz while woodwinds play. Experiment with options: full-ensemble performances; alternating groups (woodwinds playing first, brass buzzing second); alternating soloists; and more, always working to match tuning.
    3. Over time, add chorales, repertoire excerpts, and creative games.

    Require, and model, good posture and breathing techniques during the buzzing activities.

- *Inherent benefits of parallelism.* With this activity, students sound two scales simultaneously, a 4th or 5th apart. For example, choose Concert B♭ and Concert F, or use two scales representing the first piece(s) you'll rehearse. If you're about to play *The Fairest of the Fair*, play Concert E♭ (beginning) paired with Concert A♭ (trio) for a more focused, relevant version of this strategy.

    Begin by sustaining the open 4th/5th harmonic dyad with the band split in half (using any division of your choice). Give students time and guidance to tune the open interval, working to eliminate beats; then play each scale individually. Finally, play both scales together, ascending and descending, to create a series of parallel perfect 5th intervals.

    Consider applying this strategy beyond scales. Here are recommendations to help students improve intonation by hearing *parallel motion*, especially with 5ths:

    - Whether by rote or from notation, students can play a simple melody in two keys, creating parallel movement in perfect intervals. Musicians should check intonation by listening for beats during their melodic movement. Repeat at different dynamic levels, and in different octaves. Some suggested materials include "Three Blind Mice," "Happy Birthday," "America," your school's "Alma Mater," or themes from a current repertoire piece.

- For an easy version of this exercise, use a fugue's first *subject* and its *answer* simultaneously. Try Bach's Prelude and Fugue in D Minor.
- From the comprehensive musicianship perspective, these exercises provide a step toward later understanding of parallel organum.

Note: these short activities lead toward an understanding of how the Circle of 4ths can improve a band's performance. See Lisk's "The Creative Director" series for many additional suggestions.

Some Tuning Briefs

Tuning From a Specific Instrument

Whereas orchestras often tune to the oboe, that's usually an advanced player. It's unwise to assign our band's "center of pitch" role to someone struggling with both timbre and stability. Bands often favor a clarinetist or tuba player, but other options exist; directors are encouraged to evaluate all possibilities. The best answer will be a personal choice based on a variety of factors, including (at least) these:

- Who are the advanced players, with the most stable pitch?
- Have you sampled several tuning sources to compare the results of each?

Remember once again that the best "tuner" in your bandroom is *the well-trained ear*!

The "Tuning Note"

With many schools of thought, a typical question is whether to use B♭, A, or F to tune the band. Perhaps the best answer is "all of them," but it's important to know advantages and limitations of the choices.

- Concert B♭ is an open-tube note for most brass instruments, without valves (horn excepted), so it becomes an efficient pitch for tuning the instrument's full length with the main tuning slide. It is also fairly stable on most woodwinds. Therefore B♭ works in band for much the same reason Concert A is used in orchestras (where string instruments all have open "A" strings).
- Concert A supports woodwinds well—it is one of the saxophone's more stable notes—and as an open string for double bass, but it requires most brasses to use a valve or slide-position.
- Concert F is a wide favorite and tends to work as well or better than B♭ for brass instruments. Moreover, lots of great warm-up exercises are written in F major, and many sources elect Concert F as the wise choice for tuning. However, band directors should be aware of some inherent factors associated with F:

  - Flutists—perhaps the *largest* population in bands—often play flat on low F, slightly flat on top-line F, but quite sharp on high F.
  - Oboists have different tendencies for each F fingering.
  - For E♭ saxophones (often a large group), the written D can be significantly sharp.
  - Bassoons, especially with younger players, have factors frequently leading to instability on the F.
  - For most of the brass instruments (horn excluded), Concert F becomes the 3rd partial (slightly sharp) or 6th partial (quite sharp).

After considering all influencing factors, directors can then rely on their familiarity with students' abilities to select the best tuning choices for each situation.

INTONATION AND TUNING

Five Recommended Tuning Strategies for the Full Band

Note: these are only *suggestions*. Use all resources to synthesize your own full-group tuning preferences.

- A slow, sustained process using: B♭ > A > F ("Do > Ti > Sol" in the key of B♭).
    1. Tune Concert B♭ together.
    2. Drop to Concert A: brass players then check 2nd valve tuning.
    3. Drop again to Concert F: clarinetists check the throat-tone G, brass players check for sharpness, and alto/baritone saxes practice slightly flattening the 4th-line D.
    4. ". . . and, repeat!"

- Sound an open interval with some students holding B♭ and others F. This group-drone process supports the common approach of having students play an ascending tetrachord: "SOL_____ La–Ti–*DO*_____" (F_____ G–A–B♭_____).

- Tuning from principals: tune all first-chair players together first. The sound is then provided by a cohesive ensemble of only advanced players. Add players in smaller increments: "If you're seated next to the principals on either side, come in now; eliminate the beats!" Guide the students to listen as the beatless unison gets larger until the entire group is sounding. This strategy also provides a timbre model for each section while spreading the tuned unison out across the band for proximity.

- "Pass the Sound" (or, "F Around the Room") allows students to play individually or in small groups, usually starting from tubas. Pass a pitch throughout the band, working to match tuning, tone and intensity of the player(s) before. Variations include these and others of your design:
    1. A tuned volunteer sounds the pitch—a second player joins, tuning the unison to a beatless result. When the third player begins, the first stops; there are constantly two students playing.
    2. The band plays a *tutti* unison—each section plays alone, holding for four counts, stopping when the next section begins. Conclude with another *tutti*.
    3. All principal players sound the tuning note first, as described previously.

- "Tuning by the numbers"—find this detailed strategic process at [RW5.2]. This document is designed specifically to tune the lowest bass voices before moving upward through the tenor, alto, and soprano voices. This acoustics-based strategy follows a numbered, sequential procedure that can be administered by students themselves. This download is easily revised, adaptable to your preferences.

Beyond the Tonic: *Tuning the Entire Instrument*

Even when the band sounds beautiful on its "tuning note", the job is incomplete. Brass instruments' valve-slides should be tuned. Similarly, clarinets benefit from tuning at the various joints. Try *mapping* each student's intonation deficiencies (see "Intonation Map" on page 93); that task brings attention to the adjustment of the valve-slides. TIP: Be alert for mismatched clarinet barrels, bassoons' bocal length, oboe reed length/hardness and, of course, stuck slides on brasses, among many other issues.

Six Chord-based *Activities to Improve Large-ensemble Intonation*

1. *Scales in canon.* Featured in Chapter 3, the same exercise can be adapted to assist with intonation. Divide the band into equal parts for the scale canon up to the 9th. Students' listening skills will improve the most if they know where the unisons and octaves occur (boxed in Figure 5.10), and are directed toward tuning them. This sequence can be used with or without a sounding drone.

INTONATION AND TUNING

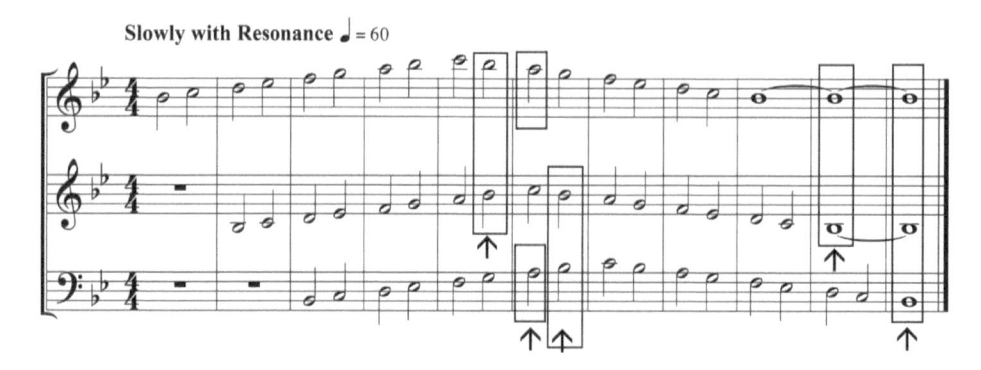

Figure 5.10 Unisons and octaves to tune during a scale-in-canon.

2. *Solfege strategy.* It takes very little time to teach students basic Solfege syllables. Provide a classroom display aligning Solfege syllables with major scale notes and scale-degree numbers:

1	2	3	4	5	6	7	8
B♭	C	D	E♭	F	G	A	B♭
Do	*Re*	*Mi*	*Fa*	*Sol*	*La*	*Ti*	*do*

Then, create four short musical lines indicated by Solfege syllables:

Soprano:	Do	Do	Do	Ti	Do
Alto:	Sol	La	Sol	Sol	Sol
Tenor:	Mi	Fa	Mi	Re	Mi
Bass:	Do	Fa	Sol	Sol	Do

The students can then memorize sequences, and play (or sing!) an "Instant Chorale" *in any key.* Over time, directors can creatively "custom-fit" these Solfege-chorales to passages extracted from your band's repertoire.

3. *The "Remington."* Named for legendary teacher Emory Remington, this is a time-tested and highly recommended exercise with many benefits beyond intonation. Optionally, sound a tonic-key drone softly so the students will hear a reference during rests. The version in Figure 5.11 is condensed to a single staff for clarity; choose your own SATB instrument assignments. Of course, the goal is always to create a sonorous, well-balanced chord:

Figure 5.11 The "Remington."

4. *A blueprint for tuning common chord qualities.* This short exercise focuses students' concentration. It supports tuning-awareness and helps to teach the sound of three common chord-types: major, minor and diminished. Musical notation is helpful but not required. Try the visual blueprint in Figure 5.12, or provide a verbal description supplemented by hand-signals, cues, or conducting. The process begins with a major chord, and each descending half-step yields a new chord: *major* becomes *minor*, and then *diminished*, before settling on another *major* chord, one semitone below the original.

INTONATION AND TUNING

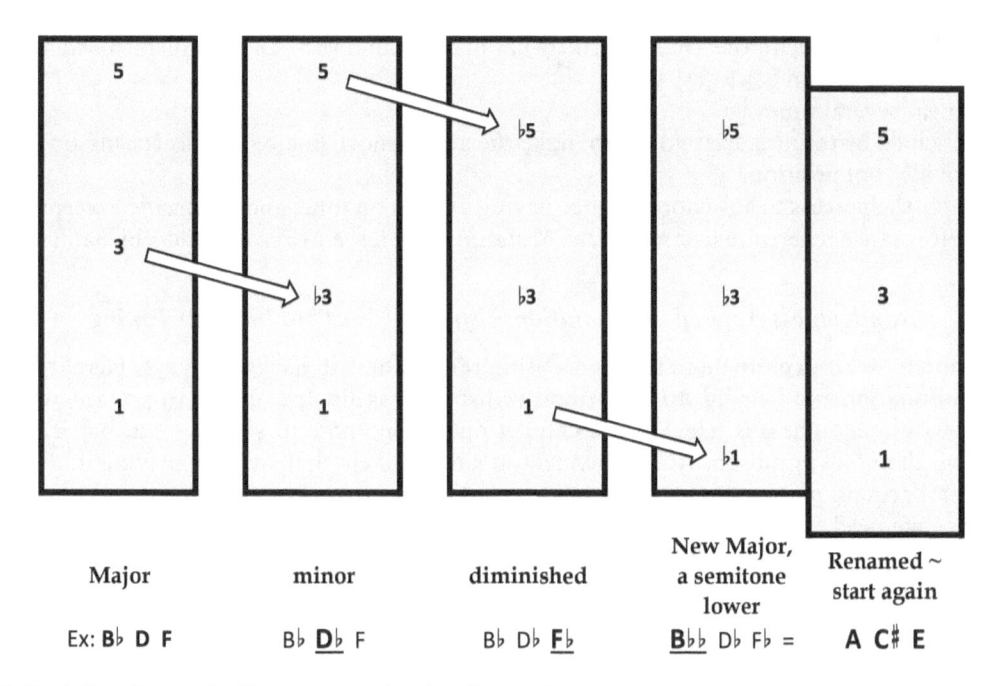

Major	minor	diminished	New Major, a semitone lower	Renamed ~ start again
Ex: B♭ **D** F	B♭ **D♭** F	B♭ D♭ **F♭**	**B♭♭** D♭ F♭ =	A C♯ E

Figure 5.12 A "math equation" strategy: maj–min–dim–maj.

As a variation, use finger signals (1–3–5) to identify which tone of the chord to change, and then point (up/down) to indicate raising or lowering that pitch by a semitone. This version can create all four main chord qualities, including augmented (M m + °).

This entire strategy goes far beyond tuning; the careful *listening* required will further support your ensemble's ongoing ear-training.

5. *Building chords from scales.* With this process, it is easy to create any diatonic chord on-site. Just add sustained tones to create a triad or even a seventh chord. Consider the example in Figure 5.13, condensed to a grand staff.

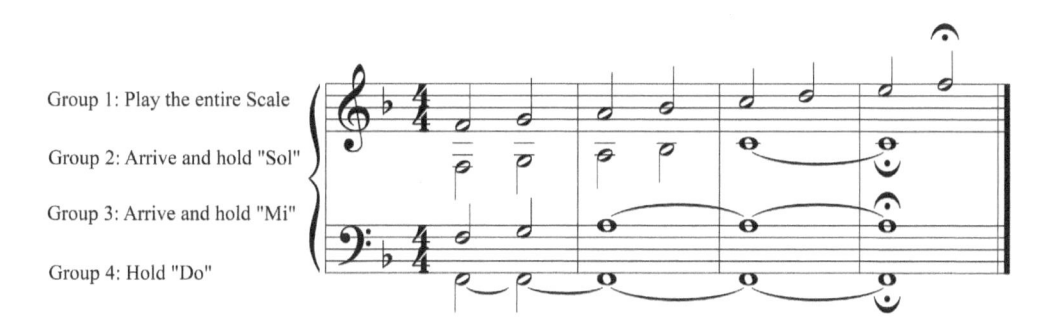

Group 1: Play the entire Scale
Group 2: Arrive and hold "Sol"
Group 3: Arrive and hold "Mi"
Group 4: Hold "Do"

Figure 5.13 Build an ensemble chord from a scale.

This exercise can be revised many ways. Using the major scale alone, for instance, try ii⁷ (re–fa–la–do), inversions of IV (do–fa–la–do) and V⁷ (re–fa–sol–ti), and others.

6. Using a sustained tone to "anchor" tuning: some chord progressions are harder for students to hear, and thus to tune. As an example, consider I to ♭VI. In B-flat, that's B♭ major to G♭ major. A well-designed strategy clarifies the chord's construction while improving its tuning.

   ○ Sustain a major triad: "Do–Mi–Sol"
   ○ On cue, Mi drops ½ step while Sol raises ½ step.

87

- With these two semitone changes, the B-flat major sound (B♭–D–F) transforms to an inverted G-flat major sound (B♭–D♭–G♭).
- Repeat several times.
- Conclude by training bass voices to make the actual move (major 3rd down; minor 6th up), to provide root position.
- Apply the process to any chord-change having a common tone, and to specific excerpts from the performance repertoire (consider *Our Yesterdays Lengthen Like Shadows* by Samuel Hazo).

Randomness Applied to Intonation: Using "Chance" to Improve Tuning

In later chapters, we'll explore more strategies using randomness in engaging ways. Here, the focus is limited to intonation and helping students improve listening skills. It can help to preface activities by explaining why randomness is relevant: we can get our tuning note to sound great, but it's rare that we'll all hold that note in unison. At any moment, it's more likely that we'll be playing in duets, trios, or other small groups: players might sound with their own section, or with a mixed collection of other instruments. We need to be in tune whether playing unisons or chords, in small groups or in the full ensemble, at all dynamics, and in all keys and registers.

Here are examples of how to use these concepts in the rehearsal (after basic tuning):

- "If your birthday is in January, please play a Concert B♭ together now."
- "If you are currently *not* wearing socks, please choose one note of the E-flat major chord and play together now."
- "Count off 1 to 12 through the entire band." (wait-time) Then, roll two dice to indicate, for example, that "Everyone with number 7, please play." Count 1 to 6 for a single die, or 1 to 20 to choose students using a dartboard.

These types of randomness strategies (several others are found at [RW5.3]) offer refreshing diversions to spot-check intonation with an ever-changing set players. Students will see these activities as a departure from the more predictable tuning alternatives. And for the director, using randomness strategies will offer inspiring ways to use your own creativity.

"The Magic Number"

This is an appealing strategy—a game, actually—that functions for many purposes. Applied to intonation, it works this way:

- With the full band pre-tuned, announce that "The magic number is 4."
- The 4th player from each end of each row should play. Therefore, eight or more random players—usually representing different instruments—will sound the pitch together as a tuning spot-check.
- After experiencing this strategy for tuning unisons, students will also accept it for checking chords from the repertoire. For example, "The magic number is 6. Please go to measure 78; hold what you have on Beat 4."

Using Measurements to Create a Helpful Challenge

This game, based on measurable tuning, has an element of competitiveness that often motivates students. Choose players randomly. For clarity, let's connect it to the magic number strategy. In your band of five rows, now you'll have ten students participating.

Ask each student to play the tuning note *alone* for a few seconds while you view the tuner. Tabulate results by writing measurements: "+10" when the pitch is ten cents sharp, and "-17" for seventeen cents flat. If a pitch is too unstable to stop the tuner, make a best-guess for that student; on the display, you might write "W" . . . "That was about 20 cents sharp, but I added the 'W' for 'wobbly.' Keep working to hold a stable, 'straight-line' sound."

Continue through all ten students; then use your list:

- "Today's total was 64; that's ten points closer to 'zero' than yesterday."
- "Today's average was still higher than our goal. Better, but please keep working on your personal tuning."
- "Kudos to players who were dead-center in their tuning! They are really helping our group sound better."
- "When we reach a tuning average of 5 or lower, I'll buy pizza for the band after school!"

This strategy enables many opportunities for the teacher's inventiveness using averages, totals, comparisons, charts, and competitions of all kinds.

Four Strategies for Alternating Full-band with Individuals (or Groups) for Tuning

Lead the band slowly through a scale, cutting off the full ensemble to leave a student or small-group playing for comparison or evaluation. Sample possibilities include:

1. The band sustains "Do" in tune. The teacher points to a student, and cuts off the full band, leaving that individual playing. Use a tuner, or ask for verbal feedback to evaluate the student's success. Repeat, choosing several students for successive attempts. Move on to the next pitch.
2. Expand the process to duets: cut off the full band, leaving only a duet and have the students listen for beats. Move to the next pitch and repeat the process. Vary the duets so students can hear instrumental mixtures.
3. Reverse the order: a soloist sustains "Do." Cue the entry of the rest of the band to join on the unison "Do". Point to a new student, who plays "Re" alone when you cut off the band. Cue the re-entry of the band to match the soloist on "Re." Continue up the scale.
4. Move from small to large: begin with a tuned soloist. On cue, all principal players enter to create an in-tune unison. Finally, cue the rest of the band. Move to "Re" and repeat the process.

Teach the Mindset of Playing in Trios Within the Full Ensemble

This is a philosophy students can employ as just one part of their vast collection of listening skills. In terms of intonation, train students to listen "to *only* your two neighbors; work carefully to eliminate beats so all three of you are perfectly in tune." By extension, these tuned neighbor-groups will interconnect across the ensemble to improve the entire group's intonation. Additional applications beyond tuning are found in Chapter 8, and you're encouraged to read "Listening to your 'Trio of Players'" in Richard Floyd's wonderful book, *The Artistry of Teaching and Making Music* (GIA Publications, 2015).

Four Strategies for Using Audio Record/Playback to Improve Intonation

Too often the obvious strategies are overlooked. Here are novel ways to use recording–playback for intonation purposes. These processes are easy, objective, and enlightening to students; further, the evidence is compelling.

- Use separate microphones to isolate two students playing the same line of a composition during a short excerpt in the context of the full band. On playback, all listeners can easily compare the pair's tuning accuracy.
- With any multitracking program, record a student playing a musical excerpt twice, three times, or more on separate tracks while listening to a reference drone. Record with a click-track only, muting the other takes. Combine the multiple tracks into one unison performance to reveal how consistently the student has managed the intonation.

- Multitracking can also highlight tuning problems related to *range* and *dynamics.* The student records an excerpt on two tracks for comparative playback. Record the excerpt as written, and compare to another performance an octave higher or lower; or, compare a *pianissimo* performance to a *fortissimo* version.
- Record a student's part along with a full concert band track on SmartMusic©, or with any other backing track. The playback offers an easy evaluation of the student's tuning.

Tune Problematic Chords Through Reduction

Some excerpts are unkind to intonation. Severe tuning problems emerge when parts are written very high or low, especially at extreme dynamics. Problems are exacerbated by odd orchestrations or thinly scored groupings, and especially when instruments are assigned to inherently bad notes. So to provide immediate improvement, reduce the chord. Transpose its notes to a "comfort-zone" where players can better control their tuning. In its most basic form, this is a two-step process:

1. Reduce the problematic chord by transposing notes to their best octaves, and tune this closed-position chord to a pleasant result.
2. Gradually send players back to their written notes

Examine a problematic moment in the band's standard literature: a very loud G major chord at Rehearsal Number 10 in Ronald Lo Presti's, *Elegy for a Young American*. The instrumental parts are written *fff* in their extreme ranges, which can result in serious tuning problems (Figure 5.14).

Figure 5.14 Tuning by reduction to the "Comfort Zone."

1. Tune *any* G major chord. Use a *Treasury of Scales* chorale, a scale-canon, or simply tell students what to play. For the most relevant process, transpose the specific Lo Presti notes to comfortable octaves for each instrument. This beautifully tuned chord becomes the basis for the next steps.
2. Move gradually—student by student—rebuilding the orchestrated chord while most of the ensemble sustains their "comfortable" pitches. Here are suggested sample options, only to spark creativity:
    - "*One* 1st flute, please move to high G; tune with your section. Now the other 1st flutes change to high G, one by one. Finish by *marking* the pitch so you'll stay in tune when we perform." Or,
    - "Everybody, hold the tuned chord at *mezzo-forte*. On cue, all *principal players* go to the written dynamic level of *fff*." Or,
    - "Let's make a comparison. First, play the tuned 'comfort zone' chord at *mezzoforte*. On cue, play the actual notes at the written dynamic level. We'll playback a recording of the results."

About the Effects of Seating Arrangements

Using the "tuning from the principals" model, it seems logical that intonation for the entire ensemble can improve when principal players are seated near each other. For example, 1st cornet next to 1st trombone, and 1st alto sax by 1st horn. But there are many factors to consider, including these:

Proximity—the distance between players affects their ability to tune to one another.

Bell direction—it is easier for students to hear bell-front instruments when seated ahead of them. Caveat: stay aware of bell-directions, and the effects on blend, balance, and all other aspects of the sound.

Stacking—some conductors enjoy tuning benefits from stacking the brass instruments; for example, 1st and 2nd horns ahead of 3rd and 4th, rather than in one line.

SATB groupings—younger students often tune more accurately when seated in a pitch-range group. For example, we could split the saxophones like this: altos by horns, tenors nearer to trombones/euphoniums, and baritone saxes close to tubas and bass clarinets.

The layout of the performance space—unconventional venues may require unconventional seating plans. Don't hesitate to adjust occasionally.

Resonance—your band will sound better if the timpani heads are in tune with the same pitches provided by other bass voices.

Section 4: Even More Strategies to Improve Intonation

Exploit the phenomenon of resonance—or sympathetic vibration—to provide students with interesting, inventive activities.

Exercises Using the Piano

When a wind student plays into a piano with its damper pedal depressed (or when the piano key is held down), the counterpart string vibrates sympathetically. The fullness and quality of the piano's "ring" provides an aural measurement of the student's tuning accuracy. Repeated efforts teach students that a focused, stable tone improves results. Piano strategies can include:

○ For arpeggios and other chord-based patterns, simply depress the damper pedal while the student plays notes of a chord.

○ Check problem notes individually: open the piano string, timed precisely to align with the arrival of one specific note played by the student. The resulting vibration—ringing on after the student has finished—demonstrates whether the tuning was accurate. Alternatively, slowly depress the (one) piano key and *hold it down* until the target note is reached.

○ Check an ensemble's chord: for example, a brass quintet's final cadence or a jazz band's "kick" chord can be played while the piano's damper pedal is depressed. The ensemble members hear the results—good or *not so*—ringing back from the piano.

○ Help a soloist tune to the accompanist: the wind musician sounds the tuning note first, prior to hearing it from the piano. Depress the damper pedal just before the wind player releases the pitch; the string will vibrate if the soloist and the piano are at the same frequency. Tip: By listening to the piano pitch first, some students have a keen enough ear to match it, even if they do so by distorting the embouchure while their instrument is poorly tuned. Find the best *tone*, and only then determine if it matches the piano's pitch.

Of course, the piano's equal-tempered tuning doesn't really match what advanced musicians encounter in ensemble playing, but it helps students refine their ability to listen and adjust for *results*.

Tuning the Large Ensemble with Resonance in Mind

Rather than tuning to a single target pitch or with a tuner, let the principles of acoustics and resonance help tune the group. "Tuning by the numbers" [RW5.2] relies on resonance to tune the ensemble from the bottom up, using *aural* rather than mechanical methods. That is, tune the tubas, contra clarinets and baritone sax before tuning the other instruments. In an ensemble with the bottom-most voices well in tune, the higher-pitched instruments can tune more easily because their pitches are already contained in the lower instruments' harmonics.

INTONATION AND TUNING

Resonance Ideas for Percussionists

With awareness of how resonance affects their section, percussionists can be integrated better into the band's blend and tuning:

- Resonance frequently causes snares to buzz during a lyrical ballad section: teach students to use the throw-off mechanism.
- Closed flappers stop the vibraphone's tone from fully ringing into the resonator tubes: teach students to rotate them to the "open" position when playing without the motor.
- Toms sometimes converge with the *room* acoustics to produce boomy sounds: teach players to eliminate a rumble by adjusting the drumhead slightly, "de-tuning" it from the room's natural frequencies.
- Timpani lugs should be fine-tuned so the head will produce the same pitch at every location; the drum will then be "in tune with itself:" teach players how to hear the drum resonating with the band. TIP: This is an excellent opportunity to teach about sympathetic vibrations by *singing* into the timpani.

Resonance for the Double Bass

With the band sustaining Concert A, the double bass player tunes the open "A" string, which should also ring sympathetically. Then, allow a moment for the student (alone) to finish tuning the other three strings. Using Concert A helps to ensure that the open strings are tuned. TIP: Warm-up chorales and etudes in E, A, D, and G will support the open strings.

A Strategy for Students in Small Groups to use Perfect 5ths in Tuning

With a trio of students tuned carefully, ask *two* players to sustain a perfect 5th drone (tonic–dominant). The third student should *slowly* play a scale, tuning every interval against the drone. Repeat until each student has played the scale; remember feedback to support the desired balance and blend.

Although listed for a trio, this process can be adapted to function well for most chamber ensembles. Try this with a brass or woodwind quintet:

- Double the tonic and dominant to engage four players, while the fifth player tunes the scale.
- Use four students to sustain a full chord while a soloist plays a scale or excerpt within the well-tuned framework.
- A soloist can also practice tuning an improvised diatonic melody over the ensemble.

A Technique to Support Intonation, using Non-transposed Scales

Direct students to "Play your C major scale," for example. By playing the same scale-name with mixed instruments, students can practice hearing intervals of a 4th and 5th. A foremost advantage of playing non-transposed scales is that students can visualize, internalize, finger and *recite* the same key signature and pitch-names.

- A "chamber ensemble" example using brass quintet: when they all play the "C major scale", we'll hear
    - "C" from tuba and trombone
    - "F" from horn
    - "B♭" from trumpets.

First, have the horn, tuba, and trombone play to create parallel 5ths/4ths (C–F). Then, the trumpets and horn play together to yield another parallel scale (F–B♭). After students are comfortable hearing the 4ths, then stack them by having all members play together. Guide them carefully as they listen for 4ths and 5ths in the new context of a *quartal stack* (C–F–B♭).

INTONATION AND TUNING

- A full band example: if we choose instrument groupings carefully, we will sound two parallel scales in perfect intervals. For instance, all concert pitch instruments and horns will sound parallel scales in C and F. Add other groups to hear scales in an extended stack in quartal harmony (C–F–B♭–E♭). It's worth noting that quartal harmonies are common throughout the wind band's repertoire.

Creating and Using "Intonation Maps" Personalized for Individuals

Musicians must know their instrument's intonation tendencies for specific notes, across various ranges, and at all dynamic levels. Players can show immediate improvements by learning the instrument's "bad" notes, along with alternate fingerings and other methods for raising/lowering pitches. These improvements can be guided, structured, and objectively measured by creating an individualized intonation map for each student; this is essentially a personal *inventory* of intonation faults. Here's how to achieve that goal:

- Provide students with a written full-range chromatic scale, each pitch having a spot to notate a measurement of its tuning.
- Teach them how to use a tuner to evaluate each pitch in terms of *cents*.
- While the student plays the chromatic scale slowly, a partner documents the tuning, writing results for each pitch on the map.

This project requires the student to "calibrate" first by tuning in the standard way until the display locks at *zero*. The player doesn't view the tuner for this exercise; instead, he holds each pitch long enough for a *partner* to record the results as *+10* (ten cents sharp), *–15* (fifteen cents flat), or *0* (in-tune). The resulting chart creates a *map* of the notes that are observed inherently problematic for that student. For best results, the student should . . .

. . . memorize problematic notes;
. . . repeat the exercise periodically, attempting to improve the results each time;
. . . assess pitches at varied *dynamics* as well.

In the following example, the first measure offers a basic method where results can be entered by placing a vertical line through + for "sharp", or ++ for "very sharp." The second measure is a bit more specific; the vertical line can still work, or the partner can circle the number-of-cents sharp or flat. The third measure is a completed model of a "multi-test" design, which can be used in a variety of inventive ways:

○ Complete Tests #1, 2, 3 and 4 shown in Figure 5.15 several weeks apart, each time working for improvements based on results from previous tests; or,
○ Do the mapping three times in the same sitting: once each at *pp*, *mf*, and *ff*.

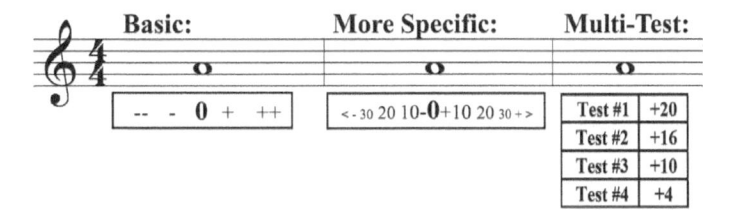

Figure 5.15 Building the intonation map.

Tip: To optimize your students' intonation education, provide written details about the general pitch tendencies common to their instruments. Look for lists showing sharp and flat tendencies for each instrument, and textual information describing methods to adjust the pitch. Many helpful resources are available in print, online, and by simply questioning a trusted professional.

Students then need a practical knowledge about options (e.g. alternate fingerings) for intonation adjustments. By knowing tuning characteristics in advance, and applying pitch-adjustment techniques, the musician can have a positive effect on intonation before the problem arrives.

Music-markings Specifically for Intonation

Your students can adjust pitches more efficiently if they *mark* the music; for that, they'll need a system of markings to identify flaws. Once a pitch is discovered to be very flat, for example, a cleverly placed symbol will alert the student to adjust the pitch, before its sour intonation arrives. Musicians invent their own markings for pitch; a workable suggestion is given in Figure 5.16 as an example.

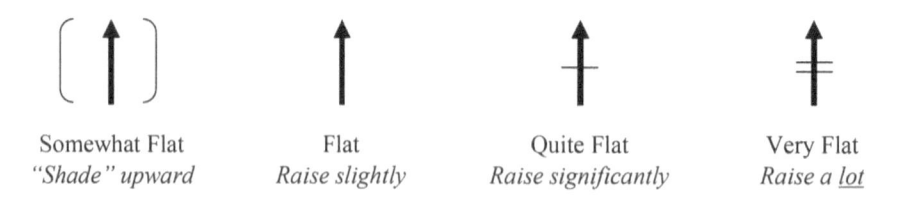

Somewhat Flat   Flat   Quite Flat   Very Flat
"Shade" upward   *Raise slightly*   *Raise significantly*   *Raise a <u>lot</u>*

Figure 5.16 Tuning arrow markings for out-of-tune pitches.

Arrows in the opposite direction, of course, are used for sharp pitches. After learning a pitch-marking method, the students then learn to "nudge" a pitch in the needed direction before making the sound. A teacher's guidance might manifest like this: "You already discovered that your upper 'F' is almost twenty-cents sharp in that chord, and you marked it. So, before you actually play it out-of-tune, *aim* flatter. How about this: 'here comes the cone; steer a little to the left to miss the pothole that's been there every day!'"

Five Additional Strategies and Resources to Promote Better Intonation

1. *Use two tuners for a special lesson.* While one tuner produces a sound, an adjacent model shows its visual LED or needle function. The student plays, listening for the beats against the sounding tuner. After a moment, turn off the sounding tuner (or gradually decrease its volume), leaving only the student's instrumental sound. The player will then notice if the gauge leaves its "zero" position to indicate inaccurate tuning.
2. *Add a duet at the octave.* The instructor can play *8vb* or *8va* with the student, rather than in a unison. The teacher's version provides a real-time target for pitch-accuracy, as well as a model for rhythm, tone and more. The octave separation helps to isolate the student's sound from that of the teacher.
3. *Accompany the student's playing, even for scales and simple passages.* Instructors with unrefined keyboard skills can still play the student's melody, or perhaps a very basic chord progression. Quality accompaniments of any kind offer important opportunities for intonation training; consider accompaniment software and digital products as well.
4. *Stay up to date on emerging technology.* Apps, games, programs, and other evolving options will surely offer additional assistance with intonation. At the time of this writing, the TonalEnergy family of applications has made an important advancement in the teaching of tone and intonation.
5. *Deliver an uncomplicated lesson about the harmonic series.* Especially for brass players, knowing tendencies of the various partials can help students choose an alternate fingering or slide-position. In Figure 5.17, a trumpet student is struggling to tune the top-space E:

Figure 5.17 Alternate fingering choices based on the harmonic series.

- 0: The open fingering for this E is the 5th partial of the C series; tuning is somewhat flat and may be difficult to "lip up."
- 1–2: Fingering with valves 1–2, the same E becomes the 6th partial in the A series, with a sharper tendency.
- 3: The same E using the 3rd valve is still the (sharp) 6th partial, but the 3rd valve is built to be a bit flat, so the resulting pitch offers another choice to the player.

As you can imagine, this entire topic can become complex for students. Although it will require creativity to design a delivery that matches your teaching-style, the results will be invaluable to the development of your students' tuning.

Conclusion: Final Thoughts about Intonation in Your Teaching

To help students improve tuning during actual performance, play in unison with students frequently during lessons. Students emulate the teacher—the exemplar—in many aspects of playing, including tone and style. In the case of tuning, playing with an experienced partner allows students to evaluate intonation on a pitch-by-pitch basis. For that reason, teachers should *not* adjust to the student's faulty intonation; we become adept at intonation ourselves, and we might feel an overwhelming need to adjust to "fix" bad tuning. Doing so will only reinforce the student's faults.

Notice that none of our strategies will guarantee that students can identify if they are sharp or flat. But that skill, while important, is perhaps not necessary for students to make improvements. By developing their awareness of beats, students can be guided easily to the next logical step: "Make a slight change. If the beats get faster, you went the wrong direction, so try going the other way. Your goal is to slow the beats until they finally go away."

The crux of this entire chapter can be distilled into an easy checklist to help students make tangible progress in tuning:

- ✓ "Can you hear the beats when you're playing out of tune?"
- ✓ "Have you learned skills to raise and to lower badly tuned notes to improve intonation?"
- ✓ "Do you know about your instrument's bad notes and other factors so you can predict intonation problems before they happen?"

These three skills, in exactly that order, will do much to help instrumentalists learn to play better in tune.

Some easy observations may yield quick-fix solutions:

- Instruments are manufactured slightly sharp: "when in doubt, pull it out."
- Look for missing bumpers, bent keys and compressed corks, and other problems that contribute to bad tuning on woodwinds.
- Frozen and sticking slides on brass instruments are major factors in poor tuning.
- At loud dynamics, and during a *crescendo*, instrument tuning often goes in opposite directions: brass and flutes sail sharp, while reed instruments often fall flat.
- An extreme push or pull (tuning slide, barrel, headjoint) usually indicates a different underlying problem.

- Important factors occasionally slip through the cracks. Watch carefully for mismatched parts; clarinet barrels that are too long/short; the wrong number of bits in a Sousaphone's leadpipe; keys/pads that are significantly higher or lower than others; severe dents; built-up gunk that keeps tenons and slides from full insertion; deposits in the chamber of a woodwind mouthpiece.
- Common problems leading to full-band intonation deficiencies include:
    - *Range/Register*—extremely high or low notes (anything outside the "comfort zone" for students) are likely to have problems.
    - *Dynamics*—not all instruments share the *same* pitch-tendencies at the loud and soft ends of the spectrum.
    - *Less-common keys and chords*— a band finds better intonation on a B♭ triad than on a B♮ triad.
    - *Known "bad notes" on instruments*—specifically, watch for how the problem-notes are scored in the band's chords.
    - And a host of other factors.

As teachers and conductors, we must be acutely aware of *all* of these considerations and more. Further, perhaps most importantly, each director should consistently convey the importance of excellent intonation: address the faults, utilize strategies toward solutions, and provide motivating feedback to acknowledge every successful step.

Still, intonation will surely be a long-term goal for all bands and the players within. "Great tuning" is not produced by accident, so seek every available resource and make use of every known strategy to help students improve. Through strategies that help to refine musicians' listening skills, improvements to many other facets of the band's performance are made more possible.

6
RHYTHM, METER, AND TEMPO

Introduction

In most cases, rhythm is correct, or it is not. Other elements of performance allow for personal variance; we expect and even *appreciate* differences in some aspects of music. In fact, listeners are often drawn to certain performers for their beautiful tone, unique style, and interpretive decisions. However, rhythm is not afforded as much flexibility: musicians should read rhythms correctly (which involves meter signatures, of course), and perform with exactness, appropriate style, and control of the pulse. As such, teachers are obligated to help students "get it right" through any means possible. This chapter focuses on strategies to meet that goal, starting with a very abbreviated look at *how* we learn and, specifically, by noting the parallels between language and music.

The "sound-to-symbol" approach is undoubtedly the strongest influence on learning language. By any other designation (sound before sign, practice before theory, understanding before notation), this is also the most natural and unobstructed path toward music-learning, especially where primary goals include enjoyment, engagement, fluency, and a lifelong love of music. David Newell says that "theoretical explanations must always *reflect* the learners' experiences—never *precede* them."[1] Rather than delving into the ample related research, however, the emphasis here will remain firmly on *activities* and *practical strategies* to help support rhythm and its components in the full-band setting. This chapter rests on three tenets:

1. *An internal sense of pulse* is crucial.
2. *Movement* is a vital ingredient in the most complete recipe for pulse, meter, and rhythm.
3. *Sound* is a productive resource for learning fluent, natural-sounding rhythmic performance.

Section 1: Building the Concept of Pulse for Rhythm

The notion that movement is important to internal pulse is not this author's invention. It seems that inner pulse becomes a predictor of rhythmic fluency; the research is abundant already. Short supportive examples are listed here:

Daniel Levitin, on "keeping the beat":
   Yes, it seems as though it's hardwired. It's because neurons synchronize with the beat of the music, and because babies go through a period of practicing motor movements and viewing the intended results as a way of training their visual-motor system. Something similar happens when we "march in time," or when we do "jumping jacks" exercises together in a schoolyard. And, as I've suggested, this was likely an evolutionary adaptation; success at synchronous group activities could have real survival value.[2]

Peter Keller, on "the importance of the innate pulse":
   In other words, some people required external physical stimulation to perceive the beat, whereas others were able to generate the beat internally. Remarkably, people who were good at

internally generating beats also performed well on a synchronisation task that required them to predict tempo changes in musical sequences. So the capacity for internal beat generation turns out to be a reliable marker of rhythmic skill.[3]

It is important to recognize that the best musicians can maintain a steady pulse independently, and they can synchronize with a given pulse, by sound (the ensemble), and by sight (the conductor). It stands to reason, then, that we can support students' rhythmic success by nurturing their inner pulse first.

Strategies to Enhance Students' Innate Sense of Pulse

- *Visual and aural demonstrations.* To start, it can be enlightening for students to experience proof that inner clocks are not all the same. These activities can confirm that, without help, we all measure time differently.
    - *A steady experiment.* We experience it at sporting events: the crowd's steady clapping accelerates until, out of control, it dissolves into a shower of random applause. As an experiment, task your students with the challenge to "keep clapping as steadily as possible." Provide a steady example, and then "1–2–ready–go." Let students work together without any assistance, while you record their attempt. On playback, they'll surely hear the fluctuation of the speed. To offer further proof, use a metronome's "tap" function to display the changing tempo of the group's "steady" pulse.
    - *One to ten.* Let a metronome sound for a few moments, instructing students to internalize the pulse: "Keep imagining this steady pulse when I turn off the metronome." Describe that you'll say "one" as you stop the sound. "Count silently in your head. When your inner voice says, 'ten,' clap once." The scattered results will prove the point. Another version of this exercise is provided later to support the power of subdivision.
    - *Disengaged conductors.* Ask two volunteers to face away from each other to silently conduct a duple pattern in view of the band. Ensure that they *start* together, but then the band can observe as their motions phase apart, following different internal clocks. For a fun supplement, split the ensemble into two teams; ask students to "Follow your own conductor for sixteen measures; clap on the downbeat of measure seventeen." The misaligned sounds will quickly illustrate the goal of this activity.
- *Call-and-response.* These rhythmic activities inherently require the students to work within a steady pulse. The teacher sings/plays/counts a rhythm, and the ensemble repeats it, in time. Remember that the "call" can also come from students; one student at a time plays an original rhythm, perhaps going down a row, and the ensemble repeats it, always in steady time.
- *Alternating sound with silence.* In *The Creative Director*, Ed Lisk presents an engaging series of exercises using the Circle of 4ths to refine the ensemble's inner pulse through a skill he calls the "discipline of duration." In short, students should sustain a sound for a number ("x") of beats in a steady pulse; then, they silently count through "x" beats of silent rest, to re-enter together, all without a conductor. We'll revisit other sound-and-silence activities later.
- *The "Cosmic Whole Note."* This activity, often used with younger children in the Dalcroze eurhythmics method, is adapted here for bands. Provide a steady pulse at a very slow tempo—perhaps 10bpm or slower. Students listen to these slow sounds, internalize their *subdivision*, and then predict when the next sound will happen. Allow students to hear several sounds: "Two more for practice, and then *clap* exactly when you think the third pulse will happen."
- *Moving into movement.* Walking is a framework for innumerable activities. Gross-motor activities are more easily developed, and are highly connected to rhythmic feel, marching, dance, and more. For now, we will stay focused on internal pulse: while walking in a steady tempo (e.g. MM=60), speak aloud together first to highlight the pulse ("1"), and then to subdivide it into groups (Figure 6.1).

RHYTHM, METER, AND TEMPO

STEP:	Left					Right					Left					Right				
Count:	1					1					1					1				
Subdivide in 2s	1		2			1		2			1		2			1		2		
Subdivide in 3s	1		2		3	1		2		3	1		2		3	1		2		3
Subdivide in 4s	1	2		3	4	1	2		3	4	1	2		3	4	1	2		3	4
Subdivide in 5s	1	2	3	4	5	1	2	3	4	5	1	2	3	4	5	1	2	3	4	5

Figure 6.1 Speak while walking in steady pulse to teach subdivisions.

Choosing *numbers* for the subdivision provides another benefit: students will understand, and feel, how to divide the abstract "beat" into equal portions, while keeping the pulse steady through walking. TIP: this strategy can easily solve problems with tuplets of all kinds. "Here's how we can fit five notes equally into the space of one beat; repeat after me." This is a quick and effective fix in the context of rehearsal sessions. In seated situations, replace stepping with clapping, patting, or foot-tapping.

- *The cosmic metronome.* We can use the metronome at one-half or even one-quarter the original speed. For example, when students are to play at MM=120, set the metronome instead to 60 or even 30bpm. Instruct the students, "*You* supply the internal subdivision, and try to stay precisely aligned with the sound." Students can only align with "cosmic metronome" clicks through extremely careful subdivision.

Section 2: Rhythm in the Ensemble—Exercises, Strategies, and Games

The musician's internal pulse refers only to the steady "single-beat" sound rather than ties, long-duration notes, or the subdivisions inside the pulse. The pulse may be a quarter-note in Common time, half-note in Cut time, dotted-quarter-note in compound meter, or something else. That information is determined by the *meter signature,* of course, found later in this chapter. Because the activities above point to the concept of subdivision, we'll move next into *subdivision activities*, regardless of meter.

Strategies to Enhance Students' Sense of Subdivision

- *Selling the importance of subdivision.* Give brief instructions, sampled here to describe this strategy: "I'll count steadily while you keep your eyes closed. Make no sound, and don't tap feet; all we should hear is the counting. At some point I'll stop, but you should keep counting silently. Clap your hands once, exactly when you think you'd hear my voice say, "TWENTY". Ready? 1...2...3...4...5...6...7...8...9...{silence}" (Figure 6.2).

The claps will be poorly aligned, of course, because students will "hear" *twenty* at different moments. "Now let's try again, but this time you should *subdivide* carefully. This will be just like before, except for your silent subdivision. Follow my example and remember to clap exactly on "twenty". Here we go."

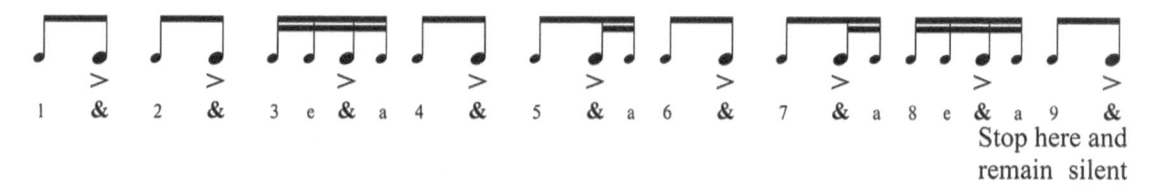

Figure 6.2 A counting game, based on supportive subdivision.

The clapping will almost surely align better when students have been provided a steady, martial framework first. Musicians can internalize subdivisions more accurately when the *offbeats* are highlighted.

- *Locating and aligning with the subdivisions.* Processes like the following examples can help students find, feel, and align with subdivisions. Note: the text may say "count," but these exercises do not promote one counting *system* over another. *Playing, clapping,* or even *patting* will be just as effective:
    - The director counts/claps aloud (using any meter) while students fill in the subdivisions; this example uses common time. The director provides the beat ("1–2–3–4–"), and students accompany with subdivisions (1-and 2-and 3-and 4-and). Tip: start with a steady pulse, but work to enhance students' attention by speeding up and slowing down, thus forcing students to align with your changing tempo.
    - As previously, but in this case students will use *only* the offbeats. The group responds between the teacher's beats by counting, clapping or playing the offbeats, as "__ and! __ and! __ and! __ and!" Again, fluctuate the tempo.
    - Repeat the previous exercise using conducting motions only, without providing audible sounds. Tip: This short activity has great benefits to your traditional rehearsal processes, as it enhances musicians' connection with their conductor.
    - Split the group in half (optionally, choose small groups or even two volunteers). The downbeats and offbeat-subdivisions are traded between the two participating halves. Conduct in fluctuating tempo; the students should maintain precise, even-sounding subdivisions.
- *Employing subdivisions during performance*: some sample training activities include:
    - "I'll conduct, and you should silently subdivide while watching. Your goal is to clap once each measure, *only* on the 'and' of Beat 3." Of course any rhythmic spot can be chosen, with or without notation. Return to this activity later, using advanced rhythmic figures and smaller note-values.

        For improved precision with the rhythmic placement, temporarily fill in sounds on subdivisions before and after the targeted rhythm. Then remove the extra sounds, leaving only silent subdivisions to place the targeted rhythm (Figure 6.3). Tip: This type of activity is effective to combat rushing.

Add some or all of the missing subdivisions:

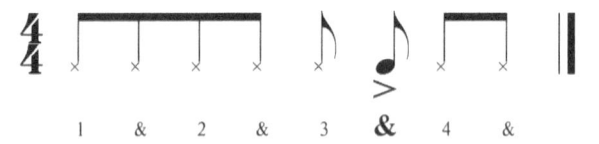

Then, "think" those subdivisions silently to place the written rhythm precisely.

Figure 6.3 Fill in the missing subdivisions.

-
    - Practice adding breath pulses to emphasize subdivisions in long notes; train students during scales at first. Playing a whole-note in common time, students fill the sustained sound with eight connected eighth-note pulses: "Too-hoo hoo-hoo hoo-hoo hoo-hoo."
    - While a selected group plays, remaining students accompany with a percussive vocal sound. Try an unvoiced "chuh-chuh-chuh-chuh" or "tss-tss-tss-tss" or the like. By stepping away, the director has an unobstructed listening opportunity, while the band uses its own rhythmic motor. Tip: This strategy supports both inner pulse and externalized subdivisions while also engaging all players.
    - Use internalized subdivisions to maintain steady time through long rests; this is a "sound-and-silence" exchange. Students will sound aloud for a few measures without a conductor, but then rest silently for one measure. We look for precise alignment when the sound begins again. Use

syllables or counting at first (Figure 6.4), but then play on the instruments. Over time, extend the length of the silences to two, three, or four measures or longer. As with Lisk's exercises, include measures of less-common and irregular meters.

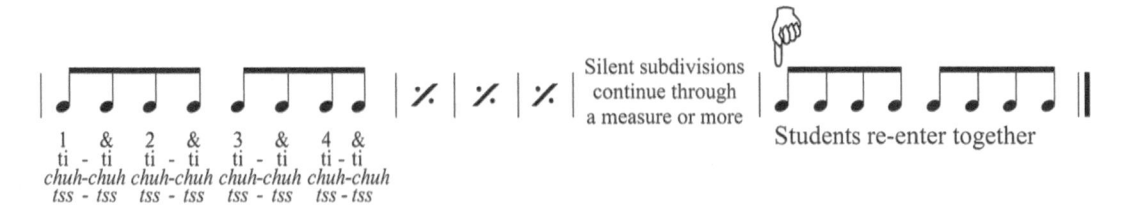

Figure 6.4 Subdivisions with sound and silence.

This is an excellent time to note: the importance of Lisk's "Ruler of Time" cannot be overlooked. Refer to *The Creative Director* series.

- Apply the previous sound-and-silence techniques to repertoire passages: "Without a conductor, play measures 1–6; stay silent for 7–8 and re-enter on measure 9." Tip: For extra engagement, record/playback these attempts. Consider the potential value of internal competition: who will do it better today—woodwinds, brass, or percussion?
- Replace longer notes with the correct number of subdivisions for each. For example, replace a written half-note with four eighth-notes; the written rhythmic values are then constructed from their own subdivisions. As a training exercise, ask one section to play repeated subdivisions in unison on the tonic note of the key while another group plays the printed passage.

Next, apply subdivisions to the passage itself. For example, Figure 6.5 shows a melody ("Full Original"), which players can replace with the next-smaller note values ('Subdivided Fill'). With subdivision, the class has several options: play all subdivisions, or tie subdivisions together to add the breath-impulse technique. Tip: Split the group into a duet—half on the melody, half playing its subdivisions.

Note: the bottom staff below introduces "bopping," a technique wherein students play only the front-end of the note without sustaining its body. This "bopping" is excellent for refining students' internalized rhythm with its focus on the precise start-time for each sound. We'll refer to bopping again.

Figure 6.5 Subdivided Fill and bopping.

This exercise helps, or forces, students to be aware of rhythmic subdivisions. Strong support comes directly from Walter Beeler: "The thing that has to be sold is that when one plays the quarter, he must learn to hear two 8ths or he won't possibly be able to come in on the next beat on time. To demonstrate the flow of 8th notes throughout, half the band should play quarters and half 8ths, and then alternate."[4]

RHYTHM, METER, AND TEMPO

- Add, then remove, audible external subdivision to accompany a passage. For example, during a repertoire passage, assign one snare drummer to add the subdivisions. Call students' attention to the sound of subdivision, which will define the duration of longer notes and rests.

    When the band's rhythms are precisely aligned, then remove the sounded subdivision. "This time, *you* will supply the subdivisions, silently. Just keep imagining the "tap-tap-tap-tap" that we heard from the snare."

- Recall from Chapter 3 that some types of instruments (e.g. handbells, Boomwhackers®) require placement of individual pitches in precise rhythmic locations; otherwise, the fluent, connected musical "whole" doesn't exist. That sort of exercise supports the development of steady pulse through subdivision. In Figure 6.6, the snare drum provides the constant subdivisions, while the rest of the band is divided into groups, collaborating to provide the unbroken musical thought. The sound is reminiscent of the "bopping" technique.

Figure 6.6 Basic bopping exercise for rhythm.

- By adding *sustain* to these exercises, we can check both precision of the rhythms, and *balance*: can we hear new entrances adequately? Many passages of this kind exist in our repertoire; approach them with subdivision, using the "bopping" technique to place the front-ends of notes, finally replacing the full sustain of each pitch (Figure 6.7).

Subdivision activities go a long way toward helping students avoid problems with rushing, dragging, and erratic time.

Figure 6.7 Adding sustain to the bopping technique, with snare subdivisions.

Strategies Using Movement to Support Rhythm and Subdivision: A Kinesthetic Approach

Walter Beeler said, "I've never taught anyone who had natural rhythm, so we have to develop it. Rhythm is a kinesthetic thing. It's a muscular thing, a form of eurythmics applied through the instrument. It has nothing to do with the mental process, and I don't think we should approach it through the mind; rather, through the body. Rhythm cannot be thought. It must be felt."[5] While there are surely mechanical and academic aspects to rhythmic mastery, movement is at the very heart of fluency. Here are additional activities to underscore the benefits of movement:

- Foot-tapping, despite debate about its importance for every student (internalizing rhythm may be a unique process for each musician), is nonetheless a great way to experience subdivisions: the tap down indicates the beat while between beats we have a natural "upbeat" with the foot in its upward position. Some elementary method books use "down-up" pictures of the foot-tapping. Incidentally, foot-tapping gives the teacher some visual evidence, even if only about the student's foot-tapping skills rather than actual rhythm cognition.
- "Clap-and-grip": this is an excellent tactile activity for ties and long-duration notes because musicians are "holding" the rhythm, almost literally! For example, students perform a whole-note by clapping once (beat 1); then keeping hands gripped together, holding through the down-up motions of beats 2-3-4-. In Figure 6.8, examine this technique applied to a typical dotted-note pattern.

RHYTHM, METER, AND TEMPO

$\frac{4}{4}$ 𝅗𝅥. 𝅘𝅥𝅮𝅘𝅥 𝅘𝅥𝅮𝅘𝅥

Figure 6.8 Dotted quarter–eighth note for clapping.

It becomes the following activity: CLAP(down) hold(up) hold(down) CLAP(up) CLAP(down) hold(up) hold(down) CLAP(up) CLAP(down) (Figure 6.9).

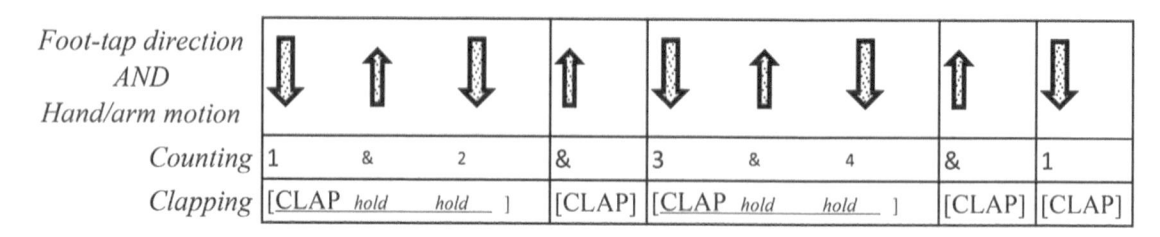

Foot-tap direction AND Hand/arm motion	↓	↑	↓	↑	↓	↑	↓	↑	↓
Counting	1	&	2	&	3	&	4	&	1
Clapping	[CLAP hold hold]			[CLAP]	[CLAP hold hold]			[CLAP]	[CLAP]

Figure 6.9 Dotted quarter–eighth clapping chart.

- Ask section leaders to model *motion* for their section members. For instance, section leaders can provide a supportive *movement* on the upbeat breath before an entrance. Thus, each section has an internal conductor.
- Be percussive with finger, key, and trombone slide *movements*. The snappy movements help to define the rhythmic precision within a steady pulse. TIP: Periodically, ask winds to play *silently*; listen for the rhythmic sounds produced by finger/hand movements alone.
- *Eurhythmics* activities enhance students' overall musical understanding and artistic expressiveness using movement. Some ideas appropriate for a full band class include the following:
    - Add vertical motion to clapping activities: the left hand, palm up, becomes the ictus plane while the right hand, clapping vertically, simulates a conductor's gesture. TIP: A standard "one–two" clapping motion easily becomes the duple conducting pattern.
    - Teach students basic conducting gestures. They'll feel a tactile connection to rhythm and meter but, more importantly, they'll also develop a sense of rhythmic placement. TIP: "The syncopation on beat 3" means much more once students know where/when beat 3 is located.
    - Use subdivisions to transform conducting motions toward a feel for asymmetric/irregular meters: in a steady, subdivided duple meter, simply add extra subdivisions. For example, $\frac{5}{8}$ meter can be felt easily with the same duple motions by feeling, and perhaps verbalizing, 1-and 2-and-*and*. TIP: By performing the patterns, students will learn to follow the conductor's motions more easily.
    - Invent kinesthetic games to strengthen the ensemble-to-conductor connection. For example, "play" a drumset-style groove using the class as your instrument. Split the class and use your two hands to guide each respective side of the band: your left hand controls clapping while the right hand controls foot-stomping on the other side. Students will enjoy it, while honing their skills at reacting to the conductor.

RHYTHM, METER, AND TEMPO

- Try a multitasking approach using feet, hands, and voice. Walk the *pulse* (or tap feet while seated), simultaneously clapping and counting/singing/chanting the written rhythms. TIP: With the feet and voice still in motion, have students perform silent finger/slide/sticking movements.
- Advanced groups gain from advanced activities. For instance, exchange rhythms, performing one measure in the feet followed by a measure of a different rhythm in the hands. Or combine different rhythms simultaneously in the hands and feet. TIP: on cue, the most advanced students can switch rhythms between hands and feet, not unlike the childhood challenge, "Rub your belly while you pat your head; now switch!"
- We can incorporate common gross-motor movement as a component in the plan to refine rhythmic fluency. Here is a sample activity for irregular meter, this time $\frac{5}{8}$ in 3+2 groupings:

    1. Start by lightly running in place, adding accents at the beginning of each group:

       R–L–R **L**–R | **L**–R–L **R**–L | **R**–L–R **L**–R | **L**–R–L **R**–L |

    2. Next, invoke the feeling of roller-skating or cross-country skiing with a series of weighted push/glide movements:

       R*(glide)* L–R | **L***(glide)* R–L | **R***(glide)* L–R | **L***(glide)* R–L |

"Building Blocks" Strategies: The Bricks and Mortar of Rhythm

It's no secret that performers need a vocabulary of rhythms recognized both by notation and by feel. Rhythm sheets, lists and books—like *Basics in Rhythm* by Garwood Whaley (Meredith Music Publications, 2003) —will serve perfectly toward meeting goals in the large-group setting. With written rhythms in view, invent creative ways to support the groupwide pulse in the rehearsal room, such as these examples:

- Play any short rhythmic passage together, nonstop (i.e. "page 1, measures 17–24, consecutively—keep going!")
- Attach an 8-measure rhythm to a scale, playing a new note of the scale on each measure of the rhythm.
- Run "rhythm relays." Pass rhythms from student to student, or section to section, always maintaining a steady pulse.
- Perform a full-group call and response: one after another, student soloists perform rhythms chosen from the printed list, and the full group responds immediately. With a metronome or percussion groove providing a pulse, the process continues with the next soloist.
- With some rhythm sheets—constructed as duets or trios—you can also create ensemble interplay by selecting complementary figures: "Woodwinds play measures 5 to 8 while brasses please play measures 1 to 4; percussionists, help us with a very steady line of 8th-note flams."
- Sound-and-silence games from rhythm lists: "Play measure 1 together. Count one full measure of silence, then re-enter together on the second measure. Continue alternating silence with sound, always with a careful, steady pulse."

Even without rhythm sheets, group activities can highlight the make-up of rhythmic figures, and the correct placements within the beat structure.

- *Use rhythmic chunking.* As with language, we can fragment rhythms to help students experience a root, a prefix, a suffix, a different tense, and the like. For example, break longer rhythmic figures into their component parts (Figure 6.10). Once those parts are performed comfortably, reassemble the full rhythm.

RHYTHM, METER, AND TEMPO

Full Rhythm

Figure 6.10 A rhythmic "chunking" process.

- *Play it incorrectly.* Correctly establish a rhythm by first playing it adjacent to its incorrect version (Figure 6.11). "Let's play the wrong rhythm on purpose. Now we'll compare."

Correct

Close ... but incorrect!

Figure 6.11 Pairing correct with incorrect.

You'll discover many creative ways to employ "correct vs. incorrect" comparisons. This exciting blank slate has unlimited potential.
- *Fill the gaps.* Put notes temporarily in the space of rests, then remove them to reach the original rhythm (Figure 6.12). But be careful—sometimes this strategy can engrain a substitute sound that could be hard to "unlearn."

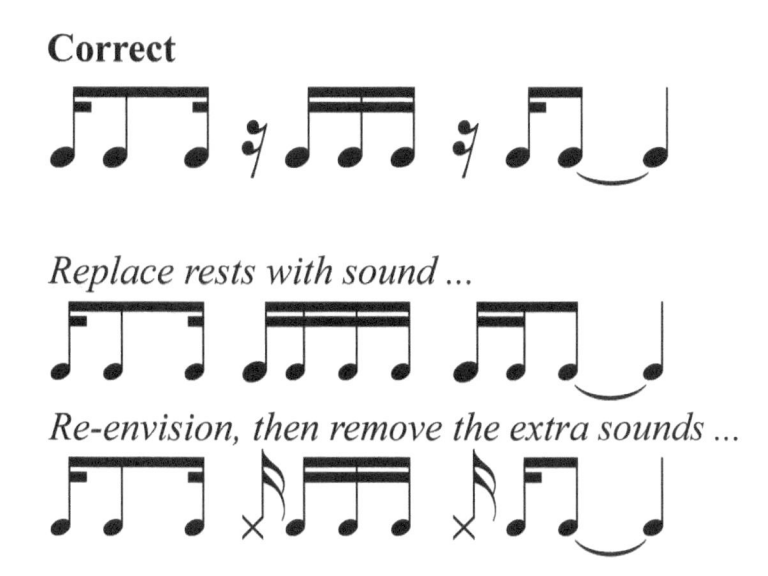

Figure 6.12 Fill the gaps.

- *Remove the ties.* Occasionally a groupwide rhythmic problem is easily solved by removing a tie. Using the example in Figure 6.13, imagine how removing the tie can help establish the exact location for the *"and"* of beat 3.

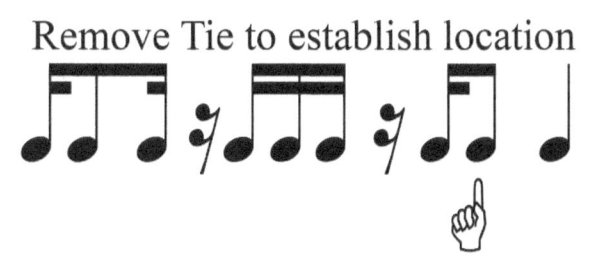

Figure 6.13 Remove the tie.

- *Deconstruct to reconstruct.* This strategy is fully customizable to match the director's most comfortable skills. Teach a complex rhythm quickly by displaying the basic building blocks of the rhythm (Figure 6.14). If the rhythm's smallest figure is the sixteenth-note, display a running line of these "least common denominators." A whiteboard allows instant drawing, erasure, replacement, and other manipulations. With this kind of process, we provide a step-by-step path from the known-to-unknown, or from simple-to-complex.

Figure 6.14 Deconstruct to reconstruct.

- *Vertical rhythmic placement* ("*bopping*"). This can help with more advanced rhythms. A rhythm can manifest with different appearances; it may even *sound* different because of its positioning within a measure. Teach the basic rhythm first, using its most common appearance and its most frequent beat-location (Figure 6.15, first measure). Play the rhythm in unison in its "main" version, and then in its other locations/appearances. With the base rhythms learned, students then follow easy steps:

    1. Play ("bop") only the first sound of the figure to correctly locate its starting position in time; rehearse/repair as needed.

2. With starting-sounds correctly placed, perform and record the full passage; playback for scrutiny by the group.

Figure 6.15 is reduced from *Eternal Father, Strong To Save* (Claude T. Smith) at Rehearsal Letter E. The same scale pattern is used in *eleven* instrumental parts, but with shifting rhythmic locations. Practice each one separately. Consider displaying notation to support your lesson. Note: the performance *inflection* might also change based on where the figure appears.

Figure 6.15 One rhythm in alternate locations.

- *Flashcards* can be extremely effective in bands if used strategically. Their greatest success depends of course on how they are employed. There may be no better current resource than David Newell's innovative book, *Teaching Rhythm: New Strategies and Techniques for Success* (Neil A. Kjos Music, 2008). Newell's five-step sequence includes *Step Three—"See It,"* which offers outstanding ideas, especially under the header, "Putting the FLASH into Flashcards."

The Metronome

A metronome is to the musician as a straight-edge is to the architect. There's no doubt that an experienced architect can produce excellent work by hand, and certainly a creative builder can construct masterpieces from poorly sketched blueprints. But the tools provide the precision. Even when students possess steady pulse skills, there are good reasons to incorporate a metronome in the full ensemble setting. This short collection of suggested strategies will provide a springboard into metronome inclusion. The following are a few strategies for using the Metronome in band rehearsals:

- *Frame the tempo.* Establish a steady audible pulse first, before playing. After a careful count-off, mute the sound immediately when the band starts. When students have completed the passage without a conductor, restore the metronome's sound to illustrate if the final tempo has drifted. Tip: Try restoring the metronome during play.
- *Play silence.* With the metronome sounding just loudly enough to be perceived, cue the band to "play" a passage, but without sound, working to align the subtle sounds of fingerings, key motions, slide-movement, and percussion air-sticking to the metronome. With experience, this strategy can be combined with sound-and-silence passes. As the metronome clicks, the band alternates measures of playing aloud with measures of soundless fingering. Use short excerpts at first, eventually extending the length. If the band maintains a steady pulse, the metronome's sound will be correctly aligned with each silence.

- *Establish incremental goals.* Create a stepwise plan for growth over time. For example, rehearse at MM=80 for a week, 90 for a week, and so on, reaching full performance tempo several weeks before the scheduled performance. For safety in the band's technical preparedness, plan sessions at a tempo faster than required.
- *Engage the subdivisions.* To provide additional anchors for the performers' rhythmic precision, divide the "beat" into halves, quarters, and, for compound meter, thirds. If your metronome is not equipped with subdivisions, use math to calculate the correct multiples/factors. For example, a metronome set to 180 is clicking the eighth-notes in a compound-meter excerpt marked MM=60.
- *Slow the metronome.* Set the metronome to one-half or one-third of the printed tempo. This is another version of the "Cosmic Metronome." For instance, use a marking of 40 to provide a sound on beat 1 of each measure when the quarter-note is marked at 120 in triple meter ($\frac{3}{4}$). The group has the obligation to pace the timing of the entire measure, or risk a misaligned arrival at the next downbeat.
- *Metro-reversal*: Hear the click of the metronome as the *offbeat*. It may take guidance to help students with this adaptation because they're strongly drawn to hearing the beat. Until you find something more comfortable, speak the word "and" on the click of the metronome; gradually insert beat-numbers between the sounds: "*and—and—and—and* 1 *and* 2 *and* 3 *and* 4 *and* 1 . . ." It may help to snap the fingers when saying "and." TIP: This strategy is particularly effective to solve rushing issues and to strengthen sounds played indistinctly on weak beats.
- *Use the tap function.* During either live performance or recorded playback, view the bpm display on the metronome while depressing the "Tap" button, aligned with each beat as performed by the band. For example, the tap might yield a changing display of 120–116–122–126–125–130–134 and so on, which can be especially helpful to demonstrate rushing during a loud strain of a march.
- *Follow the single leader.* Give the metronome to a selected individual, who uses visual or auditory means (including headphones) to stay precisely aligned with the metronome. The other students carefully watch and listen to their "internal conductor," aligning with the leader's sound. To introduce the concept, consider using one section (e.g. clarinets) following its section leader, or "all principal players" across the band following one leader. This strategy will be helpful toward refining the group's listening awareness. TIP: consider a student from whichever section has the excerpt's most important moving line.
- *Combine the metronome with recording/playback*: This is a quick and irrefutable (but sometimes humbling) process to prove to students that their pulse is imperfect. Start with the tempo carefully established by a metronome. Set up two microphones in a stereo L–R configuration. Have the band perform a steady excerpt, like a strain from a march; one mic records the full band while the other is trained on the metronome, set to a soft volume. On playback, balance the output from each channel. Students will clearly hear if their pulse is erratic. TIP: Compare two attempts of this process, one at piano, another at forte as the dynamic; students will be forced to confront a common issue ("forte means louder, but it does *not* mean faster").
- *Replace the metronome.* Employing a "human metronome" has some distinct advantages. The human version has many forms, including a single drummer; the percussion section playing a pulse or even a full "groove"; portions of the band in rotating roles (stomping/clapping/tapping/vocalizing); or other creative options. A human metronome engages more students, and offers flexibility with volume changes, easier starting-stopping, timbre changes, creating metric groupings, and more. But there are other pulse options beyond the human metronome: try software loops, prerecorded grooves, a drum machine, beat-producing apps, or YouTube videos.
- *Beware the metronome.* Be flexible with tempo. By using a range of acceptable tempo markings during rehearsals, you encourage neurological development (fingerings, stickings, articulations) within a wider range of speeds. Bonus: you can experiment with the group's zones of success and limitation. Under some unintended circumstances, a conductor might begin faster or slower than desired; by having practiced other speeds in advance, there's a bit more assurance that the performance won't crash.

Control of Tempo

Using a metronome does not guarantee controlled group adjustment of tempo within a performance (e.g. *rubato, accelerando, ritard*, and the like). Students occasionally need to regulate the pulse together but the foundation for those skills still relies on control of a steady group pulse at any chosen tempo. The following are some additional strategies targeting the group's control of Tempo:

- *Time the total voyage.* When playing a march at 120bpm, total performance duration is easily determined because it requires one second to play two beats. For example, play a 32-measure strain in Cut-time without a conductor; those sixty-four beats should take exactly thirty-two seconds. Clock the excerpt several times during one rehearsal, or on separate days; for a fun psychological experiment, compare timings from Monday and Friday.
- *Record–playback comparisons.* In compositions marked only with text indications (Allegro, Moderato, etc.), students can sample several options while selecting the final "performance" tempo. Record and playback each tempo. We'll find that students have opinions about playing at each tempo, and preferences about the best tempo to perform for the audience.
- *Play with a recording—play with the tempo.* Software accommodates this strategy, but a quick and easy method can be found on YouTube. Choose an exemplary recording and have the band play along with it, even "silently."

    1. Occasionally mute the recording while the band continues. Students must maintain a steady tempo so they'll remain synchronized in time when the sound is restored.
    2. Use YouTube's settings feature to alter playback speeds, using the 0.75 and 1.25 options.

- *Exaggerate.* Nudge the group's tempo in the desired direction—faster or slower—with speech, conducting, body movements, or demonstrations at an exaggerated speed.
- *Choose a "Quick Fix" method to save time.* Sometimes the solution is as simple as a well-designed directive or analogy. Examples are found in Section 3. For simplicity, choose a student-centered question like, "Was that too slow, too fast, or just right?" Return to the passage immediately, capitalizing on students' attentiveness.

Additional Considerations About Tempo

Many of the strategies already presented in this chapter will impact the management of *tempo*, but bands will surely still experience rushing, dragging, and unevenness. Those kinds of tempo issues are often aggravated by one or more influencers. That is, while students may exhibit tempo-control problems without provocation, a lack of steadiness can also be the result of certain characteristics in the compositions they perform. Simply knowing about those influencers will be helpful in your design of effective pedagogical plans.

For example, each piece has its unique *level of difficulty* and *technical demand*. Depending on your students, "easy" music may rush from their overconfidence; or drag from excessive relaxation. Similarly, "hard" music has its own issues; technique problems, of course, top the list of contributors. Tempo control is therefore unpredictable. The best advice is perhaps only to stay alert, and keep building your personal collection of rehearsal activities.

Here is a short list—surely incomplete—of some of the factors that may influence the band's tempo:

- *Rests*—a notorious problem. Each teacher develops instructional preferences, guiding students with favorite strategies (play, count, feel, "replace" the rests with notes, or some other instruction). Be sure the instructional plan specifically addresses rests.
- *Offbeats.*
- *Repetitive figures*—students may lose concentration as they engage "cruise control."
- *Excitement inherent in a live performance.*
- *Complexity of the setting* (in terms of polyphony, fragmentation and more).

- *Fatigue.*
- *Group-wide psychological factors* (e.g. anxiety, grief, worry, stress, pre-weekend enthusiasm).
- *Markings and notation*—we find rushing more frequently in slurred, rather than tongued, passages. There's a visual aspect in the spacing (short, "squeezed" measures compared to those with an expansive appearance); additionally, students often treat *time* differently when playing whole- and half-notes, compared to their response during sixteenth- and thirty-second-notes in the notation.
- *The conductor*—it must be said: when problems exist, we should look to ourselves as a potential cause.

Precision

Even when students have developed inner pulse, we still find that imprecision is a frequent rhythmic problem in bands. Of course, precision issues are often case-specific, but here is a short collection of helpful pedagogical ideas:

- *Provide a rhythmic framework.* As with previous subdivision activities, use a snare drum to play a backdrop. Then, the winds join the drum's careful rhythmic framework. This process is especially helpful to "glue" overlapping passages together, and to help students arrive precisely in time when the entrance is between beats. TIP: Apply the rhythmic framework to chunking and bopping activities.
- *Subtract problematic technique.* At times, an articulation, finger pattern or other technique-related issue may mask itself as an apparent rhythm problem. Separate the skills to check the rhythm alone; play the isolated rhythm as a repeating loop on a unison pitch or chord, without changing pitches. While most students continue looping just the rhythm, ask the more advanced players to restore the written pitches. A few at a time, students restore the technical content to the original passage as written.
- *Build the texture using layers.* Establish a steady pulse with a metronome. Play a single rhythmic layer at first; choose the line with the longest note durations to create the "base" layer. Add each new layer individually, moving from longer note-values to shorter. Use a metronome—mechanical or human—as desired.
- *Seek and align to aural landmarks.* With your support, students can locate other rhythmic lines to use as auditory footholds during complex rhythmic passages. As above, play rhythmic layers separately; in this strategy, however, guide students to discover similar, contrasting, and complementary rhythms. Repeat the process until students can identify and align to their rhythmic "cohorts" within the full ensemble.
- *Target misunderstood figures.* You might choose rhythms from repertoire, or create an overarching rhythmic vocabulary curriculum. For each problematic figure, devise an efficient set of solutions. For example, students who normally recognize syncopations with ease might still misunderstand the figure when it occupies a less familiar rhythmic location (Figure 6.16).

Figure 6.16 Syncopated figure in altered locations.

Similarly, extended syncopations, and tied figures, are often misunderstood and therefore lead to precision issues. Remove ties, rebuild the rhythm by combining smaller values, or choose another of your favorite strategies (Figure 6.17).

Figure 6.17 Extended syncopations: two notated versions.

- *Be watchful for approximations.* Students may play a rhythm incorrectly—something "close"—based on what they think, rather than what they read. If left unchecked, the incorrect rhythm becomes ingrained and, worse, may turn up repeatedly whenever the rhythm is encountered in other compositions. It will be the director's onus to listen carefully, making repairs immediately. Figure 6.18 is just one of many prevalent errors—the students read a triplet but instead play a close approximation.

Figure 6.18 Written rhythm and sounded approximation.

- *Build precision by unifying students' approach.* Consider featuring a correct performance by a student or section. Then, use call-and-response alternations, commenting and intervening as needed. Finish by replacing the rhythm into its context; continue feedback to help retain accuracy and precision.
- *Work at the timing of the front ends.* This helpful "vertical-placement" technique (bopping) isolates the starting sound of each note, without sustain. The resulting grid of staccato sounds will reveal any imprecisions in the alignment of attacks.
- *Demonstrate the rhythm or shape it with language.* Sometimes teaching by rote is the quickest, most efficient route to success. Walter Beeler said, "saying 'day today today' produces a natural dotted 8th and 16th feeling. The size of the 16th depends on the tune. In Spanish music, often you hear very reputable recordings with it as a 32nd. Who can say how long it is? But I've never seen a piece where the 16th really belonged to the note barred to it."[6] For the creative director, a couple of well-chosen words or sounds may clarify a rhythmic concept faster than any amount of standard pedagogy. TIP: Choose known words to address rhythmic problems of all kinds, including in irregular meters.

    5/8 as 3+2   = **ITH**-a-ca **COL**-lege |
    5/8 as 2+3   = U-ni **VER**-si-ty |
    7/8 as 2+2+3 = **MANS**-field U-ni **VER**-si-ty |

- *In extreme cases, a substitute rhythm solves a problem.* Readers may need to suspend judgment for the following strategy. Applied selectively, this technique can solve specific precision problems, often more efficiently than traditional methods. This illustration comes from the Overture to *The Barber of Seville*, where the entire band begins with a sixteen-note anacrusis in Andante Maestoso, slowly "in 8." Even with concentrated subdivision, some students still may not align their first two sounds precisely. Consider moving the opening rhythm to the downbeat to help ensure a unified start; then, re-establish the ensemble's time-keeping on the next beat (Figure 6.19).

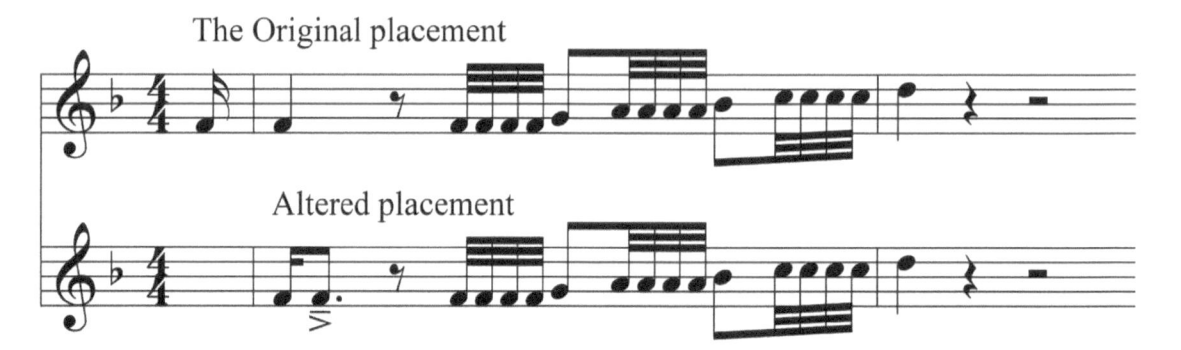

Figure 6.19 Move the rhythm to correct its precision.

The Need to Read: Symbols, Systems and Syntax of Rhythmic Notation

It's worth noting here that authors Feldman and Contzius name *sound-to-symbol* as an important impetus for the pedagogical portions of their outstanding text, *Instrumental Music Education*. Additionally, support for using the *ear* in fluent learning permeates history:

1. There is almost universal agreement about the importance of sound-before-symbol among major educational psychologists and foremost music education specialists.
2. "Music reaches heart and brain through the ear, yet we have usually tried to teach it through the eye. It was always 'look' and never 'listen.'"[7]
3. In his *Manual of Instruction of the Boston Academy of Music* (1834), Lowell Mason places the "sound before symbol" principle *first* in his list of eight foundational tenets toward the most effective music education.
4. "What I am driving at is that we have to teach all rhythms first by ear and by rote. First, we'll sing or play it to him and make him imitate it, rote style, and say 'whenever you see this notation on paper it should remind you to play that thing that we learned by ear a few days ago.' How can we ever hope to teach anything but mathematics if we approach music by the mathematical route? We try to make it too scientific and too mechanical and thereby lose the beat. Rhythm is kinesthetic, it's a feel; and anyone will accept this in a minute in a dance band."[8]
5. Evan Feldman is clear in *Instrumental Music Education*: "But as with language, students must learn rhythm by the way it feels and sounds, not by the way it looks."[9]

We certainly can use words and speech patterns as the basis for learning rhythms, and we can apply *inflections* from spoken language to help mold our students' interpretation practices. However, the elephant in the room can be avoided no longer: *we need to read*.

Musicians must perform from notation, by definition, in order to "sight-read" anything. And after listening, sight-reading is the very first step in performing a band composition. Any shortcomings in rhythmic reading will erect a barrier: students' enjoyment is delayed by the frustration of struggle. Directors are therefore obligated to teach notation-reading as a key component in the band's rhythmic plan.

This book is not presented as a primary source for teaching band students how to read notation. However, the following suggestions can supplement any chosen rhythm-reading methodology without causing a loss of allotted rehearsal time:

- *A notion about counting.* Seasoned performers will find truth in this notion: *we* rarely, if ever, use a system to count rhythms. Mature musicians recognize a rhythm and perform its sound correctly. But we still "account for" time in some way. Our rhythmic success relies on keen real-time awareness; we consider meter, the internal pulse, length of rests, precise alignment (by listening to others), and especially subdivision. Nonetheless, because every excellent musician requires those awareness skills, the teacher must occasionally intervene. Students learn from experience or observation, so the effective teacher's role might best be described as, "Do as I *model*."

RHYTHM, METER, AND TEMPO

- *Counting systems debriefed*. Examine the rhythmic notation in Figure 6.20. These are equivalent-sounding measures, chosen only to illustrate various counting systems:

Figure 6.20 Notation for counting systems debriefed.

This *sound* could be counted using any one of the most common Rhythmic Syllable systems, including these:

Ta ka Di mi	Ta–Di–	Takadimi
Du ta De ta	Du–De–	Edwin Gordon
Ti ri Ti ri	Ti–Ti–	Kodály
Ta fa Te fa	Ta–Te–	French "Time-Names", Lowell Mason adaptation

Or, the measures could be counted with instinctual patterns of natural spoken language:

Mis-sis-sip-pi   Del–ta–   *Orff-inspired*

Or, with a straightforward numbers system, including:

| 1 ti te ta | 2–te– | The *Eastman* system |
| 1 e and a | 2–and– | Traditional American number system |

These are just a few of the better-known counting systems; for the purpose of this book, the list can be left incomplete. Also, there is no mention here of counting compound meters with triple sub-divisions (Tri-po-let; 1-la-li; 1-trip-let; Ta-ki-da; etc.); again, the depth of options goes beyond the scope of this book. Instead, our focus is strategic. There are many ways to count and teach rhythm. Each can be effective, assuming the director answers these two important guiding questions:

- What works *for you*? Outstanding demonstrations rely on the teacher's fluency.
- What works *for the students*? Specifically, what has been used by previous teachers? Students may experience difficulties when transferred unnecessarily from one method to another.

It's not the purpose of this book to advocate one counting system over others. Find what works best, and utilize it when it helps.

- *Counting system considerations*
  - Every facet of the chosen counting method(s) should support your educational goals.
    - Ideally, there should be agreement among all teachers; moving from one teacher to the next, students benefit from a seamless transfer of pedagogy
    - Counting may be a crutch, but should never be a hindrance; if too complex, the system stands in the way of effectiveness
    - Whether verbal or written, the counting should provide *one* syllable per note. Consider vocal music, for example, with the syllables of its text pinned to the rhythmic notation. "Counting" is like lyrics as shown in Figure 6.21.

Figure 6.21 Syllables and "lyrics" in rhythmic counting.

A = A "typical" way students might count this rhythm
B = One syllable for each note; the words align with the sounds
C = How the counting might be penciled into the part

David Newell astutely refers to the "lyrics" of rhythmic counting in *Teaching Rhythm*. Newell writes, "A whole note does not sound ————. Therefore, it should not be counted "1, 2, 3, 4"—four separate vocal sounds."[10]

- Example C above also introduces the "parenthetical method," another common idea about writing rhythmic counts into the music. Penciled numbers are added to account for passing time during sustained notes, but only in parentheses with smaller fonts.
- All verbal counting should convey the artistic interpretation of the music; we should count expressively, including all markings from the printed music. Without the teacher's guidance, no counting system—either verbalized or written onto the music—will account for dynamics, articulations or other written interpretive markings.

○ *There should be accounting for rests*. Rhythmic errors are very often precipitated by rests-to-be-counted, rather than figures-to-be-played. Some rest-counting ideas could include these:

- Whisper "*shhh*" for rests—this is problematic because its usage has no specific duration-basis, and because it's noisy; rests are silent.
- Simply stay silent during rests—this plan lacks the specificity of time-keeping.
- Edwin Gordon (the *Music Learning Theory* idea of "audiation") asks us to think about the sound of counting, but without vocalizing it.
- A closely related idea is simply to *turn off the sound*—the students continue to count notes and rests with the same process, but the rests are silent; this process allows for "lip-syncing" the appearance of the counting, or even a fun assignment for students to "shout, but don't let me hear you."
- Any movements chosen for time-keeping (e.g. foot-tapping, air-clapping) will also function for rests.

A bonus to ponder: number-based counting systems allow students to place a rhythm *in time* (where "3-e-and-a" works to locate the rhythm directly on beat 3) which, in turn, may help players align their written rhythms with the conductor's motions.

Strategies, Tips, and Activities about Meter Signatures

In most types of music, poetry, and dance, the grouping of stronger and weaker beats into sets is an expected component of the art. Meter, however, is not the real problem to be addressed; we hear it, feel it, and most can perform metric groupings fluently. The challenge instead is that musicians must read notation within meter signatures and, specifically, that the written notes and rests will change value, depending on meter. The conundrum of the meter signature is that it removes standardizations; the "quarter-note," as an example, can then indicate a variety of different sounds:

> It is easy for us to see how ludicrous it would be if the art world changed the names of the basic colors as they switched from oil paints to watercolors. The exact same color would be called red in an oil painting and blue in a watercolor. Obviously, red has to stay red, no matter the media. In music, quarter notes have to stay quarter notes, no matter the meter.[11]

But what about the *beat*? Clearly, students will need our help.

- *A sales tactic*, sampled here, can help students understand the meter signature conundrum:
  ○ Write the word *tough* on the board: "What does that say?"
  ○ Follow by listing other words using the o-u-g-h letter combination, like *though, through, cough, bough*, asking, "How is this pronounced?" for each word.

- A script to paraphrase: "English is a complex language. Our letters sound different, depending on how they're used, and it can be very confusing. In music, the meter signature can cause that same confusion for us: notes and rests will have different sounds, depending on the meter signature in which they're written."
- *Provide visual evidence* of the problem by comparing "rhythmic homonyms": display the same *sound* in different meter signatures, like those in Figure 6.22.

Figure 6.22 Rhythmic "homonyms."

- *A follow-up activity*—provide a short, written rhythm (grab students' attention with a rhythm from the band's repertoire). Ask students to *rewrite this rhythm so it will sound exactly the same, but in a different meter signature*. As a written task, this can easily serve as an *exit ticket* to check students' understanding without a loss of class time.
- *A curricular add-on*—if it doesn't currently exist, consider adding a composition component to the band program. Rhythmic dictation activities provide an excellent foundation toward greater depth with composition (see "The power of rhythmic dictation" on page 120 for more details).

Students are more open to challenges when their curiosity is piqued by an engaging teacher.

About the Top and Bottom Numbers:
Common Views of Meter Signatures

As with their rhythmic counting systems, students will likely arrive at your room with a predisposition toward meter signatures, molded by their instruction from previous teachers. So, any of these common opinions can be effective, based on students' prior instruction:

- *Standard top/bottom method*. The top is the *number of beats* in each measure; the bottom is *what kind of note* gets that beat. Example: $\frac{3}{4}$ means there are three beats in each measure (top), and "the beat" is the quarter note (bottom).
- *Top/Bottom method restated*: The top number is how many times to tap the foot in each measure; the bottom number is what type of note the foot is tapping. Example: $\frac{3}{4}$ means we tap three times in each measure (top), and the note we're tapping is the quarter-note (bottom).

Note: these "standard" descriptions of the meter signature work very well for numeric time signatures, in *simple time*. That is, these methods adequately describe meter when there is a top and bottom number, and when it is *not* a compound or irregular/asymmetric meter. Standard methods fall short—or can even cause confusion—with meter signatures of Common time, Cut-time, $\frac{6}{8}$, and many others. In most cases it is *not true* in $\frac{6}{8}$ that "there are six beats in a measure and the eighth-note gets the beat." The next methods are better suited to address a wider collection of meters:

- *A ruler method*. This clever method transfers the meter signature to a visual ruler, from which students can see both the total length and the subdivisions of a measure. An excellent scripted lesson example can be found in Evan Feldman's *Instrumental Music Education* (Routledge 2016, pp. 40–42).
- *A fractions method*. Since students have used fractions from an early age, this method can always describe numeric meters, even in compound and irregular time, with this two-step process:
    1. Train students to read (speak) the meter signature as a fraction, without "reducing" it. They should refer to quarters when the fraction has the number 4 on the bottom. Thus, $\frac{3}{4}$ is three-quarters (not three-fourths). Then,
    2. Ask a question, phrased exactly this way: "How many beats can be in each measure?" The answer to that question will always describe one measure of music: $\frac{2}{2}$ is two-halves, $\frac{6}{8}$ is six-eighths, and "In $\frac{4}{1}$ there can be four whole notes in a measure". Note: students should not reduce the fraction, for example, by changing $\frac{2}{2}$ to "1", and $\frac{4}{1}$ to "4".
- *An algebraic method* (David Newell's *Whole Note System*). This is arguably a foolproof innovation that, at first, seems quite similar to standard top/bottom methods. It begins with "the top number is the number of beats in each measure." But importantly, "the bottom number tells how many beats are in *the whole note*." In this way, in $\frac{5}{4}$ there are five beats in a measure and the whole note gets four beats; and, in $\frac{3}{2}$ there are three beats in a measure and the whole note gets two beats. The method works for compound and irregular meters because it relies solely on the students' understanding of the standard rhythm tree where a whole-note = two half-notes, and a half-note = two quarter-notes, and so on. In his outstanding book, *Teaching Rhythm*, Newell includes a very thorough collection of activities to support, and to practice this system. The author strongly endorses Newell's *Whole Note System*. Further, the method easily supplements others without confusion if directors follow Newell's instructions.

About Compound Meters and Cut-time

Students may wonder, and some will even put their frustrated curiosity into a question: "Why do we have Cut-time?" Or, "If the composer can use the triplet bracket, why do we need compound meters?" Such questions aren't unreasonable. Again, Newell's *Teaching Rhythm* provides excellent instructional support for these topics. Additional ideas include these:

- *Another method to stimulate students' interest*. "Have you noticed that the original *Bill of Rights* document refers to the *"Congrefs of the United States"*? It looks like a misspelling, but the writing is simply "the way it was done" at the time. It is locked in history, and we won't rewrite the original. Similarly, there are several centuries of printed music using essentially the same meter signature rules; now we're obligated to learn how to read it with the original rules."
- *More history applied to meters*. Students frequently enjoy knowing the "why" answers; a short detour into history may be appropriate for some students. Briefly, everything "perfect" was once related to the Holy Trinity, represented by an unending circle. Thus the original meter signature for *tempus perfectum* (the triple grouping) was shown as a circle. And a duple meter, or *tempus imperfectum*, was then an incomplete circle; we now recognize this incomplete circle, "C", as the symbol for Common time. A vertical line through that C became "Cut" Common time, now *alla breve*. A simple web search yields much more detail.
- *Pictorial assistance with meter signatures*. Most students have seen the standard rhythm tree, where each note value subdivides into *halves*. Adding dots, the dotted whole still divides in *half*, to

RHYTHM, METER, AND TEMPO

create dotted half-notes; in turn, the dotted half-note divides in *half* to create dotted quarter-notes. At that point, however (and for only one level), the math changes and the division is into thirds. By showing students the "compound" rhythm tree, Figure 6.23, they'll easily see the subdivision into thirds, beginning at the eighth-notes. In addition:

- This graphic supports tapping/patting/clapping games to fill the dotted quarter-note pulse with its subdivisions of thirds. And,
- It's easy to provide added visual support: rewrite each dotted quarter-note into its tied form (a quarter-note tied to an eighth-note). That version provides more verification that the dotted quarter has a value of exactly *three* eighth-notes.

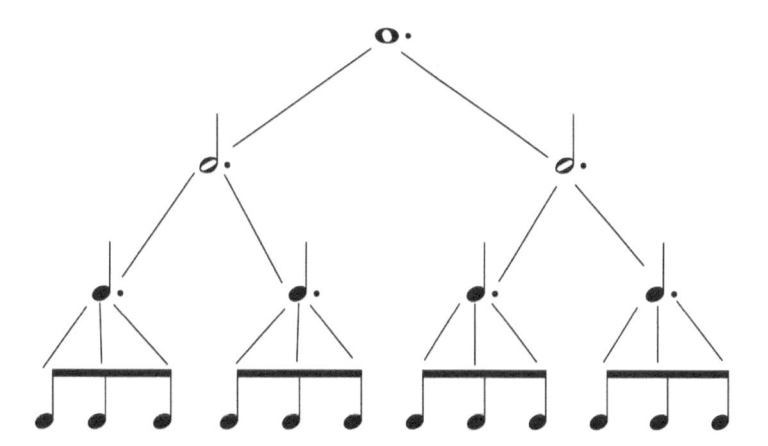

Figure 6.23 The "compound" rhythm tree.

- *Pictorial versions of meter signatures.* The traditional theory for meter signatures often causes difficulties with compound time. "The bottom number tells what kind of note gets the beat"—except when something else gets the beat! To eliminate confusion, we can replace the bottom number with a picture of a note. Be creative in leading students toward a related concept, which is "tap your foot to this note," referring to the picture. In a compound meter, students will see clearly that the "beat" is a dotted quarter-note (Figure 6.24).

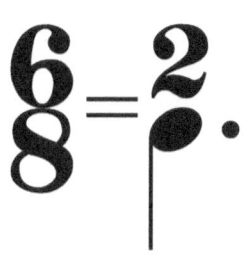

Figure 6.24 Pictorial meter signature.

- *"Sound-before-symbol" applied to compound meter.* Although this is another construct more appropriate for smaller lesson groups and younger learners, it may show up in the band class. Find a common song (e.g. folk song, children's song, nursery rhyme) that shares some of the specific compound-meter rhythms found in the band piece; sing or demonstrate the *known* first, and then show the notation.

- *The "rhythmic homonyms" approach applied to compound meter.* We already know that a *sound* can be represented in different ways, depending on its meter signature. As such, we show that a compound meter sound is easily rewritten in simple meter with triplets as shown in Figure 6.25. Exercises like this are found in many of the best-known beginning method books, and in rhythm books/lists. Find (or create) and use rhythm comparisons meeting your band's needs.

Figure 6.25 Rhythmic homonyms: simple to compound

- *Using charts to feel, count, and understand subdivisions.* The Longy Rhythm Chart (Renée Longy, The Julliard School of Music) and its Takadimi counterpart both serve as very detailed counting methods, with great attention to subdivisions and groupings. Readers can find an excellent description of these processes, and prints of the charts, in Feldman and Contzius's *Instrumental Music Education* (Routledge, 2016, pp. 42–46).
- *The power of rhythmic dictation.* Dictation promotes students' learning of rhythms and meter, and it provides teachers with objective *evidence*. Furthermore, it can be a springboard into other composition-based activities.
    - First, establish the meter signature, pulse, length of the rhythm (number of measures), and any other parameters required to complete the task.
    - Then, play or sing the rhythm while students transcribe the notation on paper. Clapping doesn't convey *duration*, so it's not as effective.
    - Consider including a "bonus-question" like, "From the music in our folders, name the composition and the measure number where this rhythm can be found."
    - For schools where the "Exit Ticket" is used, consider short rhythmic dictation exercises. TIP: Offer two collection bins—one for "I'm confident" and another for "I'm unsure." A glance at how many responses are in each bin can offer some valid information guiding follow-up plans.
    - And a dividend: rhythmic dictation is always helpful but, especially during the "observation day," it's an impressive way for non-music administrators to experience the academic content of your performance class. Note: dictation is helpful to all music learners, but it is *imperative* to the advanced musicians, especially those who are potentially headed toward college for music.

Fluency

When our students have amassed the desired skills (rhythmic precision, a strong sense of pulse, and control of tempo), we'll still need to seek an elusive goal that Beeler called "a relaxed ensemble rhythm. Even though you have drilled and spent a lot of time in your rehearsals on rhythm, the minute the band is under any kind of stress, they will revert to their old system of playing, which is a typewriter-like way of playing notes without a beat."[12]

The following are suggested activities to help refine students' rhythmic fluency:

- *Isolate the moving lines.* Give an instruction like, "Play only when you have moving lines; when you have half- or whole-notes, drop out and silently subdivide until your next entrance."
- *Eliminate excess difficulties for lower-achieving players.* As we know, sometimes an apparent rhythmic problem is more likely a composite issue involving other skills. Try altering the level of

challenge by removing articulation markings and complex tonguing patterns, but only for *some* students. When those players can concentrate fully on the rhythm and its fingering technique (without other distractions), the full ensemble sounds more mature. Caveat: altered parts must be played more softly than those with full correct markings.

- *Unaccent the strong beats.* Our good work and best intentions may elicit unwanted rhythmic concepts. That is, the movements, clapping, metronome, conductor's motions, and even the appearance of rhythmic notation are all "beat-oriented." Thus, musicians often over-emphasize the first note in each group, resulting in neglect for the other notes. Try instructions as simple as, "Let's accent all notes *except* the first one on each beat." Devise creative analogies for de-emphasis tasks.
- *Highlight note-grouping and rhythmic direction concepts.* In terms of rhythmic maturity and evenness, consider adding a subtle *crescendo* to the notes in secondary positions, as shown below, or simply follow Beeler's advice: "Once you've said 'huckleberry' (for four 16th notes) that is the end of the word and you are thinking 'stop.' If you say something silly like 'and so I do' you have to keep going to the next beat. A series of figures in rhythm must not end. This is motion. The minute we stop the motion, we stop the rhythm. Everything beyond the first note should be directed to the next note—the effect of 'and so I do and so I do and so I do.'"[13] These well-known ideas are commonplace in our instructional literature; Chapters 8 and 9 offer more detail.

Each of the previous suggestions should yield the same result: we want to reduce the immature pounding on each beat, striving instead for artistic *direction* within the moving rhythmic lines as shown in Figure 6.26.

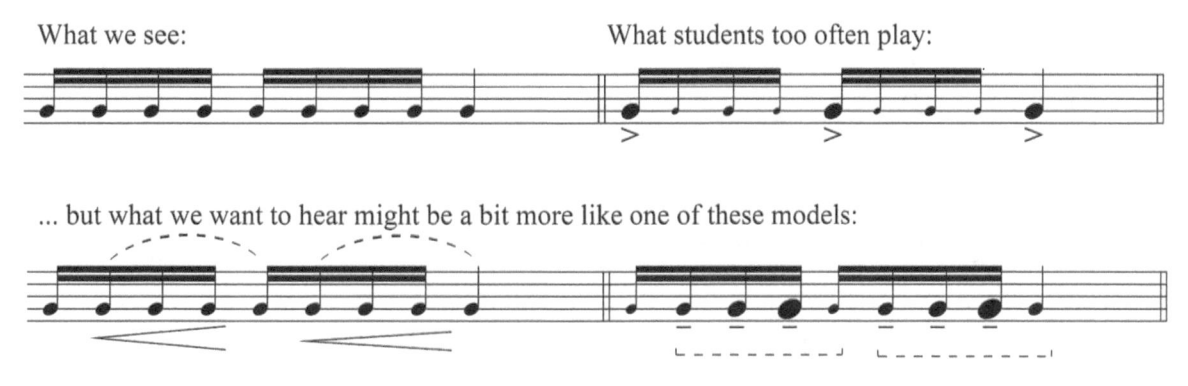

Figure 6.26 Note direction notation pictures.

- *Spend more time without a conductor.* Rhythmic fluency can mature when students' performance includes less *watching* and more *listening and feeling*. Both of these fluency factors are enhanced by playing without the conductor. We want students to listen actively during band rehearsals. Some startup activities can include the following:
    - Record an excerpt with and without the conductor; playback for comparison.
    - Hand-off rhythmic passages for recording/playback (i.e. "seniors play measures 1 to 4, Juniors play 5 to 8," etc.), expecting the segmented excerpt to connect seamlessly.
    - Loop a passage, exchanging sets of players. In this version, each group plays *the same excerpt*. The goal must still be fluency, of course, but we also work to mold a unified approach to the passage.
    - Customize a fluency challenge. For example, "We'll play measures 133–148. Your job is to speed up for eight measures, then slow down for eight measures, ending on a fermata." The conductor starts the students together, but then remains motionless.
- *Hop on–hop off.* Some members of the band play a passage continuously, while others enter and exit from the music during the continuous rhythmic movement. For example, the principal players

perform normally, while the remaining students enter only for segments of several measures each. Consider an analogy of running alongside a moving platform; we must get on the platform and back off smoothly. For a fluent sound, all musicians must maintain their internal subdivisions very carefully.
- *Managing simultaneous rhythms.* This little-known fact is largely overlooked by both players and teachers alike. In almost every passage, several contrasting layers of rhythm require players to engage different sets of motor-skills to perform them. Examine the trumpet excerpt in Figure 6.27. In this standard-looking melody . . .

    . . . the top staff shows the excerpt as the player views it
    . . . the rhythm used for *reading* is probably what the player perceives, but
    . . . the articulation patterns create an entirely different rhythm for *tonguing*, and
    . . . the *fingering* patterns result in yet a third layer of rhythm.

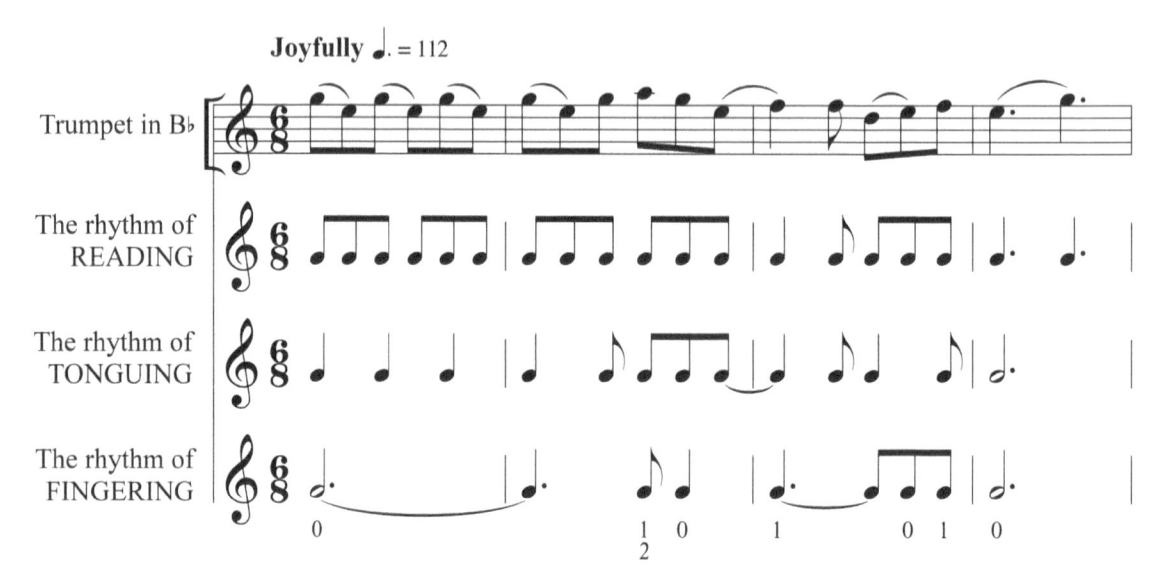

Figure 6.27 "Layers" within a rhythm.

Although this is more of a construct for instrument class lessons, teachers are advised to be aware of the phenomenon. It's visually obvious in orchestras, when individuals play with different bow directions. But, unseen among winds, difficulties of this kind may be a principal factor when the band sound lacks mature fluency.
- *The soundtrack.* Noted teacher/composer Richard Saucedo shares that his primary goal when addressing rhythm is to consider it a soundtrack that never stops. Saucedo advises directors to discuss how a film soundtrack is recorded in a studio: "Everybody has to understand that from the beginning of the piece to the end, that click track is always going. They have to feel it inside of them. There are fluctuations with rubato, but the ensemble's track has to be together."[14]

Section 3: A Buffet of Quick-Fix Strategies

How would you answer the question, "What's the difference between beat, rhythm and meter?" Consider the potential confusion steeped in those terms, and interrelated words like *time, tempo, groove,* and others. When students don't grasp subtle differences, an explanation alone can become a time-consuming quagmire. The best solution is therefore sometimes to preconceive an answer, even if it's scripted and rehearsed. The goal is to keep students engaged in effective, inspired learning. This collection of "quick-fix" strategies provides a springboard toward additional creative time-saving adaptations.

Analogies, Short-cuts, and Other Quick-Fix Suggestions for Rhythm

- *Use the band's best snare player* to demonstrate the sound of a problematic rhythm written for woodwinds or brass. If the rhythm also has articulation or technique issues, the snare can continue playing while the winds join on the passage. Finish by subtracting the snare; listen for precision in the rhythm and articulation, and evenness in the technique.
- *"Breathe together to play together."* Give this short instruction, model it for the students, and practice together. This functions for both timing *and* style.
- *Breathing for rhythm is sometimes like a jazz drummer's "kick."* That is, if the sound enters on a beat, the kick (breath) is on the beat *before*. With the sound on beat 4, breathe on beat 3. For an entrance *off* a beat, the breath is still *on* the beat before; for example, for a sound on *the "and" of 3*, we'll still breathe on beat 3.
- *"Play only when you have eighth notes"* (or sixteenth-notes, moving notes). "Otherwise, keep time silently and re-enter when the eighth-notes return."
- *"Play any note. We're looking only for rhythmic precision."* This works equally well for complex rhythms and for the precision of entrances. Students will enjoy unpredictable sonorities while they work on rhythm, without technique-related problems. Directors continue to comment on precision, articulation, note-lengths, dynamic balance, and more.
- *"Play only the first sound after a rest of any kind, then drop out and wait for the next entrance."* With this, we evaluate students' ability to count through long rests. Even with short rests, we can hear any precision problems, and the students stay engaged when not playing.
- *"Beam us up."* Traditional rhythmic notation is beamed in beat-based groups. Especially in complex figures (e.g. funk, rag, syncopations) and when *ties* confuse the reader, teach students to examine *beaming* to help calculate their rhythms.
- *Mark the pulse.* Use pencil marks, ticks, vertical lines and the like to identify the exact pulse landmarks in confusing notation. As a suggestion, taller vertical lines show each *beat*, and shorter partial-lines indicate the *"and"* of each beat as shown in Figure 6.28.

Figure 6.28 Counting, ticks, and marks: *Lights Out* by Alex Shapiro, mm. 49–50 condensed. Used by permission.

- *Assemble a composite rhythm as an "auditory grid."* Complementary rhythms often work together to create a larger "whole" which, in turn, helps musicians learn the placement of their own portions (Figure 6.29).

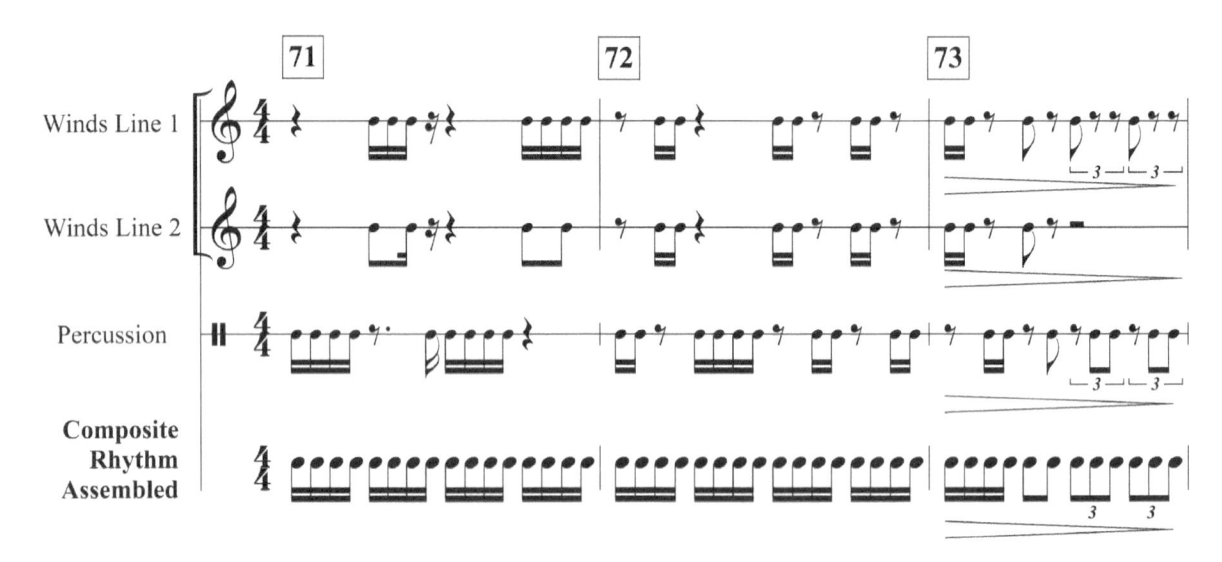

Figure 6.29 Composite rhythm strategy: reduced from *Fanfare Ritmico* by Jennifer Higdon. Used by permission of Lawdon Press. All other rights reserved.

- *A connection to foot-tapping.* Foot-tappers already have a tactile connection to the terms "downbeats" and "upbeats" because of the foot's down-up movement. For pairs of sixteenth-notes (common time), use terms like "double-downs" on a beat and "double-ups."
- *Another language connection.* We can recognize a word whether it is spoken very fast or very slowly; loudly or softly; in a high or low voice. Even when it is spoken by many different people, it is the same word. Once we know what *style* to use, printed rhythms work the same way, unchanged by speed, dynamics, register, or instrument.
- *Sing rhythms for students to imitate by rote.* Use typical jazz syllables or even nonsense sounds, but be careful to perform the correct style, length, articulation, emphasis, and all other interpretive markings.
- *Play a rhythm detective game.* For example:
  - Provide a sheet of rhythms composed by the teacher; each line has four or more very similar rhythms. The teacher plays *one* rhythm from the line; students identify which one.
  - From any rhythm sheet: a volunteer plays one rhythm call, and the entire band imitates it with the response. Then, another student identifies which rhythm (number, or line/measure) represents the sound.
  - The teacher *or* a volunteer student plays any measure from a piece being rehearsed. Other students identify where the rhythm exists in the piece.
- *Another exit-ticket strategy.* Choose a specific rhythm from the performance repertoire, asking students to "Rewrite the rhythm into several equivalent versions. Bonus points for using a different meter signature."

Analogies, Short-cuts and Other Quick-Fix Suggestions for Tempo and Meter

- *Use your voice and motions to help guarantee rhythmic success.* Count-offs and preparatory conducting motions should always be in the correct tempo and style of the desired sound.

- *Adapt these exercises*, often employed by a conductor in the first moments of meeting a band for the first time. These short processes can help to strengthen the ensemble-to-conductor bond:
    - "We'll play four *beats* on each tone of the scale. Those four beats might be a whole-note, half-notes, quarter-notes, eighth-notes, or even rests . . . watch carefully, but work together to interpret exactly what I show you."
    - "Play steady eighth notes as I conduct," but then change speeds, stretch beats, delay downbeats, and demonstrate dynamics and style. With this exercise, the ensemble becomes more cohesive, with a stronger ability to follow conducting, and with improved rhythmic awareness.
    - As above, but "Count aloud 1-&-2-&-3-&-4-&." This process can become a game or a competition between sections.
- *Make separate recordings of students or sections playing the same excerpt with a click-track.* Record on *separate tracks* using multitracking software. For playback, engage all tracks to compare the rhythmic placement of attacks and releases. Playback at slower speed for a better aural viewpoint.
- *Add temporary accent-groups* to stabilize the pulse: **1** e & a **2** e & a **3** e & a, for example. Note: use this technique sparingly, as this excessively accented sound may be difficult to undo, thus undermining other good note-grouping interpretive direction.
- *"Remove all ties; re-tongue the notes instead."* This works to identify pulse-alignment, and to prevent rushing.
- *Play with the meter signature.* Perform a written rhythm in its original meter signature (e.g. $\frac{4}{4}$). As the director changes the conducting patterns, replay the same *notation* but in different meters. For example, change the conducting to "8" and play the notation in $\frac{8}{8}$ meter. Repeat in $\frac{2}{2}$ and $\frac{16}{16}$.
- *Let all students conduct the pattern* for the passage. By feeling the conducting motions, students will be more connected to the rhythm *and* to the aesthetic aspects of the performance.
- *To combat rushing*:
    - Conduct *too slowly* on purpose; exaggerate the slow end of the tempo, even if you appear to *drag* behind the band.
    - Stop conducting. *Mime* instead with slow, deliberate body motions.
    - Remove slurs; tongue the passage, then reinsert slurs.
    - Stop the band, asking only "Is that too slow, too fast, or just right?"
    - "Play everything within each beat as slowly as possible . . . but without slowing the beat."
    - "You're rushing . . . try *dragging* instead. Slow us down."
    - "Don't be first to the dance. Be fashionably late, but be sure to arrive before the door closes."
- *Some directives that can work equally well for separate purposes:*

To discourage *rushing* . . .	To discourage *dragging* . . .
Stay on the back side of the beat	Be on the front side of the beat
Go as slowly as you can go . . . *without dragging*	Go as fast as you can go . . . *without rushing.*
Delay!	Anticipate!
Be like a suffix at the end of the word	Be like a prefix at the beginning of the word
Be *almost* too late to get into the Prom before they close the door	Be the very first to arrive at the Prom when the doors open
In this passage, you're sitting in the *last* car of the roller coaster. You're taking the same ride, but you'll be last to start and last to finish. Enjoy the ride!	In this passage, you're sitting in the *front* car of the roller coaster. You're taking the same ride, but you'll be first to start and first to finish. Enjoy the ride!

- *The Swan parallel*—adapt this short script to your style:
  - "Think of this scene—the sun is barely up, and you're looking out over the motionless surface of a pond. There, in the morning mist, you see a single swan gliding across the water. Now, what *adjectives* can you use to describe the scene?"
  - The students will offer words like *smooth, elegant, graceful, serene*.
  - "But do you know what you can't see? Under the water, the swan is paddling like H-E-double hockey sticks! Its elegant control requires constant, vigorous work, unseen under the surface."

A short exercise like this can help convey the importance of active timekeeping, subdivision, and constant attentiveness.

Other ideas for offbeats (especially the fast ones):

- In wind parts, with ties across the bar—try using language, substituting words with a matching rhythmic placement. For example: (-up) <u>GID</u>dy (up) <u>GID</u>dy (up).
- In wind parts, after or surrounded by rests—to avoid misalignment with the pulse, add an occasional *sound* to replace the rest on a downbeat, such as in Figure 6.30.

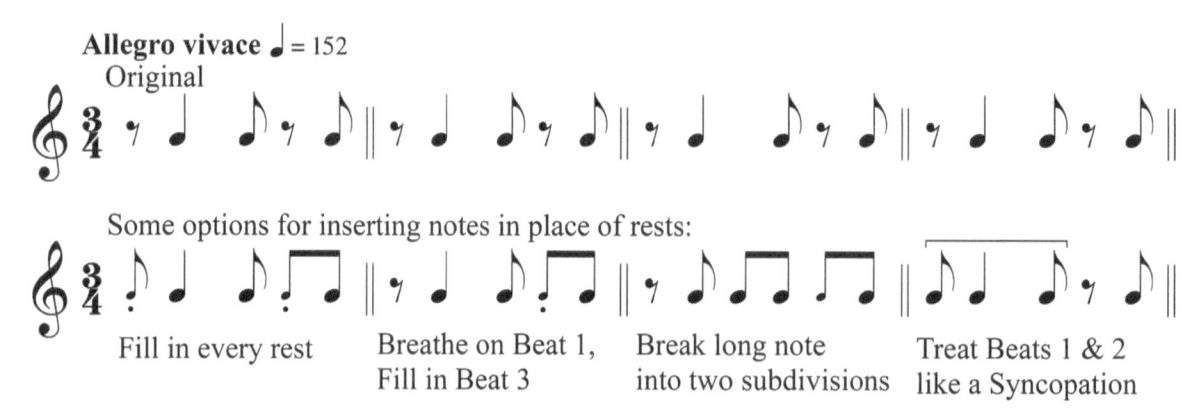

Figure 6.30 Adding sounds to help place offbeats.

This technique will be helpful against *dragging*.
- For percussion, "airplay" the rests (or play the rest lightly on a thigh) in order to use a familiar R–L–R–L sticking alternation. For example, the right-hand stick strikes silently off-the-head, while the left hand plays the offbeat normally, on the drum (r L r L—r L r L).

In Conclusion

In conclusion, it seems that "in conclusion" is far from the truth when we speak about teaching rhythm. If there's a main theme to Chapter 6, it must be that there are many ways to solve the same problem. Ultimately, our goal is to help all students reach *independence* with their rhythmic reading, understanding, and performance. Perhaps the best recommendation is simply to continue your reading, research and observations (Newell's *Teaching Rhythm* is an outstanding innovation), always searching for efficient ways to meet your students' needs and your own educational goals. The most effective teacher will never stop growing.

These compelling thoughts, quoted from Walter Beeler, distill the importance of our rhythmic instruction into just a few words:

We say unthinkingly "play what you see" and if a youngster plays what he sees he would give you a most unnatural picture most of the time. What you mean is "play what I see when I look at this, after 20 years' experience." When you examine it carefully, almost no music is really played the way it is written. All notes in a group look the same size or weight, but they are not played that way.

Any player's musicianship can best be measured by his rhythmic poise. A conductor cannot do anything about a player's rhythm. That has to come from within each player's system.[15]

Notes

1 David Newell, *Teaching Rhythm: New Strategies and Techniques for Success* (San Diego, CA: Neil A. Kjos Music Co., 2008), 38.
2 Daniel Levitin, "The Music Moves Us—But How?" interview by Dan Falk, *Knowable Magazine*, https://www.knowablemagazine.org/article/mind/2018/music-moves-us-how.
3 Peter Keller, "Rhythm on the Brain, and Why We Can't Stop Dancing," https://theconversation.com/rhythm-on-the-brain-and-why-we-cant-stop-dancing-56354.
4 Walter Beeler, "Improving the Sound of the Band." This version first appeared in the WASBE Newsletter, reorganized and edited by Mark Fonder, http://www.timreynish.com/conducting/conducting-articles/improving-the-sound.php.
5 Beeler/Fonder, "Improving the Sound of the Band."
6 Beeler/Fonder, "Improving the Sound of the Band."
7 Annie Jessy Curwen, *The Teacher's Guide to Mrs. Curwen's Pianoforte Method (The Child Pianist)*, Curwen's edition 5048 (Curwen & Sons Ltd., 1913), 8, https://archive.org/details/teachersguidecur00curwuoft/page/n3/mode/2up/search/through+the+eye.
8 Beeler/Fonder, "Improving the Sound of the Band."
9 Evan Feldman and Air Contzius, *Instrumental Music Education with the Musical and Practical in Harmony* (New York: Routledge, 2016), 21.
10 Newell, *Teaching Rhythm: New Strategies and Techniques for Success*, 121.
11 Newell, *Teaching Rhythm: New Strategies and Techniques for Success*, 83.
12 Beeler/Fonder, "Improving the Sound of the Band."
13 Beeler/Fonder, "Improving the Sound of the Band."
14 Stephen Meyer, ed., *Rehearsing the High School Band* (Delray Beach, FL, Meredith Music Publications, 2016), 64.
15 Beeler/Fonder, "Improving the Sound of the Band."

7

PERCUSSION

Introduction

This chapter offers strategies and suggestions designed to address six important premises about percussion, briefly described below:

1. Percussion is very different from other sections. Percussionists must master an extensive array of skills, and then should rotate through instruments to keep the skills refined. Students must also manage a substantial inventory of equipment. Above all, percussionists must stay attentive during sometimes long periods of inactivity.
2. Many directors have at least some discomfort with percussion. Statistically, the director is not a percussion major, and hasn't played much as an ensemble percussionist. Because percussion instruments require many different techniques, various clefs, and specialized notation practices, directors without keen curiosity for percussion are at a disadvantage.
3. Collegiate percussion courses often fall short. Even if taught by a world-class performer rather than a graduate assistant, methods courses can lack the "band director" perspective, gained only through relevant work experience. Regardless of the instructor, most will agree: a semester-long course is too short to address pedagogical necessities effectively.
4. The percussion section is a *collective* unit—an "ensemble-within-an-ensemble". Percussion, like the wind sections, needs *balance*. For percussion, however, balance differs for each composition. It is counterproductive to "hide" less-skilled players deep in the section. The *best* band requires well-rounded percussionists, with able players for every instrument. Remember that most percussion instruments are really *solo* parts.
5. This anomaly is arguably found only with percussion: while wind players usually know intuitively how to teach their major instrument and provide for its needs in the band setting, even the brightest, most skilled percussionist might not glean the director's perspective solely through participation. Performing in a band does little to ensure that percussionists know how to teach and *manage* the section within the context of the whole program. The most effective director is skilled at many tasks not always apparent to percussion players, including the art and science of part-assignments, rotation of parts, selection of repertoire, and many other aspects related to *teaching* percussion.
6. Percussionists, like other musicians, are individuals who want to be treated as such. This "basic human need" treatment is necessary for students to enjoy an engaging and fulfilling musical experience, and yet it may not be in the director's comfort zone. But, if percussionists sense that the director gives more (or "better") attention to wind-player peers, their progress slows and behavioral problems can evolve.

As with teaching their secondary wind instruments, directors can become outstanding percussion *teachers* without a mastery of performance skills. Therefore this percussion chapter does not focus on pedagogy for each specific instrument. For instructional information, turn to Gary D. Cook's

Teaching Percussion (Schirmer Books, 1998), Richard Colwell, Michael Hewitt, and Mark Fonder's *The Teaching of Instrumental Music* (Fifth Edition, Routledge, 2018), and other exceptional texts. Rather, the emphasis here is to offer procedures, organizational strategies, and supplemental teaching techniques beyond the typical focus of methods courses. These strategies are suggested to catapult non-percussionist directors toward becoming more effective teachers, while developing a great working relationship with this complex and often misunderstood section. An additional goal is to forge a stronger bond among individuals within the section, and section to section with the wind players.

Section 1: From the Podium—
The Director's Duties and Influence

A peculiarity of percussion is that, unlike most kinds of musical instruments, making a reasonable sound often requires no formal instruction. While it seems easy to play a woodblock, directors must not be misled. Gary Cook writes, "Therefore, an attitude is needed toward playing and teaching percussion instruments that is as musical and sophisticated as one that would be cultivated when approaching any wind or string instrument."[1] This attitude is entirely within the control of directors, starting with the organized environment we provide—and the way we treat percussionists—even when our personal performance skills are lacking.

First, it is productive to adopt a philosophy of support and assistance; that is, "What can I do *for* the percussion section, since it's the backbone of my ensemble?"

Careful Consideration of Percussion during Repertoire
Selection and Programming

Percussionists' skills, motivation, enjoyment, and even behaviors can be molded by the experience we provide. With sixteen percussionists, perhaps your concert theme shouldn't be "Bach Chorales: Alpha to Omega." From a wealth of available literature, conductors should match at least some pieces specifically to the percussion section.

- *Match pieces to the number of players.* Without much to play, players lose interest. But with too many parts to cover, players experience stress.
- *Match pieces to the inventory of instruments.* While loans are possible, of course, avoid pieces that are highly reliant on instruments not readily available.
- *Match pieces to students' skill levels and specialties.* This is more fully addressed later.
- *Balance the concert program.* Try to assign each percussionist meaningful parts in almost every piece.
- *Allow for variety in programs.* Not every piece in a performance must be fully instrumented; the players and audience alike may appreciate occasional music with lighter percussion scoring.
- *A helpful project.* In your digital library record, add a category for the minimum number of required percussionists for each work. With the search/sort feature, you can then easily find titles to support seven, eight, or even more percussionists, while also programming solid literature with only four players. Volunteers with good instructions can do this work for you. Also, remember to use printed and online sources regarding percussion in band repertoire.

An Overview before Making Part-assignments

In the finished design, every musician has a specified role in each composition. The director then monitors the roles, rotating assignments to offer a variety of opportunities and challenges to each student.

However, the wide diversity of instruments may prompt both preferences and apprehensions among percussionists. A player might love playing only his favorite instruments, avoiding instruments he can't play well. Without the director's intervention, some players could be repeatedly consigned to the same small auxiliary roles; worse, they might be left out entirely. Directors should therefore always oversee the percussion assignments. Even if a trusted section leader prepares an excellent draft, the director should still be able to approve, revise, or entirely veto assignments.

The next subsection describes some important tasks required to design percussion assignments. Because the project can be complicated at first, these tasks are presented in a sample sequence that will prove successful. Of course, this is just one template to revise as desired.

A Five-step Guide to Percussion Part-assignments

With no standardized rules to address every possible situation, percussion assignments will become a personal choice for each director. This section will supplement your current ideas, while providing a checklist leading through the entire percussion assignments process.

Important preliminary considerations prior to assigning roles:

- *Look ahead*—even with a careful literature-selection process, it is important to be fully organized (folders, lists, charts) before assigning the various performance roles to students.
- *Recognize your personal opinions in advance*—the work will reflect your preferences about doubling, rotating, expectations, providing supplemental parts, and more.
- *Know your students well*—assigning roles will be more beneficial to the overall education by considering students as both musicians and people.
- *Steward the first experience carefully*—remember that first impressions are powerful. In some rushed situations, you'll distribute parts before finishing the percussion assignments. If a student "claims" a part, it can be uncomfortable to reassign it later to someone else, even for sound reasons. TIP: rotate parts one or more times during the first sessions, thereby limiting the perception that a student will play a specific part.
- *Protect the printed parts*—if parts are distributed before assignments are diagrammed, be sure to collect them. You'll need the parts for several steps in this process.

Step 1: Dissect Each Composition's Percussion Needs

The part-assignment process requires listing all instruments to be played. For each instrument, consider . . .

. . . *the level of skill required*—the difficulty is perhaps the most essential factor in choosing a player for each part.

. . . *the extent to which each instrument is used*—for example, there is *one* triangle stroke in Holst's *Hammersmith*; a student assigned to "triangle" will count three hundred measures of rest.

. . . *whether instruments can be combined*—in *Hammersmith*, one player could cover triangle along with bass drum and gong.

. . . *if it must be shared between players*—make careful notes for reference. For example, a suspended cymbal might be notated on both Percussion 1 and Percussion 2 parts; will that affect where the cymbal is physically placed?

. . . *the format of the parts*—some compositions use generalized part sheets (e.g. "Percussion 1"), each with several instruments. Others provide different parts for each principal instrument—snare, bass, timpani, mallets—with accessories listed on one or more separate pages. Sometimes percussion parts are in a score format, with each instrument on a different staff. Each format presents its own consideration for the part-assignment process.

PERCUSSION

RESOURCES

We don't need to reinvent every wheel; resources are available to assist with percussion part assignments. First, consider asking people who have experience making assignments for the kind of literature you'll program: local colleagues, nearby college directors, or even advisors on web-based discussion forums (consider the Percussive Arts Society: www.pas.org). Of course, it's handy to have a hard-copy reference: an important publication is Russ Girsberger's *Percussion Assignments for Band & Wind Ensemble* (Meredith Music, 2005). Other websites are also highly recommended, including www.ThePercussionRoom.com and www.vicfirth.zildjian.com.

WORK FROM THE PARTS

While the conductor's score serves as a resource, look at the percussion *parts* for the best view of the roles. Using the parts will streamline directors' work, while helping to avoid potential pitfalls. The parts offer a quick, uncluttered look at everything you'll need to know. For example, technical challenges for the timpani player in Hanson's *Chorale and Alleluia* may be overlooked in the conductor's score. But the part clearly reveals a difficult problem: the timpanist must tune to *twelve* different pitches over shifting harmonies, with almost no rests!

From the parts, we easily see doublings, page-turns, frequency of rests, and the difficulty level. *It helps to view all parts simultaneously*, which can require a large workspace. Remember again that you'll need to do some homework *before* distributing music.

A PARTS-ASSIGNMENT CHECKLIST

A checklist can guide your work. Always adjustable, yours might look something like this:

A. List the percussion *parts* by name/label. Examples:

  ☐ Snare Drum, Bass Drum & Cymbals, Timpani, Mallets
  or,
  ☐ Percussion I, Perc II, P III, Mallet Percussion, Timpani

B. From each part, list the instruments to be played. For example:

  ☐ Percussion I = Snare Drum & Tambourine
  ☐ Percussion II = Bass Drum, Sus Cym, Cr Cym, Gong
  ☐ Etcetera to fit the format of the composition

C. With all instruments listed, assess each for its *difficulty*. Label each instrument for difficulty. Suggestion: *A* for Advanced, *M* for Moderate, *E* for Easier. "MA" indicates Moderately Advanced. The skill-level required to perform an instrument will help while matching students to each role.

  Your scratchpad now shows the names of all parts ("Mallet Percussion II"), and the instruments on each part, along with a basic rating of difficulty: Bells (M), Vibes (MA), Chimes (E).

D. Determine the minimum number of *players* required to perform the piece. The answer sometimes doesn't come from simply counting instruments; additional observations are required:

  ☐ Find the thickest *vertical* scoring on each part. Are two or more instruments played simultaneously? If not, can a single player cover everything on the sheet by changing instruments? If there are stacked sounds, however, it might still be possible for a skilled player to cover two instruments (e.g. bass drum with a *mounted* crash cymbal).

PERCUSSION

- ☐ Examine the *linear* arrangement of instruments, considering if an individual could play multiple instruments. Evaluate:
  - *Time* to change (instrument, grip, mallets)
  - *Physical spacing* within the setup
  - *Difficulty* (the "mallets" part might show an easy chimes passage, followed by a very difficult xylophone line).

Step B of the checklist will help you ascertain how much each instrument is used, which could expose the possibility that one player could cover multiple instruments. Also, make a note when one instrument is included on separate parts: if toms are shown on Percussion I and II, a decision is required about the instrument's physical placement (for sharing between players), and about whether a single player can cover toms from both parts.

Your work in step D determines how many players are required to perform the concert. If that number exceeds your membership, it may be feasible to enlist someone to cover a role during one piece. You might also pencil in subtle changes to accommodate the section's size. In other cases, the number of required players will indicate rethinking your choice of repertoire. This step also requires balancing the personal educational philosophy, mentioned earlier, with the needs of the music (e.g. will students "sit out" or will instruments be doubled to increase participation?).

TIP: Keep a printed version of this work in the score for reference during instruction, then file it to minimize future work. Enter the number(s) of players into the computerized library to guide future repertoire selection.

A review of this checklist, and an editable prototype can be found at [RW7.1]: Percussion Assignments, Part I: Preparatory work by the director.

The following *sample* blank copy shows information gathered by using the checklist. This version is only a template to inspire other options. The "back-up" column will be explained later in Step 4.

AMONG THE CLOUDS Brian Balmages (8 players minimum)

Player   *Back-Up*

_____ _____ Bells (MA)
_____ _____ Chimes/Vibraphone (M-MA)
_____ _____ Perc I: Bass Dr (E)
_____ _____ Perc I: Snare Dr (M) and Finger Cymb (E)
_____ _____ Perc II: Triangle, Cr Cymb
_____ _____ Perc II: Sus Cymb
_____ _____ Perc II: Tamb, Wind Ch
_____ _____ Timpani (M+)

Your blank should work to draft part-assignments that help the band's performance while also supporting each percussionist's individual development.

Step 2: Consider the Student

Beyond the students' skill-level with each percussion instrument, other key attributes are helpful when designing part-assignments.

- *Recognize each student's unique educational needs.* Each student's innate aptitude and strengths–weaknesses are important factors guiding percussion assignments. But students are also distinctive in their learning styles, likes/dislikes, and willingness to accept challenge. Alert directors recall these details about each returning student. To expedite familiarity with *new* students, consider these options:

- a basic discussion/interview with students
- a portfolio, checklist, or report from the previous teacher
- a baseline skills evaluation (snare drum, timpani, mallets, auxiliaries, drum set, reading and more)
- the student's responses to self-analysis questions: on the resources website, see files [RW7.2] "Students' Self-Analysis" and [RW7.3] "Percussionists' Track—Setting up the Lessons"

- *Assess self-awareness, confidence, and especially students' ability to work together as a section.* With a cohesive section and disciplined students, directors may have success delegating work to the percussionists themselves. Still, subtle vigilance is advisable. See [RW7.4] "Percussion Assignments—1st Task—September." By observing students through this short project, you'll determine how much intervention will be needed.

Step 3: Match the Students' Educational Needs with the Percussion Roles

The best plan leads to outstanding performances. Just as importantly, through continuous encouragement from the director, part-assignments also foster development of each student as a well-rounded percussionist. Steps 3 and 4 are designed to use part-assignments to help cultivate versatile percussionists.

- *Encourage students to engage in their learning, and to take risks.* Students' perceptions can obstruct their own progress. Worse, if percussion roles only reflect students' preferences and their own perceived strengths and weaknesses, some students may be typecast into limited opportunities. A student might say, "I hate playing timpani," in part because of previous bad experiences. Use the percussion assignments to provide opportunities and instruction leading to that student's success on a basic timpani part.
- *Consider students' strengths, weaknesses, and needs.* Somewhat self-explanatory, if a piece requires an advanced mallet player, you must know who can and cannot perform it. But a student without advanced ability still deserves *opportunities*. The part-assignment process itself can drive the percussion curriculum: we provide varied opportunities to promote comprehensive skill-development.

    - Assign a simple bells/chimes part to the person without mallet strength.
    - A moderately easy snare drum part can be assigned to the mallet or timpani specialist who hasn't yet mastered rolling skills.
    - Assign a two-drum timpani part without tuning changes to the student developing a better ear for pitches, or to someone just learning to read bass clef.

In short, use assignments to help educate the students. Carefully avoid parts that are far too difficult or exposed, which can spoil the experience for both the players and for the entire ensemble.

Suggested project: let students *participate* in the parts-assignment process. On the resources website find [RW7.5] "Self-Assignment Guidelines." This checklist leads students to choose primary and back-up roles. By following the steps as outlined, it's possible for students themselves to design workable Section assignments, again with the director's observation and final authority.

Additionally, we offer a sample Percussion Assignments Worksheet at [RW7.6]. This kind of document shows the title, parts, instruments, and level of difficulty for every percussion role in the planned repertoire. It is useful to view each instrument's difficulty while matching students to roles.

PERCUSSION

Step 4: Assign Back-Ups and Doubling

In most cases, a "back-up" is assigned in case the primary player is missing. Anyone who has lost an important percussionist from a performance will appreciate having an understudy ready. But the importance of back-up assignments reaches even further.

- *The philosophy of "Back-up" assignments.* If every student is assigned primary *and* back-up parts, then . . .

    . . . no one "sits the bench"; all students have meaningful roles.
    . . . all percussionists are *on task*, stationed at an instrument, engaged in the learning, contributing to the rehearsal. Directors can use substitution to allow back-up students to have time with the ensemble.
    . . . a student with no primary role is still stationed with another, often stronger, percussionist who can act as a mentor. The back-up player observes and participates in a guided-learning situation.
    . . . the back-up player may be the stronger percussionist, tutoring the primary player. For example, an advanced snare player has the "back-up" role on a moderately easy snare part, but serves as a mentor to the less-skilled "primary" player.
    . . . the ensemble is more prepared for unexpected absences because each part has at least two trained players.
    . . . directors with a large percussion population can program pieces with fewer parts-than-people, because percussionists are given more opportunities to play.
    . . . back-up playing can be individualized or assigned by rotating groups ("A-Squad, step back please; B-Squad, let's begin at the Coda.")

- *Doubling.* Besides back-up roles, doubling also keeps multiple players active. Snare drums, mallets, and other selected instruments can be doubled to some extent without serious musical detriment. Further, use drum practice pads to keep players involved without risking a cacophonous sound. TIP: While the director may elect to avoid doubling in performances, the process supports learning as well as better behavior during rehearsals.

Step 5: Provide the Written Part-assignments Chart

The assignments chart is indispensable for organizing the students and the smooth flow of percussion activities. With it, students have a clear view of specific roles, and a guide to their needs (music, instruments, mallets, setup details) for every composition. They also see a total listing of equipment needed, along with what must be covered during another player's absence.

The flow of percussionists covering parts is a dance that should appear smooth, systematic, and effortless.[2]

- *Design the chart.* Blank designs are easily found; the recommended format uses *Players' Names* and *Composition Titles* as the header labels. Then, the "field" cells show assigned roles for each player in each composition. Regardless of the format, the efficient chart provides the quickest possible view of assignments.

    The format sampled in Figure 7.1 allows students to view other players' roles, which is helpful during absences. Your chart will also reveal when a student is left "tacet," and when the student is assigned to the same part in multiple works.

PERCUSSION

Students	FOLDER #	Brazilian Sleigh Bells	Chant and Jubilo	Fate of the Gods	With Good Will and Glad Tidings
Aaron	51	*Back-up P3: Bongos with Austin*	SD	Sus Cym	Sus/Cr Cymbals
Alan	52	P1 - BD	Sus Cym	Aux Perc: Vi	*Back-up SD*
Alexa	53	P1 - SD	Glock	Timp	Sl Bells & Mark Tree
Allison	54	P2 - Claves	BD	Mallet Perc	Be
Andrea	55	P2 - CB	*Back-up Glock*	Tenor Dr & SD	Timp
Andrew	56	P3 - SusCym	*Back-up SD*	BD & Mark Tr	BD
Aria	57	P4 - Sl Bells	Tri	Chimes	*Back-up Timpani*
Austin	58	P3 - Bongos	Timp	Aux Perc: Tam-Tam, Tamb, Hi-Hat, Bell Tree	Temple Bl & Tri
Avery	59	P3 - Maracas	*Back-up Bass Dr*	Cr Cym	SD

Figure 7.1 Sample part-assignments chart excerpt.

Consider using a common set of abbreviations to save space: SD, BD, Ti, Xy, and the like. Tip: An outstanding blank chart by Bruce Pearson and M. Max McKee is offered at www.bandworld.org.

Finally, save more time by including a listing of instruments for the entire collection of pieces shown on the chart. This checklist will help prepare the percussion section for each rehearsal.

- *Display the chart.* Part-assignments should be displayed in clear view of percussionists, in multiple locations as needed. Include the percussion cabinet, closet/locker area, and perhaps on music stands. In addition, every player's folder should have a copy. See [RW7.7] for a sample "Master Percussion Assignments Chart."

- *Use the chart.* The entire conception of the part-assignments (preceding Steps 1–4) will help to drive students' instruction toward a comprehensive skill set. Roles are clearly defined in an organized structure. The design and display of the chart promotes an outstanding goal: "to make disorganization impossible."
- *A distilled review of part-assignments, and some extra quick-fix tips*:
    - Think carefully about the section and its members when choosing repertoire, and when designing assignments
    - List instruments before distributing music; identify instruments that cannot be covered by a single player
    - Rate the difficulty for parts; this practice helps students know what to expect before choosing a role
    - Organize assignments first, then display the chart in common areas; put a copy in percussion folders, and keep one in your conductor's folder. Regardless of the suggestions/models provided here, any format will work if it communicates details clearly and efficiently
    - List the part-name ("Percussion I") as well as the instrument(s) to play from that part ("Tri & Tamb").
    - Pencil the instrument name(s), or circle the pre-printed names on each student's part, usually at the top left corner of the page.
    - Train and monitor the section leader for this role; delegating tasks carefully can save enormous amounts of time.
- *Philosophical support.* A comprehensively designed percussion assignments process allows every student to stay engaged in the music-making, playing a wide variety of parts. Behavior may improve as well: students with well-defined responsibilities will have neither time nor incentive to misbehave.

On the Choice to Amend Parts

While rehearsing a piece with minimal percussion, subtle revisions can keep percussionists more involved without changing the composition's character. There is some debate about this, but there *are* justifiable reasons to rewrite parts—or compose new ones—when it helps students' development.

A repertoire model demonstrates this philosophical suggestion: *Air for Band* by Frank Erickson is too beautiful to be missed, but the percussion is extremely limited. For rehearsals, and perhaps performances, consider adding parts to support the music while also keeping percussionists active:

- Marimba can play the double bass line, rolled with soft mallets.
- Vibes and bells play any concert-pitched part; consider doubling the melody at times.
- A sparse timpani part provides bass support at important harmonic moments.
- Similarly, well-chosen chimes notes support the harmonic structure.
- Bass drum strokes can join printed cymbal crashes at climax moments.

This modification engages at least six additional players; initially only two percussionists played. Notice that this plan provides support for pitch-reading and mallet skills. Re-writing has many purposes, including musical support of other band sections, but the recommendations here focus on educational and behavioral development of the percussionists.

Section 2: In the Bandroom—The Students' Environment

We already work to provide an organized and efficient bandroom—a welcoming space that elicits students' pride each time they enter. But percussionists have unique and vital roles, and a vast amount of equipment to manage; their work can be simplified with a customized environment. Accordingly,

Percussionists are apt to be more successful if we think carefully about their needs: we can support them with careful choices about folders and music, equipment and storage, and more.

Strategies to Help Organize the Percussion Music

Even when part-assignments are provided clearly, a young section can sometimes seem chaotic and confused. Additionally, percussionists in the average school ensemble are traditionally more likely to misplace music. The situation can improve dramatically with director interventions, such as the following:

- *Label folders and store them strategically.* Common options include these:
    - Store percussion folders with *all* other band folders, in score order for quick access. Or,
    - Store folders in or near the percussion section, apart from the winds. With rapid access to folders, percussionists have more time to get themselves and their gear ready for the rehearsal. By allowing percussionists to avoid lines at the folder cabinet, both the beginning and the end of the rehearsal will be more productive.
- *Every percussionist can benefit by having an individual folder.* In this system, for example, Aaron's parts go in Aaron's folder, with Aaron's markings on them. Consult copyright policy and contact publishers for extra parts. Note: the author recognizes that this approach is specific, and that many bands are fully successful with their own folder plans. Most of the following bulleted text is adaptable for any plan but is designed with individualized folders in mind.
- *All music has the player's name penciled on it.* Other information can be added as needed, as in the following suggestions:
    - Circle the instrument(s) to be played.
    - Label sticks/mallets needed for each part.
    - Add textual notes where helpful (e.g. "pick up triangle beater").
    - With several players' roles shown on the same staff, pencil brackets to highlight assigned parts for each.
    - Consider penciling a guide for timpani tuning; whether by text or symbols, the student should know which drum to choose for the new note, and when to make the change.
    - Occasionally a student plays excerpts from Percussion II, before moving to a different instrument on Percussion III; consider adhesive notes or a written roadmap. Note: these situations may also affect the section's setup.
- *Additional documents for the folder*:
    - the part assignments chart
    - a diagram of the basic section setup
    - curricular forms (help-sheets, rudiments lists, timpani tuning materials, etc.)
    - a personalized guide-sheet—this is a clear listing of "what I play on each composition." Tip: Find an editable template at [RW7.8] "Personal Folder Assignments Guide."
    - a section responsibilities sheet, described later.

Attention to part-assignments and folders can ensure that all percussionists have the materials, guidance and skills needed for success.

Strategies to Help Organize the Percussion Setup

The setup of instruments, trap tables, and stands is another personal decision. Many resources are available; for the scope of this book, the principle is simply that the layout should work well. In a generalized view of a common setup, mallet instruments usually remain closer to upper woodwinds and/

or other melodic instruments, while timpani may be found near tubas and other root-producers for harmonic reasons. Bass drum and its battery partners are often centered to keep the pulse equidistant from all players.

However, there are too many variables to standardize an arrangement that "always" works. The setup is guided by the number of percussionists, the layout of the bandroom, and other factors. It changes to reflect repertoire, and occasionally requires an enlarged collection of items. Because the percussion arrangement will be customized for each band, these suggestions are designed to assist with *any* setup:

- Percussionists, like other performers, should find equipment organized and in good working order when they enter the space. Directors and students have shared responsibilities in that goal, addressed with more detail in the next sections.
- Allow *space*—percussionists require room to walk, perform, move, and store instruments.
- Provide extra music stands where needed. When one student plays several larger instruments, the printed part is easily carried to an empty stand at the new station.
- Be inventive with storage options—repurpose other items for efficiency:
    - Clear shoe-storage boxes and over-the-door shoe holders for small instruments.
    - Carpet samples and towels for a quiet exchange of sticks/mallets.
    - Velcro, Command® strips, etc. for temporary attachments.
    - More suggestions are found at [RW7.9] "Bandroom Hacks & Shortcuts" file.
- Adjust the setup to support players' *visual*, *aural*, and *spatial* perspective:
    - Percussionists must see the conductor and music clearly. Be watchful of lighting, distance, and obstructions (tuba bells).
    - Percussionists are typically farthest from the podium; be sure instructions are loud enough, and that players can hear each other, and the winds, adequately.
    - Look for management issues with small auxiliaries: a student may need a trap table or other help to transition between instruments. Be resourceful—solutions may be as simple as a towel on a music stand, or a trap case, a stool, or a waiter's tray with a plywood topper.
    - At times, percussionists may be unable to turn pages; be thoughtful about their music-reading, offering advice and extra music when required.
    - When players share, the equipment or even people may need to be close together.
    - When one player covers several parts, a "pod" arrangement may allow efficient access to several instruments. Note: sometimes one student's pod intersects with another, placing shared instruments within reach of both.
    - Observe students' physical size; an instrument's height or angle may need adjustment.
    - When instruments are musically "paired" (e.g. bass drum and crash cymbals), encourage players to stand adjacent.
- An essential practice related to the setup—post the rehearsal schedule so percussionists will know which instruments to prepare first.
- Similarly, plan some rehearsals specifically with percussionists in mind—consider choosing pieces based on the needs of the setup. For example, if the needs are extensive but vastly different for two major pieces, consider rehearsing those pieces on different days.
- Obviously not every possibility can be addressed here. Be observant; your attentiveness demonstrates to students that you feel their needs are important.

Strategies to Help with the Percussion Culture

Wind players come to their seats with instruments, music, and accessories. They are ready for the rehearsal. But uniquely, every percussionist performs tasks affecting the entire section, and the rest of the band. More than in any wind section, the percussion section always functions best as a unit; it is a team, with its own special internal leadership. James Doyle says, "A culture of teamwork enhances the attitude of a section and ultimately their ability to perform together."³ The following suggestions will foster that "culture of teamwork" within the band.

- Be an *advocate* for the percussion section:
    - *Protect their space and equipment.* Percussion instruments are not toys; special techniques are needed to play them, and they are stored and maintained in specific ways. By allowing non-percussionists to play them at will—potentially mistreating them—we send a message. Your players feel supported when they are invited to help develop policies.
    - *Treat percussionists as the musicians they are.* With your words and actions, and your musical expectations, acknowledge percussionists as you do any others. Expect every section to perform confidently, musically, and artistically.
    - *Involve* the percussion section in the warm-up process in a musical way (see Chapter 3, Section 2). And when they are not involved, give percussionists clear instructions to keep them engaged.
    - *Choose feedback carefully.* Although perhaps difficult for less experienced "non-percussionist" directors, it is important to give instructional feedback with the same level of specificity given to players of the "major" instrument. A few minutes of homework will yield great returns for everyone.
    - *Help percussionists manage time wisely.* When the rehearsal pauses (e.g. to address a woodwind tuning issue), give concise instructions to percussionists: what they should do, how long they'll have to do it, and what will happen next for them when the rehearsal resumes.
    - *Provide for their needs.* Percussionists often require extra time to change instruments or mallets, retune timpani, or move to a new space. Be patient and supportive.
    - *Highlight their special skills for peers.* Consider featuring percussionists by demonstrating rhythms to help other sections. Remember that winds can share the "human metronome" function (e.g. keeping time with clapping).
    - Similarly, help wind players to recognize and appreciate percussionists' *logistics*. An entertaining "choreography" often results from special equipment needs, multiple assignments, and students' movement throughout the section. Consider highlighting it with a description, allowing wind players to watch percussionists during a particularly difficult sequence.
    - *Train percussionists' peers for compassionate integrity.* Discourage students from turning to look at a percussionist after an inevitable error; even if a crash-cymbals mistake is "a bit" more obvious than a wrong note in 3rd clarinet, there is no place for humiliation.

- Provide strategies to help the percussion section *develop its team identity*:
    - *Expect that section tasks will involve every member*:
        - The setup—provide a diagram; agree on a time-allotment schedule.
        - The tear-down—allow time; expect a careful, complete result.
        - Organizing, packing, and moving for trips and competitions—this extensive process is fraught with opportunities for mistakes; provide a careful checklist, offering both supervision and praise. A sample, editable checklist is available at [RW7.10] "Percussion List for Trips."
    - *Strengthen the full-band bond using percussion buddies.* These are volunteers from other sections who agree to be trained by percussionist partners. After training, they occasionally help with specific tasks. Examples of percussion buddies' tasks could include setting up cymbal stands, removing/storing timpani covers, assembling a drum-set, and transporting instruments. Even if percussion buddies are not employed often, the concept builds a relationship between percussionists and their wind-playing peers. It will prove immensely helpful for efficiency at a

festival, adjudication, offsite performance or even a school concert when the stage is shared by multiple groups. Consider offering perks to volunteers.
- "Self-management": *A plan for leadership, equipment-management, and structure within the percussion section.* This model relies on a prerequisite organizational plan for percussion inventory; label the locations of instruments in the cabinet, drawers, lockers, shelves, and closets. The result is a well-organized section where equipment is stored and maintained regularly.

    - *Ownership and responsibilities*—if your cabinet/closet has a lock, cut extra keys, assigning one to *each* percussionist. Because access is limited to solely the director and the percussionists, they will be more apt to care for equipment: students' level of responsibility will rise toward your expectations. Having a key is a privilege to be withheld when needed.
    - *Site assignments*—these non-performance tasks are different than part-assignments. Each percussionist chooses (or is assigned) a short task, and a back-up role for peers' absence. Each task is thoroughly described and takes only moments to complete. An adaptable sample is posted at [RW7.11] "Section responsibilities chart."

        With complete control over how many tasks to create, directors can assign a role to every percussionist: for twelve percussionists, we simply define twelve unique tasks. Each student then has partial ownership of the section, and directors can easily monitor the accountability of all individuals.

Section 3: In Lessons and Sectionals

The pedagogical choices for percussion lessons will reflect the teacher's philosophy, prior experience, curriculum, availability of methods and materials, etc. However, there's no doubt that true percussionists should be able to perform a majority of instruments with ease. The philosophy is applied through action: "If we want a snare specialist to be able to play mallets, *we teach mallet skills to the snare player.*" Therefore, all materials chosen for use in the curriculum should support the plan to create *multitalented* percussionists. For example:

> For next week, prepare just the first line of Solo #1 (snare drum) from the Albright book. We'll work at that etude for a few minutes, and then we'll see how you do with tuning perfect 4th intervals on timpani; I'll give you a sight-reading etude using those intervals. After that, I've got a fun multiple percussion piece to try . . . hey, let me give it to you today; see what you can learn on your own before next week. I'll give you a short quiz on finding pitches by name on the marimba (Chris, can you remind us how to find "C" on a mallet instrument?). If we can get all of this done, it will leave time to work together on the NoveltyCicles piece for the Prism Concert.

A well-rounded approach requires care and planning from directors, but it's worth the work.
Remember the *essential questions* that drive your instruction:

- "What should my students know or be able to do?"
- "How will I determine if they know it (can do it)?"
- "What is my response-plan if they *don't* know it?"

With an important follow-up:

- "And, for those who already know it, how can I extend/advance their education?"

Toward developing versatility in your percussionists, the curriculum of study should cover all types of instruments for every student. If that curriculum is not yet in place for you, start with the strategies suggested above (management and part-assignments), or select from them to supplement any existing curriculum. The suggestions in Sections 1 and 2 have been directed at percussion within the full band setting. But without a curriculum, non-percussionist directors might experience some daunting apprehension about sectionals and small-group lessons: "I can't play these instruments, so how am I supposed to *teach* them?" Here are several brief descriptions of helpful strategies.

1. *Incorporate band literature in lessons and sectionals.* Once students are rotating through diversified part-assignments, the repertoire becomes a logical choice for content during lessons. You'll be within your comfort zone, conducting, but in closer proximity to the students, so you'll observe even more about their strengths and limitations.
2. *Keep students working at multiple instruments*, whether using band literature or not. Try a basic rotation, visiting several instruments within each class period. While some advance preparation is required, rotations help organize your teaching while also structuring the students' learning. These are among many variations of the rotation idea:

   - Break sessions into segments, giving 50% of the activity to the "major" instrument, and fill the remaining 50% with alternate instruments and ensembles.
   - Choose an ensemble that includes several distinct types of percussion: snare drum, timpani, mallets, and battery (BD/Cyms), or auxiliary parts. Rotate through stations, repeating the ensemble as needed to give each player a rounded experience. Discuss the results, prompting students to recognize their strengths and voids.
   - *Teach the audition sequence* required for honor bands. Materials typically entail etudes, excerpts, or solos appropriate for a multi-skilled percussionist. This is an excellent, resourceful choice even if the student has no plans to audition. The experience carries inherent self-esteem benefits, when directors get to speak encouragingly about the student's possibilities.
   - *Rotate players* through the stations carefully organized in Dr. Eric Willie and Dr. Julie Hill's *All-Inclusive Audition Etudes* (Row-Loff Productions, 2017). This work is exceptionally well suited to developing comprehensive percussion skills. It is available at the JH and SH levels, with text assistance and video samples helpful for *any* instructor.
   - *Be inventive with approaches.* Search for instructional literature offering a comprehensive approach. Some other notable examples include: *The Drummer's Daily Drill* by Dennis DeLucia (Row-Loff Productions, 2010); *Percussion with Class* by Douglas B. Wallace (The FJH Music Company Inc., 2008); *Audition Etudes* by Garwood Whaley (Meredith Music Publications, 1982); *Alfred's Drum Method* by Sandy Feldstein (Alfred Music, 1982); and *Percussion Section Techniques* by Grimo and Snider (Meredith Music Publications, 1993). A comprehensive method will also be helpful to you in your professional growth.
   - *Establish a setup that allows rotations for sectionals and lesson classes.* With instruments in a circle or square, students have quick access to all stations and can move smoothly from one to the next. Beyond lesson classes, this kind of physical layout also supports fun activities like those found in drum-circles: call-and-response activities led by the teacher or the students themselves, "trading-fours," improvisations, and groove-based exercises (the teacher might say, "Everything you play should sound like *Funk* and we'll keep this steady *Tempo*; one-two-ready-go!"). When an engaging exercise is discovered, directors shepherd students to other stations for experience on new instruments.
3. *Exploit the power of intrinsic motivation.* Consider using games as motivation for students to accept multiple roles. This is suggested as a longer-term project, perhaps over the course of a month, marking period, or semester. The author invented "Percussion 21," described in the following, to motivate students to prepare four different excerpts—snare drum, timpani, mallets, and multiple

percussion. Any name of your own will suffice (e.g. *Percussion Yahtzee*, *Drum Rummy*, *PARcussion*). You can design your own adaptation from this basic design:

- Each etude is labeled with a number rating its difficulty from 1 (easiest) to 10 (most difficult). Note: the author used *Audition Etudes* by Garwood Whaley. You may also extract excerpts from any literature, including your concert repertoire.
- Students prepare four different etudes of their own choosing.
- Students are required to reach at least 21 points by adding the values of the four chosen etudes (note that each student self-selects assignments).
- Perform all etudes, either as a "recital" in class or alone for the director.

  The teacher's preparation is easy: just choose a point-value for each excerpt's difficulty, and provide a written chart to accompany the printed music. A sample is available at [RW7.12].

  Students typically select a more difficult piece (thus, a higher point-value) for their stronger instruments, but they'll still need to use other instruments to meet the point-goal. The game offers a hidden psychology: during their selection process, students sample *more of the etudes* independently than if given specific requirements.

  Optionally, offer recognitions (e.g. the highest point total; most outstanding musical performance; best memorization; earliest date of completion).

4. *Consider strategies for multi-ability classes*. Students at vastly different skill-levels require individualized instruction within the same class. Percussionists can play each other's assignments. Suggestions include:

   - While a less-skilled student plays an easy snare drum assignment, the more advanced students offer support by playing along, either on a drum or pad. Then, during the advanced student's assigned etude, the novice(s) can participate by playing bass drum, cymbals, a repeating rudimentary figure, or even a simplified complementary part written especially for the lesson.
   - When a mallet specialist is grouped with a snare specialist, assign *two appropriate etudes* to each: advanced music for the "major," easier music for the "minor" instrument. In the lesson, for example, a Level 5 snare drum student plays a Level 2 mallet assignment, while the mallet-specialist plays along in support. Then, reverse roles.

   With a cleverly designed multi-ability strategy, all students remain engaged at almost all times.

5. *Consider the metronome* during percussion lessons. Although sometimes difficult to hear, eliminate volume problems by . . .

   . . . focusing on the metronome's LED display (easy during memorized excerpts)
   . . . choosing a drum pad
   . . . patching through an amplifier.

   Note: the metronome can provide incremental measurements of students' skills—list varied metronome markings as speed-goals for designated skills, then maintain an ongoing chart of percussionists' progress.

6. *Record percussion performances for playback and evaluation*. Recordings allow multiple hearings but, more importantly, students almost always exhibit greater concentration when they know they're being recorded. Consider altering the playback speed:

   - A *slower* playback highlights the student's clarity and evenness.
   - Use a *faster* playback to hear the intended tempo if the student's skill-level necessitated a slower performance-speed for the recording.

7. *Seek and create resources*. As we know, directors may be unable to perform at the level required to provide a motivating example. Alternative demonstrations can include:

   - Vocalize percussion sounds using appropriate nonsense-syllables.
   - Engage advanced students to provide demonstrations for others.

- Consider hiring (or bartering with) a percussion professional to work with your students.
- Use media resources of all kinds, including texts, recordings, charts, DVDs.
- The internet offers myriad benefits, including video lessons, professional demonstrations, and percussion-specific websites.
- In YouTube's "settings," choose slower playback speeds to view technique problems with clarity.

8. *Solos and small ensembles* can provide a core curriculum in the absence of other plans. A special project suggestion: find excellent video samples on the internet and save each link as a QR code. Attach QR codes to each title page in the music library. While percussion students peruse music, their smartphones can link them immediately to demonstrations.
9. *Consider the benefits of marching percussion music.* Marching compositions can provide percussionists with educational concepts and experiences beyond those found in most traditional band music.

    - Snare drum parts are more based on rudiments, so students can immediately see the relevance of their rudimental lessons.
    - The depth of the scoring provides opportunities to a larger number of players.
    - Doubling is supported on more of the instruments.
    - Multi-tom parts are great fun—not unlike "marching drumset"—and offer opportunities to practice cross-sticking and controlled double-bounce techniques.
    - Finally, even crash cymbals and bass drum parts are interesting; a student playing one pitch in a piece scored for four tonal bass drums requires impeccable pulse, along with enhanced listening and reading skills.

    Whether your school has a marching band or not, percussionists will benefit from playing marching band music. With that experience as a catalyst, try adding percussion ensembles of all kinds, including street cadences, body percussion pieces, or even "trash can" features. Students enjoy the ensembles and will become much more independent as musicians.
10. *The "Rudiments Inventory."* An invention of the author, this is a self-driven snare drum rudiments checklist to help students learn, memorize, and master rudiments. Additionally, this device creates a visual inventory of skills, where checkboxes indicate all speeds at which students can perform each rudiment. The full document is found at [RW7.13]—an excerpt is shown in Figure 7.2.

P.A.S. #	**Rudiment Name & Notation** * = *Part of the Original 26*	**Link to Video Lessons & Practice Tracks at www.vicfirth.zildjian.com**	Memorized by Name?	Achievement BRONZE	Achievement SILVER	Achievement GOLD	Achievement PLATINUM	Achievement DIAMOND
21	21. Flam Accent (> 3 > 3; LR L R RL R L)	https://vicfirth.zildjian.com/education/21-flam-accent.html	❑	❑	❑	❑	❑	❑

Figure 7.2 Excerpt from "Rudiments Inventory."

Section 4: More from the Podium—Rehearsals and Performances

All aspects of our work during rehearsals and concerts can affect students' behavior and performance. Percussionists may feel that their participation, and perhaps even their worth, is limited; without the director's careful planning, some students might experience entire rehearsals with not much more than a few bass drum strokes or cymbal crashes. Unsurprisingly, it's possible that some percussionists feel like "forgotten members" of the band. Positive outcomes result from applying a basic educational philosophy:

- Design a structured environment where each student remains productively engaged.
- Provide meaningful and appropriate activities to each student.
- Offer high-quality feedback, chosen carefully to meet each student's needs.

These provisions apply of course to all students in all sections. But percussionists—whether in lessons, rehearsals or concerts—will prosper more fully when they are organized, kept active, and of course when they *enjoy* their participation. Most of the previous suggestions, especially the organizational and part-assignment strategies, are designed to improve all aspects of performance, so it is the onus of the director to maintain the attitude of "podium-to-percussion awareness." The following tips will review and add to what has already been presented.

A "User's Guide" to Apply Earlier Suggestions

- While it's helpful for percussionists to participate during band warm-ups, there are always exceptions. If not performing, they might be working at setup and assembly. But it may be destructive to leave them unattended, without instructions.
- If you use an established warm-up "routine" for winds, consider employing percussion rotations during that segment to develop versatile skills in all members.
- Part-assignments clarifications:
    - *Rotation*—this is a constructive way to "force" students to maintain concentration in the rehearsal; when not playing, students must be attentive, knowing they might be asked to step in at any moment.
    - *Back-up*—students should be given time during rehearsals to perform their back-up roles.
    - *Tutoring* and *mentoring*—regarding back-up assignments and doubling, directors are encouraged to use tutoring and mentoring practices by strategically pairing less-skilled players with classmates who are slightly more advanced. Pairing keeps multiple students engaged, which is a great benefit to directors with a large Percussion section. Pairing works well when students are friends but at different skill levels.

Tips About Your Wording and Delivery

With regard to your verbal instructions, be careful to consider special circumstances. Be specific with details, and allow time for percussionists to make their equipment changes:

- "Let's go back to Rehearsal Letter B"—percussionists might require different equipment at Letter B. Whereas wind players simply look elsewhere on the page, percussionists might need to change timpani tunings, move from a marimba to chimes, set brushes aside, pick up drumsticks, change the position of the snare throw-off, and so on. Percussionists need specificity, and time.
- "Let's jump ahead to the key-change"—the key change is not shown on battery parts, so the instruction is meaningless for most percussionists.
- Directors can support students' awareness by choosing language wisely. Rather than using teacher-centered directives like, "yes/no, louder/softer, choose a harder mallet," instead choose more student-centered prompts, such as "Did you notice?" "What will happen if?" "Did you like the way that sounded?" and the like. A common instruction like, "Use a softer mallet," can easily convert to a prompt requiring students to apply their musicianship, such as "Try for a warmer sound to match the clarinet section there; listen to the clarinets first, and then see what you can do to improve the blend." This example perfectly illustrates a point that inspired the very inception of this entire book; that is, this kind of motivational delivery may be learned through

experience, self-reflection, and by observing master teachers, conductors, and clinicians. Language, chosen wisely, helps transform students from "member-players" into thinking, artistic, comprehensive musical performers.

More Tips Regarding Percussionists' Engagement

- *Provide additional varied experiences*—mallet players can read any concert-pitch part; choose flute/oboe parts for treble, and trombone/bassoon/tuba parts for bass clef reading. Or, target a specific rhythm in the brass section, by asking battery percussion players to play the rhythm while viewing the pitched wind-players' parts.
- *Seating changes* are addressed in more depth in Chapter 8. For percussionists' benefit, simply reverse the band, so all students face the opposite direction. Now in the "front," percussionists will hear things differently, while feeling "featured." Meanwhile, the rest of the band, conductor included, enjoys a different perspective of percussionists' sounds and physical techniques they employ.
- *"Percussion day"*—this *fun* project requires an easy-level marching percussion feature with full-band accompaniment. Create a blank chart offering multiple openings for wind players to sign up as "percussionists for a day." Your new percussion section might accommodate as many as 20–30 players by heavily doubling snare drums, bass drums, cymbals, quads, mallet parts, and all auxiliary percussion. Borrow extra instruments for this special event. Rehearse the piece as normal, leaving some original percussionists in place as mentors. The one-day collaboration strengthens bonds between percussionists and their peers, and offers a new and enlightening perspective to all participants.

A Random Sampling of Additional Suggestions

- *Percussion storage.* You've labeled your cabinet and other storage locations; *expect* the students to replace equipment in the right spot after every usage.
- *Leadership in percussion.* Select, train, and supervise officers wisely. Section leaders and principal players might be different people in any section. Regarding percussion, the most successful section leader is dedicated, organized, responsible, intuitive, and detail-oriented; additionally, percussion section leaders may be more effective if well liked by peers.
- *Plan speeches with percussionists in mind.* Schedule your longer monologues to allow time for percussionists to complete the changes required for the next piece; especially in concerts, this practice keeps the audience engaged during a time-consuming process.
- *Elevate the small instruments.* A portion of an audience's excitement about the percussion section relies on *visual* perceptions. Even when instruments can be heard, raising the triangle, maracas, cabasa, claves, and other small instruments helps listeners enjoy the parts because they can (or *think* they can) hear them better. Elevating the instruments also improves players' posture, view of the conductor, careful play-position, and more.
- *Watch out for acoustic anomalies.* You may have reduced the volume of snare, bells, triangle, tambourine, and cymbal crashes during rehearsals because their high frequencies sounded loud in the band room. But from the back of the auditorium stage, many things can be different. Be vigilant with listening, and flexible with the adjustments, which might include changes to volume, student locations, positioning of curtains/reflectors, or substitutions of instruments and beaters.
- *Visit the percussion section*:
  - In rehearsals, consider leaving an aisle through the seating plan so you can reach the percussionists whenever needed.
  - In concerts (especially for off-site adjudications), visit percussionists after the first selection to quietly discuss the need for changes; players may need to know "The bass drum is too boomy; muffle it more," "We can't hear the snare clearly on this stage," or "We lose the timpani articulations in this space."

- *Help timpani students with markings.* Even when a timpani part seems uncomplicated, a student may appreciate assistance with tuning or special sticking techniques. Put a notation (symbol or text) on the part indicating which drum to tune, and when; write in sticking patterns when cross-sticking or double-strokes are required.
- *Hold a dress rehearsal specifically for percussion.* This could be a short walk/talk session taking only a few moments, but supports percussionists as they consider, "Can you make it from here to there in time?" "Did all instruments make it to the stage, and are they in the right spot for the first piece?" "Can you see well enough?" (sometimes the stage setup offers new obstructions, or insufficient lighting). A dry run can yield success at the right time.
- *Think of "Plan B."* More than in any other section, a missing percussionist or instrument can have serious consequences; have a plan in advance.
- *Demonstrate skills for students*—but *only* when you can provide an example that is correct and musical; otherwise, choose alternate teaching techniques to convey the message.
- *Remember to view the parts!* If this step is skipped in the part-assignment process, you might not be aware of grave difficulties. For example, Symphonic Dance No. 3: "Fiesta" (Williams) puts all percussion on a single score-style part but, after the first page, the instruments are not labeled. Be aware of the special circumstances that arise in percussion more often than in any other section. Add clarifying markings as needed.
- *Salesmanship in a demonstration tops the lecture approach.* For example, the desired claves sound requires a special grip. We can give a detailed explanation, or we can show a fun demo to students—"I'm using the same grip you just used; how do you like this sound?" Then, turn your back to the student, concealing the corrected grip while you model the characteristic sound. The student will immediately be more interested in learning the correct grip!
- *A worst-case scenario anecdote.* This is just one of many possible disasters, but you're urged to read and remember this carefully. The director selects music with percussionists in mind, and works carefully, giving each student a rounded slate of assignments. Rotations and doublings offer opportunities to every student. But as the concert approaches, two of the pieces really need more practice in the wind sections, so the director decides to postpone those works. Then, the "cut" collides with the director's choice *not* to double percussion assignments. An angry parent reveals the surprise: "I bought my son his concert clothing. I switched my shift at work to be here. I drove through traffic, and I just sat through the entire concert, only to notice that my kid never played a single note!" Be extremely thoughtful with planning and with all choices; "cuts" and other changes can have big consequences to the percussion section.

Final Words About Extra Obligations of the "Non-percussionist" Director

It must be stated: we become better ensemble directors when we improve our personal percussion skills and understanding. A significant number of first-year band directors have never played percussion in an ensemble, nor have they reached performance-level skill on anything more than the basics required by their only semester of collegiate study.

- We'll be more respected by our percussion students *if we have experience from their perspective*: spend some time playing percussion in a community band, during summer graduate study, or even in your own band while someone else conducts.
- A related thought: require every Student Teacher to play in your percussion section when not conducting.

Until we have experience from within a percussion section—or, more importantly, until we have *the vocabulary to instruct students correctly* in the wide variety of percussion techniques—our effectiveness as ensemble directors may be compromised. Therefore, it is strongly recommended to continuously seek answers, education, and experiences.

- Ask for guidance from local colleagues. Be willing to "barter" your way to excellence: trade your expertise with that of a percussion-major friend.
- When you accompany students to an honor-band festival, or when you observe a rehearsal, spend time behind percussionists. View the roles from their perspective, carefully noting how they play, how they manage equipment and, just as importantly, what they do when they're not playing.
- Listen to a good recording while watching the percussion parts, with the goal of hearing what the printed notation should sound like. Then work to develop those skills, and devise strategies to teach them to students.

While this chapter merely scratches the surface of directors' needs, we'll finish by listing a few voids common among non-percussionists. The following can be adapted as a checklist if preferred, but *add to it* as soon as you encounter a new unknown (there will be plenty of those!).

We need to know . . .

. . . how to get the most appropriate sound from snare drum rolls.

- Understand the difference between *rudimental* and *orchestral* rolls, and the application for each type at various tempi.
- Learn how and when to *end* rolls, especially to separate adjacent, untied rolls.

. . . how to listen to and evaluate a student's performance while following the music notation, just as easily with percussion as with woodwind and brass performance. Seasoned percussionists might be surprised to know how many non-percussionists simply get "lost" in the notation, particularly with advanced snare drum music.

. . . grips appropriate to all instruments (e.g. how timpani differs from snare; various three- and four-mallet grips for mallet instruments).

. . . how tone and response for each instrument is affected by:

- the choice of stick/mallet
- the placement of the stroke (where is the "playing area" for each desired effect?)
- various methods of playing (e.g. a "dry" staccato sound from tambourine), and
- the condition of the instrument.

. . . how to *calculate* stickings:

- Does the mallet excerpt require *all* L–R alternation, or some double strokes (LL, RR), and where?
- Should the snare drum figure be played with all separate strokes, or are some passages better with double-strokes or rudimental stickings instead?
- When should the player use crossover stickings in timpani passages?

. . . the mechanical aspects of percussion, including:

- changing and adjusting heads
- regulating tension of snares and snare drumheads for tone and response
- securely adjusting percussion stands for angle and height
- gripping crash cymbals, claves, triangle, tambourines, etc.
- tuning timpani, setting timpani heads to the best "primary" pitch for each size drum, and calibrating the tuning gauges
- tying triangle loops and crash cymbal straps
- emergency repairs.

. . . about various parts and accessories (e.g. sleeves and felts for cymbals; internal/external mufflers; mounting hardware for auxiliary instruments).

. . . about harnesses, carriers and stands of all kinds for marching percussion.

... playing techniques and "grooves" for drumset as well as congas, bongos, timbales, and other Latin percussion instruments.

... and this is only the *short list!*

As with all other musical skills and technical achievements, the best approach is simply to keep working at it systematically, with patience. By providing an organized approach to percussion as a *section* and to percussionists individually, you'll reap benefits in many facets of your program, and you'll have fun with the experience.

Notes

1 Gary Cook, *Teaching Percussion* (New York: Schirmer Books, 1988), 48.
2 James Doyle, *The PAS Educators' Companion, Volume 2*, The Percussion Arts Society, https://www.pas.org/docs/default-source/default-document-library/pas-ed-companion---volume-2-full.pdf?sfvrsn=6&sfvrsn=6.
3 Doyle, *The PAS Educators' Companion.*

8

IN THE REHEARSAL

Section 1: From the Podium

Introduction

The large group Rehearsal is probably the most efficient setting to educate students and build the total program. Almost everything we teach in smaller settings can also be included in the full rehearsal. There, we communicate expectations, establish discipline, and motivate students en masse. Each director's behavior demonstrates a unique mixture of seriousness and humor; strictness and tolerance; urgency and patience; expectation and acceptance; knowledge and curiosity. Whether intentionally or not, the director's teaching strategies will influence students as they formulate character traits and practice teamwork processes, all of which can ultimately define how they'll function in society. One of the controllable factors in this influence is feedback, so it's logical to begin with an overview of the director's verbal and nonverbal communication.

Regarding the Director's Feedback

This entire chapter will be supported by one basic precept: *positivity works*. Positive feedback, if chosen wisely and used selectively, can enhance the effectiveness of any rehearsal strategy about to be discussed. The most effective feedback will be . . .

- . . . *specific.* The best guidance includes specificity. A detailed description of a success serves as both a compliment, and as motivation for continued improvement. For example: "Yes! Trombones remembered 4th position for the D in that passage; it sounded *so* much more fluent this time!" Ambiguity (like, "good job!") might provide a brief feel-good moment but cannot show explicitly how to meet goals.
- . . . *sincere.* Praise is a proven motivator if sincere and not overused. *Insincere* compliments—like frequent flattery—can have negative effects over time. Sincere praise should be given when it is deserved; teachers are advised to seize those opportunities. Correspondingly, honest criticism can still be encouraging if the requisite comments are delivered with optimism and careful language. Teachers should be very selective with words, phrases, inflections, and facial expressions.
- . . . *ongoing.* Progress occurs, by definition, through a series of successes. Once feedback is given to identify it, each success helps motivate students toward new, additional successes. Beyond feedback from the director, of course, students are also influenced by self-evaluation, comments by adjudicators and peers, sincere applause, and even the most subtle of facial expressions. All feedback will prove more meaningful than test results and performance "scores."
- . . . *focused on the task.* The comment should emphasize the task, the process, and even the succession of efforts, while also leading the students further forward toward other advancements. Work for comments that foster a mindset of efforts toward systematic growth. For example: "The flute section's tone and accuracy in the high-register passage was so much better today; whatever you're doing in your personal practice, keep it up because the results are showing! OK, this time let's try for a longer phrase with even more artistic inflections." A basic talent-based comment ("Wow,

you're really good at the high register!") can hinder improvement because students feel a sense of final accomplishment rather than growth.

... designed to highlight the process rather than the result. Our efforts should motivate students to consistently use their own best strategies, rather than just offering comments like, "You came in first place" or "You earned a superior rating."

It is clear, however, that good teaching also requires very frequent critical commentary, which is unlikely to be perceived by students as "positive." The most effective teachers admirably demonstrate an ability to deliver uncomplimentary feedback that remains motivational. Their wording is succinct, articulate, and relevant. It specifically targets errors and issues in terms of how they affect the musical goals, but the language is carefully selected to inspire, and never to defeat or offend.

A template for motivational feedback:

1. The compliment—"Good job! I heard obvious progress since our last rehearsal..."
2. A motivational clause—"... but if we really want to improve even more ..."
3. The specific "next-step" instruction—"... we'll need to work at shaping this phrase beautifully. Now that we've got it technically correct, let's work to give our audience a 'goosebumps' moment. So, try this ..."

In the hands of a master teacher, "feedback" and "detailed, goal-oriented music instruction" can be one and the same. The success lies largely in the communication. Here's a lighthearted listing of the ingredients in a recipe for "band director effectiveness":

> One-third of your effectiveness comes from your knowledge of the literature (band music, composers, time-periods and styles, solos, method books, exercises, and other resources).
>
> Another third comes from your knowledge of the instruments (techniques, inherent problems, special fingerings for special purposes, intonation characteristics, mouthpieces/mallets/equipment).
>
> But *the final 95%* is based on your delivery as the teacher (your communication skills, your humor, your actions and reactions, your engagement of each student, your motivational strategies and so much more—in short, what makes you "you" in the eyes of the students).

Section 2: More on the Rehearsal Environment

Even as students enter, much of the director's philosophy is already evident through predetermined components of the band program (e.g. policies, room readiness, displays, management style). Although perhaps self-explanatory, here are just some of the pre-rehearsal considerations, with special tips for each:

- *The displayed rehearsal plan* is imperative to students' readiness, especially for percussionists. TIP: Post the details as early as possible to encourage self-motivated students to practice vital passages.
- *The set-up*—chairs, stands, lighting, and equipment should be planned and fully prepared before students arrive. TIPS:
    - Offer incentives to volunteers to serve as stage crew members. A trained team can prepare the space daily, and can streamline the setup and striking of concerts.
    - Consider including aisles to allow quick travel from the podium to any section.
    - Post a diagram of your setup, with a note to encourage re-setting by custodians or visitors sharing the space.
    - *Instrumental Music Education* (Feldman and Contzius, chapter 11) offers an excellent and thorough instructional guide.
- *Leaders' roles should be* chosen wisely, clearly defined, and trained beforehand. [RW8.1] is an editable sample listing of band officer positions. TIP: Each student leader should have specific responsibilities, many of which can be employed as the band enters the rehearsal.

IN THE REHEARSAL

- *All other needs* (e.g. tuners, supplements, handouts, reeds, supplies) should be planned for efficiency. TIP: Murphy's Law brings a malfunctioning instrument to you just moments before the downbeat. Have a plan.

Entering the Rehearsal

The flow of traffic can promote, or hinder, efficiency in a rehearsal. Even some elements that are ostensibly insignificant may provide time-management benefits when systematically designed. While this is not a suggestion to micromanage, a strategic approach to the following room-related components can encourage productivity:

- *The director* chooses all aspects of his/her own role. Reflect appropriately about where to stand, how to greet band members, and your routines prior to the downbeat. These choices highlight your personal style, and surely help to define your students' experience. TIP: Delegate specific pre-rehearsal roles to student leaders; their help saves the director's time for meaningful tasks.
- *Music folders* deserve thorough attention. An organized plan can expedite students' readiness. TIPS:
    - To further accelerate readiness, one student in each section can care for that section's folders.
    - Plan the folders' contents: besides the compositions, determine whether folders should include extra resources (e.g. warm-up or technique books, fingering charts and rudiments lists, chorales, tuning guides).
    - Periodically inspect folders; confirm that contents are complete, and look for unnecessary "stuff" that leads to disorganization or even damage.
    - Insisting that folders are returned to organized storage gives the director quick access for distributions, collections, inspections, and other changes. However . . .
    - Have a plan in place for students to take folders home for practice!
- *Lockers and all other equipment storage* should again be designed with a prudent eye toward efficiency. TIPS:
    - If lockers are grouped according to instrument Sections, are they physically aligned to the seating plan? Avoid clogging traffic by minimizing the need for students to cross others' paths.
    - For lockable storage compartments, you may need to regulate the locks; use school-provided locks or collect combinations from all students.
    - When storage is not lockable, seek a design for security.
    - Labeling is important. Mom: "I'm here to pick up my daughter's trumpet." The director should know exactly where to find it.
- *Cases* can cause disorder or, worse, can become a hazard; provide guidance for management during rehearsals (e.g. leave large cases in lockers; store smaller cases under chairs during the rehearsal). TIPS:
    - Cases should be labeled, both for inventory of school-owned equipment and for protection of personal belongings.
    - Above all, ensure that your case-management (like all other physical aspects of the room) conforms to the school's safety procedures.
- *Extra equipment* (reeds, oils, mutes, etc.) can be managed to an extent by trained leaders. Avoid excessive disruptions by carefully delegating tasks to officers.

Minimizing Time Lost to Management Procedures

With your group's trusted leaders in trained roles, much of the daily procedural routine can be delegated to students. Other tasks can be automated. All choices lead to the same goal: an engaging rehearsal that maximizes the time-on-task.

- *Handouts* can be streamlined with orderly distribution plans: add materials to folders or place on music stands before students arrive; stack materials at the entry door, or ask section leaders to distribute.
- *Attendance* is an obligation, and your plan should be matched to your circumstances. In many cases, the task can be managed by a single student or even section leaders. Of course, the director should always double-check the results before submitting the official report.
- *Rehearsal announcements* often reach closed ears if delivered in a mundane way. Plan announcements for maximum results in minimum time. Methods can include, at least, a handout, a poster or other visual display, a student reader, or digital methods. Important announcements must be stressed and probably repeated; consider Remind.com or other digital contact delivery for imperative information. TIP: Load announcements, the rehearsal order and other information into a rotating slideshow.
- *Collections*, except for money and personal information, can be automated. Try a labeled box, bin, or envelope in a specific location; a shelf; a wall-mounted office tray; a dedicated lockable box (especially good when attached or otherwise fixed in place). TIP: Students can be easily trained to use an inexpensive indexed office sorter to turn in forms that must be tabulated/alphabetized anyway. Note: Any collection of money (specifically) or other sensitive information will require a careful plan, perhaps involving multiple adults and an extra layer of security.
- *Other tasks*, well, there will always be more! In short, a thoughtful "routine" can streamline the start-up process for improved efficiency. By delegating specific parts of the routine to trusted leaders, the teacher can greet students, finish obligations, listen and observe, and still be available for emergency repairs. Meanwhile, student leaders often enjoy the enhanced responsibilities.
- And by the way, if you're reading this thinking, "When are we going to get to the rehearsal stuff?" then you know what your students feel when "things" get in the way of the music-making!

Important notes: we can understand more about the power of our bandroom environment by examining some key quotes from Harry K. and Rosemary T. Wong:

> A well-managed classroom is a task-oriented and predictable environment.[1]

> Half of what you will accomplish in a day will be determined before you leave home. Three quarters of what you achieve will be determined before you enter the classroom door.[2]

> The most successful classes are those where the teacher has a clear idea of what is expected from the students and the students know what the teacher expects from them.[3]

> The number one problem in the classroom is not discipline; it is the lack of procedures and routines.[4]

Caveat: "routine" is a concept that, if mismanaged, *could* begin a death-spiral for the band program. Keep the bandroom fresh and motivating.

Section 3: General Rehearsal Methods—The Big Picture

In their early work, inexperienced conductors tend to lead students through long sections—perhaps the entire piece—and then provide simple feedback, sometimes as little as "that was pretty good; let's do it again." With experience, conductors soon realize that a more effective rehearsal requires diagnosing faults, and providing activities to improve the performance. By adding the "diagnosis-repair" segment, the basic play-through session becomes what is commonly termed a "Macro–Micro–Macro" rehearsal method. Feldman and Contzius's *Instrumental Music Education* offers an excellent description, relating the conductor's approach to that of an auto mechanic, who listens to the car to diagnose problems, then makes the repair/replacement procedure, and finishes by re-evaluating the car's performance.[5] The authors continue with excellent models demonstrating how the technique may manifest in an actual rehearsal (see "Zoom-in" examples, Feldman and Contzius, pp. 192–194).

But of course, we discover this same basic approach manifested in countless other professions, where the following processes are applied:

1. Evaluate
2. Diagnose
3. Prescribe (and after allowing time for the prescription to yield results) . . .
4. Follow-up/Re-evaluate (which often indicates a different prescription)

Return to #1 and the process begins again.

The sequence is largely the same for medical doctors, athletic trainers, and of course for band directors. We design our "prescriptions" guided in part by what we already know about our students: their aptitude, previous achievements, attention span, additional musical activities, age/experience, home support, and more. Occasionally, other professions utilize special tools, technology, or tests to dig deeper into the needs of the "patient." And whereas a doctor continues to learn about the effectiveness and side-effects of various therapies, over time the band director accumulates a greater collection of strategies for the "Micro" portion of the process—more tools for the tool chest. Before exploring specific strategies, the following is a brief "big-picture" overview.

"Big Picture" Rehearsal Methods

- *Beginning-to-end play-through.* Self-explanatory, this method is more prevalent at opposite ends of the preparing a piece. Choose a play-through in the early days for basic learning, and just prior to a performance to build comfort while refining the artistic components. Then, with the "middle" sessions mostly dedicated to isolating problems (over either a few days or many weeks), the long-term rehearsal arc also displays a macro–micro–macro scheme. TIP: Use play-through performances frequently to simulate a concert, intensify students' attention, and build endurance.
- *Start–stop.* When we hear an error (especially a bad one!), it feels natural to stop immediately. Perhaps the most prevalent method, especially among younger directors, this "stop–repair–restart, stop–repair–restart" process can be very efficient for solving problems. But such a fragmented approach can also undermine the desired fluency of a full-length performance. TIPS:
    - Alternate the start–stop method regularly with longer periods of uninterrupted playing. Continuous play helps to sculpt the cohesive performance, but it can also enhance students' behavior and enjoyment: sometimes students *just need to play*. Therefore, we should resist trying to fix "everything."
    - When resuming an excerpt after a pitstop, consider starting a few measures early, and continue beyond the end of the target excerpt. While we may "lose" a few seconds, we also enhance students' understanding of the passage in context, and we strengthen the transitions (common problem-areas for younger groups).
- *Isolation.* Of course, a large part of the teacher's job is to repair errors, and that generally includes isolating the sections or individuals needing help. Then, we apply specific teaching strategies to the isolated sections. TIPS:
    - By isolating the band's specific needs, we can use short focused segments in almost any rehearsal; just a few moments spent on "hit and run" goals can be very helpful.
    - Caveat: too much time allotted to isolation carries risks (students feeling singled out; peers sitting idle).
- *Thick-to-thin funneling.* This approach also isolates problems, but more gradually; each attempt removes another leg from a support system. With a target in mind, lead the full band several times through a passage. Build confidence with the large group, and then use "subtraction" to reach the objective:
    - "Let's hear the brass section at Letter L."
    - "Now, upper brass alone—just trumpets and horns."
    - "Good. Could we please hear just trumpets? Let's play measures 73–88."
    - "OK, we should check the rhythm in measure 87 with 2nd trumpets."

You've moved from the full band, to a family, to a section, and finally to a small group or even individuals. After each pass, design your remarks thoughtfully to fortify the desired performance characteristics; each subsequent group molds its attempts on the feedback given to the previous. TIP: This method uses group-security to help students feel more comfortable playing alone, if even just for short passages. Meanwhile, besides simply isolating problems, we keep more students engaged for a longer time.

- *End-to-beginning overlap.* In this method, we rehearse the end of a piece first. Choose a section near the end (the Coda, the final rehearsal letter, or the entire recapitulation) as the first step toward learning the full composition. As soon as that section is comfortable, back up; add an earlier excerpt—even just a few transitional measures—and let it connect into the material students have already learned. For example: rehearse "Letter U to the End" first and, when ready, back up to start "8 measures before U," and then back to begin at "Letter T" and so on. The end-to-beginning method offers early strength at the end of a piece, which is what audiences hear last! TIP: Class disruptions are inevitable and rehearsal time is of the essence; use this strategy to help avert an uncomfortable "crash" at the end of the performance.
- *Metronomic steps.* Widely used by soloists, this method follows a sequence of benchmarks based on tempo. For example, work at MM=80, then 92, 104, 116, and continue throughout an established time-period. TIPS:
    - Plan to arrive at the performance tempo as early as possible.
    - At each tempo marking, make thoughtful observations about students' needs, leading to realistic choices about follow-up work.
    - Consider practicing at a *faster* tempo than needed.
- *Sight reading.* True "sight-reading" happens only once for each passage. But the process used during sight-reading with the full band is a concentrated method we can employ in other ways. In a typical adjudicated sight-reading, there are timed study periods preceding the non-stop reading. Some festivals have a silent-study period (players and the conductor separately) followed by a non-playing instructional period where "anything goes" (e.g. clapping, singing, Q&A, students teaching others). Others have a general explanation period followed by a summary explanation period. The important element is that the teaching happens at a compressed rate; your words, signals and activities are chosen for efficiency. TIPS:
    - Search online for U.I.L. Sight-Reading Rules. Study the instructions and direct your band through the process. For best benefits, record the session for your own later review.
    - Apply the *pace* of these efficient processes to other portions of the rehearsal, even several weeks into the learning process.
    - Author Shelley Jagow names a "Blitzkrieg Rehearsal" method and recommends employing it for two to four minutes each time it is chosen. "The pacing of instruction quickens, the performance standard becomes more critical, and the general energy of the rehearsal intensifies."[6]
- *Alternative rehearsal methods.* There are many other general techniques, of course, and some are self-evident, including *clapping* (and other movement-based activities); *listening* activities; *talk-through* performances (which may include silent-play movements, "air-play," "finger-play"); and *no-conductor* performances. These approaches can be used almost anytime, without special changes.

Other extremely effective methods may involve additional planning or even a physical change to the set-up:

- *Sectionals*—If used during the class/rehearsal period, extra rooms will likely be needed. TIP: See [RW8.2] to download a sectionals structure that can be run effectively by students themselves.
- *Pods or other sub-groups*—this plan requires advance work to establish small-group seating throughout the space. The director designs a seating plan according to parts (e.g. 2nd clarinets), SATB mixed groups, predetermined chamber groups, or something else. As the students play, they

work together in new ways and hear from an altered perspective. Importantly, the performance can be counted off, conducted, or student-led; all options allow the director to circulate for effective, close-up observations.
- *Alternative seating plans*—some, detailed in Section 4, can be managed within the rehearsal period without changing the room. Other plans will require some setup (e.g., reverse rows; in-the-round; rotating parts).

So what happens next? Your bandroom environment, processes, and logistical details are designed carefully. With careful reflection about your students' needs, you've chosen your repertoire wisely. And through score study, you've found the excerpts where you believe players will experience greater difficulty; these discoveries offer guidance toward potential rehearsal needs. Additionally, after developing an aural concept of each piece, you have a basis for the interpretive portions of the teaching. You have a set of traditional and alternative rehearsal approaches in mind.

But where do you go from there? How will you proceed in rehearsals after the initial reading? What processes, strategies, and activities will be the most effective in the arc leading toward a masterful, artistic performance? The answers become more obvious through experience, but can be kick-started by adapting suggestions like those presented in the following section.

Section 4: Rehearsal Strategies

As the next section offers a collection of rehearsal strategies, readers should consider an important point: Any process encountered in Chapter 8—along with what you already use or will develop in your future—might be of secondary importance compared to the personality with which you deliver it. The author maintains that the "what" is often not as important as the "how." That philosophy becomes more obvious in Chapter 9. Note: rehearsal strategies associated with specific topics (e.g. rhythm, intonation) are found in those chapters.

Part 1: Student-Centered Learning

A word on the student-centered approach: it is beyond the intent of this book to deeply explore historical movements and educational theories. Here, we'll just note that the basic principles of student-centered learning align with the author's original purpose.

Just as we want students to be engaged in learning that is self-motivated, cooperative, personalized, and competency-based, we also hope to enjoy our own teaching while using creative approaches to meet each student's needs. And, for both the director and for the students, there is a goal of becoming a lifelong inquisitive learner, always looking forward to the next achievement. We should never stop learning. Another purpose of this chapter, therefore, is only to inspire your search for additional teaching strategies.

Student-centered "Independence" Strategies

To be an excellent contributing member of any group, each student has a responsibility both to himself and to all others in the room. And the best pathway to meet both personal and group obligations is through *independence.* Although learning independently is a lofty goal, it is probably the single most important long-term objective in education. Meeting that objective requires teachers to gently expect students to manage their own counting, rhythmic entrances, mastery of skills, and all other components of music group membership. Our work should lead toward the last part of the "I do ⇨ We do ⇨ You do" model: demonstrated independence.

The amount of conducting you provide has a strong effect on the development of independence. Here are some general conducting/directing suggestions all designed to leave most of the responsibility on the student:

- Conducting *less*—instruct students simply to "keep playing" while you stop conducting, walk away, observe/listen, then return and resume. Wean students from reliance on the conductor. Your feedback, however, remains important.

- Conducting *without cueing*—provide the basic patterns including style, dynamics, and other musical elements, but expect students to manage their own rhythmic entrances.
- Conducting *only* the expressive components—convey *musical* elements through dancing, miming, facial expressions, and other physical methods, but without providing the metric pattern.
- *No conducting at all*—certainly, expressive meanings can be conveyed without any standard conducting gestures at all! Some excellent models include the following:
  - *Silent rehearsal*—direct students with any silent method such as hand signals, a marker on a whiteboard, body movements, or any other nonverbal means. Think of this like charades (*Pictionary, Guesstures, Catch Phrase, Hoopla*, etc.), where the "conductor" will provide clues, and the band responds.
  - *Modeling*—play or *sing* (especially) a demonstration of the desired musical objectives; go far beyond notes and rhythms, instead using your modeling to convey the emotional content of the passage. The most effective conductors do not just "conduct," just as the finest teachers do not rely solely on "lecture." Singing can provide everything required for students to absorb the artistic aspects of performance.
  - *Emotional connections*—use stories, analogies, and super-charged adjectives and adverbs to shape the band's next attempt at a passage they've just played. You might also refer to a scene from a film, a description of a sporting contest, or an emotion drawn from experiences you know are shared by most students at the age-level of your band's members. Or, display another type of artwork, asking the students to "Look at this, and then play the music with the feelings you get." With forethought, you can pre-plan these moments days or weeks in advance. Author Shelley Jagow offers an excellent description of the Analogy Rehearsal.[7] This is an especially beautiful way to help students reach beyond technique to find the artistry and emotion (for more ideas, refer to Chapter 9).

Additionally, other types of rehearsal activities work strategically to foster independence:

- *"Structured chaos"*—give students a brief but specific time-period to practice, either alone or with stand partners; "Anything you need to review before we play the passage together. It will be noisy, but please use the time to improve your own personal playing. Work out the problems. You'll have exactly sixty seconds; go!"
- *Metronomic increments*—this specific plan is designed to assist students' independence, while building self-awareness of limitations, without danger of embarrassment: "We'll play this passage several times, moving gradually faster toward the final performance tempo. I'll tell you the metronome markings each time, and you should notice the speed at which you start to make errors." Offer support in small-group lessons, reminding students about other helpful techniques including partial passages (dropping some notes), sharing the passage (e.g. juggling half-measure portions with the stand partner), revising the passage to accommodate a missing skill, or in some cases playing "tacet" for a short time.
- *A "help sheet" for ensemble musicians*—posted as [RW8.3], this blank document provides a template for students to create a study guide for a specific composition; they'll list vocabulary, find technical challenges, create skill-goals and develop a personalized plan for improving their own performance.

Tips to Help Support Students' Awareness as Band Musicians

With experience and maturity, the student performer will develop an increased self-awareness in musical and technical terms. But the same student will also become more cognitive of his/her relationship to the rest of the ensemble. Here is an overview of what we already do in typical band rehearsals, and how each common activity supports the student's development.

These common activities in band rehearsals are influential toward . . .

. . . knowing one's *fit*—we provide balance/blend exercises, with emphasis on listening (to immediate neighbors; to the section; to principal players; across the band).

... knowing one's *role*—throughout rehearsal activities, we give labels to various functions: a solo/soli; a melody/countermelody; rhythmic accompaniment; harmonic underpinning; motives/answers; basslines, and more.

... knowing one's *strengths and limitations*—the guidance and feedback given during isolated rehearsal moments will accumulate to help build the students' self-concept. Caveat: be thoughtful about individuals, especially when comparing them to others. While too many criticisms without kudos can be defeating, nonetheless directors have the power to comment on a student's performance "this week" in contrast to "last week". Growth-comparisons can be very motivating for students' perception of their abilities.

... knowing about *others*—among the most exhilarating aspects of band membership is the musician's interaction with others in the group. Moreover, because ensemble-playing offers unique elements not available in solo performance, it is incumbent on the director to highlight those group interactions throughout the rehearsals. Examples include:

- After singing a demonstration, ask students to "Please play if you have that part."
- Alternatively: "Let's hear that beautiful 2nd Clarinet line at measure 25," followed by "Now let's hear everyone who has that line."
- An approach requiring musical reasoning: "Can we hear the melody at measure 78? Ah, that's right—it's the saxophones and horns. But I wonder who has the countermelody there. Please play if you think you have the countermelody."
- And to develop a cohesive interpretation within the ensemble: "Listen to the trumpets at measure 96 . . . if you have that same line at measure 104, it's up to you to match the articulations, dynamics, and phrasing that the trumpets just demonstrated."

Activities of this kind will keep students attentive, while engaging their listening skills and rehearsal awareness. When not playing, the students should be listening.

- *"Listen like a Judge."* Whether all students listen to a recording of the band, or several representatives rotate out to the audience role, the task may be described as such: "Listen like a Judge would listen, with critical ears. I'm *definitely* going to ask you to provide suggestions, so if you don't think you can do that, raise your hand and say 'pass,' and we'll give it to someone else. When you come back, have at least *one* helpful suggestion to offer: a) to the whole band, b) to me, as the conductor, and c) to your own section."
- *Play from a score.* Ask students to play their parts by reading from a score, which could be displayed on a SmartBoard, chromebooks, or other devices. Encourage students to notice how their parts relate to others. TIP: Choose your own *marked* score to highlight the conductor's work.
- *Combine skills* for a multi-layer experience. For example:
  - Each student claps the rhythm while singing a passage.
  - One stand partner sings while the other plays.
  - Hum/sing while fingering the parts.

Three Strategies for Starting a New Piece

- *The first reading* of a piece provides a perfect opportunity to practice the "sight-reading adjudication" process. One model is described here:
  - Distribute the parts (perhaps face-down on the music stand as students arrive, with notation hidden); when students are ready, give a verbal introduction to the task.
  - Apply timed prep sessions, allotting five minutes to each segment. First, a study period for the conductor and students (the conductor with the score, and students alone, or cooperatively sharing ideas); you may choose to point out main features like the tempo, the key signature, and the transitional elements. The second session features concentrated, fast-paced work together, which can include singing, clapping, fingering, and all other non-playing methodology; the director's comments should be concisely worded.

IN THE REHEARSAL

- o Perform the piece, without stops if possible. Alternatively, you might pre-select a portion of the piece, leaving other excerpts for later usages of this strategy.
- o Record the effort and scrutinize the playback together. TIP: Ask students to finger along, silently accompanying the playback of their first attempt. This step often allows students to recognize errors independently.
- *Apply the "structured chaos" approach* to the new piece, rather than first playing it together. Give a specified time-period (2–4 minutes) with brief instructions. Then, allow students to explore it with stand partners or even with section leaders and full sections. Students may look it over, search for "fun" parts, discuss and ask questions, and clap or play passages. The next step is also flexible: play it with the full ensemble or choose to put it away after this browsing period, allowing it to "simmer" before playing it together.
- *Use students' input to chart the course.* Provide an organizer or study guide with which students can evaluate the new piece compared with their own skill level; [RW8.4] offers an editable sample. A portion of the assignment is to "identify difficult areas . . . put rehearsal letters (formal sections) in an order by difficulty, with the most challenging passages first on your list." That self-study helps students to recognize their own personal practice needs. But, for the conductor, the students' observations will guide your rehearsal plans to address the challenging areas first. We don't always have to begin at the beginning.

Part 2: The Director's Style, Delivery, and Choices

Communication and the Director's Delivery Style:

Think for one moment, imagining "The most effective, inspirational and magnetic conductor I've ever observed."

Almost surely, your choice is in large part due to an obvious mastery of communication. All words, gestures, and expressions are impeccably chosen, and the result is complete engagement of the students. Much of the finesse seems instinctive—almost magical—for these gifted individuals.

But other aspects of the director's delivery are more tangible, and can be enriched through a careful strategic approach. Here, we'll look mostly at the clarity and specificity of the instructions, leaving discussions about *artistry* for Chapter 9.

- *A basic overview.* Instructions are best delivered fluently, with words chosen to match the players' age, interests, and level of understanding. Further, spoken directions should be clear and articulate, and loud enough to be heard by the most distant students. Experienced directors seem to temper their instructions away from the authoritarian perspective of "I need" and, instead, they sculpt their instructions based on the requirements of . . .

    . . . the music: "It seems that the musical phrase is only half-done, so let's not breathe there."
    . . . the composer: "Holst was clear with those accents; let's play more marcato there."
    . . . the listeners: "The audience won't be moved if we rush that passage; be patient."
    . . . the full ensemble: "We're going to need a lighter style in that passage."

    Simple instructions are also very effective, of course: "Breathe together on Beat 1."
- *Talk less(!) and show more.* With great thanks to Philip C. Chevallard, Ret USAF, ensemble players can respond very well when the feedback is limited to "six words: slower, faster, shorter, longer, softer, and louder."[8] In many cases, those simple instructions can deliver the essence of the message.
- *Communicate instructions efficiently.*
    - o *The location*—guide students from the first words spoken. Avoid confusion, hidden details, and extra words: "We'll start—hmm, let's see, how many measures, um, 1-2-3-4-5 measures before . . .". Students cannot act until hearing a specific landmark. Instead, start with the landmark and choose wording wisely. It becomes, "Find Letter G. Count with me before

G, 1–2–3–4–5 measures before G. Let's hear all clarinets and bass clarinet starting at the fifth measure before G." TIP: By leaving the *who* instruction until last, you've maintained the attention of the entire band, and the non-playing students will arrive at the same location for listening and other activities.
- *The player(s)*—be specific, whether referring to a large group of "all woodwinds" or a selection of "Clarinets 2 and 3, and bass clarinet." TIP: Keep more students engaged by adding a forward-looking instruction, like "Everyone finger along please. We'll get to your section in just a moment, so stay ready."
- *The objective(s)*—tell the students exactly what to do, with specific instructions about musical elements. For example: "Accent the syncopation, and let's put more space around all notes. For now, please play it a little louder than written." That's enough of a goal (*"What do I want students to do?"*) to allow your feedback. They'll play it and, based on your listening (*"How will I know if they can do it?"*), you'll be able to follow up with your next step (*"What is my response?"*). TIP: These moments might provide the best measure of your effectiveness as a teacher—can you convey instructions efficiently, and give relevant, motivational feedback? Most importantly, are you able to move the band's skills and artistry constantly along a path toward improvement?

- *"Before, after, and during"*—*before* the band plays, we provide instructions and a statement of the objective. *After* the passage, we provide feedback that is accurate, honest, and encouraging. But we can also influence the performance with feedback *during the passage*: in some instances, it is most efficient to convey ideas *without stopping*. For example: turning toward the flutes, "Whoops, we agreed not to breathe there." TIP: Avoid excessive talking during the playing. Although comments can help in small doses, some students will be distracted, and others may be unable to hear you. Rely more on gestures, facial expressions, and signals.
- *On pacing*—students' attentiveness is largely a product of the rehearsal pacing. But good pacing is also dependent on the director's real-time awareness, and the intuitive recognition of when a new activity is needed. There are too many unpredictable variables to establish a concrete plan that will always work. TIPS:
  - In general terms, the macro–micro–macro approach is both reliable and flexible, starting and ending the session with full-group activities, with detailed work between.
  - Try to build enthusiasm for the next rehearsal by ending with something successful, that is also well liked by students.
  - Including the standard parts of the session (attendance, warm-up, tuning, announcements), plan activities to allow variety in the experience. Each activity should be designed for its relevance toward meeting a specific objective.
  - After each rehearsal, make reflective notes that include your evaluation of how the group responded to your pacing; use those observations to guide follow-up planning.

Successful rehearsals require thoughtful planning, and the most effective rehearsals offer pacing that keeps all players engaged. On the other hand, pacing might not be an issue at all if the rehearsal is planned and executed carefully, based on clear goals.

Rehearsal Strategies Based on the Director's Delivery

- *Leave the podium*—sometimes the quickest way to meet an objective does *not* involve conducting. Leaving the podium allows you to . . .
  - . . . observe, listen, and make notes, unimpeded by conducting gestures or score-reading. Each new location also provides a unique listening perspective.
  - . . . promote independence by the ensemble and its members.
  - . . . encourage refinement of students' awareness and listening; simply removing the conductor requires players to listen more than watch.
  - . . . use alternative physical or facial expressions to convey interpretive ideas.

IN THE REHEARSAL

- . . . adjust music stands, instrument positioning, visual obstructions and the like.
- . . . visit or join a section.
- . . . offer specific assistance to students.
- . . . demonstrate percussion techniques.
- . . . check students' markings.
- . . . assist with repair/maintenance issues.
- . . . keep players on task; proximity is a solution in itself.

- *Establishing the ensemble-to-director connections*:
  - *Training the peripheral vision*—with instruments secured, ask students to look forward, wiggling one finger in front of their faces. "While you stare straight ahead, slowly rotate your hand toward your side. Notice that you can see the movement even when you're not looking at it. Now, look *only* at the music on your stand, but notice what I'm doing up here. You can see me even when you're not looking!"
  - A *"following-technique" challenge*—this is a skill-building exercise. Physiologically, it takes time for eyes to relocate and refocus. This brief description of the challenge may also be used as your instructions: "At least once in every measure, look up at the conductor then back at your music, even if you don't feel it's necessary. 'Check in' every measure, and find your way back to the printed page efficiently. Try it twice-per-measure to strengthen your visual tracking skills." You can watch students' eyes, or perhaps you can assign that task to one member of each section.
  - *"Sound from the mirror"*—conductors use this strategy, unnamed, very frequently. The concept is similar to children's kinesthetic imitation games, and actors' improvisational warm-ups, where a follower mirrors the motions of the leader. In our case while conducting, we fluctuate the tempo, change dynamics, indicate phrasing, and show other elements to build the ensemble's eye-contact and "following" skills. This exercise is exceptionally valuable when forging our connection to a new group, and during warm-ups, scales, chorales, and unison passages.
  - *Mirror strategy options*—these additional activities strengthen students' listening:
    - "Don't look at the conductor." Part one: use only peripheral vision for sensing the conductor's motions, keeping eyes on the printed music. Part two: the principal players follow the conductor, while the rest of the players follow their respective principals.
    - While principal players follow the conductor, all other music stands are raised to block the conductor from section-players' view. Consider turning section-players' chairs to face the principal player.

Ten Rehearsal Strategies Based on Alternative Seating Arrangements

We can modify the seating arrangement for a variety of student-centered benefits. Some options require advance work to change the setup; others will accommodate standard seating plans and therefore could function as a brief activity.

1. *Mix up the seating* for a basic version. It could be chaotic without guidance, so be careful to give parameters and a time limit. For example, "When I release you I'd like you to change seats. You'll go to another chair, away from your section's normal location. If you share a folder with someone, you will still sit together, but somewhere else. You'll have exactly 60 seconds to find your new spot. Protect your instrument; move carefully and silently. Go." The novelty alone will be enough to recharge students, adding something "special" to the day's work.
2. *Reverse the instrumentation*, moving flutes and clarinets to the back, and back-row players to the front. And a similar but faster alternative . . .
3. *Turn the winds around*. In this case, the seated rows of winds will be facing the percussion section. You might conduct from a centered location in or near the percussion.
4. *Apply standard Choral seating* where the setup features SATB groupings. For example, the leftmost end of the band would be all soprano instruments (1st flutes, oboe, clarinets, trumpets, and

IN THE REHEARSAL

bells). Then, moving across alto and tenor instruments, the right-most end of the band is reserved for bass voices. Groups 1 through 4 (using McBeth and Lisk models) will work well.
5. *Redistribute each section's leadership* by rotating parts within the section or, for a subtle version, move several "1st" players to play along on the 2nd and 3rd parts.
6. *Rotate rows* (e.g.1–2–3–4 to 2–3–4–1 to 3–4–1–2) throughout the rehearsal, or on successive days, or even "periodically". Each rotation provides students with a new perspective, and a revised opportunity for you to evaluate all students.
7. *Choose a shape*, as simple as a circle ("in the round"), or a box around the room's perimeter; although this requires some moving of chairs, it also allows the conductor to be surrounded by the sound and, for behavior purposes, equidistant from all students.
8. *Space the winds throughout the audience seating* if you have access to the auditorium during the rehearsal, with percussion placed logically. With vast spacing and reverberant sound, students are charged with a new and heightened need to watch and listen.
9. *Move the band deep onto the stage*—perhaps even facing the back wall—and then, for a contrasted listening experience, close the main curtain and all other curtains, entirely surrounding the band. Once enclosed in a dry environment with the band's reverb minimized, all details are more easily heard: articulations, tone quality faults, note lengths, and phrasing choices are revealed.
10. *Remember the value of discussion* in all cases—"What did you hear today that we don't usually experience?"

Part 3: Discovering Errors and Determining a Response

It is imperative that we develop the ability to immediately hear problems and to have strategies in mind to fix them quickly. The presence of this skill is one of the most apparent differences between experienced and inexperienced teachers. Those with less experience will eventually get the problems solved. It just takes them longer to find and fix the errors. The resulting rehearsal down time creates boredom, invites discipline problems and a host of other things, none of which are good.[9]

Although error-detection seems to come quite naturally for some, most directors will require time, relentless concentration, and an accumulation of experiences to develop auditory finesse. Use your own chosen strategies to support error-detection endeavors:

- *During score study*, rely on the types of procedures that definitively increase the likelihood that you will detect performance errors:
    ○ Audiate, solfege or sing each part; if possible, play the instruments to experience fingerings, slide movements, and stickings.
    ○ Examine the printed *parts* for page-turns, notation issues, and technical difficulties.
    ○ Analyze vertical structures for chord-tones, extensions, and dissonances; to determine if a pitch is "wrong," we must first know whether it was written by the composer.

- *Rely on repetition, using the big picture general rehearsal methods*—each replay of a passage provides another opportunity to listen; students are very tolerant of repetitions if the objectives are clearly stated. When you suspect any issue, design the next activity carefully, further isolating the problem to clarify your listening.

- *Record the band*—recording for playback is highly recommended for many reasons. For error detection, a recording allows time for repeated hearings. A recording eliminates the many obligations required during a live rehearsal, so the director can listen with composure. TIPS: Recording/playback makes it easier to . . .
    . . . discern correct from incorrect
    . . . compare the recorded excerpt (students' performance) to your *aural concept* (the model for the eventual performance)
    . . . devise subsequent rehearsal activities to address what has been heard.

161

IN THE REHEARSAL

Note: beware of a common cognitive error—that is, during the rehearsal, sometimes directors hear what they "think" rather than what is actually happening. It's possible for our *aural concept* to give us an inflated impression of the band's live performance. We can use the record–playback process to learn more about the acuity of our own hearing.

- *"Stop looking, and listen"*—listen without watching the score. Removing visual distractions enhances the aural sense. Consider standing, without conducting at all, to simply listen. It's remarkable how much more even a novice can hear by listening without interference.
- *Use students' input about errors and concerns*—we may encounter situations when there are several concerns—perhaps too many to accurately hear and address. Tɪᴘ: A "members choice" approach can plot the course of instruction while also extending the length of time students will maintain attention (i.e. if they get to choose the activity, they'll be more willing to do it). Again, each repetition offers a new opportunity to listen. For example, "Section leaders, are any passages or measures causing difficulty for your section? We can stop to work on them."
- *"Repair, improvement and maintenance"*—once errors are detected (and musical concerns are noted), the director then needs to decide when to schedule each objective. It is unwise to use rehearsals solely as "problem-solving" sessions; that scheme guarantees a lackluster experience for students, and is the reason we plan variety in our rehearsal activities. However, we can't overlook the need to repair errors, improve musical expressiveness, and maintain the work we've done. To avoid reliance on the stop–repair–restart method . . .

    . . . *keep paper or a device at the podium.* Jot brief reflections during the rehearsal; the list helps your memory, and guides the follow-up planning. Further, the process helps convey your expectations because you'll tell students how to act during your writing.

    . . . *dictate into a handheld recorder* or smartphone for later listening. Consider the value of recording *during* the passage to collect musical evidence for planning.

    . . . *write on sticky notes.* Pencil the objectives and plans onto the note, adhered to the page adjacent to the concerns. Tɪᴘ: Some rehearsals can be driven entirely by the notes. Affix notes

Measures / Rehearsal #	Intro	A	9-12	33-36	63-64
Rhythm	Tpts/Hns				
Notes / Accuracy					All Low Br
Technical Problem		Tbns		Fl Trills	
Tuning			All WW		
Balance / Dynamics					More countermel.
Articulation		"			
Interpretive / Artistic				Change 2nd Rpt.	
Other					
Ideas/Plans					

Figure 8.1 To keep organized planning notes during the rehearsal.

IN THE REHEARSAL

to protrude from the page, giving each a priority number in pencil to further organize the rehearsal order. When the objective has been met, remove the note; consider moving it to a "review page" for a later check-up session.

- *Logging rehearsal plans in real-time*—a chart can organize notes during score-study or, more specifically, during a rehearsal to reinforce your own recall (Figure 8.1). This is valuable for in-class usage, and for both short- and long-term planning. When you encounter a concern but have no time to address it, use the chart to efficiently diagram your plans for later. Used as one part of the rehearsal process, this chart-method efficiently answers the question, "Exactly what will I say to the band when we stop?"

Rehearsing Separate Excerpts Concurrently: How and Why?

Introduced in Chapter 2, combining separate excerpts into a single rehearsal-pass is an efficient and time-saving strategy to teach important rhythms, fragments, motifs, and concepts to a larger group, rather than singling out a small faction while others sit idly by. This strategy supports comprehensive musicianship because performers become more aware of thematic material and how one's part relates to others. The excerpts in Figure 8.2 are in different keys so, combined, they yield a "duet" of parallel major 3rds. Note: the excerpts are not exactly the same, but those subtleties can help the development of the lines, as students can be told, "Your rhythms are not alike; let's make sure you and the audience can both hear those differences distinctly."

Figure 8.2 Dakota Fanfare (Erik Morales). Copyright © 2010. The FJH Music Company Inc. (ASCAP). Used by permission.

It's a good bet that you'll find excerpts in most compositions for which simultaneous rehearsal is helpful, especially when earlier material is restated. Additionally, engaging more players contributes to better behavior, and helps in unifying musical *style* across the ensemble.

- *Modifying compositions: why and how*—we are always obligated to the music and its composer, but there are valid reasons to delicately revise a composition. The choices are driven by this philosophy: *students deserve to experience high-quality music*. Sometimes our group's attributes are not matched to the needs of the composition. Slight modifications can therefore help students succeed while also improving the quality of the performance, without changing the character of the original composition. For example:

- *Incomplete or imbalanced instrumentation*—use substitutions. Suggested substitution ideas (e.g. tenor sax or euphonium for trombone) are easily found. Or, import players: supplement the group with students or even adults. Internal moves can help, as when a flutist covers a mallet part.
- *Missing solo instrument*—rescore for a reasonable substitute instrument (or rely on cross-cueing if provided). In cases where the solo line exceeds the player's skill-level, consider <u>doubling</u>, or perform it as a section soli.
- *Dynamic problems*—after other interventions, thin the number of players to achieve a better decrescendo while maintaining the best tone and tuning; restore (or add) players for a more dramatic crescendo. Encourage students to conceal entrances/exits by tapering and, when needed, by eliminating articulations.
- *Intonation problems*—displace octaves for select students (specifically, those without control of tuning in extreme registers).
- *Clarity problems*—again, thinning is sometimes an answer; just as often, a subtle change of written articulations can clarify muddled technique.
- *Technique limitations*—first, we encourage practice, and we help students with our best teaching strategies. However, students may encounter passages that are simply too difficult at the time. Rather than rejecting the composition entirely, or performing it as written—with inevitable errors—we can make some subtle revisions based on the processes detailed below:
    - *The need*—when literature is chosen based on the band's median skill level, lower-skilled students frequently face limiting challenges. The *modifications* approach serves the

The COMPLETE Original ~ *Keep practicing to see if you can master the excerpt as written ...*

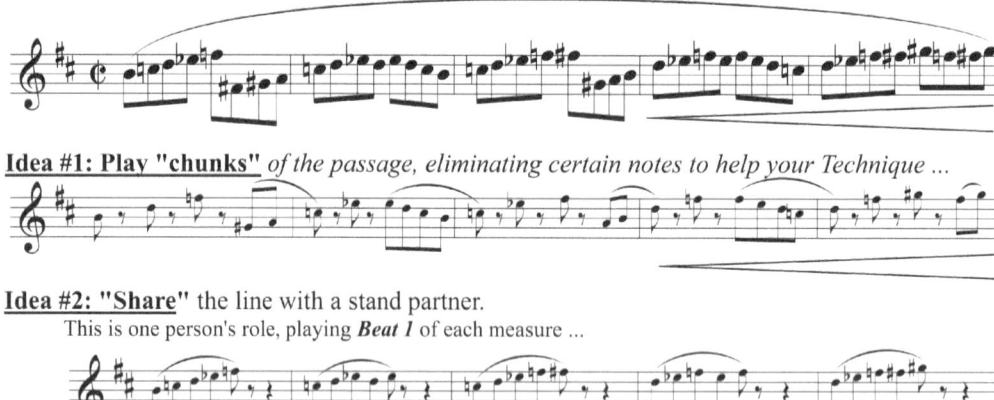

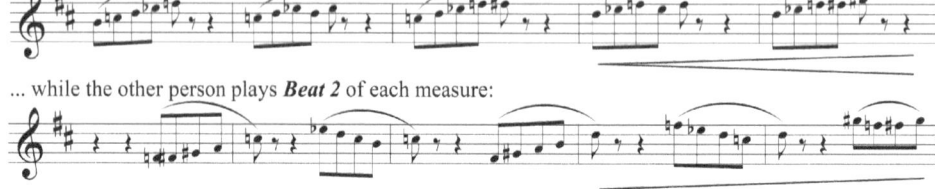

Idea #1: Play "chunks" *of the passage, eliminating certain notes to help your Technique ...*

Idea #2: "Share" the line with a stand partner.
  This is one person's role, playing **Beat 1** of each measure ...

  ... while the other person plays **Beat 2** of each measure:

Idea #3: Play _NEARLY_ everything. *You'll decide how much to leave out...*

For ALL strategies: Your chosen plan should always fit the music perfectly;
  it should *contribute* to the music, never interfering with others' work.

Figure 8.3 A first intervention: teach the student his/her own strategies. This example uses an excerpt from *October Colors* by Robin Linaberry.

individual, the ensemble, and the listener. Used selectively, modifications also respect the composer and the spirit of the work.

- *The interventions*—the easiest "modification" to address a technique challenge is for the student to do it independently (see Figure 8.3). This plan aligns with the aphorism that concludes with, "Teach a man to fish and he'll eat every day." So this first process can help the student to develop a unique approach to modify a passage, independent from the teacher.

Other basic processes can be easy to demonstrate, and for students to apply on their own. As they progress, students learn to customize their approaches independently. What works perfectly for one student can of course be difficult or impossible for another. The student assimilates personal strengths and weaknesses with strategies leading toward success (see Figure 8.4):

Even after much practice, a young player might not be able to manage these over-the-break fingerings:

Here's a subtle revision that can give the student some success, without affecting what the audience hears ...

* Use Alternate B (right side-key)

Figure 8.4 *Fate of the Gods*, by Steven Reineke, clarinet part, mm. 68–71. © Birch Island Music Press. Used with permission.

BASSOON: Original notation with two optional revisions

Figure 8.5 *Eternal Father, Strong To Save* by Claude T. Smith, bassoon, mm. 8–13. © Claude T. Smith Publications, Inc. Used with permission.

Students are not always self-sufficient, of course. Occasionally the teacher may need to intervene with written revisions. In that case, the best plan begins with a scrutiny of the student's skills. Evaluate the excerpt for its technical difficulties, and compose a revised passage tailored to meet the student's needs.

Additionally, it is efficient to *format* the notation while creating the revision. Figure 8.5 offers options to a less-skilled bassoonist in a difficult fingering pattern. With almost no extra time, the revision could be formatted to match the exact staff-size, measure lengths, and spacing of the original. Then, it becomes easy to lightly tape the revision onto the original—a literal cut-and-paste job!

Five Additional Rehearsal Strategies to Promote Student Engagement

Students' learning, progress, and especially their *enjoyment* will be more significant when they are actively engrossed in the music-making process. The following strategies offer such engagement:

1. *Rotate parts*—determine first what you'd like students to do, and then word your instructions carefully. This process allows students to play a different part for a short period of time. As a simple option: "Stand partners on the left side, stay in place; stand partners on the right side, move to a different part. Now, let's replay the excerpt we've already 'perfected' . . . can you make it sound *exactly* as good?" Your guidance is needed to avoid pandemonium during the move. But the important lesson is, "What did you learn from that?"
2. *"Divide and Conquer"* using sub-groups (instrument families, sections, students' grade-levels, 1sts, 2nds, 3rds, randomness groups):
   - Play the target excerpt with one group alone.
   - Each new group is asked to duplicate the achievements of the previous. For example, the first group worked to bring out moving notes, also adjusting the dynamics of sustained notes. The second group replicates those concepts, but is additionally directed to emphasize beat 4, while eliminating barline breathing. Each ensuing group adds a layer to the product.
   - Direct two or more groups together, applying all accumulated concepts.
   - Finish with the entire ensemble reassembled.
3. *Isolating musical elements*—students will perform all aspects of the passage except pitches: play rhythms, articulations, dynamic changes, phrasing concepts, etc., on an unchanging unison or chord. Discuss the success of each element, then restore the written pitches with a heightened sensitivity to the improved elements.
4. *"Bopping" applied to excerpts*—bopping, detailed in Chapter 7 to help build rhythmic independence, can enhance the clarity of almost any passage. But it can also improve the players' concentration. Some additional usages include:
   - One featured section plays as written; other members bop *only* the first pitch after any written rest.
   - A portion of the band sings (or hums, or claps). The remaining members bop the first note: of every measure, of every fourth measure, of each new rehearsal number.
   - Bopping is applied to note "weights," where a sustained note = *p*, and moving notes are bopped more loudly (quarter-note *mf*, eighth-note *f*, sixteenth-note *ff*). Note: this is especially helpful for moving notes to be heard in Chorale excerpts and contrapuntal passages.
   - Bopping as a relay: "Percussion please play your parts exactly as written, but softly. All wind players will 'bop' for four measures and rest for four measures. Woodwinds 'bop' measures 1 through 4, and brass players 'bop' measures 5 through 8. Woodwinds 9–12, Brass 13–16. Ready?"
5. *"Linking" and "overlapping"*—all performers alternate playing with silence. The goal is a smooth, balanced connection from one set of performers to the next. This strategy can be applied to partial-groups of all kinds.

- Linking examples—a group plays four-measure segments (1–4 and 9–12), resting while a second group plays 5–8 and 13–16. Or, the right-side stand partner plays measures 1–2, while the left-side partner plays 3–4.
- Overlapping example—each group plays four measures and rests two measures, but in a reverse order as shown in Figure 8.6.

Measures >	1	2	3	4	5	6	7	8	9	10	11	12
Group 1	PLAY			>>	REST	>>	PLAY			>>	REST	>>
Group 2	REST	>>	PLAY			>>	REST	>>	PLAY			>>

Figure 8.6 Play–rest overlapping.

In this process, the full ensemble is sounding tutti in two-measure segments. Charge the students with the obligation to "Make it sound as beautiful and complete as possible."

Additional Rehearsal Tips Based on Singing

"Becoming a better singer is not the most direct path to becoming a trombonist, but it may be the most effective."[10] There are only good things to say about singing in instrumental music; concurrent study in vocal and instrumental music helps students immensely in both endeavors. And using movement and listening activities only improves the sophistication of the musician. Here are just a few ways we can access those benefits through singing in the band rehearsal:

- *Singing during the warm-up.* Chapter 3 offers ideas about singing. If students can find comfort with humming, singing, basic solfege, and hand signals during the warm-up session, those techniques are then easily applied to other parts of the rehearsal. Sing for the students, and with them, as often as possible.
- *The singing director.* Singing from the podium is an expeditious, inspiring method of instruction, likely the most direct path toward the interpretive aspects of music. And when the singing comes from the director, students accept it as a "norm" of the classroom; their own willingness to sing follows.
  - *To build the eye-ear connection*—"Many of you have this melody; see if you can find it on the page. Then, play it the way I'm singing it."
  - *To model and contrast interpretive styles*—"You played it like this" [sing the imitation] "but I think Vaughan-Williams wants something more like this" [sing the interpretation]. "Let's try it that way."
  - *To replace extra words*—singing can be much faster than a wordy verbal instruction. For example, sing a pitch or line, and ask students to "Play if you have this sound."
  - *To demonstrate balance or tuning concepts*—ask students to play a perfect 5th drone, while you sing the third of the chord. "Notice that just one person providing the 'third,' even softly, is enough for us to hear this chord as major or minor. That's why a dynamic marking of *mf* can sometimes be too loud; the 'third' tastes better in small amounts!" Or, "While Whitney and Chris *play* the Perfect 5th, I'll *sing* the major 3rd. Listen while I make it sharper, then flatter. Hey, do you notice the chord sounds better when the third is lower?"
  - *To expedite learning of all kinds*—arguments against rote-learning don't acknowledge that ours is an art and science of sound rather than facts and processes alone. As such, the most direct path to understanding is often through modeling with sound. Sing a rhythm to teach a rhythm; sing a style to teach a style. Nearly all musical concepts can be taught, conveyed, or supported by singing.

- *The singing band musician.* Singing is the first and most reliable tool in the student's music-learning collection, and offers the easiest access. Singing provides variety and sensitivity within the rehearsal; further, it extends the length of activities without depleting players' endurance:
  - *Separate the tasks to isolate technique problems*—students perform just the fingerings and slide-positions while singing the part.
  - *Sing the parts*—these three words describe a large topic! Treated briefly, here are several outstanding suggested activities:
    - Sing the parts rather than playing. For example, "All students who have the melody, please sing it." Or, "We've just played the Chorale section; let's sing it now, using 'loo' as the syllable."
    - This call-and-response template is an effective "concept conduit" to transfer ideas from the teacher's demonstration to the students' understanding: the director sings a model > the students sing the response > then they play the response, applying the targeted musical features. As an intermediate step, the playing can be restored gradually: "All principals play; everyone else sing" or "Sophomores and seniors play, 9th and 11th grades sing" (see "randomness" exercises, later in this chapter).
    - Standmates alternate roles: one plays the part while the other sings. This may stand alone as a helpful strategy, but it also allows the director to ask for, "singers only" and "players only." Students then exchange roles to repeat the process. This activity can hatch engaging discussions.
    - Transfer the bopping technique to singing. Try a split, with half of the students playing the front-end of the note (instrumental bopping) and the other half singing with the full sustained values. Give singers a syllable like "dome", where "do-" is the articulation and "-ohmmmm" is the hummed sustain.
    - While most members are singing a passage, some others (principal players, perhaps) can be instructed to "hop on—hop off", playing a measure and then resting. In *The Rehearsal Toolkit*, Feldman and Contzius describe "Audio Anchors": while singing longer excerpts, band members are asked to play the downbeat at every new Rehearsal letter.[11]
  - *Singing to improve audiation*—this "musical imagery" is crucial to deeper learning, and to excellence as a performer. Strategic examples include:
    - For tonal sensitivity: after the sound stops, "Let's sing the 'Root' of that last chord" or ". . . your own note in that last chord."
    - For more accurate entrances, especially helpful for brass players, highlight an "anchor" note in the scoring, and use it to help players predetermine their next sound. "Horns, can you hear the 1st clarinets in that chord? Sing their note. That's the next pitch you'll play after your 16-measure rest." Or, "Let's listen again to the very last note of the March. Based on what you just played, *sing* the first note of the next piece."
    - For more precision in sight-reading: "We're about to read a new piece. Let's just play and hold your first pitch; now sing it. Now, just finger along and *sing* while I conduct the first thirty-two measures, even if it's not very accurate. Then we'll play it."
  - *Singing to mold the performance*—this is another fertile field of exciting possibilities; here are four examples of creative ways to use singing to meet specific performance goals:
    - To refine an unusual chord change, "Play your parts, but stop after the first chord. *Sing* the second chord."
    - "If your repeat section says '2nd time only,' let's *sing* the parts while fingering through the first time."
    - For some pieces, this excellent diversion helps develop pulse, melodic interpretation, tuning, and harmonic awareness: instruct "melody" students to sing the melody. Teach other students how to compress their parts (bass notes, rhythmic chords, oom-pa-pas) into a single sustained tone to create a long chord. "Now, all harmony instruments, please play (or sing)

your sustained chord; change the pitch when you get to the chord-change at measure __. Melody players, *sing* your melody over the sustained chord progression." Groom their interpretation of the melody through singing. Finish the sequence by playing the full passage.
- "Let's check our group's concept of tempo. Sing your parts for the first eight measures. Then *imagine* (audiate) your next eight-measure sequence in total silence, before resuming the sound. Will our entrances line up?"

Additionally, *listening* is inherently different while singing. For instrumentalists, their listening occurs in layers along with technique, articulation, music-reading, and more. Singing affords an unobstructed opportunity for careful listening. But, of course, listening skills are fundamental to independent musicianship, so we should include guided listening tasks prominently in the rehearsals.

Supplementary Tips to Support Listening in the Rehearsal

- *In-class listening tasks.* Directors guide listening tasks during every rehearsal, even unwittingly, with verbal descriptions and prompts. For example, "Listen for other instruments playing your part; I'll ask you who they are in a moment." "After we play the passage, point to the section you feel has the most important part." "Raise your hand if you can say which measure has the most serious tuning problems."
- *Listening guides.* But at other times, an actual listening guide can help to drive the instruction. On the resources website you'll find two samples to spark creations of your own:

  1. "Listening Guide for Specific Repertoire" [RW8.5]: this document encourages critical listening by prompting students for responses. It is also an excellent option for days when, "I hurt my finger in Phys Ed class and can't play," or "Um, I forgot my instrument."
  2. "Listening Guide for Guest Performers" [RW8.6]: this is used to enhance listening (and behavior) when a visiting group performs; it can also serve as an extra-credit assignment for students attending an offsite concert.

- *Record–playback ideas.* Hearing one's own performance is sometimes humbling, but a recording is also the best way to listen objectively, without the obstacles and distractions of playing.

  - Record your band's performance several times throughout a preparation cycle, from the first "baseline" through the final concert. Play and discuss those versions in class. Do students recognize the improvements?
  - Record an excerpt during a rehearsal. Play it immediately, offering prompts to guide the listening. For example: "Together, let's describe three important goals." Clarify the goals, instructing students what to write into their music. Rerecord the excerpt, then play both recordings in succession to determine if *we* have improved.
  - Select an exemplary recording in advance; cue it to the excerpt you'll target with your band. Record your band playing that excerpt; play it back, immediately followed by the professional version. Discuss differences before returning to the rehearsal.
  - If software is available, choose a slower playback speed to hear rhythmic precision, placement of articulations, and releases more clearly.

- *Plugging the ears to "listen."* Use a finger to gently depress the tragus, covering the ear canal. This partial blockage decreases the collection of higher frequencies, and greatly reduces the reverb. The altered perspective allows listeners—conductor and students alike—to hear layers of the group differently, and can clarify articulations, releases, and other aspects of the performance.
- *Expand the concept of "playing in trios."* This was described in Chapters 4 and 5 to refine the group's tone, blend, balance, and tuning; we can link it to many other musical goals. When students are comfortable with the concept, shift their aural focus to other sources ("Listen to Principal players" / ". . . the Bass note" / ". . . the Solo line" / ". . . other people who play the same note as you"). Then apply the concept to numerous goals of your choosing.

IN THE REHEARSAL

About Customizing Rehearsal Strategies

A director's capacity to identify errors and make interpretive decisions is critical during band rehearsals. But in the makeup of the "most effective director," perhaps the one element of paramount importance is the intuitive ability to *get results*. The effective director recognizes a problem, evaluates it in terms of the students' skills, and designs an outstanding activity to improve the performance, keeping the students engrossed in the process. Those activities are frequently custom-designed for each piece.

The design of rehearsal strategies is instinctive for some. For others, perhaps the best advice is also the easiest: find trusted colleagues who have taught the same piece and ask them about their experiences. What problems were encountered, and what methods were chosen to solve those problems? The following paragraph exemplifies that kind of exchange with composer Alex Shapiro commenting on a problem-solution sequence in one of her own compositions:

> Paper Cut is an electroacoustic wind band piece which has the musicians not only playing their instruments, but playing sheets of printer paper as well! The piece has been performed thousands of times since it premiered in 2010, and I've noticed that there are two brief passages that, despite having simple rhythms, manage to trip up the vast majority of ensembles. During the paper playing "call and response" sections beginning at bars 20 and 28, musicians often tend to rush, and get far ahead of the accompaniment. Here's a helpful technique: as each group lowers their arms after playing their tapping figure, have them subtly continue to tap the "answer" rhythm in their laps, while the responding players raise their arms and play their tapping parts. The musicians can even be encouraged to move their feet or bodies with the pulse, so that they truly feel it. This may help to keep everyone from rushing into their next entrance, and therefore keep the band aligned with the track.[12]

While it's not always feasible to communicate directly with the composer, other trusted teachers *can* help by sharing their strategies.

Part 4: Games and Diversions

When asked by parents, "What did you do in school today?" it is not likely that a student will respond, "We took twenty minutes to tune a D-flat major chord in band!" But "meeting an educational objective" can still be fun and engaging, worthy of dinner-table conversation. Some strategies in this category include:

- *Elimination games.* All players stand to play an isolated excerpt together (be inventive for players who cannot stand). Using the "honor system," students sit down after making an error; however, seated students should continue to play. Give feedback for improvement, and then repeat the challenge. Monitor students' reactions carefully to keep the process constructive and never uncomfortable. Acknowledge the achievement when most students can remain standing.
- *Rotating Out.* A scripted sample—"I need six volunteers . . . No, I'm not going to tell you why you're volunteering! . . . OK, you six people, go into the audience and listen while we play." To start, just allow them to go out. When they come back, ask them general questions about their discoveries. They'll probably say "I heard parts I never heard before", "People sit with bad posture and it's easy to see," or "Can't hear the trumpets" (or maybe even "Wow, those seats are nice!"). Later, give them a written list of listening-goals.
- *Friendly competitions—"intramural music"*
    - "Let's play measures 33–64 *four* times in a row, without stopping. The first time is seniors only; the second time is for juniors, third is sophomores, with freshmen last. Who will sound the best? What else will we notice?"

IN THE REHEARSAL

- ○ "Let's hear grades 10 and 12 together; now 9th and 11th grades."
- ○ "Woodwinds and mallets will play first; now brass and battery percussion." (See "randomness" later for more ideas.)

- *Play the passage without leaders.* Specifically, eliminate the principal players. A logical sequence might be:

1. The full band plays the passage.
2. Several alternations—principal players alone, followed by all others, and repeat.
3. Reassemble the full band.

- *Two strategies to refine the cooperative team approach:*

1. In an excerpt where several instruments share a melody, ask each section to play only a portion, but with seamless connections to the players before and after them. "Let's split the melody. Flutes please play measures 33–34; clarinets 35–36; saxes and bassoon 37–38" and so on. Record the result and play it for students' critique. Then restore the melody to its fully scored version with everyone playing; again, record/playback and discuss.
2. On a passage from your repertoire, split the band into four equal-sized groups (e.g. "quarter-segments" left-to-right). Those groups might play the excerpt separately for side-by-side comparison, or they might share it as previously by playing only a portion of the passage and "passing it on" to the next group.

- *Perform to an online audience.* With technology appropriate to your situation, "live stream" a performance during the rehearsal period. The "audience" possibilities are innumerable.
- *"Recital day"* offers a performance opportunity to the band's soloists and chamber groups. This is a miniature chamber music concert, with peers as both performers and audience. The director has an opportunity (and an obligation) to guide behaviors.
- *Using principles of randomness in the band classroom.* In Chapter 4, we described several tuning strategies based on randomness. Applied to daily rehearsals, randomness erases monotony while keeping students alert, attentive, aware, and even entertained. The focus remains on the director's ability to meet chosen goals.

Randomness Strategies for Band Rehearsals

- *The fastest approach* is probably the teacher's off-the-cuff descriptor: "Please play if your first name has two syllables . . . if you're wearing red . . . if you have shoes with laces" and so on. An advantage is that the director can use "apparent" randomness to choose specific students, because you've already made observations about the student(s) you hope to hear.
- *Count-offs applied to rehearsals*—instruct the group using the numbers of your choice ("Let's count off, 1 through 5, to create five groups"). Then,
  - ○ "OK, let's hear the excerpt played by only the people with number 4."
  - ○ Use additive layering by having "all students with #1 please play . . . let's *add* #2 players . . . #3 . . ."
  - ○ Your creativity offers infinite options.
- *Devices*—select the random player(s) using dice, a bingo cage, coin flips, or a "draw" from a container. For the "draw," consider giving a numbered ticket to each student, ripped from a perforated roll of matching pairs; as the rehearsal proceeds, you can pull a ticket as many times as you'd like throughout the session.
- *Use an app or software*—helpful digital tools continue to evolve; it is easy to find a random picker, student generator, random number, and other apps and add-ons. There are many options within "Flippity" (https://flippity.net/). With the free Wheel of Names web-based tool

IN THE REHEARSAL

(https://wheelofnames.com/), enter your own names or even band sections (e.g. 1st flutes, 2nd flutes, 1st clarinets), then tap to "spin." The targeted skill or excerpt is then performed by randomly selected students.
- See [RW8.7] to play The Great Dartboard Challenge.

Section 5: Additional Quick-Fix Tips

- Tempo quick fix—simply ask students, "Too fast, too slow, or just right?"
- Pulse quick fix—ask students, "Are we staying steady? If not, are we rushing, dragging, or a little bit of each?"
- Rhythm quick fix—choose "any note" (students love this). Either from notation or by rote, repeat the rhythm until correct. Return to "the written note."
- Musical motion quick-fix—similar to the bopping method, students will play only their moving notes, emphasizing their importance. Sustained pitches are bopped with no sustain, or they may be sustained *pp*.
- Attentiveness quick-fix—invite guests often. New eyes and ears in the room enhance focus.
- Consistency quick-fix—let the students set the group goal of three, four, five, or more acceptable repetitions of a known passage. Sometimes called the "coin" or "paper clip" method, any manipulatives can be placed on one edge of the conductor's stand: with each correct passage, slide one item to the *Success* side.
- Invert the pyramid—in the discussion of balance (see Chapter 3), we played the SATB balance incorrectly as a model of how *not* to sound. Apply this process to the composition. Additionally . . .
- Demonstrate the "incorrect" to sculpt the "correct"—this is a helpful strategy for almost any musical element: rhythm, dynamics, breath locations, articulations, and even expressive choices. It is also effective when students have already made an error. An instruction like, "Oh, let's do that again, exactly as you just played it," can be the catalyst toward working on repairs. Also, the process can germinate a cooperative effort to democratically choose interpretive ideas.
- "Why did we stop?"—asking that question aloud enhances awareness, encouraging students to recognize basic errors. Guide students toward responding even when the technical elements seem "correct," because students should also notice when music lacks expressive elements.
- Marking music—"We're humans, and humans forget. Mark it in." Markings, however, may be more meaningful when conceived by the students. For example: "That was much better; I think we found a great balance and dynamic-level for that passage! Now, can you do it that way *every time*? Please write in a marking that will remind you." Add extra descriptions as needed.
- Section-comparison exercises to reach consensus about concepts: listen to each section as the students perform their interpretive contributions. "How did we feel about the saxophones' phrasing?" The director's questioning drives the group toward democratic agreement about musical choices.
- Propagation: in this strategy, we feature individuals or groups who can successfully demonstrate the musical goal, and then we spread it out through the ensemble. "Let's hear that [chord/note/passage] with *only* the principal players. When I give you the next cue, *add* the very next chair. Match the tone, volume, and tuning so you're playing a perfect unison with your neighbor. New cue, next seat. Can we get through the entire band without hearing major problems?"
- Director's confidence, part 1—score study sessions can help us to pre-answer questions likely to be asked. (Clarinetists ask, "How do we finger the high A-flat to B-flat trill?") But because we can't know everything, it's valid and acceptable just to be truthful: "I can't remember, so let's use resources and work together to figure it out. Then, help the band by making sure your entire section learns that important skill."
- Director's confidence, part 2—hopefully you'll never experience "the ultimate train-wreck" during a concert. But if (when) it happens, it will be comforting to have pre-planned remarks prepared with careful forethought during a moment of poise. Remember Murphy's Law.

Final Words About "The Rehearsal"

Distilled to its bottom-line philosophy, this chapter has been designed to promote these principles:

- The full-group rehearsal can be a highly efficient venue for music education.
- Meeting objectives is dependent on planning, strategic delivery, and careful feedback. Success is not accidental.
- The best rehearsal processes are even more effective when the students are *engaged*.

Therefore, we work to keep as many students as possible engaged in all components of the rehearsal. Apart from our music performance classes, nowhere in any educational setting will the student-to-teacher ratio be so high in a single room (often 150 to 1, or even higher!). And yet the goals can still be met consistently by a poised director who uses feedback to the students' advantage.

Notes

1. Harry K. Wong and Rosemary T. Wong, *The First Days of School* (Mountain View, CA: Harry K. Wong Publications, 1998), 88.
2. Wong and Wong, *The First Days of School*, 91.
3. Wong and Wong, *The First Days of School*, 143.
4. Wong and Wong, *The First Days of School*, 167.
5. Evan Feldman and Ari Contzius, *Instrumental Music Education: Teaching with the Musical and Practical in Harmony* (New York: Routledge, 2016), 191–192.
6. Shelley Jagow, *Teaching Instrumental Music: Developing the Complete Band Program* (Galesville MD: Meredith Music Publications, 2007), 187.
7. Jagow, *Teaching Instrumental Music*, 187.
8. Gary Stith, *The Conductor's Companion: 100 Rehearsal Techniques, Imaginative Ideas, Quotes, and Facts* (Delray Beach FL: Meredith Music Publications, 2017), 21.
9. David Newell, *Teaching Rhythm: New Strategies and Techniques for Success* (San Diego, CA: Neil A. Kjos Music Co., 2008), 129.
10. Feldman and Contzius, *Instrumental Music Education*, 16.
11. Evan Feldman and Ari Contzius, *The Rehearsal Toolkit* (New York: Routledge Textbooks, Taylor & Francis, 2011), https://routledgetextbooks.com/textbooks/9781138921405/additional-chapters.php.
12. Quoted from an email from the composer, June 17, 2020.

9

THE "INTANGIBLES"

Introduction

"Make music," the Teacher says. "You're playing it very well, but I don't *feel* anything. Find the *art* in your music!" And the students stare blankly, because expressiveness involves performance skills that are not always instinctively learned, and can be enigmatic to teach. Even a flawless delivery of notes, rhythms, articulations, and dynamics cannot be considered "artistic" without something more. The artistic performance includes—or perhaps it requires—a variety of vague "gray area" skills and responses. But is it actually possible to teach students how to control and manipulate subtleties for expressive and emotional performances? "Yes!," the teacher says.

If performed expressively, music has the capacity to convey sentiments, to tell stories, and to evoke emotional responses. This special chapter attempts to demystify the interpretive aspects of music performance. Rather than trying to find the elusive "It-Factor," the approach here will be to examine some of its more tangible components separately.

Section 1: On Principles of Artistry, Phrasing, and Interpretation

Music teachers rely on a set of almost universal concepts to nudge students toward expressiveness. These "rules"—sampled in the following in no prioritized order—should be viewed as generalizations, but they bring results. Even if the performance feels artificial or mechanical at first, these pseudo-artistic steps can provide pathways toward the goal of interpretative musicianship.

Guiding Students Through Their Performance Practices

- *Avoid breathing on barlines,* and anywhere interrupting the musical phrase. Breath-spots should be chosen for interpretive reasons rather than solely because of a need to breathe. Until students learn about cadences, use simple prompts like, "Is this a question-and-answer? Is it a complete thought or a partial idea? Does it sound 'final'?"
- *Choose the "important" note(s) within each phrase.* Use a subtle *crescendo* leading toward the peak note, and *decrescendo* away from it. In fact, a default plan is simply to put a "rise and fall" on the phrase, whether or not peak notes are identified.
- *Give direction to musical lines,* moving "toward" some notes and "from" others. Performers should rarely use "*at*" as a musical descriptor, strong endings excepted.
- *Employ these common performance practices to support musical "direction":*
  - Moving notes are more important than static notes: the shorter the rhythmic value, the more important the note is to hear. Generally, play moving notes louder.
  - Upbeats should lean forward: even a multi-note anacrusis benefits from dynamic direction leading toward the beginning of phrases.
  - On long notes, reduce volume after the attack, and *crescendo* slightly toward the release: the *crescendo* can be more pronounced when the long note is followed by shorter notes and rhythmic movement.
  - *Crescendo* on dotted-notes and on tied-notes, especially when crossing a barline.

- *Shape music's intensity using tempo and volume:* faster/louder to increase intensity, and slower/softer to decrease.
- *Add a subtle crescendo rather than backing away from dissonances:* by emphasizing the dissonance and its resolution, the performance discovers the music's tension-and-release.
- *Listen specifically for expressiveness in the students' work.* Record the performance; as an objective listener during playback, do you hear something more than notes and rhythms? Can you clearly hear the emotions you thought were added to your performance? If the answer is "no," exaggerate the effects.

Performance Practice Perspectives from Other Sources

Evan Feldman, in *The Rehearsal Toolkit,* advises:

> Moving Notes Forte, Sustained Notes Piano: Directors often instruct students, "Bring out the moving lines." A step beyond this is to ask students to play all moving notes forte and all sustained notes piano. Reinforce this technique so individuals are literally toggling between forte and piano depending on their rhythm. Eventually ask students to smooth out the exaggeration.[1]

Richard Floyd describes musical movement based on longer and shorter note-values ("white" and "black" notes, respectively) as such: "White notes sustain the music while black notes connect the music."[2]

Mark Fonder offers the following:

> Also, in Bach chorales, accidentals often signal a movement of the tonal center in some way. If your line contains an accidental, it is possibly a nonchord tone creating harmonic tension, which with more motion, will resolve. Be sure your voice is heard.[3]

Bobby Adams advises that bands can improve technique, while making wonderful musical discoveries, simply by *probing*. While some may see it simply as "repetition,"

> the process of probing automatically improves technical passages without drill. Working on technique is not fun, probing is. Some suggested probing techniques include slow practice, manipulating tempo changes, the use of exaggeration in dynamics, weight of notes, accents, hesitating, anticipating, stretching, and playing a piece in a totally different style.[4]

Remember Craig Kirchhoff's *The Plus and Minus System,* described in Chapter 4.

Shelley Jagow describes a method for students to use hand motions to feel a musical effect: "A 'punch' in the air may depict marcato, a 'sweep' in the air may depict legato, and a 'tap' at the air may depict staccato."[5]

Gregory Rudgers teaches students to *feel* the phrase: with students holding hands around the perimeter of the space, he tells them to "gradually tighten the grip of their hands for 8 counts, and then gradually loosen the grip for 8 counts."[6] After several silent repetitions, Rudgers then engages one advanced player to perform an artistic phrase; the remaining students, linked, share the tangible *feeling* of the motion.

Guiding Students Through Their Intellectual Processes

- *Imagine that your music accompanies a story*: can you tell the story through your performance?
- *Play as if you are talking*: speech uses inflections, pauses, volume-changes, and other components so naturally. Can you apply those components to your playing?
- *Pick an emotion* (happiness, anger, love, etc.) that describes your music: how can you use your performance to help listeners feel that emotion?

- *Play as if your music describes movement:* is it a dance, and what kind? Do you hear walking or running? Are you moving up a hill, or down? What would the conductor's motions look like?
- *What color is your music?* Are the sounds light or dark? If you painted your music, what colors would you use? Will the color stay mostly the same, or will you need a variety of colors?
- *What is your goal with this performance?* If you heard a professional play this piece, what would sound different? Can *you* interpret it like the professional?

Section 2: Making Logical Connections to Speech and Reading

Speaking in our primary language, we employ a natural combination of pauses, stresses, upward and downward inflections, variations of tempo and pitch, and other conventions. Some of these concepts are instinctual and some learned, but are always employed to convey meaning more effectively.

Thought-to-speech is immensely more intuitive and fluent than *print-to-speech* (reading). Students learn effective speaking habits simply by imitating the speakers heard daily. But it is more difficult to gain fluency at the transfer of symbols on the printed page into believable speech. Teachers must intervene to help students apply symbols like punctuation into fluent delivery.

Music performance can be viewed through the same lens to an extent. While some students intuitively add interpretive elements in their improvised or memorized music, they may have difficulty applying printed musical markings into fluent performance. Moreover, even when students can synthesize common music symbols into their playing, they must still learn to *add* their own meaningful markings to the printed page.

Music interpretation, however, is more advanced than a print-to-speech reading. Music artistry requires a synthesis of reading, feeling, and *writing*. The music teacher holds the additional responsibility of training students how to mark their music, including what specific markings to use, when to write them in, and for what reasons. The following highlights a special correlation between punctuation and musical markings, all for fluency of performance whether speaking or playing.

Three Easy Demonstrations for Students

1. *Read* a short passage, avoiding all punctuation marks. Read with a flat, unaffected delivery, without inflections. Students will notice the missing elements easily.
2. For enhanced effect, *alter* the punctuation: add, delete or *move* the punctuation marks. Display both printed versions—the original and the revision—and then read aloud. Students will easily hear (and enjoy!) the illogical consequences. A follow-up conversation might include, "Now, how can we mark our *music* with symbols that will show us how to play it, just as easily as punctuation marks show us how to read?"
3. To easily introduce the correlation between punctuation and music markings, begin by comparing *commas* to *breath marks*. The comma (,) makes us *pause* in our reading. Luckily, it looks much like the breath mark (') which, likewise, results in a separation or pause. Students will recognize the similarities easily. Then, expand the concept to include other grammatical relationships.

Punctuation and Music Markings: A More Advanced View

Other punctuation marks and common *text*-marking devices (especially those which affect *interpretation* of the reading) can be compared to *musical markings*. With an extensive collection of music marking choices at their disposal—added to other creative options that you will share—students can use pencils to "draw artistry" into their music. Figure 9.1 contains some suggested examples.

A logical follow-up to this exercise will include questions ("What punctuation mark would you use in that musical 'sentence'?") and instructions ("*Pencil in markings* to ensure that we'll play our interpretation the same way every time").

THE "INTANGIBLES"

Basic conceptual *Meaning*	Punctuations and other common text markings to convey the meaning	Potential relationship to these musical markings (among others):	*Musical Meanings; Common Terms*
Full stop; end of idea; final downward inflection	Period .	 G.P. *fine*	Any "End"; End of the piece, movement, or phrase (a stronger phrase-ending
Partial stop; pause; upward inflection; incomplete idea	Comma , Semi-colon ; Colon : Dash - Question mark ? Ellipsis ...	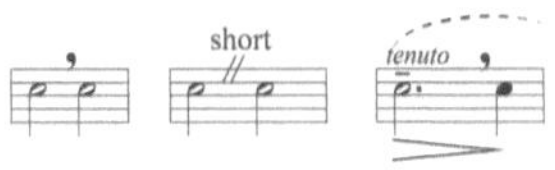 short / tenuto	Phrasing Breath; Pause; End of a phrase (weaker); Separation between two musical ideas or sections; Half-cadence; Antecedent phrase; "false stop" continuing to next phrase
Accentuation or Emphasis (shorter values)	Exclamation mark ! **Bold** (letter, symbol or syllable)	 fz sf sfz sub.f rit. ff	Accent (shorter); *ff-ff* dynamics; musical point-of-emphasis; "punch"; top of a *crescendo*
Emphasis (longer)	**Bold** (word or phrase) Underline Larger font	 Soloistic "To the fore" ff	Accent (longer); *ff-fff* dynamics; "Solo/Soli"; "To the fore"; *Bring out*; *Sforzando*
Other Long Emphasis (setting a phrase or idea apart from its surrounding ideas)	Brackets [ ] Parentheses ( ) Italics Quotation Marks " "	 Subject	*Maestoso*; theme or *Subject* (as in a Fugue); *Marcato* (longer sections); *Obbligato; Sonoro; Deciso*
To link a split word between lines	The Hyphen -	**V.S.** **Attacca**	"Volti Subito" ("turn quickly"; get to the next page right away); Go directly ahead
Possession *or* omission of characters (as in a contraction)	The apostrophe '	*(Less relevant to music notation)*	-
Other - 1. To replace *or*, and 2. to list equivalent words	The slash /	*(Less relevant to music notation)*	-

Figure 9.1 Making musical connections to speech, writing, and reading.

Beaming, Grouping, and Context Clues

Performers read notation that has been standardized over centuries. Music-readers are conditioned to recognize rhythmic figures more easily when beat-groups are identified by beaming. Non-standard beaming makes for tricky rhythm-reading, even if the notation "adds up" mathematically. We simply learn to respond better to conventional (and thus predictable) choices in music notation.

To illustrate the oddity, "writ ean ysent enc eon th ebo ard" with incorrect spacing; ask a volunteer to read it. Just one simple sentence provides an engaging way to convey the lesson: reading has an undeniable effect on *performance fluency* in music.

But the focus of the next exercise is not really on *reading* at all, because we can see that the student *did* read the sentence, though hesitantly at first. Rather, this engaging tactic is designed to attract students to the search for artistry, hidden in the notes. The author created this strategy for personal use during honor-band experiences, to provide exceptional students with something *beyond* simply "performing quality repertoire at an exceptional level." Further, the author counts this among his most effective rehearsal processes.

1. Start by displaying the following text, or something similar of your own design:

   Them—Us—I
   (CIA) Nmu: Stk
   Nowh Owtog Ro
   Upno . . . Teswit
   Hart is, Try?

2. Provide a description of the challenge. This scripted version offers a model for adaptation to your style: "This is why we're here. You'll probably understand soon by yourself, and I'll guide you toward figuring it out, but we've got to know together: *this* is our goal, and *this* is what will make our concert a wonderfully moving event for everyone. So, if you already know, please *don't* tell us aloud—tell us with your work, but don't say the answer out loud. Just by a show of hands, how many of you already know exactly what this means?" [Remind them not to speak aloud.] "Wow, that's great! Come see me on our first break, and I'll let you know if you're correct."

i). Load the rehearsal with your favorite *interpretation strategies* to

- shape a phrase
- avoid poorly placed breaths
- choose and emphasize important points-of-arrival
- highlight principles of tension and release.

Use excerpts from the literature, or a standard warm-up, or even a scale or chorale. During these exercises, refer to the display occasionally: "This is what we're doing right now . . . do you understand yet? You *will* soon!" Tip: On behalf of the backbone of your band, you're urged to keep percussionists engaged with this process as well.

ii). Once you've addressed your favorite interpretive topics, and you've worked to stimulate students with many kinds of prompts, then you can reveal the "secret." Display the new version:

>The musician must know
>how to group notes with artistry.

"This" [point to a space] "is what happens when you interrupt the phrase by breathing in an illogical spot."

"And this" [point to a misplaced large-case letter] "is your sound 'sticking out' as you play too loudly, or with poor tone."

"And this might be the worst . . ." [choose the colon, the question mark, or the ellipsis] "This is a great example of how you can distort the entire artistic meaning of the performance by misdirecting your musical emphasis."

"You see? The answer was in front of you the entire time, but you couldn't understand it. And maybe you couldn't even read it, because it was poorly presented. It had the right letters, but none of the other important components needed to clarify *meaning* for us."

"In music, we are obligated to provide our listeners with *meaning* in everything we perform. Notes and rhythms are like letters and punctuation . . . they can be 'right' without being 'meaningful'."

Paraphrase this of course to reflect your style. Then, return immediately to additional and more advanced strategies to reinforce students' artistic understanding.

With an abundance of research highlighting the language-music connections, this suggested diversion relies instead on simple observations about our human experiences:

1. When we read, we recognize words rather than letters and characters.
2. Further, we require *groups* of words, and context, to fully understand *meaning*.

But while this lesson is surely effective, another component of expressiveness is also easily demonstrated with engaging strategies: in both language and music, meaning is further clarified through *emphasis* and *inflection*.

The Art of Emphasis

This strategy effectively demonstrates that each performance can project a unique meaning based on performers' choices. We use inflection and emphasis to sculpt musical phrases in the same way we rely on those elements to clarify the meaning of speech. In brief, by altering the *emphasis*, we can modify one short sentence to convey several alternative messages. Read the following sentence, using inflections as shown. Even young students recognize that each utterance creates a different meaning. More importantly, though, each version also indicates a unique direction which, in turn, will elicit a different kind of response:

1. *We* can play beautifully.   [*Others*, however, may not have that ability.]
2. We *can* play beautifully.   [We're confident!]
3. We can *play* beautifully.   [But, gosh, don't ask us to dance.]
4. We can play *beautifully*.   [Did you see Mr. L *crying?!*]

This short illustration is an excellent pathway toward controlling musical artistry through conscious choices. Until students develop independence, we simply guide them toward appropriate artistic choices. Decisions made *democratically*—even about interpretive elements—will "stick," because students are invested in the choices. Therefore, rather than dictating "put a breath mark there" or "play that note louder," consider using group-based approaches like questioning, prompts, comparisons, and students' input.

Many outstanding conductors use some version of this method, because it works. The author first encountered it in Nilo W. Hovey's *The Selmer Band Manual* (Selmer, 1955), which in itself is a wonderful resource, and revised it over the years to fit his own teaching. The brief preceding version works well, and quickly. But for a more deeply engaging and even entertaining sequence, choose a longer sentence. Then, lead the group through a preconceived question-and-answer sequence to demonstrate these truths:

- A nine-word sentence can convey *at least* nine different meanings.
- Similarly, a musical line can convey an infinite set of meanings, dependent on the delivery.

Display this sentence in writing: *I thought you would drive your car to Chicago*, and lead students on an engaging journey through at least nine different implied meanings. [RW9.1] offers a scripted lesson plan.

The importance of the lesson is this: by applying *emphasis* and *inflection* in selective ways, we can convey specific meaning with our musical performances.

Section 3: Additional Instructional Pathways to Musical Artistry

Applying Basic, Predictable "Rules" to Chorales

Earlier, we explored some common guidelines (the "rules") leading toward expressiveness in music performance. Those concepts become more practical when they can help us to perform our music the same way every time. And that, of course, requires musicians to *write markings* into music. In this strategy, we'll use the flute part from *Warm Up #21* (Linaberry, 2002), unmarked at first. But the process can be applied to any chorale.

First, lead the ensemble through any chorale, reminding students about the components of expressive playing. At first, without any written expressive markings, the musical line might sound as bland as it appears (Figure 9.2).

Figure 9.2 Chorale line without markings.

Repeat the chorale over days, or even weeks; each time, instruct students on *specific* markings to pencil into their music. You might engage the help of your section leaders to make sure the markings are entered. To finish the lesson . . .

  . . . choose an exemplar from each section, or mark parts yourself
  . . . copy and distribute the model parts
  . . . conduct the group through an expressive performance of the chorale, asking students to specifically follow the pencil markings.

Bonus: by making a baseline recording of the first attempt, it will be fun and effective to *compare* a recording of this latter version; the students should recognize the results of their efforts. The student-marked version *might* look like that shown in Figure 9.3.

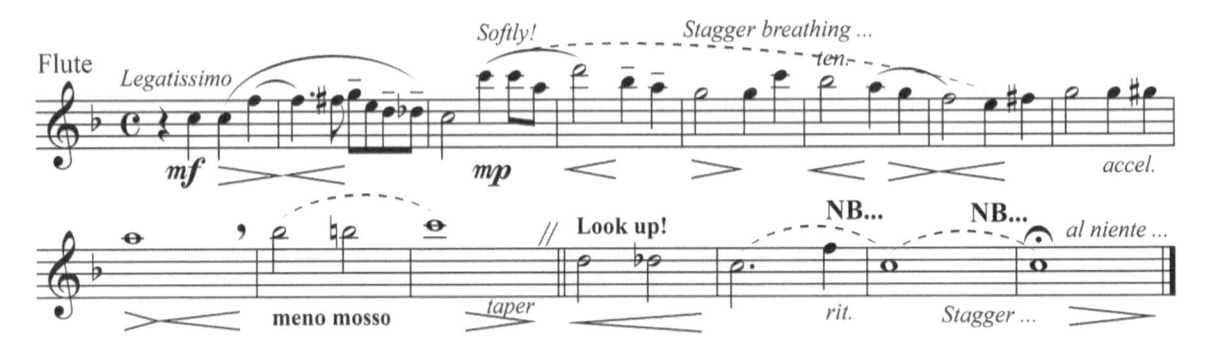

Figure 9.3 Chorale line with expressive markings added.

This lesson, "The power of the pencil," reinforces the importance of writing markings into the music.

Evaluating Interpretive Playing

A recent educational adage claims that *if it can be measured, it can be improved*. If true, then we should be able to use a rubric to assess the various components of expressiveness. Then, we can evaluate musicians' interpretative skills by applying an objective numeric scale to a chorale (or any other legato passage), with qualifying descriptors so students can learn from the exercise. Here is just one example as a prototype for further experimentation.

Element and Rubric descriptor	Element Assessment Score
Breathing	
Breath spots are chosen wisely, and *executed* artistically	= 4
Breaths are *mostly* chosen for musically appropriate reasons	= 2
Students breathe on barlines or at other random spots, without considering effects on musical expression	= 0
Musical Direction/Inflection	
Smoothly connected, with obvious artistic choice of direction/inflection	= 4
Some instances of artistic direction/inflection choices	= 2
There is no evidence of conscious choices affecting direction/inflection	= 0
Performance Interpretation	
(Observance of markings, from both symbols and text)	
Expressively performed, with artistic observance of all markings	= 4
There are attempts to observe markings, with some oversights	= 2
No apparent understanding of (or observance of) markings	= 0

Customize your approach to address specific interpretive skills, using language extracted from your own teaching style. Other skill categories can include tempo, basic rhythm and note accuracy, tone quality, vibrato for soloists, and any other expressiveness ideals that you deem important. A numeric rubric is not always warranted; consider a simple checklist to demarcate that the band does or does not demonstrate the element.

TIP: This type of exercise, though valuable, may be better if included only as a "periodic examination," rather than a frequent expectation. By highlighting students' deficiencies *regularly*—and by speaking about emotions *unemotionally*—we risk damaging the very enjoyment we hope to foster in musicians. Remember that the "what" in teaching may not be as powerful as the "how," so be mindful of how students perceive your delivery.

Establishing Purpose: A Method to Encourage Students' Discovery of Their Artistry

An engaging way to introduce this approach begins on YouTube: search for "How Music can Change a Film" to display how a single scene will convey an entirely new message each time a different soundtrack is applied. It's easy and enjoyable for students to observe that the basic character of a scene (e.g., comedic, thoughtful, foreboding, tragic, triumphant) is portrayed more by music than by visual means. These short examples can demonstrate how to cultivate that awareness in rehearsals:

o *Song and dance.* Some venerated conductors will say that, at its basic level, all music is either "song" or "dance." But if our composition is a song, is it a love song, fight song, lament, celebration, or something else? And if we are playing a dance, we'll need to define exactly what kind. We have interpretive choices at hand to fill in the story's blank spaces. TIP: With any dance, it may be especially enjoyable for students to watch a willing director miming the movements. And for a song-like piece, class activities involving highly descriptive language (e.g. adjectives, scene portrayals, analogies) are also very effective. In both cases, the director's creativity plays a central role.

o *Provide background details.* Determine together if the composition is designed to tell a story, as program music hopes to do. If so, how can we use interpretive choices to provide detail to our story? Let's have "more intensity here," "subtle rubato there," and perhaps "a longer space after that fermata, so the listeners can absorb the last phrase a little more." TIP: If it is not a programmatic work, however, the same types of descriptors can be used to shape the band's performance.

o *Access the group's collective creativity—a fun project for students.* Even with a decidedly programmatic piece, it can be productive to engage students' imaginativeness. For example, pieces like *Cry of the Last Unicorn* (Rossano Galante) and *The Light Eternal* (James Swearingen) are musical depictions of stories. Consider withholding the story, often found at the beginning of the score, until the work is partially learned. Then, provide a class project as an assignment, an option, an extra-credit opportunity, or even an interdisciplinary "creative writing" task shared with the English teacher: "This piece tells a very specific tale. Let's see what *you* think the music is saying. Write a short essay to share your version of the story: what do you think is happening? Does the story have characters? Is there a conflict-resolution sequence? Does it describe an item, visual scene, historic event, or something else?" The submission doesn't have to be "correct"; there can be many interpretations. Through this endeavor, students strengthen their understanding of the relationship between musical interpretation processes and literary devices. And it's both fun and engaging.

o *Establish the purpose.* This is a supplementary project, beyond musical aspects of the rehearsal, but the diversion may be worth the short time required: provide students with a standard "real estate" listing. They'll read details about the house and its surrounding property including size, number of rooms, whether it has a walk-out basement, and if it has replacement windows. They'll learn if the property has highway access, a fenced-in yard, a security system, and if it's in a development or a rural setting. Those details are all important to the realtor trying to sell the house. Then ask students to "reread the advertisement again, but from the perspective of a *robber*." Students will see details in a new way. Likewise, our musical interpretation is based on choices that we make, and those choices are prescribed by our purpose. What do we hope to convey to listeners? In just moments, students will discover more fuel to drive the group's work toward a collective artistic interpretation.

The Creativity of Delivery: Metaphors, Analogies, Stories, and Descriptions

Here is the better-known portion of a quote from *De Poetica*: "The greatest thing by far is to be a master of metaphor." In terms of teaching music, few would disagree with Aristotle. Indeed, the most outstanding and memorable conductors are described as such, probably more because of their communication skills than for any other characteristic. They reach students.

But Aristotle continues, "it is the one thing that cannot be learned from others; and it is also a sign of genius, since a good metaphor implies an intuitive perception of the similarity in the dissimilar." Sadly, no book, this one included, can realistically teach how to become a master of engaging communication. The command of metaphor, analogies, stories, and descriptions is an elusive *art* that might never be taught nor learned, but it will be recognized at every encounter. TIP: This is a compelling reason to observe other teachers often, because in teaching, as with other professions, our excellence stands in part on the shoulders of influencers. Share and exchange with colleagues. And when you encounter a true master, "beg" and "borrow" (avoid outright stealing) but then carefully modify their material, adapting it to suit your style, and your students' needs.

Connecting to Students' Interests

"Human thought processes are largely metaphorical."[7] With a metaphor, students understand one concept in terms of another. Both metaphors and analogies are particularly effective when the teacher chooses a reference that intersects with students' shared experiences and interests. We can improve the effectiveness of our communication by connecting to the students' interests; we deliver the same material, but with subtle assistance from connections that draw on those interests.

Directors learn very quickly that the age and make-up of students can provide a rich collection of communication magnifiers. That is, a middle school director might relate musical goal-setting and perseverance to video gaming, where getting from one level to the next is a prideful achievement. Similarly, learning a helpful alternate fingering equates to finding the game's hidden tool or "cheat code" for advancement. But a high school director might relate the same musical discussion to a skill-building workout in a favorite sport, or to the intricacies of studying for a driver's test.

In 2015, the author heard a particularly charismatic guest conductor deliver a well-timed two-word compliment to students after a remarkably good passage: "Hashtag—WOW!" and the players responded with prideful smiles. But in a different year, the same comment would be either meaningless, or stale and clichéd. TIP: Stay aware of trends, pop culture, local traditions, and players' shared interests.

Choose Engaging Imagery

Use knowledge about your students to help construct the most magnetic approach. Think of the most engaging analogues you've even experienced. You'll remember what you felt when playing for a preeminent conductor, or when you observed a particularly enthralling clinician. You'll recall successful (and failing!) choices from your own work as a teacher, hopefully drawing from your written log of personal favorites. There's no doubt that most effective directors share this lifelong goal: to build an ever-expanding personal repertoire of engaging communication strategies. While assembling your own collection, refer to other examples:

- Review "The Swan Parallel" (p. 126).
- Search the internet.

- Collect successful imagery from music education books and journals.
- If not overused, inspirational quotes serve an engaging purpose; they are easy to find and, if chosen selectively, can be as meaningful and entertaining as analogies.
- Read "Nuggets" in the next section for some specific motivation.

Match the imagery carefully to the needs of the group:

- A college or community band responds easily to unadorned descriptions: use the bassoon section as the model; copy their articulation style and note-lengths whenever this figure shows up in your part.
- Younger students might benefit from expanded imagery: "OK, for this passage, we're like a team, all playing with the same ball. The size, shape, weight, and texture are always the same, regardless of who has it. When someone passes it to you, keep it unchanged until you pass it to someone else. We're all working to move the same ball down the court."

By matching the delivery to the needs and interests of the band, you'll increase your effectiveness. Exemplary band director Bobby Adams offers a perfect description of the musical experience in the bandroom. This single sentence encases the director's delivery, the band members' performance, and the use of imagery as the conduit: "If done correctly, playing music—alone or with others—is not unlike walking the highwire: Total engagement, constant adjustment, or disaster."[8]

Section 4: Tying It All Together

Nuggets of "Intangible" Wisdom in Brief: Some Philosophies and Quick-Fix Plans

- "Good phrasing necessitates approaching and generally receding from a natural climax or high spot. Succeeding phrases of a similar nature must be handled in a refreshing manner to avoid monotony."[9]
- Remember the "default" plan—identify the most important note(s) in a musical phrase, mark them (perhaps with an asterisk) then apply shaping procedures.
- Low searches for high, and high searches for low.[10]
- Follow a "contour-based" phrasing plan—as the pitches go higher, get generally louder, reversing the plan as the pitches descend.
- Occasionally reverse the contour-based plan for comparison, where high becomes softer and low becomes louder. Incidentally, this may not be your final phrasing choice, but it offers good support to the pyramid of sound. Occasionally, for comparison, play a flattened, monotonous phrasing without dynamic direction of any kind.
- Teach students to "breathe when neighbors are *not* breathing." That may be an abstract concept for some. But there are other, more manageable, methods to erase the feeling of unwanted barlines. Consider adding breath marks with penciled initials to couple each mark with its player: "RL" after beat 2, and "PM" after beat 3. Or, ask students to breathe in chair-order. The goal is to help wind players learn to control an uninterrupted ensemble sound.
- At *pianissimo* and *al niente* releases, let the sound "evaporate."
- Play the music, not the instrument.
- The smaller the note value, the louder the dynamic—another description of emphasizing moving notes within each line.
- Facial expression is a potent communicator. Without words, what does your face convey to students?
- Choose conducting motions that shape the music. Combined, your hands, face, fingers, and body motions should help deliver the one-and-only message you collectively want listeners to hear.
- Model the *style* before the downbeat. Every interpretive concept can be communicated through gestures, descriptions, your count-off and other verbalizations, even before the music begins.

- Work together—conductor with ensemble—to discover the music's meaning. Bobby Adams calls it "probing." He wisely counsels us that asking students whether music is "happy" or "sad" is only a partial question. "But suppose in this instance the piece is discovered to be a sad piece. Therefore, the next question is, "what kind of sad?" Is it sadness related to death, a disappointment, a longing for something in the past, loneliness, regret, etc. This, too, has to be discovered."[11]
- Share conducting and movement exercises with students to experience the feeling of interpretive elements like resistance, tension and release, a *molto ritard* in a big *crescendo*, the development (growth) of a phrase, and *decrescendo*.
- Stock up as a learner—in terms of interpretation, it may be more important for the "conductor" to study adjectives and adverbs more than cut-off gestures. And, your facial expressions and acting skills may be as important as words. Read a story, watch a movie, hear a joke, learn a dance, and then put those emotions into your delivery.
- Remember the power of . . . a pause. In conjunction with inflections, these two expressions can be perceived quite differently by students: "I think that's great!" compared to, "I think that's . . . great."
- Again, the importance of recording/playback for evaluation cannot be overstated. When a unified approach has been chosen, record the band's performance and play it back. Do we hear the details in the story?
- Practice applying expressiveness strategies to a piece that has already been learned very well. Without technique issues cluttering their performance, students are free to concentrate on interpretive aspects. Perform the same excerpt using several different interpretations; record and compare the results. Can students clearly hear their choices?
- With your performance of a single passage, use interpretive skills to . . .

    . . . express love
    . . . scold the listener
    . . . question someone, with insistence
    . . . beg, plead, cry
    . . . convey confidence, discontent, sadness, anger.

A Random Sampling of Additional Suggestions

In a chapter entitled "The Intangibles," the possibilities are unlimited. It is unlikely that such a chapter can address every available option, so the segment below offers just a small selection of additional thoughts, all designed to foster the search for artistry in the performance.

- *More on dynamics.* Earlier we discussed substituting *numbers* for dynamics, referring to numbers for their measurable, incremental value. Notice now that numbers 1 through 10 will be comparable to a volume controller on audio devices. Thus, "play at a level of 5" indicates a dynamic "halfway between the softest and the loudest." Or, we can choose 1 through 6 to align with our most common dynamic levels: *pp, p, mp, mf, f,* and *ff*. With a numbers-based dynamic scale, we can train students to manipulate their dynamic control. For example: "1 is as softly as you can play with good tone; 6 is as loudly. . ." and then guide the band with statements like, "I know you're all marked *mf*, but in this passage let's ask Clarinets to play at a 4 while saxes and percussion drop yours to a 2."
- *More on connections.* "Art" in music can be discovered through the probing, or it can be reproduced, imitated, or created anew using our collection of performance practices. We know that music is responsible for supporting and perhaps *creating* the character of film and live experiences. But artistic choices in music performance can also be influenced by comparison to other artworks. Instead of reading the composer's program notes, for instance, we can reference a painting, sculpture, tapestry, or book to provide details of the "story." TIP: By creating a detailed narrative in advance, you can supplement the band rehearsals with interesting and engaging discussions.
- *More on special experiences.*

> *"Can we have today off? We just had our concert last night."* Rather than taking a day "off," use the opportunity to re-energize students by exploring exciting alternative activities:
> - ☐ Evaluate the concert recording with a detailed critical-listening guide.
> - ☐ Replay the same literature, rotating part-assignments.
> - ☐ Sight-read a new piece.
> - ☐ Start applying details to long-term literature.
> - ☐ Replay a known work, choosing a new interpretation.
> - ☐ Play music at a very easy technical level as a vehicle for artistic experimentation.
> - ☐ Your additional ideas can provide a rejuvenating experience.
>
> *Consider including a sight-reading session on a concert.* It's a fascinating process for the audience and, if managed carefully, it can also serve to amplify the band members' concentration. Similarly, program a chorale or other expressive piece without a conductor. Performing successfully *sans conductor* involves every layer of independence from each musician, and promotes the deep awareness skills we hope our students will develop.
>
> *Include a "special experience" during a concert.* A Prism Concert, we know, offers unparalleled prospects for exploring unconventional music, lighting, spacing, pacing, and other components of live performance. The very nature of a Prism Concert gives more *ownership* of the event to the performers. And, with some thought, we can include innovative plans to supplement students' musical experience; these short examples may spark further ideas:
> - ☐ Offer extra opportunities to engage students (as composers, conductors, designers, score-readers for lighting scene-changes).
> - ☐ Foster collaboration with other school groups. For example, the Art Department might present its annual art show around the auditorium, or could help create a slide show of appropriate artworks to accompany a live performance of an Impressionistic piece.
> - ☐ Provide a multi-media performance. Students at the middle- and high-school levels might especially love *The Haunted Carousel* (Erika Svanoe) with its iPad "theremin" solo; creative options then include featuring a beloved music teacher as the soloist, adding movement and choreography designed by the students, or designing special lighting effects to support the music. [RW9.2] is a downloadable list of suggestions.
> - ☐ Collaborate directly with composers to augment the students' experience. When the author featured *Lights Out!* (Alex Shapiro), the composer offered to communicate with the band members; written, email, and virtual messages can provide a wonderful "special" experience for the students.
>
> *"Why Music Matters"*—this is a compelling demonstration by Jack Stamp, easily found on YouTube. Try an easy adaptation using a known *Treasury of Scales* chorale. Ask students to consciously play *one* error. In a fifteen-measure chorale, a single error yields a "score" of 93.3%, an "A" in academic terms. And yet the sound is unacceptable. Thomas Duffy's clever composition demonstrates the concept on a concert. Try, "A+: A 'Precise' Prelude and an 'Excellent' March."

Section 5: The Power of the It-Factor

A recurrent theme throughout this book is that, while strategies can be very effective, the *most effective factor* may be the teacher. Carl Strommen says, "It's the chef that counts."[12] That is, with all other "ingredients" equal—practice, fundamentals, instrumentation, desire among students, private lessons—some bands still perform better, with more beautiful tone, and an obvious artistic expressiveness. The most important factor to those bands is *you*; the director makes the difference. So regarding the strategies and activities you'll employ, the most lasting results depend on how *you* deliver the message. TIP: Revisit Chapter 8 with a new perspective after reading "The Intangibles."

- *The "art" of the teacher's delivery can rely on the wording.* An adage attributed to Roosevelt, among others, says, "Comparison is the thief of joy." It's certainly possible that comparing one's own achievements and circumstances with those of more gifted, more fortunate people can be emotionally draining. But it's also true that comparison can effectively illuminate the path to improvement. The difference lies in the delivery, once again. Because we use comparisons so frequently in teaching, it's wise to consider the implications of what we say, and how.

    With careful wording, teachers can avoid the negative connotation of questions like, "What's not good about yours . . . why was theirs better?" Instead, try "Here's what makes your performance good . . . yours already had this strength and this triumph, but theirs had [another element]. Let's try it again, imitating the better parts." And of course, deliver it with optimism and enthusiasm.

    Remember that, for many students, awareness of specific attributes in a musical performance hasn't yet developed. For them, critical listening is still an abstract. Instead of "What do you notice?"—which may lie beyond their cognitive capabilities—try, "Do you know what they did well? What did you like? Can you tell me what made theirs sound better in that passage?" These reworded questions serve as prompts to help mold and focus students' responses during comparative listening.

    Then, follow with (as an example) "Now, can you do that? Let's try it, and then we'll listen to the recording. Did yours sound better this time?" Some students simply don't notice performance features as easily as others do, and require further prompts. Similarly, the teacher must notice that some wording-choices work better to evoke responses; the process should be personalized for students. This skill improves over time for teachers who stay alert.
- *Getting to the "It" of the "It-Factor."* This book has mentioned *It* more than a few times: some directors just seem to have *It* while perhaps *It* eludes others. The director with *It*—charisma, perhaps—can easily be identified. She, or he, enthralls listeners, eloquently spinning a simple story into a "can't put the book down" moment. He, or she, is confident yet without arrogance, because of a focus on others rather than self. This director is both interested and interesting, and yet it seems that listening is as important as talking.

    "Yes, this is how I want to be!" But can it be learned?

    In the business world, this special charisma is often called "executive presence." We know athletes who demonstrate it, and it's easily identifiable in a public speaker, politician, host, chairperson, and others; for those with *It*, anyway, it's obvious within moments. Or, it's obviously missing. Sometimes it seems that some people just have *It*, but perhaps they work persistently. This quest will always require looking inward.

    Some will say that *It* is simply an attitude rather than a skill. But confident, radiating charisma has components; each of those is worthy of reflection, and practice. Just as we separate students' skills and musicianship into components for practice, we too can work at each piece of the larger puzzle in the constant pursuit of better, more engaging delivery in the classroom.
- *Desirable characteristics guiding the music teacher* (a.k.a. more components of the *It Factor*): observations of expert role models will reveal that the most inspirational music teachers—the *great* ones—seem to share a common set of qualities, some of which are condensed into a sample listing below. These descriptors may provide the adhesive to hold your rehearsal-design choices together. *The outstanding band director . . .*

    - *. . . is affable.* This is a consistently fair and kind person who follows The Golden Rule. This teacher exudes an indefinable magnetism, constantly inspiring and almost never intimidating students.
    - *. . . models—and expects—musical, technical, and behavioral fundamentals.* This teacher is a consistent personification of classroom objectives.
    - *. . . sets goals which are logically chosen* based on the group's demonstrated skill-level. Therefore, goals are achievable in a stepwise skill-development trajectory to avoid frustrating over-expectations. Each goal is its own reward: the "carrot" is dangled where it can be reached.

    ... *is guided by the music.* This teacher determines the course of the rehearsal more by the music than by errors, and errors are addressed in terms of how the music is affected.

    ... *offers enough repetition to ingrain desired results.* The teacher helps students achieve, not just once but with a "Practice makes permanent" mentality.

    ... *also remembers to include through-performances.* The teacher maintains performance-mode by simulating the concert, which in turn refines students' attention and endurance.

    ... *observes the students' responses and alters the rehearsal activities accordingly.* The effective teacher intuitively knows when to provide breaks, tangents, anecdotes, and other relevant activities, helping students to maintain attention while *enjoying* the process.

    ... *involves students in decision-making where appropriate* to keep the focus on the music, but steers the eventual choices toward acceptable options.

    ... *reviews fundamental skills within the wording of new instructions.* This teacher is adept at providing feedback and directions, stacking new objectives atop a supportive review of earlier achievements and expectations.

And, perhaps above all other qualities, the effective band director ...

    ... *is a master of communication, feedback, and motivation.* This teacher is eloquent yet succinct, conveying concepts verbally and nonverbally with equal effectiveness. Everything the teacher does, says, and demonstrates during a rehearsal is meaningful. With this in mind, the best band directors also regard their personal professional growth as *continuous*, for life: always learning, always adapting.

Notes

1 Evan Feldman and Ari Contzius, *The Rehearsal Toolkit* (New York: Routledge Textbooks, Taylor & Francis, 2011), https://routledgetextbooks.com/textbooks/9781138921405/additional-chapters.php.
2 Richard Floyd, *The Artistry of Teaching and Making Music* (Chicago: GIA Publications, Inc., 2015), 108.
3 Mark Fonder, "Teaching Harmonic Tension and Resolution," in *The Conductor's Companion: 100 Rehearsal Techniques, Imaginative Ideas, Quotes, and Facts*, ed. Gary Stith (Delray Beach, FL: Meredith Music Publications, 2015), 36.
4 Bobby Adams, *Music: From Skill to Art* (Chicago: GIA Publications, Inc., 2015), 51.
5 Shelley Jagow, *Teaching Instrumental Music: Developing the Complete Band Program* (Galesville MD: Meredith Music Publications, 2007), 109.
6 Gregory Rudgers, "Teaching Students to 'Feel' the Phrase," in *The Conductor's Companion*, ed. Stith, 86.
7 George Lakoff and Mark Johnson, *Metaphors We Live By* (Chicago: University of Chicago Press, 1980), 6.
8 Adams, *Music: From Skill to Art*, 50.
9 Walter Beeler, "Improving the Sound of the Band." This version first appeared in the WASBE Newsletter, reorganized and edited by Mark Fonder, http://www.timreynish.com/conducting/conducting-articles/improving-the-sound.php.
10 Ed Lisk, *Intangibles of Music Performance* (Delray Beach, FL: Meredith Music Publications, 1996), 31–36.
11 Adams, *Music: From Skill to Art*, 56.
12 Garwood Whaley, *The Music Director's Cookbook* (Galesville MD: Meredith Music Publications, 2005), 108.

10

WRAP-UP

Without question, no single source can provide every solution to every problem you'll encounter. But the book has stayed true to its mission: to offer a vast collection of tips and pedagogical strategies that can be used immediately, without further training. Even so, there have been some notable voids so far in the text. This chapter visits other important topics, even if superficially, to offer guidance toward additional self-reflection and professional growth.

Section 1: Curriculum Matters

You may work with a curriculum that has been carefully vetted, tested, and modified when needed. Or perhaps you're in the early stages of writing or revising curriculum, with a partial plan in place. Still other readers have no curriculum at all. It is beyond the scope of this book to delve deeply into curriculum, assessment, grading, and policy issues. Much of that is predetermined by each unique situation.

This section targets directors without an established curriculum. This collection of strategies can supplement any current curriculum, but it's really designed for directors who need "something," and quickly. Ponder a few common questions:

- What repertoire and level of difficulty should my band play?
- How do I grade the students?
- What is the instructional content of my instrumental classes?
- What assessments can I put into place easily?
- How do I manage program tasks like placement auditions, expectations/assignments, goal-setting, and record-keeping about students' skills?

Curriculum

This section presents some ideas directed toward programs where no written curriculum exists. Without records from the previous year (e.g. from "feeder" colleagues), then one of the first tasks is apparent: "Level" your students, assessing their skill-levels to evaluate individual needs.

We ultimately have the same goal whether teaching a novice or a superlative musician: let's start with what you can already do, and then set a plan for *improvement* including specific objectives and target dates. You'll need printed music to accomplish this task; consider these sources:

- *Sight-reading* diagnoses students' strengths and weaknesses quickly. Sight-reading books are available for each instrument, and for the full-band setting. If those materials are not available, other resources easily adapt for sight-reading assessment:
  - *Method books*—these don't need to be "the" books used in lessons. You can simply flip through numerous books; find exercises to build the progression you'd like your students to sight-read. TIP: Using method books and other printed matter, spend a rainy summer day creating your own sight-reading curriculum.

WRAP-UP

- *Band repertoire*—craft a sight-reading task comprised of excerpts from band compositions, sorted easy-to-difficult. Include a variety of meters, rhythmic figures, high- and low-range passages, chromatics, and especially technical demands. While students read through excerpts, make notes about their needs. TIP: Choose demanding excerpts from compositions you hope to perform with your band. While discovering students' skill-levels, you'll collect evidence guiding repertoire selection. You can then discard, or postpone, pieces deemed too difficult for a majority of players.
- *Online sight-reading*—at the time of this writing, notable examples include SmartMusic®; Finale's sight-reading worksheets; Sight-Reading Factory® (www.sightreadingfactory.com); and other web and digital sources. TIP: Selectable options allow difficulty and other characteristics to be predetermined. Notably, Sight-Reading Factory® is based on filters, so you can choose exactly which types of attributes students will read.
- *Original compositions*—write or find short etudes representing the targeted skills; transpose for each instrument. All students (battery percussion excepted, of course) will be playing the same music. TIP: Use this project to refine your own notation-software skills; save your work into a well-organized library.

○ The Watkins-Farnum Performance Scale© can be an excellent pillar to support any band program for players of any age, from beginners to professionals. This is a wonderful method for kick-starting the recommended Evaluate>Diagnose>Prescribe process. Created in 1954, the Watkins-Farnum Performance Scale is a reliable standardized test for evaluating instrumental performance skills. The test consists of short etudes, arranged in order of progressive difficulty. Starting with whole- and half-notes/rests, each subsequent etude adds increasingly advanced skills. While it evaluates sight-reading, the test also exposes strengths and weaknesses quickly and objectively. TIP: This device can also be used effectively for auditions, seating placement, tie-breakers and, if desired, grading or recognitions. See [RW10.1] for a thorough discussion.

○ *"How far can you go?"*—with subtle guidance from the director, students can define their own goals. It is a quick, straightforward way to create a syllabus for a month, term, or year, and will be customized to each student's needs. The self-created syllabus is easily enforced because it's elective, rather than mandated by the teacher: the student creates the goals. And it's organized well enough to drive the instruction all year, or until determining together that a new path is needed. Here's a basic structural outline that you can adapt to your situation:

- *Gather* materials—prepare the session by selecting printed music from method books, etudes, excerpts, and even solos, at approximately the difficulty you estimate will be best for the students.
- *Describe* the process—let students know that they will choose their goals, assessments, and timeline. At the end of the session, students will have chosen what to play, the "due date," and how they will be assessed. TIP: Allow students to choose one short test-piece; the director chooses another.
- *Guide students* through the task—give step-by-step assistance. For example: "If you already know everything on that page, let's just play a bit, but then move on. Search for music that challenges you, but that you could achieve by your chosen deadline. It's important that you don't skip any skills: music learning is cumulative." But, retain the power of veto if their goal-setting is too easy, or too advanced.
- *List goals* clearly—keep careful records. List (for example) a page number, an excerpt of specific length, a metronome-marking for a solo, or even a set of added rudiments or alternate fingerings/slide-positions.
- *Share a description* of the "successful" performance—consider a specific rubric, or just describe how you'll determine together whether the goal is met.
- *Design* a series of stepping-stones—choose a schedule of benchmarks to help plan successive lesson sessions.
- *Allow an "out"*—students' personal goal-setting is often a case of "I bit off more than I can chew." So, allow for students to fail a bit without devastating consequences. Keep the positive reinforcements flowing while you work together to redesign the goal/date.

- *Subtle steering* of students toward skills and etudes that align with your own philosophy and expectations can be beneficial; or, toward goals that build the skills required to perform your chosen band repertoire.

    Although this description is rather long, with practice you can lead students through the goal-setting process within just one school-length instructional period. The result is not limited to having a syllabus in place; a better outcome is that students take ownership of their learning. They choose a successful path rather than having unattainable goals assigned to them.

- *The Objectives Sheet*—a quick, organized model allowing students to choose personal goals. The methods used to guide students in their goal-setting can have a profound effect on their progress, enjoyment, and self-esteem. This suggestion is driven by a basic educational truth: a student can achieve more when he wants to! Therefore, the most helpful process prompts students to identify specific goals, personalized to their own needs. Students start by recognizing current skills, using that finite information to set their future goals. Examples might include:

    - (On a musical staff) Show your comfortable high- and low-range limits.
    - (Using a metronome marking) How fast can you tongue sixteenth-notes . . . on a single pitch? . . . on a scale or musical line with moving pitches?
    - List fingerings/positions/rudiments that you need to review often, but haven't mastered yet.
    - Based on your own current skills, list "x" goals you hope to meet, and choose a target date for each goal.

Note that these student-designed objectives require reflection. They become so-named "SMART" goals because the objectives are *Specific, Measurable, Attainable, Relevant*, and *Time-bound*. In Chapter 8 (p. 156), we discussed an ensemble "help sheet." In this case, we can use the student's individual input to formulate a personalized "Goals Sheet," found at [RW10.2].

- *PACE—the Performance Achievement Cumulative Evaluation*. This suggestion can be reproduced independently after reading the description below. Or, go to the resources website [RW10.3] for more details.

    It's not uncommon for teachers to feel disorganized. In terms of students' skills and achievement levels, the question that structures our follow-up planning is plainly this: "Who can do exactly what, and how well?" In other words, it is valuable—perhaps imperative—for directors to know the skills, deficiencies, and cumulative experiences for each student. With a digital skills-based curriculum in place (e.g. SmartMusic assignments), the answers are only a click away. But in the absence of another plan, consider PACE. This program provides teachers with a cumulative record-keeping device individualized for every student: a teacher will finish the year knowing exactly what each student has achieved.

    The *Performance Achievement Cumulative Evaluation* is a blueprint providing musicians with an organized set of skill-goals. Designed to be completed in no more than two-to-four minutes during each session, PACE uses rubrics to assess and track data for common performance skills including:

    - scales (of all kinds), arpeggios, and other basic figures
    - rudiments for battery percussion
    - sight-reading as an objectively measured skill
    - level-of-success on the ensemble music (the student's part in any group's literature)
    - solos.

- *The Three-Tiered Assessment Model*–from *Habits of a Successful Band Director* by Scott Rush, this is just one example of how "tiers" can be designed as achievement levels. These tiers, like terraced benchmarks, each provide a list of skills and expectations. The plan serves as incentive toward students' self-motivated improvement. The three tiers are labeled Intermediate Musician, Advanced Musician, and Master Musician. Further, Rush offers an example of how each tier (i.e. each set of achievements) can be used to formulate a grade.[1]

Grading

Again, perhaps you work where an existing grading policy functions well and has weathered all challenges. If not, however, this topic goes well beyond the depth of this book, especially because there can be no "one size fits all" standard. Readers are encouraged to thoroughly consider various models of grading, some of which are listed in the following with comments about implications beyond grading (additional outstanding discussion is provided in Evan Feldman and Ari Contzius's *Instrumental Music Education* (Routledge, 2016, chapter 8)):

- *Portfolios*—beyond grading functions, portfolios provide a method for archiving artifacts including recordings, adjudications, writings, compositions, and much more. TIP: Consider passing the final portfolios to graduating seniors; they will surely treasure recordings from their beginner and intermediate years!
- *Tiers* and *accumulation* (of points, of skills)—tiers may also be viewed as "status levels" that are earned through demonstrated skills. Merit/demerit plans offer even more options, and the record-keeping can be combined with portfolio methods. TIP: Consider the value of recognition—even if only a verbal "shout-out"—for students reaching each new tier. Displaying lists of achievers can boost your program's motivation, if carefully managed. Adapt tiers to reflect your school colors and mascot (e.g. the Blue Musician, the Gold Musician, and the Spartan Musician).
- *Subjective methods*—subjectivity is often the source of discontent and disagreement. TIP: Locate rubrics that attach numeric values to carefully worded descriptors. In that way, a performance qualifies for a narrow, specific grade range only if it can be described with phrases from the rubric (e.g. "fluently, confidently," "correct rhythms," "only 2 to 4 errors," "measurably better than last week"). Also, subjectivity contains inherent opinion, so involve the students in a guided discussion about their performances.
- *Objective methods*—objective grading is probably the easiest to design, to calculate and, in the event of a dispute, to substantiate. TIP: Some objective processes can be delegated to student leaders, with careful oversight. Trained students can help with simple check-off performances, make-up work, and basic tabulations.
- *Philosophical considerations*—each policy must carefully delineate which components will be included in the grading calculations. Some elements will require a philosophical choice before being included in grading processes: practice, extra credit, effort, aptitude, "unforeseen circumstances," and transferring to a new instrument. Examples:
  - a *practice* report has an inherent question of honesty. A digital-activity method, such as SmartMusic assignments, can authenticate the practice.
  - even with an entirely objective policy, the student who changes from saxophone to oboe "to help the band" should not be penalized when unable to perform new skills at the "expected" level.

The genesis of a helpful plan lies in conversations with colleagues at other schools. Especially regarding teachers at cohort schools of the same basic size and community characteristics, ask the simple question first: "What is the grading policy for band at your school?" Most will describe it, and will probably share a copy with you. Your evaluation of their policy reveals that follow-up questions are necessary:

- If you grade performance, do you have a trustworthy rubric you could share?
- If attendance (outside the school day) is a part of the grade, what are your provisions for illness, emergencies, pre-existing conflicts, and make-up opportunities?
- Do you have a band handbook in place and, if so, are students asked to sign a contract? And most importantly,
- Does your policy have the proven support of your administrators?

Interesting scenarios arise in terms of grading, not only because of *subjectivity*, but also because unique conditions apply to music that have no equivalent in other disciplines. For example, Algebra grades certainly do not require attendance at a "math performance" from 6pm–9:30pm. And yet membership in a music group assumes extra-curricular hours.

WRAP-UP

The complicated scope of music grading becomes apparent to most teachers within just the first months of work: "I got a 96 for "Tone" but I really think it's at least a 98, and all my friends think so too. My parents are really angry." Or, "but Mr. L, I *did* tell the coach about our band concert. The only other pitcher has a broken arm, and tonight is the play-off game. What do I do?"

Directors are advised to give comprehensive forethought to this important policy-design task. It may help to involve your *constituents* to an extent (department teachers, students, and parents); as with other policies, it will be difficult for students to argue with a plan they've helped to design. This recommendation eclipses all others: the grading conversation *must* include your administration. School officials should expressly endorse your grading plan. Administrators will appreciate their involvement, and your role in their preparedness, if they need to talk with an unhappy parent.

> TIP: See the resources website [RW10.4] for sample rubrics and grading policy documents. You'll also find an innovative model that evaluates both "process" and "achievement"; this version is a matrix that addresses both progress *and* effort.

Other Policies and the Handbook

If you haven't inherited a successful band handbook, be careful with its design. Many of your successes and hardships can ultimately be traced back to your own policies, and how they were communicated and practiced. While there may be exceptions to this generalization, it's wise to administer your policies and consequences to *behaviors*, and not to students. Otherwise, you risk that your community might perceive favoritism or bias. Work for fairness, with equal treatment of all students. TIP: The careful work you put into the grading policy should be matched by special attention to expectations, absences/excuses, seating order, solos, rotations, behaviors, and so on. An easier solution is to adapt others' successful models into a hybrid handbook fitting your needs.

Section 2: Organization Matters

To this point, our discussion has addressed strategies for music folders, distributions/collections, lockers/cases/equipment, daily processes, and the percussion section overall. Peruse the "Bandroom Hacks & Shortcuts" file [RW7.9], for a large collection of additional organizational tips. This section offers even more supplementary suggestions toward improved efficiency in managerial aspects of the band director's job.

Some Cheap (and Free!) Organizational Strategies

- *Library, filing, and categorical storage*—working simultaneously with several large ensembles along with chamber groups and lesson classes, directors deal with enormous amounts of music. Even with highly organized processes in place, we can still find piles of disorganized music that appear and infiltrate our spaces. "I know you collected all this stuff last June, but I found this folder when my brother left for college." Without a plan for these situations, directors may be overwhelmed by random parts that accumulate with solos, method books, warm-up collections, and countless other pages of printed music in an unmanageable mess. TIPS:
    - Make sure the library is well organized—pieces are filed well, and the listing is printed and computerized. Note: if all sheets are stamped and numbered, they can be filed by anyone.
    - Create "holding areas"—bins, shelves, cubbies or the like—categorized and labeled carefully to fit your needs (e.g. Bands, Marching, Jazz, Solos, Small Ensembles, Lesson Books).
    - Train volunteers to transfer mismatched parts from the "holding area" to their correct locations.
- *More about sorters*—beyond our earlier mention in Chapter 8 ("collections"), inexpensive office sorters can be customized for music. Label each leaf of the plastic sorter (Score, Piccolo, Flute 1, Flute 2, Oboe 1). Train students to slide parts into the matching leaf. When all parts have been

entered, stabilize the stack and slide the sorter out. The set is now reorganized into one pile! TIP: Save your own time. This task is fun and engaging for students.
- *Common organizational tools*—be inventive with tools like labels/stickers, cover-sheets, QR codes, and color coding. TIPS:
    - Add a cover sheet to each library title (or computerize the details) to archive performance dates, contest results, special needs, or reflective notes about the experience of teaching the piece.
    - File the concert program, adjudicators' evaluations, help-sheets, and program notes with the set.
    - Find an exceptional recording of the piece; attach a QR code (or emerging technology) to the set so you and students can listen without removing the piece from the library.

    Note: More innovative suggestions are found on the "Bandroom Hacks & Shortcuts" file.
- A *"listening station"*—with QR codes, we can display links to our students' music. TIP: Train students to scan the codes with devices when exiting. Many students may be heading toward an extended bus ride, and could use the time for listening.

Processes and Philosophies

- *Utilizing volunteers effectively*—people occasionally ask, "How can I help?" Sometimes, however, the eager helpers arrive at a stressful time. Manage others' willingness by maintaining a self-explanatory "to-do" list of simple tasks. Then, even in your busiest moments, you can capitalize on volunteers' offers.
- *Completing ten hours of work in 10 minutes* (it's not a myth!)—the setup for this unique process is time-consuming, but the results are beneficial to you, and highly engaging for students. Create a careful, simplified description for each task; then number the tasks, or print each to its own small sheet. Task descriptions might be as easy as "there are four microphone stands on the stage—fold and return them to the audio storage room," or "dust the trophies." Construct single-person tasks, as well as jobs requiring groups. You'll find plenty of tasks (think of the bandroom, stage, practice rooms, showcases, and storage areas); create enough to engage all students simultaneously. Hand out all task-descriptions, and watch the magic happen. Bring pizza.
- *Organizing band sections effectively*—section leaders are in place; perhaps the principal players are different students. Continue the organizational structure by offering well-designed responsibilities to others in each section (folders, stands, attendance, collections, mutes).
- *Passing out and collecting music*—for distributing music quickly, separate the set into correct numbers-of-parts for each section; for example, twelve clarinet stands. "Jog" the parts, alternating the direction of each instrumental section. Then, it becomes fast to hand flute music to the flute section leader, and so on through the band. Reverse the process for collections, with one easy stipulation: distribute all unassigned, leftover parts before starting the collection. For example, give unused alto clarinet parts to the clarinet section. With all parts distributed, and the file-folder empty, the section leaders then put parts in score order; the clarinet section quickly creates a stack of E-flat, 1st, 2nd, 3rd, alto, bass, contra. The director simply collects the reorganized stacks in score-order.
- *Strategizing inventory*—storage and labeling ideas are also found on the "Bandroom Hacks & Shortcuts" document. Additional problems arise during trips, and especially at the end of the year. TIPS:
    - For trips, create a detailed listing of all equipment, and the name of the student(s) responsible for it. See [RW10.5] for an editable sample.
    - Pre-plan your instrument-return process carefully, including a schedule of dates. Communicate with administrators early about the inevitable June question: "What do we do about missing instruments?"
    - Repair and maintenance, while necessary of course, is a significant time commitment for band directors. [RW10.6] is an innovative form guiding students to evaluate instruments before

returning them. It will save considerable time to know from the player, "There's a screw missing from the E-flat pad guard; it plays a high 'A' when I finger 'D'; I can't insert the neck easily—it really sticks."
- Collect serial numbers, brand/model details, and general descriptions for every student's privately owned equipment. Maintain a careful listing, which proves invaluable when instruments are missing or damaged.

Software and Technology

While this book is not designed to focus on technology, several important thoughts shouldn't be overlooked. These suggestions are offered specifically to *save time*. TIPS:

- Be extremely careful with digital storage. The virtual space needs an ordered structural design to save retrieval time. Back up files periodically. Be watchful about securing confidential matter, especially in cloud-based systems.
- Learn to use the "Find" function in every program.
- Explore options in your messaging and communications endeavors. These options will be helpful for reminders, updates, and especially cancellations.
- Similarly, consider the vital benefits of a digital total-management system like the Charms Office Assistant, or an equivalent.
- Try a specific but *very* helpful project: "100 personalized Lesson reminders in under two minutes!" [RW10.7] offers a step-by-step guide.

Section 3: Leadership Matters

As a group, musicians are among the most responsible, cooperative, and motivated students in schools. Consequently, the leadership structure can extend deeply throughout the population. The top echelon of music students will qualify for the major leadership roles. But by expanding opportunities to more students, a greater sense of *ownership* goes to a larger portion of the band. Entire volumes are written about leadership within school groups, and we all share an unspoken obligation to learn and grow. The truly effective classroom management skills, however, cannot be conveyed in short suggestions.

Special Note: Readers will notice the absence of named "classroom management" strategies. That is no accident. A band director's classroom management sense is undeniably interlinked to the overall successes of the program. It is the author's opinion that improved classroom management comes with time, care, and experience. Further, good management is deeply rooted in . . .

. . . careful, consistent work on the band's "culture"
. . . immersive engagement of students in a productive classroom environment
. . . being the best possible role model (which must include preparations, actions, *reactions,* follow-through, and adaptation)
. . . good (flexible) pacing
. . . a dose of the "It Factor"
. . . and many more sometimes undefinable contributors, discovered over time

For our purposes, here is a short set of selected thoughts which may prove helpful to the band's leadership structures:

- *The band's culture*—recall the notion that "positivity works" in the rehearsals. That same view, coincidentally, is the cornerstone of an enthusiastic *culture* for all band members. We work to build an optimistic, collective mindset where all students feel welcomed, successful, and valued equally. The philosophy trickles from the top, eventually permeating the entire membership. This approach is the very reason "we" refer to "us" rather than to "me." TIPS:
  - Training leaders is crucial, but, guide them vigilantly.

- Richard DuFour's *Professional Learning Communities at Work* (Solution Tree Press, 1998) offers relevant suggestions we can apply to help stop our needy students from "falling through the cracks."

○ *Leadership: a select population*—the band's "officers" typically include the president, treasurer, secretary and other common titles (section leaders, drum major, field captains and so on). But these roles, whether elected or appointed, are not standardized; choices are flexible to fit each unique program. TIPS:

- Regardless of titles chosen for various positions, every role should be carefully described to make it meaningful. Refrain from choosing "figurehead" positions.
- A sample "Officer Positions" document is posted at [RW10.8].
- Some situations benefit from a more inclusive leadership structure. Consider adding a "cabinet"; in this tree-like structure, each main officer leads a team of dedicated cabinet members.

○ *Leadership: options for all students*—the band culture you promote will guide your overall leadership design. Some brief examples engaging larger numbers of students can include: mentors, stage crew, lights/sound/recording workers, librarians, equipment managers, and committee members. The latter can work on fundraisers, program design, publicity, concert planning, clerical work, and so on. TIP: Remember to strengthen the student leaders by involving them in daily processes.

○ *Designing class "rules"*—we know that involving constituents in the design of classroom procedures can be beneficial. Unanimous agreement to all "terms" makes it easier for any necessary consequences to be applied. Your program's overall culture will be fractured if your own student leaders undermine your required decisions. TIP: Consider the importance of open two-way communications between the director and the student representatives. It may be helpful to include a few moments of candid discussion on every agenda for meetings of officers.

○ *On mentoring: strategies and structural design*—for assisting less-skilled players, helping with make-up work, and leading sectional rehearsals, trained mentors provide an important role. Mentors can be pivotal parts of the entire program, helping students with transitioning from one level to the next. TIP: Engage mentors to help with events at other buildings; a trained high-school mentor can model for the intermediate or beginner bands, and even assist with their performances.

○ *Two sample supportive projects*—go to the resources website for [RW10.9] "The Great Exchange" (students will enjoy this very much) and [RW8.2] "Goals-Based Sectionals Guide." The latter editable document provides a blueprint for effective student-run rehearsals.

Section 4: Competition Matters

This section will not debate arguments for or against competitions. But even when a director elects not to pursue adjudicated band events, competition and rivalry are almost always inherent in music groups. Some members earn first-chair while others do not. Some are selected for solos, or to be recognized with awards. Some feel an internal rivalry equating to, "our Section is better than theirs." Through millennia of history, leading right into the chairs of our band rooms, competition is inevitable in the human condition. However, the same can be said for *cooperation*.

It is helpful to recognize competitiveness and learn to harness the better parts of its power. The following brief examples highlight the value of exploiting competition for motivational purposes.

- *Beware of "popularity" and other biases*—popularity contests, unfortunately, may be a factor in elections and officer positions; it's likewise a human tendency to use bias, popularity, and preferences in decision-making. The issue is perhaps no greater than during adolescence. Therefore, directors are advised to be constantly cautious about bias. Unearned (or undeserved) positions can break the group's emotional bonds, and we should be watchful for all types of bias anyway. TIP: Ask colleagues to scrutinize your work thoroughly (audition processes, rubrics, election policies), looking for any ways it could be misinterpreted or manipulated.

- *Avoid the "zero-sum" game*—we try to avoid situations wherein "the way for someone to win is for someone else to lose." This destructive equation inevitably holds back bonding, as well as music-making. In the worst-case scenarios, we find that some students will drop out entirely if results don't go their way. And sometimes, we also need to accept that those students' attitudes might be irreversible. TIP: Consider rotating roles among equally-deserving candidates and/or doubling or sharing parts. You may even prefer to offer re-seating auditions throughout the year. For example, inheriting a band with ten saxophonists, the director asks for a "balanced section," but the students firmly respond, "My parents bought it for me, and I'm playing it. I'm an Alto saxophone player." With no other quick resolution, we can pursue temporary assignments, and then "We'll rotate; right after the first concert, if you still want to play Alto, it will be someone else's turn to play Baritone sax."
- *Be specific with descriptions; objective with comparisons*—choose rubrics and audition processes that support objectivity. Simple binary observations help during auditions: "does this clarinetist command the fingerings for altissimo D and E-flat needed in that passage?" A straightforward yes or no may disqualify a student from a "1st clarinet" part in the top band. TIPS:
  - Consider splitting the audition requirements, with one set of obligations for students "to perform the seating audition," and a second, more rigorous, list "if you want to audition for a 1st part within your section."
  - Over time, develop a multi-tiered chart describing each skill expected for membership in an advanced group, and for playing 2nd or 1st parts within that group. From it, students will know if their performance skills can meet expectations.

- *About seating placement and auditions*—auditions are laced with underlying problems, and it will be rare when students unanimously agree with results. Take care to design exactly how to reveal audition results. Students may accept some methods more easily than others; it may be valuable asking student officers for opinions about the "announcement" (*not* regarding results, since that is your jurisdiction). TIPS:
  - Screened auditions support anonymity, helping eliminate claims of bias.
  - If possible, engage other adults in the hearing process
  - Consider the value of challenge auditions.
  - This process can be applied in select instances and, again, eliminates bias (for example, "tie-breaker" among three very hopeful candidates):
    1. Ask a neutral person to *record* students playing the excerpt; that helper delivers recordings to the director, labeled only as "A," "B," and "C."
    2. After hearing the recordings, select a short portion that clearly delineates the best performance from its 2nd and 3rd place counterparts. Cut/paste those short excerpts to a single recording, A then B then C consecutively.
    3. If appropriate for your situation, play the comparative excerpts for the entire group. When results are announced, there will be no questions: "Although all three did really well, the best performance on this specific date was clear: Congratulations, Player B!"
  - *Rubrics can support your goals*—an anonymous audition may not eliminate all discomfort, but it usually minimizes complaints. An additional building-block toward fairness comes from the rubric used for evaluations. Trusted colleagues can offer options; ask for testimonials about favorite evaluation sheets. TIP: To supplement your choices, we've posted several models at [RW10.10]. There, you'll find (among others):
    - A "quick and easy" scoresheet; while some subjectivity is involved, it functions under most circumstances.
    - A standard basic rubric for instrumental music.
    - A weighted scoresheet, editable to give extra value to the element of your choice.
    - An innovative rubric allowing effective comparison when students have self-selected music at different levels of difficulty.

- *The case for anonymity*—while screened, recorded auditions can address most issues, anonymity can also utilize competitiveness to support intrinsic motivation: assign a unique number to each student. Then we can display results (e.g. PACE scores, Watkins-Farnum results, or any other numerical scores), without identifying names. Sort the display. Students, knowing only their own code numbers, can view the display without embarrassment. "I'm about a third of the way down, but that's good since I'm only in ninth grade. I wonder if I can move higher next time?"
- *The case for self-driven options*—without question, the average human approaches a likeable task with more energy and excitement; the response becomes true enjoyment when people get to do *what they choose*. Students face requirements, so it can be very motivating to provide them with "opportunities" to balance the mandates. TIP: Not all students will choose to pursue extra endeavors, but some will find them enticing. And students who participate in special opportunities bring residual benefits into the entire program. Examples include tiered status models, honor bands by-audition-only, summer music camps, private study, external competitions, and special acceptances (e.g., Macy's Great American Marching Band; the Honors Performance Series at Carnegie Hall).
- *Brief words about awards and recognitions*—sooner or later, most teachers contemplate intrinsic/extrinsic motivation, recognitions, awards, rewards, encouragement, and esteem-building strategies of all kinds. It's a topic worthy of more than short paragraphs can offer (for an excellent discussion, refer to Feldman and Contzius's *Instrumental Music Education*, chapter 16). For our purposes, here are a few TIPS:

  - Appreciation is a basic human need. Praise and recognition—when the comments are sincere and justified—are essential elements in outstanding businesses, and the same is true for members of your band. No one enjoys feeling unimportant or marginalized.
  - Your band's pre-existing honors plan should be continued, unless there are justifiable reasons to dissolve some portions.
  - Moreover, if these components align with your philosophy, consider the power of certificates, medals, lists, peer-selected honors, displays like an "Achievements Wall," "Student of the Month" and other such recognitions.
  - The most effective motivation is often not an extrinsic "thing." In fact, a simple compliment or verbal recognition can boost morale. You'll find that the group's *esprit de corps* is a vital ingredient in the recipe for success.

Section 5: Other Matters

Clearly, a single book cannot address every component of the band program. Attempting to do so would be unsuccessful. In this section, we add just a few more small but significant puzzle pieces. Although each entry is brief, the reader is urged to consider how it might be expanded and adapted for a customized usage.

- *On 'residual income"*—"Wow . . . Your low brass section sounds terrific! How do you get that sound? What method books do they use? Do they take performance tests? How can I get *my* low brass players to sound that good?" Sometimes the answer is no more complex than, "They're just good players." Excellence begets excellence. Think about how much of your personal growth can be traced to influencers in your current and past experiences. Being inspired by a more advanced player in undergrad school has probably had lifelong benefits on almost every reader. Work to retain the best players, and create opportunities for them to pass their skills on to others. TIPS:

  - Promote the extra and advanced experiences consistently.
  - Start the mentoring processes early: send your best players frequently to work with younger students.
  - Bring professionals into your rehearsals.
  - Seek combined-band opportunities with outstanding groups.

A specific project: ask volunteers to record a narrated lesson/performance to share with younger students. For example, an advanced student performs an intermediate solo for others, stopping occasionally to discuss "A special fingering that really helps in measure 84," or "Watch out for that passage . . . be sure the tonguing aligns with your fingerings." Or even simple inspirational comments, delivered enthusiastically, like, "I love this solo, and I *really* love playing this part!" Build a collection of these recordings to motivate older students, and inspire the younger ones, as one way to cultivate the band's excellence.

- *Unusual retention problems and solutions*—it's understood that students may move away, lose interest in band, experience insurmountable class conflicts, or succumb to peer pressure. Other problems will arise, however, so be inventive with solutions:
  - "I love band, but I have to quit. I always get a '100' in band, but it drags my GPA down. My friends are taking all AP and Honors courses; they're weighted higher than music classes." TIP: Secure approval from administrators to design an Honors-credit track in the program, offering "extra value for extra, higher-level work." Colleagues and cohort schools can suggest models; see [RW10.11] for a prototype.
  - "I've been in both bands, but I'm going to quit the lower band so I can fit an elective in my schedule." It is important to retain elders' influential leadership in younger groups. TIP: Offer a "special experience" to older students. Perhaps the senior flutist would enjoy playing mallet percussion in the younger band, or the principal clarinetist would revel in playing contra-alto.
  - Sometimes an underlying problem may go unnoticed, but could be solved easily with help. For example, a student who drops out of band may be embarrassed about lacking transportation to evening events.

- *Special offerings*—with infinite options available, consider how "extras" might provide attractive supplements to your program. Students may find extra enjoyment in trivia contests, daily music theory facts, quotes-of-the-day, "Today in Music History," social events, games, ice-breakers, or musical riddles. The advice here is only to increase the magnetic pull into the band room.

- *About persuasiveness*—a teacher with an engaging style certainly has advantages (see Chapters 8 and 9). Sometimes, however, students may benefit from a form of inspirational persuasion, which might also be called "salesmanship." There is no suggestion of trickery here. Rather, a persuasive teacher recognizes students' apprehensions, and then uses subtle methods to erase them. Just one illustrative example could be this: for a student who "refuses" to learn an alternate fingering—using the saxophone as an example, ask the student to play a passage of G to B♭, specifically using the *bis* key. Alternate rapidly between those two fingerings, like a tremolo. "Now let's try it with 'your' B-flat fingering. No, faster—like you just did it. Hey, this means you can learn a new fingering in under one minute and it will work better than the fingering you've used for five years! Oh, there are lots more of those tricks, and each one is really helpful. Do you want to learn others?"

- *About literature selection*—this is yet another topic for which outstanding resources already exist. An excellent reference may again be found in *Instrumental Music Education* (pp. 141–164).
  - For repertoire selection, the author comfortably recommends online blogs and bulletin boards: other directors in a vast network are ready to share successful recommendations with you. Ask trusted colleagues for literature recommendations, including the important question, "How did your students *like* the piece?"
  - Utilize publishers' and online retailers' extensive music selection guidance. We sometimes balance hopeful purchase intentions with a dwindling budget; while considering titles, deposit potential purchases into a "hold" list, frequently provided on the webpage.
  - Seek online examples of other schools' concert programs, along with all-county and other honor band repertoire lists. Refer to literature lists in books, journals, and on the websites of organizations like the National Band Association.
  - To supplement your score study, search for program notes, teaching guides, and other assistive materials like those found in GIA's *Teaching Music Through Band Performance*; there's no

need to reinvent every wheel. However, your own insightful observations are central to the effectiveness of your teaching, and to your unique interpretation.
- Many directors successfully select repertoire in advance, but the alternate perspective remains student-centered: you might not be able to choose the most appropriate literature for your band until you "know the band." Each year's band may be very different compared to the previous year. The changes in membership will, in turn, bring changes to instrumentation balance, skill-level, average level of confidence among students, and other characteristics.
- To avoid potential discomfort, ask your school officials if they have defined a specific policy on the performance of patriotic and religious music.

Section 6: Your Influence Matters

We know why music is needed in schools. Every major professional music association has researched the matter. Music advocacy groups offer well-documented support. Students, parents, teachers of other disciplines, and administrators universally recognize that engagement in music supports excellence in other areas. Communities, colleges, and businesses are aware that well-rounded students, having excelled in music, will bring desirable talents to the table. All of that is no mystery. Tip: Find "Quotes on Music Education" at [RW10.12].

But these well-known truths have another implication as well: *you* matter.

> What will alumni remember about their time in band? Will the philosophies and concepts you've demonstrated show up later elsewhere . . . in boardrooms, operating rooms, counseling rooms? Hopefully, they'll be found in kitchens where your students are parenting the next generations.

There is no suggestion here that music teachers are responsible for every outcome in society, but this much is true: everything you do and say, and everything you put in print, will have a trickle-down influence on those with whom you come in contact. You matter. It's wise, therefore, to reflect on your philosophy and its implications on the total band environment.

With the choices we make, we are providing an artistic environment to our students and community. And the environment itself sometimes conveys *philosophy* better than anything else can, including the director's academic training or performance skills. Be careful, therefore, with every controllable aspect of the program's *design* and *presentation*, because you are presenting a picture of you to your students and their parents.

Here's just a brief overview for your consideration:

❑ *The first contact*—whether in person, by phone, digitally or otherwise, it should be a positive experience. The lasting influence of a first impression is undeniable.
❑ *A band handbook and policies*—(see Section 1 as well) this all-encompassing document, whether printed or available digitally, addresses many of the other topics on this checklist. Your transparent communication of policies and expectations will be key to many aspects of your job. For an excellent and thorough resource, refer to *Instrumental Music Education* (chapters 7 and 20). Tip: Besides our sample handbook [RW10.13], many can be found with an online search; adapt to fit your band's needs.
❑ *Communications*—will your band have a website, phone-tree, social media presence, Remind (or other app) notification plan, or mass text-group? If so, have a plan that includes oversight, frequency, management, and outcomes in case of misuse. Similarly, will you prepare a newsletter? Consider the format and frequency of delivery, and then add it to your task list. Whatever the chosen method of communication, keep it updated and current. Tip: Some apps offer a "schedule" feature to pre-plan automatic communication updates.
❑ *Correspondence* (both its content and its quality)—everything you put in print is open to scrutiny. Be careful of spelling and grammatical errors, and be sure your numbers, dates and other details are correct (the first time!).

- *Your digital presence*—in this millennium, care for your digital footprint is a no-brainer; nothing discovered by your students and families should be distressing or awkward.
- *Bulletin boards, posters, displays, and signage*—are they attractive, clear, informative and welcoming? TIP: Offer the design and upkeep as a project for trusted student leaders; they'll develop pride for their work.
- *Room preparedness*—when they enter, will students feel both proud and inspired to do their best work?
- *Organization*—the wisdom of the adage, "a place for everything, and everything in its place" can't be overstated. You'll be remarkably more efficient and less frustrated when you're organized. Students will feel more comfortable when they're not enveloped in clutter and disarray.
- *Calendar of events*—work carefully to create a slate of events that are educational, relevant, challenging, memorable and captivating for the students. TIPS:
  - Important: choose dates as early as possible, working as a committee with other school entities to avoid conflicts with major events.
  - The "best" number and scope of events will be different for each community. If your calendar includes too many events, the students and families ("chauffeurs") could experience exhaustion and saturation; the overfilled schedule might become a factor in students' withdrawal from band. Without enough events, however, students might lose the incentive to work, or their excitement about being a member of the group.
  - Recognize that students have loves and pursuits outside of band; serious conflicts with other major events should be avoided.
  - Leave flexibility to accommodate unexpected events (e.g. a celebratory parade or special dedication).
  - For some types of "extra" events, consider polling your members/families before agreeing to the performance; be willing to *decline* the event if it's destructive in any way to your band.
  - Be vigilant: some events may be viewed as exploitation, using students' time and talents to benefit someone else's agenda.
- *Traditions vs. initiatives*—while it's admirable to be innovative, new teachers are advised: change is often difficult. Think carefully before replacing traditions with your own new ideas, because the students might not accept the changes as eagerly as you'd hope. Students will give you clues regarding how they feel about aspects of the program. It may be advisable to move methodically when making major changes, even if the initiatives will eventually prove to be outstanding decisions.
- *The ways you refer to students and colleagues*—simply put, the golden rule applies here. What you say about someone often reflects more about you than about that person.
- *Your portrayal of the band's "ownership"*—in almost all cases, you'll gain a more dedicated and cooperative following if you speak in terms of "us," "we," and "our band", rather than "I," "me," and "my band". Your students will respond better when they feel that "we're all in this together," including the director.
- *About you*—like it or not, it's a normal tendency for humans to judge others. That means *you* will be judged by not just your appearance (including facial expressions and professional dress), but by your character traits as well—your promptness, reliability, honesty, integrity, poise/composure, and so much more. Be a leader.

Almost no one with interest in education would wonder, "Why bother with perspectives like this? Why do strategies and engaging activities matter?" It only requires a few moments as a teacher in front of a group of students to know the answers. In our case, as music teachers, we know that every student's performance affects the overall quality of the band, so we must reach every student.

One Biology student can fail the class miserably, with no effect on peers; they can still excel. But a music group—like many teams—breaks apart at the weakest links and, of course, there is no one "sitting on the bench." For a fun and relevant reading, search online for Jamie Vollmer's *The Blueberry Story* (https://www.edweek.org/education/opinion-the-blueberry-story/2002/03), which stresses our need to teach all students in all circumstances. Greatly shortened and paraphrased, we can't just toss out blueberries that don't meet the company's standard.

So the great objective remains: find every conceivable method to reach, help, and inspire every individual player in the band. We may be dealing with a "forest" of students, but if the forest is to reach its full potential, we must visit, inspect, feed, trim, and fertilize each of its trees regularly. Regardless of how small or poorly rooted or misshapen it may be, when one tree flourishes the entire forest feels the benefit. And that is why strategies, tips, and engaging activities will always matter in the most effective band director's rehearsal room.

Note

1 Scott Rush, *Habits of a Successful Band Director* (Chicago: GIA Publications, Inc., 2006), 175–176.

11

THE SCHOOL MARCHING BAND PROGRAM

Christian Carichner

This chapter is dedicated to all things marching band. As stated before, we already have access elsewhere to thousands of pages of outstanding material by renowned educators. This section presents additional teaching and organizational strategies designed to be simple, and easily implemented. While you may not win your state championship by following all these suggestions for one year, you may encounter less stress about your program each fall—something we can all appreciate. As always, these suggestions represent only a jumping-off point to spur your further ideas.

Development of a New Marching Program

Schools without an existing marching band in the past may begin developing a program, typically with input from three sources:

1. The director, of course, who represents the students' needs and wishes.
2. Administration (including athletics).
3. Parents (who may bring an historical community perspective).

It is paramount to have detailed discussions among all three of these stakeholders to ensure success of the fledgling program.

- *Set expectations*—determining primary goals for the band is an essential first step to all other planning—timelines, budgets, staffing, show design, recruitment, and so on. Timelines are not always necessary from the beginning, but a discussion of the end product is important. Will this be:
  - a competitive band, designed to win a state championship?
  - a hybrid pep band, with a few sets of marching for Friday night halftime shows?
  - a parade band?

- *Be thoughtful about resource requests*—based on stakeholders' input, be judicious with requests for resources. Is there equipment that you can use in other facets of your program (front ensemble equipment?). Are there other programs in the school (or your feeder program) that could benefit from resource acquisition (sound systems being used for school dances/theatre productions or convertible tubas being transitioned to home practice horns after marching season?). For a first-year program, determine what is *essential*, and have a plan for phasing in more resources over the coming years.

- *Consider the concept of mastery*—year one might dictate that you want to master basic elements of marching such as posture, step-off technique and timing, understanding how to interpret drill coordinates, and techniques such as forward and backward marching. It is essential to remember that in year two, not only will you have the challenge of adding additional elements of marching to the returning members, but you will also have to get all the first-year members "caught up" on skills that it took last year's members the entirety of the season to master—*and* to introduce the new concepts from the second year to these first-year members. It may be prudent to develop a

"step-by-step" process for you and the instructional staff with measurable goals and achievements outlined by year/season.
- *Be prepared for failure* (and celebrate success!)—a wise old teacher once asked me—after a very successful year—"Would you be satisfied if next year went exactly the same?" My immediate reaction was "Of course not! It would mean I didn't attempt to improve and that the students grew complacent with a similar standard." So, I set about by looking at every facet of the program and targeting areas of growth. This laborious process was exhausting to develop, and did not reflect any of the current successes we were enjoying. I put my "progress" blinders on, and was so dismayed at the end of the next season when not only did we fall short of my "goals," but also other areas of our operation were less successful. The lesson was never to underestimate the difficulty of spinning several plates before you add a lot more. I would have been perfectly happy with a "similar" year compared with the year we had.

Substitutions and Mini-Recruiting

Let's face it—not every band has the perfect instrumentation. Success often breeds fertile recruiting grounds, but so does reaching out to students who are interested in unique situations where they can be of service. Here are some helpful substitutions:

... *At the top*—one excellent piccolo player can add needed clarity to woodwind technique moments, but be wary of making it a permanent addition if quality players are scarce.

... *On the bottom*—baritone sax for the win! The baritone saxophone does wonders to enhance the bottom end of the band. It is particularly useful when placed within the drill alternated with tuba players (tuba-bari-tuba-bari-tuba). Baritone saxes provide a clear articulation point with a bit more "punch," and the tuba sound helps to round them out.

... *Never fear the front ensemble!*—recruiting new students to help cover parts on synthesizers or other instruments is acceptable, and becoming more common. Also known as the Pit, this is also a great way to recruit "non-band" kids into your program from the Chorus or Orchestra, or by talking to local piano teachers to identify students who might have the aptitude for band.

... *On the battery*—although marching drumlines provide a wonderful component, plenty of bands are extremely successful without a battery, relying instead on stationary players in the pit. Not only are battery instruments expensive to maintain (equipment, sticks, heads), they can be difficult to recruit if numbers are a problem. With low numbers, no funding for additional staff, and perhaps even some discomfort teaching battery percussion if it is not your native instrument, you can be just fine with an enhanced front ensemble. TIP: Try placing the stationary front ensemble strategically *on the field*—a helpful visual trick to "enlarge" smaller bands.

... *On the drum major*—choose drum majors carefully, considering leadership and musical strengths. Directors often (rightfully) choose their best musicians to be drum majors, thus taking the horn out of their hands. TIP: In special cases, keep the drum major involved musically by considering innovative options, which might include performing a solo from the podium

Assembling a Show as a One-Person Team

It may seem overwhelming to create the entire marching production as a one-person "team," but it can be done with great success. These suggestions may guide your plans:

Start with the Music Selection First

Choose music that is moderately challenging *but attainable* by your students. If you are the sole instructor, understand that you serve as music teacher, designer/choreographer, and drill instructor simultaneously. Allow yourself time for all elements of the job.

When selecting music, directors should acknowledge the delicate balance between what the students can play "right now" and music that would "stretch them." Keep in mind that marching while playing is not innately easy; it is often the "great equalizer." If your new students are remarkably skilled, their high level of achievement will be a pleasant surprise and easier music will not impede their growth. An important reminder:

> You do not hold students back by choosing achievable music that allows them to feel accomplished, satisfied, and proud of their level of success. Creating "that feeling" that students have when they accomplish something together is an incredibly important part of your job as their band director.

In summary: the music is the guiding force behind a show concept, especially for smaller programs and smaller budgets. There are many fantastic shows you could purchase (and preview online for free) that would do the majority of your "show planning" for you. Alternatively, you could listen to the music for a "vampire" show, but decide to "spin" the concept in another direction (e.g. "The Raven" by Poe). That is entirely possible, as there are no restrictions on the show's *concept*. It is easy to use pre-programmed music, modified with a more abstract concept. For instance, when designing a football halftime show, this is a terrific way to be budget-conscious, appeal to the audience, and involve your students in the show selection by encouraging them to find arrangements online. However, while it is less expensive to choose three stand-alone songs "packaged" together with breaks between, often these selections were not composed with a through-line in mind. That disconnect can cause difficulty with the next phase of show design, and is often panned in competitive environments.

Storyboard Your Production

If you are creating a competitive show, this is a necessary next step in your process. For non-competitive shows, you may choose to skip this step and proceed to conceptualizing drill.

There is no standard way to storyboard the production. Some designers use massive Google documents, shared between captions/staff/other designers; these documents break the production into moments, sometimes as small as 4 or 8 counts at a time. The spreadsheet identifies sections/elements that are the focus for each segment. Examples include . . .

. . . what costuming is used
. . . tempo
. . . the "goal" toward which we're building
. . . staging suggestions/limitations
. . . which voices should be playing at each moment to assist in character development.

While you as "sole designer" may not require such detail, it is so helpful for rehearsal purposes. Educators get hooked on student success—and we should! It is exciting to notice, "Wow! They got so much better at the section we rehearsed today!" This exhilarating feeling is very motivating toward planning the follow up rehearsals. However, it is equally easy to have rehearsed and improved a segment, but lose sight of its focal point and goals. For example, you give careful attention to getting a set to "hit" but, in doing so, you overlook that your main goal was to build a "moment" on the other side of the field, and you've left it under-produced.

The important message here is to use a storyboard to guide your rehearsals. Clean from the areas/stages of focus first, then toward the outside of the field. Clarity of your moments will help the audience invest in your performance and, in turn, your students feel rewarded when a crowd signals its approval.

Drill Design

Remember that many outstanding resources are available to assist you as you embark upon a drill design. If you are the sole designer of the drill for your students, consider the following elements:

- Focus on staging first: getting the right people to the right places at the right time is critical to creating your "moments."

○ Consider *timing* and listening environments: work carefully to create environments where a "pulse pocket" is easily established and maintained. Sketch pictures and shapes that can be manipulated to help the ensemble perform more easily in time. While you may sacrifice some field coverage or velocity, the most important element of a marching band is to move and play with precision. Directors are dissatisfied when their *concert band* falls apart, or "tears," especially during an adjudicated performance. Similarly, if the marching band explores overly difficult movement, expansive drill, expensive props/costumes, and exceptionally hard music—all at the expense of an outstanding performance—the director is not fulfilling a music educator's most important obligations.

Uniform Selection

When programming your show—especially for a new program—uniforms are a chance to make your band look very professional, very "on-theme" or both. Remember, that uniforms are very expensive—and often for a reason. They are well constructed to make your students look great. While employing your band parents to create/develop uniforms for your students may seem budget-friendly, it is often a "you pay for what you get" scenario and may not achieve professional-looking results.

Quick-Fix Strategies

Not intended to be an "exhaustive" list, here is a collection of helpful rehearsal strategies that can help to address common problems with marching bands.

Music Performance Strategies

- *Timing*—band directors universally struggle with teaching timing. This suggested strategy improves timing by eliminating other variables first (e.g. fingering technique, rhythmic complexity, dynamics), and helps to create "spheres of influence" by focusing on a core set of players in a small field-spread. For example: start with the players no more than ten yards from the drumline and not behind them. Wind players to the sides and in front of the drumline will play a "chunk" of the music (e.g. 32 counts, 4 sets), but only using Concert F, or another comfort-range note from the key of the passage. Play only quarter-notes—or whatever pulse guides the marching—at a mezzoforte level. This stripped-out version allows performers to focus exclusively on the pulse; moreover, it allows the director to give detailed feedback on the timing. Meanwhile, students not currently playing can be directed through "cleaning projects" by other rehearsal technicians, so no time is lost.

  As repetitions improve, begin to include more students, expanding the "spheres of influence" outward. Eventually, all students are performing the quarter-notes in time, with feedback, instruction, and accountability. This exercise also illuminates the listening environment for your front ensemble; pit players learn where specific voices are coming from on the field, and perhaps which ones to trust.

  Gradually reinstate the "real" music, repeating the "spheres of influence" method, or in an "even/odd drill numbers" way, or any other innovative strategy.
- *Groove exercise*—this activity is *fun*! A leader (you, drum major, section leader) uses headphones and a metronome to conduct a specific show tempo, perhaps chosen from your opener, just before the band takes the field; the rest of the group "sings" quarter-notes. The leader (a "DJ") can then call out "eighth notes!" or "triplets!" or another subdivision. Have fun, playing with dynamics too throughout. At times—following a big *crescendo*, perhaps—have the students break out into a "groove," with everyone "freestyling" their own rhythms/sounds/beats . . . but always in the steady tempo. It should sound like a dance party! Encourage students to move freely and dance. With some practice, the students can alternate between the "grooves" and the quarter-notes to build tempo maintenance.

  Fun story: the 2007 DCI championships used a policy (unusual at the time) of having groups complete their warm-ups at schools/parks a few miles from the Rose Bowl. Pat Sheridan, Sam Pilafian, and I—sharing a strong belief in the groove exercise—split our corps onto the three busses, and each held our own "groove session" during the short ride to the stadium. When the corps got off the bus, they were all dancing together . . . *in time*! They were all of one mind, and when they took the field the opener tempo locked in place.

Sound Production Strategies

Louis Armstrong once said "If ya ain't got it in ya, ya can't blow it out." Tone quality in marching band has *so much* to do with breath production/support. Unfortunately, many directors may approach their work with a short-sighted philosophy of, "I don't need to practice breathing, I've been doing it my whole life just fine." At some point, each musician has discussed the topic of breathing, and/or has been taught some forms of breathing exercises. In marching band, the physical demands on performers continue to grow exponentially each year; also, more than ever our shows include electronic amplification. The notion that breathing is just something to be done as a warm up—or is altogether unnecessary—is putting your students at a disadvantage. Therefore, directors are encouraged to highlight breathing for its improvement of tone, and to develop breathing exercises for use in each rehearsal. With its meaningful and specific exercises with proven success for marching activities, the preferred resource is considered to be Patrick Sheridan and Sam Pilafian's *The Breathing Gym* (Focus On Music, 2002).

- *"Wind horn"*—have students or sections perform their passages with wind, sometimes called "air and valve." Players should pay close attention to the quality of the inhale, the consistency of the exhale, and they should listen for attacks/releases from their vantage point. Despite not audibly playing, much can be learned from what was formerly known as a "visual rep." Note: do *not* encourage "hissing" air—while it may be easier to hear and "clean," this is not the optimal air stream students should use in their horns to produce a great sound. Remember—we are a result of the habits we practice.
- *"Low E"*—play this pitch (the lowest note possible on the instrument) as a "one-note" version of the rehearsal passage to encourage *maximum air at minimum compression* (or else the instrument will not speak). This exercise will neutralize students who try to "force" the sound; they cannot simply "blow harder" to contribute. They must learn to refine the air column and speed for the horn to speak beautifully. This exercise promotes relaxation and full breathing, and a side benefit is usually a bigger, more resonant sound on the reset.
- *Run in place*—lightly running in place prior to starting a rep will elevate students' heart rate slightly. Marching musicians must learn to control the heart rate throughout the show (or parade). The heart rate during a full run-through of the "closer" will be very different than after a simple 16-count warm-up segment. Running in place can simulate what they will experience at that point in the show.
- *Assign breathing exercises during rests*—in an effort to slow heart rates, you may suggest an *In 4—Out 4* pattern during rests, and a timed inhale prior to an entrance. This should be practiced along with the drill to instill outstanding breathing as a *habit*.

Visual Rehearsal Strategies

- *Form vs. dot*—we all fear the "dot diver"—the student who values being "correct" ("That's my spot") more than the appearance of the pictures our audience should see ("Get in the form!!"). However, having students memorize and perform the "dot" will still provide stronger results in the long run. Peripheral vision is limited on the field and, for timing purposes, players must watch the drum major/conductor. Train each student to memorize step sizes and dot locations; many helpful apps are available to assist with this, UDB being among the best. As music educators, we excel at teaching music performance strategies: the "how to" of music. We must apply this same care to performance of the drill.
- *Plus One/Minus One*—this technique is particularly effective for improving the "cleanliness" of your drill. Have students march the 16-count set, taking one more step toward the next move

("plus one"). This allows us to assess/improve the vector or direction of the "plus one" step, and helps to teach the new step-size for the upcoming move. Additionally, this can help to teach musical "release" points while practicing wind horn or playing reps, as well as horn moves and weight/balance shifts. By having students "freeze" in the "plus one" position, you can assess and correct the aforementioned points. Further, you can then have them re-set to "minus one" so they understand how to get *from* the previous drill transition *into* the next transition. This further accentuates the step size and direction change differentiation. Once this technique is established, have students "stay in time" for the *plus one/minus one* "game." It would look like this:

<16 ct. transition> <*Plus 1 (2, 3, 4)*> <*Minus 1 (2, 3, 4)*> <next 16 count transition>

With this method, you'll link together several sets for a longer segment, *cleaning as you go*. This set-to-set variation can take time for students to learn to use it, but is very helpful when used from the beginning of the season. Encourage students to vocalize "*Plus One . . . Minus One*" during their work.

- *Formalize structure of each rep ("Assess, Adjust, Relax")*—to emphasize an efficient order of operations during your rehearsals, work with a *procedure* at the end of each rep before giving feedback. Allowing a reflective moment for students to assess their own work is important to their development and growth. Consider this suggested process:

    - *"Assess"*—have the students "freeze" in a position such as *plus one*, *minus one*, or feet together. Students should assess how far away from their dot they are before moving to it. Encourage them to estimate the distance, dividing by the number of counts in that move. This allows to students to gain insight into, "I need each step to be about one inch bigger," for example. While not exact science, it is something quantifiable that they may try on their next set without requiring individualized instruction for every repetition.
    - *"Adjust"*—have the students (still with horns up) move to their dot. Encourage them to observe the form, taking note of other students around them. Observe the correct interval between two people and their relationship to yardlines, gridmarks, and vantage points.
    - *'Relax"*—horns to a *carry* or *parade rest* position, followed by feedback from the director, rehearsal technicians, and/or student leadership.
    - *'Reset"*—"Let's get better with more information!"

- *Right foot is most important (push)*—assuming the band steps off with the left foot, stress the importance of the *right* foot when teaching the first step. Encourage students to *push* with their right foot platform to promote better balance and weight-transfer for the first step. Otherwise, students may just be placing their left foot in front while keeping their weight back over the right foot. In general, the weight focused on the platforms of the feet will prevent lazy step-offs.
- *Subdivision of the foot*—by instructing students how to *subdivide* their foot-shape, you will notice an immediate improvement in the timing of their marching. It helps to teach them to align their *crossing counts*—that is, the "and" of the beat, when the ankles "cross" from a profile view. Even more importantly, subdivision of the foot-shape will improve their pulse and musical timing. The corner of the heel is precisely on the beat, and the tip of the toe is on the next beat, and so on. Practice this exercise at a moderately slow tempo (just fast enough to maintain balance easily) (Figure 11.1).

"ONE"	"ee"	"and"	"ah"	"TWO"
Corner of the heel	Arch of the foot	Ball of the foot	Platform/Toes	Toe Tips

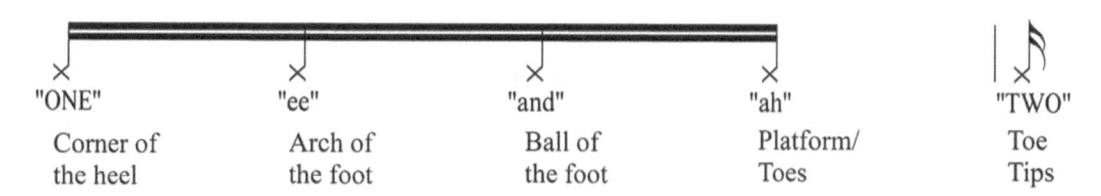

Figure 11.1 Subdivision of the foot-shape.

- *Build the triangle*—for wind instrument carriage it can be productive to teach the *basic* position without the instrument. This tactic allows the teacher to give a detailed definition to each student, and emphasizes the important concept of "uniformity." When it's time to have individual instrument breakdown (flute, clarinet, sax, etc.), this is a great chance to "gift" some instruction time to your section leaders or other instructors in smaller, instrument-specific groups.

Have students begin by putting both arms directly forward, parallel to the ground, with palms down. Next, bring the hands to the face, making a fist with the right hand, and covering that fist with the left hand. Forearms should now be perpendicular to the ground and parallel to their upper body, while elbows stay at shoulder-width. Generally, this creates an accurate *triangle* for instrument carriage. Wrists should not "break" and should act as natural extensions of the arms. Broken wrists are the biggest cause of the incorrect angle in instrument carriage. TIP: Aligning the left thumb knuckle precisely with the student's nose will achieve more uniformity.

Band Commands

In general, it is best to avoid quick commands such as "set" or a very fast "band ten hut." These quick, jerky commands often cannot achieve the desired result of *uniformity* because students are deprived of reaction time. Try signaling the command by a metronome beginning, or a longer count off. Think of so many visual/dance classes, where the start is preceded with 8 beats to get a *feel* for the rhythm: "5. . . 6. . . 5, 6, 7, 8." Some suggestions beyond the typically known commands could include:

- "Tweet Tweet Tweet"—this can be verbalized or provided by a whistle. The three *tweets* are the first three beats of a five count sequence, for example, "Tweet, Tweet, Tweet, Go, Bears!" Where the horns could snap up or come to attention on "Bears." Both "Go" and "Bears" are vocalized by the membership, and the tweets come from a leader. Further, the "Bears" can be the first count of four mark-time counts before a repetition starts (which allows time for a great breath, too.).
- "Band, horns are Up"—similar to the *tweets*, this can be done in whatever tempo matches your performance:

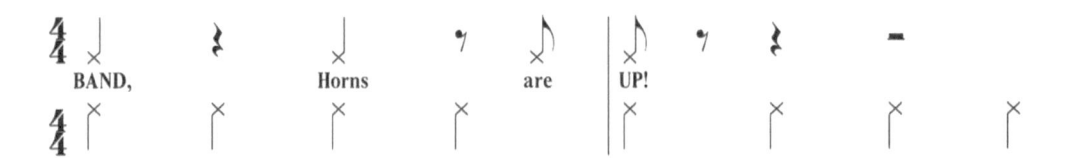

Figure 11.2 Band, horns are Up!

The "are"—here, on the "*and*" of beat four—serves as a preparatory subdivision. Students can vocalize the "up" and, similar to the *tweets*, the "up" happens on the first beat of four mark-time counts before a repetition begins.

Managing the Other Elements of a Marching Band Program

Parades

Parades are often an essential civic function of a school band. They are terrific for visibility within the community, allowing the band to be experienced by residents who may not attend a competition or football game. For many of us, parades often happen at inconvenient times of the year based upon weather and holidays (including summer parades when school is not in session). More than likely, your parade is not a competitive element within your program, so most of this section focuses on "functional" parade ideas. However, if your program has competitive parade marching, it would be wise to consider the following ideas as part of your preparation and simultaneously adapt competitive field-show design ideas into your parade package. TIP: For competitive and non-competitive schools alike, it is a convenient reminder to the community about the excellence of your program when a parade is close to a public budget vote.

Concept

It is important to evaluate the *purpose* of the parade; talk with the parade organizers about what they are looking for. An illustration: when I took our band to Normandy for the annual D-Day ceremonies, it included a town parade in St. Mere Eglise. After weeks of practicing, we had refined our gate turns, the precise horns up/down movements, and all other aspects of our very "serious" formal presentation. We reached out to organizers just before leaving for France, asking for special instructions. They replied, "Just one thing—make sure the kids have fun. This is our town's favorite event every year, with jugglers and candy, and visitors from hundreds of miles away. They don't want a 'stuffy' band—we want to have fun!" Well, fun is often what a college band does best, so we reverted to our "normal" game-day parading and the organizers raved. We as musicians need to remember—sometimes it's most important just to "give the audience what they want." Your reputation as a great band director is often enhanced much more when citizens see your students having fun and engaging with each other and the audience—as opposed to having the most precise and "sharp" band in your town— where your band is the only band!

Programming

I have never met a band director who said, "We are so prepared for this parade—we've had more than enough rehearsal, and there is no chance of this falling apart today." So it begs the question: why should parade music be difficult? Look for the following traits when selecting good parade literature:

- instantly recognizable by listeners
- easy to memorize quickly
- flexible instrumentation (and the melody is doubled often)
- *repeatable* (multiple endings; easy to start over), and *repetitive* (for development of visual routines for colorguard)
- has a "clapable" beat for audience engagement (this also allows the color guard to easily spin)
- is appropriate for the parade (e.g. patriotic, holiday).

If finding music is an issue because of your budget, I suggest public domain. A terrific resource, www.bandmusicpdf.org, is regularly updated with full editions of public domain music. Furthermore, the United States Marine Band has been working to publish public domain versions of all Sousa marches. A simple Google search will also help you find other public domain works. At the time of this writing, www.musescore.com is a free music notation software that also has an online library of arrangements in a publicly available forum. You must do the leg work to determine which songs are public domain eligible, for the site often has many copyrighted songs. These arrangements often need some care to fix errors, but with public domain music, the majority of the work is done for you.

Personnel

Ideally, you have perfect instrumentation, and all equipment needed for a parade. For the rest of us, read on.

- Suggested setup

    Banner/Flags
    Colorguard/Auxillary
    Drum Major(s)
    Trombones
    Baritones
    Mellophones
    Trumpets
    Sousaphones/Tubas
    Drumline
    Saxophones
    Clarinets
    Flutes.

    If you are missing a section from this suggested staging, just consolidate.
- Drum major(s): if yours are purely symbolic, place them right behind the banner to greet the crowd. If they are used often for signaling, it may be productive to have them *alongside* the band for trombones, trumpets, and drums.
- Auxiliary instrument recommendations:

    - *Bass clarinets* could march between saxes and clarinets if the weather is favorable and the equipment is in "good" condition; keep the high-quality instruments indoors.
    - *Baritone saxes* can march intermixed with the tubas.
    - *Oboes and bassoons* are best left indoors. Include students in one of the other roles mentioned elsewhere in this chapter, or ask if they'd like to learn a new instrument for the parade.
    - *Sousaphones* may be missing from your school. If you have only concert instruments (tuba), consider using a golf cart or perhaps a district maintenance vehicle that is easily cleaned up. Additionally, you could march an electric bass or electric keyboard the same way, if it can be done safely. A small, quiet generator (easily rented) will power electronics for the parade route.
    - *Percussion* is a special problem. Without adequate marching percussion equipment, and the appropriate carriers, you could employ "toy" percussion (claves, cowbells, slap sticks) or have creative students develop their own percussion instruments for use in the parade.
- Colorguard and twirlers significantly increase the visual presentation of a band in a parade. If you are lacking in numbers, consider reaching out to local dance schools to gauge their interest in partnering on developing a routine.

Rehearsals

Planning an effective parade rehearsal often has numerous challenges and obstacles. Here are some strategies for overcoming them:

- No access to track or streets:

    - Use an adjacent parking lot (e.g. bus garage; student parking lot).
    - Use a hallway near the band room, or the band room itself.

- Use an auditorium, or especially the cafeteria. With many students, you have hands to move lots of equipment quickly (tables and chairs); use those resources to leverage against things you don't have (rehearsal spaces).
- Use clean-release painters tape—marking a *path* or even *step-sizes* across the floor is a great rehearsal strategy when you are limited in facilities.
- At some point, you should insist (politely) that your students need at least one good practice-run before a parade, for safety reasons. Parades can be physically tiring; students need to understand what it will be like so they can mentally and physically prepare. This might require a rehearsal after school, before school, or even bussing to an alternative location, but the district should accommodate those needs if officials have the expectation that you march in a parade on behalf of the school.
  TIP: Be nice to the janitors and secretaries—at all times. They are often the ones with the keys to everything you need. Know their names, their birthdays, their families. Having these co-workers on your team will help you move the mountains that need moving.

○ Weather problems—with parades, like any other outdoor marching band activity, weather is always a huge factor. Band directors have an important mandate to care for students' safety and for the condition of instruments. Prepare your explanations in advance, starting with a *discovery* mission: speak with your athletic director about pre-written weather-related conference rules and other policies limiting play. Provide your school officials with an evidence-based assessment of how instruments are affected by temperatures and types of precipitation. You ultimately want to align with *your community* and with what you know will be supported by administration. TIP: Include a communication plan in your weather policies.

○ Loss of concert band rehearsal—creative folks will think about all sorts of possibilities for asking students to give extra time outside of concert band to prepare for a parade or other auxiliary performances. It is important to consider balance for the lives of the students, and whether or not you value a public appearance for your ensemble.

To Wrap Up

It is important to value a parade within the culture of your program. It is simultaneously important to put thought into your *perspective,* and manage your expectations accordingly. If *you* have fun putting the parade together, and the *students* have fun rehearsing and performing it, then parading will be an asset to your program instead of an obligation.

Pep Band

Pep band is another of the most visible ensembles in your program. Often, you may be requested (or "volun-told") to perform for basketball, volleyball, soccer, or various other sports. For some bands, pep band is the main component of their contributions at football games too.

Stadium Setups

While there is no "official" way to stage your band in bleachers, there are a few helpful guidelines:

- Be sure to consider the game "experience" for fans seated near the band. Sousaphones create a "restricted viewing" experience for fans. Additionally, while many spectators *love* being near the band, some may find that the band's volume affects their conversation or ability to hear announcements. Consult with your athletic department on the best location in the stands to create a great experience for your students and the fans alike.

- Evaluate your band's needs carefully, including power (e.g. for amplifiers), water availability, bathroom access, and the like. Additionally, you need a way to get your students in and out of the stands quickly and more importantly—safely. If your budget allows, having stands for your marching percussion makes their performance much better. If you choose to go with a drum-set instead, consider asking band parents to build a safe platform that can reside in the stands and is removable to limit off-season wear and tear.
- Design a setup that is not too wide, nor too deep, so your students have a better chance of playing together. If the setup is a taller rectangle (most common), I would consider having your percussion in the middle, or at the beginning of the "top third" of the rectangle. It is helpful to locate the percussion at the "heart" of your stadium setup. Seating the woodwinds behind the percussion allows for the brass to be up front (where they can cause the most havoc on the field!) and listen "back" for the percussion. Using this set up, there is no great place for sousaphones other than lining each side of the band with them (if you have several).

```
┌─────────────────────────┐
│                         │
│    Woodwinds [Back]     │
│                         │
│         Perc            │
│                         │
│         Brass           │
│                         │
│    Conductor [Front]    │
│                         │
└─────────────────────────┘
```

Uniforms

There is considerable latitude given to pep band uniforms. When deciding upon a uniform for your band, you'll have to weigh initial costs, maintenance costs, and storage—in addition to design costs, a production timeline, and sizing concerns.

○ *T-Shirts* are the cheapest option, and are easy to produce quickly. Specific sizes are available for each member and assuming students keep their shirts, there is no issue with maintenance costs or storage. Cons: T-shirts' comfort is limited by temperature; they can often look "sloppy" and have a short life span, so you'll need to re-order each year.
○ *Polo shirts* are still relatively affordable and easy to produce quickly; they are often reusable, and can become the "brand" or style of your group. Cons: There is a maintenance issue if re-used; they still have a limited comfortable temperature range, depending on long-sleeved or short-sleeved.
○ *Jerseys* are more durable, and there are many styles available. They provide a distinctive look or "brand," and can often be layered underneath for added weather ranges. Cons: Maintenance costs and storage space can be an issue. Students will often want to keep these after graduation, so replacements and re-ordering ease should be considered. These can be very expensive depending on design choices.

Styles

There are infinite ways to operate a pep band for your school community. Traditional styles resemble a basic marching band set-list with more "chants" and "cheers" incorporated into the repertoire. More progressive styles today are using DJ's, Abelton-based equipment, intense amplification, and other innovations. Ultimately, you must choose your group's style based on your budget and preferences/abilities as a director. Here are a few considerations:

- *Follow the rules*—consult your district and conference guidelines for what is "legal" and what is "illegal."
- *Consider portability*—for tournaments, travel, and pep rallies, consider how you might make the band easy to set up quickly in a variety of places/locations.
- *Consider the environment*—while some schools may choose to let a band run "rogue," it is best to have a group that you would be proud of if their "chants" were written on the front page of the newspaper. Even with remote potential for concern, it's probably best to leave out a chant no matter how "funny" it may seem. Follow good sportsmanship guidelines and make your community proud of your group at all times—not just when the team is winning.

* * *

In summary, there are a multitude of ways to operate a successful marching band. It is imperative that you treat the marching band experience with the same passion and care anyone would treat a concert band experience, or any other music education experience. A marching band has an intoxicating draw for many student musicians who are otherwise indifferent about other elements of music education. When done well, it develops a higher level of self-confidence in students and is incredible exposure for your program to the general public. Treating the marching band "beast" with respect will help your program reap the rewards of invested students for years to come.

12

CONDUCTING THE SCHOOL JAZZ ENSEMBLE

Daniel Fabricius

During the years that I taught in public schools I also mentored forty-three student teachers, who brought widely varied levels of knowledge and proficiency in the area of jazz education. I was able to provide a unique situation for them with two middle school jazz ensembles and two high school jazz ensembles, all scheduled as curricular classes in adjacent rehearsal rooms. While this small upstate-New York town was certainly not the center of the jazz universe, our efforts focused on high-quality authentic jazz experiences for students with little exposure to professional live jazz.

In this chapter I will address prevalent issues with teaching the school jazz ensemble, including instrumentation, setups, literature selection, and style. Teachers—even those with little or no jazz experience—will find numerous valuable ideas and solutions to common challenges with teaching soloists and rehearsing ensembles, all with a goal of helping students excel at performing this American art form.

Jazz Ensemble Instrumentation

An important consideration for the school jazz ensemble is instrumentation. While some schools may have an abundance of players, others may not have enough to build the standard minimum instrumentation, which is considered to be:

- Alto Sax 1 and 2
- Tenor Sax 1 and 2
- Baritone Sax
- Trumpet 1, 2, 3, and 4
- Trombone 1, 2, 3, and 4
- Piano
- Guitar
- Bass
- Drum Set.

Your school may have nearly perfect instrumentation but with voids in certain sections. Or, like some schools with developing programs, there may be students who want a jazz ensemble experience, without playing "standard" instruments. Fortunately, there are solutions to instrumentation issues:

- Many publishers produce jazz ensemble music with parts for an array of extra instruments.
- At the easier difficulty levels, it is common to have fewer divided parts; for example, many charts have just two, rather than four, trumpet parts and trombone parts.
- Some publishers' jazz charts have full instrumentation, but also indicate the essential parts allowing performance by groups with incomplete instrumentation.

Regarding publishers' instrumentation options: these practices don't apply to all publishers, nor often to more advanced music which has fewer options available. Directors occasionally need to modify charts independently. There are plenty of "adaptable" charts available for easier music, usually identified as levels 1 through 4.

Instrumentation decisions can also be influenced by the philosophy of the director. Yes, I have adjudicated large jazz ensembles comparable in size to a concert band with thirty or more players. This situation is certainly appropriate for younger players, especially when many students are learning fundamentals of jazz. It is also appropriate to double some parts of an ensemble. Numerous factors can affect the instrumentation, but decisions should reflect what is best for the band and for each student.

Literature Selection

Finding the best literature for the teaching situation may be one of the most daunting tasks for a novice jazz ensemble director. These are important decisions, often requiring research. Here are several steps that may help to find the best match of music to the ensemble:

- Start by knowing all performance dates; count the number of rehearsals available to prepare for each performance.
- Determine how much music to expect for each performance, including limitations (e.g. the total time on stage).
- Evaluate the ensemble objectively, making a realistic appraisal of the instrumentation, the capabilities of the strongest and weakest players, and which students might play improvised solos.
- Do you have an ongoing list of pieces you hope to teach? Is there a goal for the group to perform at a specific level of difficulty?
- What is your budget to purchase music? Can you borrow music or use charts you already have in your library?
- To begin selecting music for your performances, consult your state's recommended music lists, and the recommendations offered on vendors' webpages. Also ask for recommendations from trusted colleagues.
- The process of reviewing music takes time and diligence. Use internet resources to study scores and listen to recordings, making notes about pieces that appeal to you the most. Will these pieces also appeal to students and to your audience?
- As you narrow your choices, consider the following specific factors for your students:
    o rhythmic vocabulary
    o stylistic and tempo capabilities
    o current reading skills of the players (e.g. key, accidentals)
    o comfortable range of the brass players
    o instrumentation variables
    o whether the harmonic progressions match the players' improvisation skills.
- There are many compositions and arrangements suitable for developing jazz ensembles. The trend seems to be either "easier" arrangements of compositions by notable jazz artists; original compositions based on (or inspired by) famous pieces; or, original educational pieces, available at every level of difficulty. For many years writers have been providing "educational" pieces that emphasize specific jazz elements without excessive difficulty. Search for pieces meeting your criteria, but also consider the importance of students being exposed to historically significant jazz artists.
- If you are considering more advanced literature, note that some charts use expanded instrumentation; it is common to find that players may need to "double" on additional instruments. The following instrumentation variables are used quite frequently in jazz ensemble pieces:
    o use of various mutes to present an array of timbres by brass players
    o specified usage of either electric bass or acoustic bass
    o addition of an electronic keyboard or synthesizer

- - addition of vibraphone
  - addition of auxiliary percussion instruments
  - soprano sax replacing 1st alto sax
  - saxophone players doubling on other woodwinds, especially flute, piccolo, clarinet, or bass clarinet
  - addition of a 5th trumpet part
  - addition of a 5th trombone part (often a bass trombone)
  - trumpet players doubling on flugelhorn
  - use of effects on electric guitar
  - use of a vocal soloist.
- Plan performances to include a variety of jazz styles. Avoid programming pieces with similar tempo or style. Consider the three broad categories of jazz styles: swing, rock, and world music. The roots of jazz are in the swing style, but jazz ensemble music is now influenced by other cultures and emerging trends. There are many examples of diverse styles at all levels of difficulty. For example, swing, cha cha, hip hop, funk, odd-meter rock, mambo, and many others. Challenge yourself and your students to learn several styles each year.

Performance and Rehearsal Setups

Throughout my career I always came back to using what is considered a "standard" big band setup for performances:

- Looking at the stage, the rhythm section is on the left side.
- The wind sections are on the right side in three rows, with saxophones in the front, trombones in the middle, and trumpets in the back row.
- The order of the saxophones (from the left): Tenor 1, Alto 2, Alto 1, Tenor 2, and Baritone. I always provided low-profile music stands for the sax section to use in rehearsals so that their sound was not blocked. Consider using "band front" stands in performances to accomplish the same result, adding a professional look.
- The order of the trombones (from the left): 2–1–3–4 (Bass Trombone). The four players should be seated (preferably on a short riser) so that each player is between two of the sax players in the first row. Position the trombonists' music stands so that the player can see the music, but the bell is not blocked by the tray. I suggest players place the stand to the right of their slide. Remind players to keep bells up, aimed toward the audience.
- The order of the trumpets (from the left): 2–1–3–4. The players should stand in a row behind the trombone section (preferably on a slightly higher riser). Adjust music stands to an appropriate height with the tray nearly flattened so that the trumpet bells are not playing into the stand. As with trombones, keep bells up, aimed toward the audience.
- Important: the "lead" players from the wind sections (Trumpet 1, Trombone 1, Alto Sax 1) are all in line. The "lead" trumpet player's sound should be audible to all wind players, and all wind players must learn to listen toward the center of their sections to hear balance, intonation, articulations, and jazz nuances.
- Notice that the common soloists (Tenor Sax 1 and Trumpet 2) are closest to the rhythm section, so they easily become part of a jazz combo when playing solos.
- Drum set should be next to the trumpet and trombone rows.
- The guitarist should be in the same row as the saxes; put space between the guitarist and Tenor Sax 1.
- The bassist should be adjacent to the ride cymbal of the drum set. In addition to close proximity to hear the drums, the bassist should have visual contact with the drummer as well as the pianist.
- The piano (or keyboard) should be placed next to the guitarist. It is best if the pianist is positioned to easily see the conductor, bassist, guitarist, and drummer.
- Vibes and auxiliary percussion are commonly used in school jazz ensembles. These instruments can be positioned in any remaining space within the rhythm section.

- Be prepared to alter the setup to accommodate tighter spaces in some performance venues. Remind musicians to listen carefully in performance, and even more so in an altered setup.
- Photographs and video examples of jazz ensemble setups are readily available. Directors should consider the unique size and instrumentation of their group to choose an appropriate setup.

Over the course of learning music, students spend a lot of time in rehearsal. Using altered rehearsal setups is a great way to add variety to the process and to enhance student learning. Consider using modified rehearsal setups such as:

- a "box" formation, with the director in the middle and sections playing toward each other: this setup allows each section to clearly hear what other sections are playing.
- a totally "scrambled" setup, using random seating and placement —students often enjoy this setup because they get a different perspective from each different position. Note: this setup also stresses everyone's need to watch, listen, and respond in different ways.
- Use primarily the traditional setup when the group is approaching a performance.

Always stress that players need to listen across the band to hear the various components of a composition. The goal of all players should be to learn everything about the pieces—not just their own individual parts.

Understanding Jazz Styles

Jazz music emerged from New Orleans in the early 20th century. At that time it was easy to identify jazz through three main characteristics: Swing rhythm, the use of Syncopation, and the use of Improvisation. These same characteristics still apply to the jazz music of today. Whereas syncopation and improvisation can appear in other types of music (e.g. in marches, and in Baroque music, respectively), *swing rhythms* are unique to jazz.

For inexperienced student musicians, and for novice teachers, difficulty with swing rhythms may be both a stylistic and a notational issue. We use the phrase "swing the eighth-notes" to describe subdividing each beat into a triplet; however, the notation is not written as triplet-based rhythms, as shown in Figure 12.1.

Figure 12.1 Swing style example.

Note that there were no "rules" when musicians started playing jazz. The common performance practices evolved over time. See the explanation of swing notation "rules" in Figure 12.2, each with a notated performance example.

All "rules" come with exceptions; here are the common exceptions in swing:

1. Fast tempo (Bop)—eighth-notes become *even* as tempo increases.
2. Slow tempo (Ballads)—eighth-notes are *even* unless otherwise indicated.
3. Latin/Rock—eighth-notes *and* sixteenth-notes are played *even* and short unless otherwise indicated.
4. Double-time swing (characterized by the bassline in eighth-notes) – sixteenth-notes are interpreted like swing eighths; eighth-notes are interpreted like swing quarters; and so on.

Jazz Rhythms – Examples of the Rules

1. Three or more eighth notes in succession are played legato with a swing rhythm (2/3 of a beat / then 1/3 of a beat).

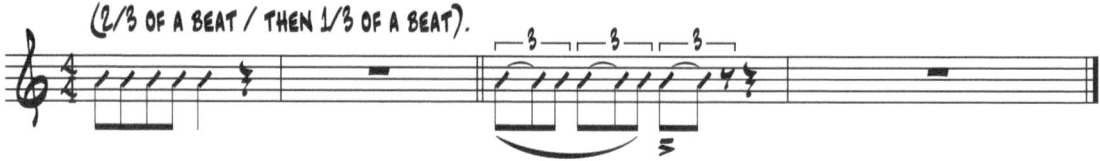

2. Eighth notes followed by rests are played short and accented.

3. Swing quarter notes that occur on the downbeat are played short (2/3 of a beat).

4. Swing quarter notes (or two eighths tied together) that occur on the upbeat are played short and accented (1/3 of a beat).

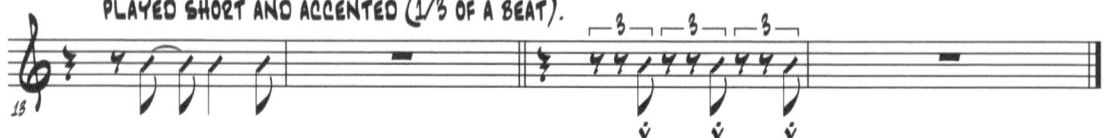

5. Triplets, sixteenth notes, and anything longer than a dotted quarternote are all played concert style.

Figure 12.2 Swing rhythms: examples of the rules.

It is often necessary to emphasize reading swing notation when teaching less experienced ensembles. Your group's warm-up could include a call-and-response; the focus on swing interpretation can be very effective when the conductor provides aural examples, either by playing or by singing with any comfortable form of rhythmic syllables first. Then the students play the rhythms on a specified pitch. Rather than reading the notation, students are instead focused on the distinct stylistic sound of each rhythm.

A great way to instill concentration and develop students' reading skills is by displaying the cliché rhythms (see examples in Figure 12.3) on a white board or projection screen; point to them while students play. Applying these rhythms to warm-ups and other exercises will help train students to read and then interpret rhythms correctly when encountered in jazz ensemble literature. Figure 12.3 contains several examples of cliché swing rhythms.

Figure 12.3 Common "cliché" rhythms in swing.

Rhythm exercises are important to reinforcing rhythms found in other styles of jazz music as well.

Jazz music is filled with special effects not commonly found in other music. Directors need to help students understand and create these unique, authentic sounds. The conductor must know the symbols used to notate jazz effects and, more importantly, be able to explain or demonstrate their sounds (Figure 12.4). Jazz music is based on aural traditions; therefore, students will likely learn these effects best by hearing examples first, followed by a "how to" lesson. There are many online videos to use for instruction.

JAZZ EFFECTS

FALL   QUICK-FALL   SHAKE   GLISSANDO   RIP   DOIT   SCOOP   BEND

Figure 12.4 Effects commonly used in jazz.

In the early days of jazz, this new music was wildly popular in the United States, eventually spreading around the world. As more people sought to experience jazz, the original American art form was influenced by music of many other cultures. Now, there are numerous "rhythmic grooves" within each of these three main categories – swing, rock, world music. There are countless printed resources and recordings available to help student musicians and directors understand specific styles within each of these categories. The following section contains a list of common styles found among jazz ensemble arrangements.

Common "Rhythmic Grooves" Found in Jazz

Swing	Rock	World Music
Medium Swing	Medium Rock	Bossa Nova
Bright Swing	Fast Rock	Cha Cha
Up-tempo Swing	Funky Rock	Nanigo
Driving Swing	Half-time Rock Feel	Samba
Relaxed Swing	Slow Funk	Batucada
Easy swing	Swing/Funk	Mambo
Swing with 2-Feel	Slow Rock Ballad	Classic 2-Beat
Jazz Ballad	Funky Shuffle	New Orleans 2nd Line
Shuffle	Hip-Hop Groove	Reggae
Jazz Waltz	Disco	Calypso
12/8 Feel	E.C.M. Groove	Soca
Odd-Meter Swing	6/8 or 12/8 Feel	Merengue
		Bolero
		Songo
		Mozambique
		Salsa
		Tango
		Beguine

Teaching Jazz Improvisation to Soloists

While improvisation is a major component of playing jazz, creating original ideas within a jazz composition may be difficult until students develop a vocabulary of figures from which to draw. Teaching improvisation within the full rehearsal is very beneficial to these developing players. It requires only a small amount of rehearsal time to outline the parameters and then to allow players to try improvising. Some students will be inspired to work more on their own, or to seek additional lessons outside of rehearsal. During my career I always appreciated when students were excited about improvisation but never had the expectation that everyone in the band would excel at this skill, or that everyone would even feel comfortable trying to improvise in front of others. Although solos are traditionally expected by specific instruments and included in their parts (e.g. tenor 1, trumpet 2, piano), any instrument can play any solo part in a jazz ensemble setting.

Conductors often need to provide extra encouragement to students about improvisation, but my experience is that while several students will make the effort to improvise, other students in the band will remain very happy to just play their written parts. I generally provided feedback to soloists in rehearsal but also offered extra help to soloists outside of rehearsals. Students will likely need extra help with solos that include extended harmonies and altered chords. It is essential to provide students with resources to practice improvisation on their own. There are numerous play-along recordings students can use to practice improvisation, and I sometimes found it necessary to create my own play-along recordings. Since the resources and technology are available, I believe that students mostly need individual practice, time to listen to great soloists, and feedback from a teacher.

Here are several specific ideas to help directors provide additional assistance to potential student jazz soloists:

- The most useful information to student improvisors is knowing what pitches work best. There is no substitute for learning the chord tones and scales of the music they are playing. Many publications include "solo sheets" to provide this information to musicians. These are useful tools; directors may need to create versions for pieces that do not include solo resources.

- Students need to learn a repertoire of melodic and rhythmic ideas. There are many books of common jazz licks, and transcriptions of solos recorded by great artists. An important part of learning to improvise is hearing what great players have recorded and then learning to speak the language of jazz through imitation.
- Although improvisation is a primary characteristic of jazz, many beginning-level charts do not include improvised sections. In this case, "open up" the chart to allow improvisation by just repeating the form of the melody, replacing the melody with improvisation.
- Many intermediate charts are written exclusively for educational settings, and include "composed solos." While these samples can be helpful to young players as they work on their improvisation skills, conductors should expect students to actually improvise as they develop and begin to play more advanced music.

Nearly all solos will be performed by instrumentalists in the jazz ensemble. However, it is also very common to feature vocal soloists with jazz ensemble accompaniment. When featuring a vocalist consider these points:

- A student who is a great vocalist is not necessarily a great jazz vocalist. The conductor or vocal coach will likely need to help the vocalist with singing in the jazz style. Encourage student vocalists to listen to professional recordings, noticing how to alter rhythms, embellish the melodic line, and present each phrase of the song. Students may need to be coached on connecting with audiences and using the microphone.
- Find music that matches each soloist's abilities and vocal range. Recent vocal solo arrangements include music for both a male and a female key.
- Expect soloists to memorize songs for performance.

Another type of coaching involves working with *instrumental* soloists on how to perform ballads. For ballads, I suggest selecting exceptional student musicians. Train the instrumental soloist using the same goals presented in the preceding first bullet for vocalists. An instrumental ballad can similarly be more exciting when performed from memory.

Jazz Ensemble Rehearsal Strategies

I believe that most band directors tend to emphasize the large-group rehearsal over other components of our job. It should be our mission to anticipate what students need to learn; provide meaningful, sequential rehearsal activities; offer the best possible feedback; and work efficiently toward presenting excellent, engaging instruction. Our goal is to present performances of high quality. Much of what we do to accomplish this goal requires thorough preparations before entering the rehearsal room. We need to be secure with our own understanding of the music and the skills that musicians need to develop during rehearsals. This portion of the chapter provides concrete strategies and ideas to help with planning effective rehearsals.

The Warm-up

All instrumental ensembles should begin rehearsal with a warm-up activity. In a school setting, students rarely have time to warm up before the rehearsal. Wind instruments literally need to be warmed up in temperature to be tuned. Student musicians also need time to concentrate on concepts such as embouchure, tone quality, and intonation before rehearsing the literature. We all know that wind players should practice long tones first, but part of our jazz ensemble warm up can next add other elements such as rhythm, style, articulation, and dynamics. The jazz ensemble presents the unique challenge of implementing the rhythm section into the warm-up activity with goals for each of those instruments. Figures 12.5 and 12.6 provide several warm-up exercises utilizing the Circle of 4ths as the primary material. Using "the circle" is a common warm-up for concert bands but these two examples have been adapted to include the jazz rhythm section with specific directions for each instrument.

- Be able to play this excerpt in all keys of the Circle of Fourths

- Melodic instruments: concentrate first on balance, blend, and intonation. Focus next on rhtyhmic precision and clear articulation so that the group presents a unified interpretation of the style.

- Guitar: play either "Freddie Green style" (Quarter-note comping) OR play the melody.

- Vibes: play the melody.

- Piano: play the 3rd & 7th (minimum) of the tonic chord. Also, "fill in" with short melodic material during the rests in measures 2 and 4.

- Bass: play a walking bass line (all quarter-notes) over the four measures. Work toward a smooth transition to each new key by approaching the next chord (root) by half-step or whole-step.

- Drums: Play swing time throughout with emphasis on beats 2 & 4 on both the ride cymbals and the hi-hat. Try different ways to reinforce the rhythm played by the ensemble. When appropriate, use the left hand on SD and/or the right foot on BD to comp as you play time. Mark the start of each phrase by playing a transitional fill in the 4th measure..

Figure 12.5 Jazz ensemble warm-up: long tones (Bossa Nova groove).

- All - begin at B♭ (concert pitch) on the circle and proceed through all pitches playing the same pattern as written above

- Melodic instruments - concentrate on balance, blend, and intonation

- Guitar - comp the chord using the rhythm notated rhythm (or use a variation)

- Vibes - play the long tones

- Piano - try various voicings of the major 7th chord, Play a short melodic fill in the second measure

- Bass - use the rhythm indicated and play roots and 5ths in each key

- Drums - Play the indicated Bossa Nova groove

Figure 12.6 Jazz ensemble warm-up: three-note melody in swing style.

Other Rehearsal Considerations Beyond the Warm-up

- Expect all sections to balance and tune notes of any chord. Young students often play softer when they have "strange" sounding notes, but those notes are usually important (color notes, extended harmonies, or altered chords) and need to be tuned with attention to proper balance. Emphasize tuning for notes of longer duration during melodic lines as well.

- Give specific directions about releases, asking players to mark music as needed.
- Ask players to vocalize their rhythms with emphasis on musical elements, then add fingerings, then playing the instruments.
- It is common for individual sections or soli groups to play alone during rehearsals. Consider asking one or two rhythm section instruments to join that group. For example, "We need to hear the saxophone soli beginning at measure 98. Bass and guitar please join them."
- Listen carefully to soli parts, making sure each voice is balanced.
- Emphasize that all students play "in time" by using an amplified metronome in rehearsals. Professional musicians must often play with a click track in recording sessions; student musicians also benefit greatly from this activity.
- It is often necessary to amplify soloists, and rhythm section instruments frequently use individual amplifiers. Using amplification in performance requires the group to have rehearsal time using the gear first; student musicians can become confused by the additional volume.
- Record rehearsals; review them to check for previously undetected errors. Play portions of rehearsal recordings for the band to hear; ask them to evaluate the recorded performance.
- Students need to hear examples of great bands. Providing listening experiences is time well spent, whether in class or as a homework activity. Consider creating a guided listening worksheet for students to complete after they listen.

The Role of Each Jazz Ensemble Player

The following rehearsal suggestions address the entire wind section and the separate saxophone and brass sections.

Wind Section

- Since the scoring is often truly "one-on-a-part," less-experienced players may have difficulty balancing harmony notes in chords. Stress the importance of every note being heard at the correct volume, and that players on the "inside parts" need to take ownership of those notes.
- Section players should use a straight tone during unison passages unless vibrato is the common practice for a specific style.
- Sections should play softer when in unison, and each player should concentrate on blending with the section.
- Parts played as background during improvised solos are often too loud. Keep track of the overall volume; adjust as needed.
- In tutti passages, rehearse clarity of articulation as opposed to volume. Tutti passages sound stronger when played with clear articulation from all players.
- Know the intonation tendencies of all instruments; be prepared to give students solutions to play in tune.
- Emphasize performing jazz style and jazz effects with clarity. All players must match in their presentation of every sound.

Saxophones

- Saxes generally need to improve projection, balance, and intonation. Investigate jazz mouthpieces, ligatures, and reed setups to help students work toward producing a characteristic jazz tone.
- Listen from 10–15 feet away to confirm how the saxophone section sounds compared with the brass and rhythm sections.

- The saxophone soli section is an important part of many arrangements. Saxophone players need to project their sound even more during soli passages. Each player must match in rhythm and stylistic interpretation and the section must be balanced. Consider asking players to stand tall for soli passages and to "play directly to the back wall" of the performance venue. Challenge players to make soli passages even more impressive by memorizing for performances.
- Players in advanced ensembles should consider learning to double on flute and clarinet. Invest in stands for the various woodwinds.

Brass

- Essential mutes: straight, cup, harmon, and plunger.
    - Players may own their mutes, but it is good to have a supply of school-owned mutes available. Consider also supplying attachments to hold the various trumpet mutes on music stands.
    - Bucket mutes are sometimes specified; if not available, students can play "into the stand" or cover the bell with cloth to replicate the sound.
    - Plunger mutes bring character to melodic passages and provide a unique effect when used by the entire section. Student musicians may need instruction on how to execute open and closed (o and +) sounds with the plunger.
    - Make sure players know how mutes will affect their projection. A mute can greatly diminish volume, and players will probably need to be reminded to play louder to maintain desired balance.
    - Since mutes also affect intonation, students will need to know how to adjust tuning when muted.
    - Mute-changes can be a cumbersome and problematic task; directors may need to help troubleshoot solutions.
- Trumpet players are often required to double on flugelhorns in jazz arrangements; problems can arise when picking up a cold flugelhorn long after it was warmed up and tuned. Players must be aware of potential intonation problems caused by temperature. Tuning can be improved when players are reminded to blow warm air through the instrument before playing. If flugelhorns are not available, players can "play into the stand" to replicate the desired sound. I recall the first time I requested funds to purchase a flugelhorn and having a conversation with the building principal about the purchase. He did not know what a flugelhorn was, but after our conversation he realized that it was an important jazz instrument and that one of my goals was to eventually have a set of five flugelhorns in our inventory. He was excited to help acquire a set of flugelhorns and to also attain other goals once he understood the benefits to our students and the value that I placed on new initiatives.
- The fourth trumpet and lead are often scored in octaves; ask the lower octave to play strongly to provide a solid foundation for the lead player to hear.
- Trumpet players often need time and help to gain proficiency with notes in the upper register; be aware of range limitations when selecting literature. If aspiring to play advanced literature, conductors should provide guidance and inspiration to help players achieve upper-register confidence. Developing the upper range requires specific practice techniques. Encourage potential lead players to play without excess mouthpiece pressure, to use enough air, and to devote time to range development in their individual practice. Lead players also tend to use mouthpieces designed for playing in the upper register.
- The lead trumpet is generally the only player in the band to use vibrato during tutti ensemble passages.
- Trombone slides must move freely and all players should work on smooth legato tonguing.
- The bass trombone is often a vitally important part and is frequently assigned soloistic parts or it is paired with the baritone sax and/or string bass for important soli lines. Otherwise, the player must balance with the trombone section.

Secrets of the Rhythm Section

Teachers should have some proficiency playing all of the instruments they teach; and although band directors learn to play secondary instruments through music education classes, it is likely that rhythm section skills were not fully developed. My experience with both colleagues and many student teachers is that they were very humbled when they took my advice and sat down behind a drum set or picked up a bass guitar. It is not too late for any of us to learn new skills.

I believe that the best school jazz ensembles have rhythm section players who work well as a unit and have learned to respond to what they hear from other instruments as they play. I also believe that "fully notated" rhythm section parts for an arrangement can be useful but also allow student musicians to rely too much on reading skills instead of learning some simple rules—and then using their musical intuition—to create their parts in the ensemble.

One of the life-changing events of my musical development as a high school student was attending a concert by the Elektric Band led by Chick Corea. I had already heard recordings of this group but watching the interaction of the players on stage that evening made a great impression on me as a player and as a future teacher. As a drummer I had been jamming with friends and had already learned various jazz standards by ear. I had learned on my own that I needed to pay attention to what others played in order to contribute my best to our combined efforts. However, at this concert I witnessed amazing musicians take this simple idea to an extreme level. They were not encumbered by reading music and it was apparent that they were communicating very effectively by watching and listening and responding to what others in the group were doing. I was fortunate to have a brilliant high school band director who often used the phrase "Watch, listen, and respond" in our rehearsals. Little did I know that this would become one of my own teaching phrases.

I always emphasized the importance of reading ability to rhythm section students but also stressed the need for them to learn the notes outside of rehearsal so that we could concentrate on creating the music when we were together. Just like the continuo players of the Baroque era, proficient jazz musicians can read minimal notation to create their parts in an ensemble. For the members of the jazz rhythm section it is essential for them to improvise their parts with an understanding of common practice.

- Start by suggesting that rhythm section players memorize the chord changes for just one song. They need to know the form of the song—the chord progression and the number of measures in each section; for instance, "12-bar blues" or "32-bar AABA." The task of eventually memorizing an entire song should be fairly easy since the same chord changes and song form will be repeated throughout. For example, playing a "blues in F" will require memorizing only twelve bars. Yes, players can still follow along in the music so that they are aware of any parts to be played as written. Players should soon grow accustomed to the repetitive nature of their role as they become aware of the structure of the composition. For instance, here is the form information of a hypothetical arrangement:
    - introduction (4 bars)
    - two choruses (12 bars each) of the melody—first chorus by trombones; the second, by the saxes, has a brass counter line
    - a section of solos (12 bars, repeated as much as needed)
    - two choruses of sax soli (12 bars each)
    - two choruses (12 bars each) of trading 4-bar solos between tutti horns and drums
    - D.S. to the trombone/sax melody sections (12 bars each)
    - a composed coda to complete the arrangement.

- It is likely that once the rhythm section players memorize the 12-bar blues chord progression, they could play the entire chart, only occasionally checking in with their notation. Rhythm section players will notice improved listening and more watching each other while everyone else will probably

notice a better accompaniment from the rhythm section. Memorizing more songs will probably seem easier after this initial exercise.
- Since inexperienced players of harmonic comping instruments may feel the need to play all the time, the conductor will also need to keep track of the "density" within the rhythm section accompaniment. Try to limit comping to just two instruments at a time with the goal of helping players stay out of the way of each other. Also keep track of the *rhythmic* comping on drums and percussion. Advanced players can often work out comping issues independently.
- Some arrangements intended for "younger" players often still include "advanced" harmonies. Directors may need to simplify harmonic changes, or supply "custom-written" charts or tablature guides for less-experienced guitarists and pianists.
- Remind rhythm section players to evaluate their own roles, noting how they fit in with other rhythm section instruments. They should also notice when their instrument might have an "opening" to play something special when melodic instruments leave space to be filled.
- Make sure instrument amplifiers (guitar, bass, keyboard) are positioned behind the player so that the students can clearly hear their own sound along with the rest of the band to accurately adjust amp volume.
- There is a potential for many balance issues within the rhythm section. Listen for imbalances between the rhythm section and the full band, the various wind sections, or soloists. Remind the rhythm section to play at a combo volume when soloists are playing. Conductors may need to be especially firm about the volume of amplified instruments.
- Perhaps the most important learning activity for rhythm section players is to copy specific skills that professional players do in performances captured in recordings and videos.
- Create opportunities for the rhythm section players to play together in other situations, such as in a *modern band*, accompanying choirs, jamming regularly, or creating a combo.

The following subsections contain some additional suggestions for each rhythm section instrument.

Piano

- Use either an acoustic or electronic instrument. In some performance venues, an acoustic piano may need sound reinforcement.
- Since student pianists may be more accustomed to reading exact notation, offer extra assistance to help free them of their need to "play as written."
- If a chart has a "fully notated" piano part, coach the player to interpret the music authentically:
    - Leave out any left-hand parts that double the bass part (unless there is not a bass player).
    - Comping parts are often "over-written" so feel free to simplify the rhythms.
    - Coach pianists to learn the melodic lines and to comp more actively when the melody has rests or long notes.
    - Sometimes charts will indicate a suggested chord voicing with just long note values. Use the voicing but add characteristic comping rhythms.
    - Play melody lines as written if doubled in other instruments.
- Encourage pianists to memorize the chord progression and then teach them a few basic rules of jazz piano voicings:
    - Most comping can be done with the right hand centered on middle C. There are plenty of available reference materials focusing on chord voicings for piano.
    - Pianists can often use just two or three notes of any chord. For example, when playing dominant 7th chords the pianist will sound great by literally playing only the 3rd and 7th of each chord.
    - Some pianists are likely to play all chords in root position; make sure players are aware of voice-leading concepts, minimizing drastic leaps between chords.

- The player can move to the upper register sometimes to make the piano more prominent when there is an opening in the texture.
- The pianist can also bring out parts by playing octaves in both hands.
- It is fine for the pianist to just rest and wait for an opening when the winds are featured in a tutti passage or shout chorus.

Guitar

- Jazz ensemble guitar parts are often a mixture of chord symbols and melodic lines. The melodic lines are often soli passages with other instruments and, when played in proper balance, is a wonderful scoring effect. Be persistent about guitarists learning to play melodic lines, always stressing that guitarists need to read staff notation in addition to tablature or chord symbols.
- Some publishers include supplemental materials for guitarists (e.g. voicing suggestions notated as tablature). These are helpful to get young players acclimated to jazz harmony and playing proven chord voicings. Encourage students to memorize a few jazz chord voicings and apply what they've learned in one song to other pieces.
- Student guitarists often do not yet have a concept of the desirable jazz guitar sound. Strive for an acoustic sound using minimal amplification, but students will need instruction about setting the amp. Avoid over-using treble or bass tone controls; use little or no reverb. Stress to players that the guitar needs to balance with other instruments. Young guitarists often play too loudly on easy or familiar songs but will then turn the volume down too much when playing melodic lines because they lack confidence with reading.
- Be prepared to provide extra assistance to guitarists about comping styles. Even very young guitarists can learn to comp in the style that Freddie Green used with the Count Basie Orchestra. There are plenty of resources and online videos that will be helpful.
- Watch the movement of the player's hand on the neck; excessive movement usually indicates the need for alternate voicings to provide smoother voice leading.
- Encourage guitarists to self-tune quickly before the rehearsal by plugging into an electronic tuner.

Bass

- While the electric bass may be the instrument available to your school or student, the acoustic bass is the instrument of choice for most jazz charts. I suggest adding an acoustic bass to your school inventory if possible. Electric bass players can usually adapt quickly to the acoustic bass.
- Even if using an acoustic instrument, it is recommended that an amp still be used. Make sure that the player is aware of amp settings, and be prepared to adjust the amp to the sound you prefer as the conductor.
- Nearly everything played on the bass in jazz is pizzicato, so the student bassist needs to have a concept of pizzicato tone. Remind the player to "dig in" or "pull harder" on strings to get a characteristic tone. To avoid a "thumpy" tone the player must play with efficient and coordinated left-hand legato movements. The pizzicato technique will still provide the space between notes, but the tone will be more resonant.
- It will be important for jazz bass players to learn how to create a walking bass line from chord symbols. Stress this skill, helping bass players use published or online resources. Suggest approaching chord changes at each bar line by half step or whole step to create a connected sound between chords.
- Although every player in the jazz ensemble is responsible for playing "in time," due to the nature of their traditional roles the bassist and drummer must work together to help everyone feel the steady pulse. Some refer to the bass, ride cymbal, and hi-hat as "the magic triangle." In swing-style playing, the drummer takes beats 1–2–3–4 from the bass, the bassist takes beats 2 and 4 from the hi-hat, and the drummer coordinates the ride and hi-hat.

- The bass is essential in jazz ensembles; however, in its absence, the bass notes can be played on an electronic keyboard.
- As with guitarists, encourage the bassist to self-tune quickly before the rehearsal.

Drum Set

- Drum set players should be aware of essential roles they serve in a jazz ensemble:
    - provide a steady pulse in conjunction with the bassist
    - play "grooves" matching the composition's style
    - reinforce rhythms that are played by the ensemble
    - help other players know exactly when to play ensemble figures by providing "setups"
    - emphasize the dynamic scheme, leading the band's dynamics from the drum stool
    - make all aware of phrase endings by improvising connector fills when appropriate
    - provide rhythmic interest in the swing style by keeping time, and also comping rhythms on both the snare drum and bass drum
    - provide an aural inspiration to other players in the ensemble.
- The drummer may have a difficult time seeing the director due to the setup, music stand placement, or parts of the drum set blocking the view. Stress the importance of "checking in" with the director; help the drummer find solutions.
- Drum parts for jazz charts (like piano) are often "over-written." The drummer often needs help deciphering notation because drummers are expected to improvise much of their part. Listen to recordings with student drummers; coach them to copy sounds of notable jazz drummers.

Vibraphone

- The vibes are usually considered *optional*, but including this instrument adds another interesting color to the jazz ensemble.
- Parts can include both melodic lines and chord symbols for comping.
- More advanced players will need to use four-mallet technique to effectively play chords.
- Vibe parts are often included with published arrangements; if not included, consider using a flute, guitar, or piano part. Directors can also create "custom-written" parts if a vibe part is not available.
- The contemporary trend is to not use the vibrato (the motor) in the jazz ensemble; however, vibrato can sometimes be effective on ballads featuring this instrument.
- Be sure that the vibes player comping doesn't create an overly "dense" texture if there is already a piano and guitar in the band. Be prepared to limit which instruments are comping.

Auxiliary Percussion

- Auxiliary percussion parts contribute much additional flavor to jazz arrangements. While it is especially common to add percussion to world music grooves, avoid overusing percussion just to keep players busy. For example, conga drums commonly provide rhythmic comping in some swing style grooves, but would be out of place and uncharacteristic in arrangements styled after the Count Basie Orchestra.
- Research world music grooves to find appropriate rhythms before adding percussion parts; then be sure that any added parts enhance the total arrangement without conflicting with the drum set part.
- Provide "custom-written" parts for extra percussionists or suggest that players experiment by writing their own ideas onto a copy of the drum set part.

The Role of the Conductor

This chapter has already included many specific strategies for jazz ensemble conductors but there are a few additional suggestions regarding how the conductor should lead performances.

- There is usually no need for the conductor to lead a jazz ensemble in the same manner as a concert band regardless of the age, experience, or development of the group.
- Do not use a baton.
- Once a piece is started, players will focus on the pulse from the rhythm section so there is no need for conductors to indicate pulse.
- On stage it is acceptable for the conductor to get out of the way; stand to the side of the band if there is nothing to show them.
- Conduct as much as needed in *rehearsals*, gradually withdrawing from conducting everything as the group gets closer to a performance.

The primary responsibilities of the conductor are to:

- provide the tempo and to start the composition. There are plenty of live concert videos of conductors counting off the start of the composition. Snap your fingers on beats two and four while speaking a count off, such as: 1 - - - | 2 - - - | 1–2 – | 1 2 3 4 |
- provide clear direction for tempo changes, fermatas, or the end of the song. These could all be conducted.
- provide important cues. The conductor needs to be aware of the form of the chart and indicate entrances and releases as needed.
- listen carefully, signaling adjustments to the balance and dynamic levels with subtle gestures.
- manage microphones if used. Be prepared to reposition mics during songs to accommodate each of the soloists.
- receive applause at the end of the song and to acknowledge soloists.

ABOUT THE CONTRIBUTORS

Christian Carichner serves as the Associate Director of Bands and Director of the Cyclone Marching Band at Iowa State University. He oversees all aspects of the Athletic Band program including the 350-member Iowa State University Cyclone Football "Varsity" Marching Band, Men's and Women's Basketball bands, Volleyball Band, Wrestling Band, and State Storm. In addition to his athletic band duties, Christian also conducts the Symphonic Band, teaches the Marching Band Methods course and instructs the applied Tuba and Euphonium studios. While serving as director of the Cyclone Marching Band, the band was awarded the prestigious Sudler Trophy—the highest honor bestowed upon a collegiate marching band in the United States. Christian served for many years as Brass Caption Head for the Phantom Regiment and the Academy Drum and Bugle Corps, as well as a lead brass instructor for the Aimachi Marching Band from Nagoya, Japan. Christian holds degrees in Music Education and Performance from Ithaca College and in Music Performance from Arizona State University where he studied with Sam Pilafian and Patrick Sheridan.

Daniel Fabricius currently serves on the faculty at Binghamton University as conductor of the Wind Symphony and at Ithaca College as an adjunct lecturer in Music Education. He had a long and successful career as a school band director in upstate New York and has taught in several areas of instrumental music, including concert band, jazz ensemble, marching band, pep band, and chamber music ensembles. Daniel has served the New York State School Music Association as an All-State adjudicator in both Percussion and Jazz and is also a Major Organization festival adjudicator for bands, orchestras, and jazz ensembles. In addition, he serves NYSSMA as the Instrumental Jazz Reviews editor of *The School Music News* and is the Jazz Ensemble Editor for the *NYSSMA Manual*. He also served a two-year term as the chairperson for the NYSSMA All-State Instrumental Jazz Ensemble. He is highly regarded as a conductor, percussion performer, and music educator.

Robin Linaberry retired after thirty-five years of distinguished work as Director of Music for Maine-Endwell Schools (Endwell, NY), where he conducted all aspects of this highly regarded high school band program. Robin supported the future of music education by hosting and mentoring nearly forty student teachers, and he served as an Adjunct conductor/instructor for Ithaca College, Binghamton University and SUNY-Broome CC. He is a state Chair for The National Band Association, conductor of the award-winning Southern Tier Concert Band, and Head Director Emeritus for the American Music Abroad Red Tour. His recognitions include special citations from MENC (the "Nationally Registered Music Educator" status), NYSSMA, the New York State Band Directors Association, and the "ASBDA-Stanbury Award" for the Northeast United States. He was the peer-chosen recipient of the "Founder's Day Award" and the "Golden Apple Award" for excellence in teaching in his district. He now works frequently as a conductor, performer, clinician, private teacher, adjudicator, and consultant.

INDEX

Page numbers in **bold** designate increased relevance to the term.

101 Rhythmic Rest Patterns (Yaus, Grover C.) 47

accommodations/modifications: for learners' needs 2, 44, 156, 163–165; for musical purposes 71, 160, 217, 230; for balance 132, 214; to increase engagement 136
acoustics: and ensemble tone 57, 59, 68; and tuning 85, 91; for rehearsals and performances 75, 92, 145
Adams, Bobby 66, 76n6, 175, 183–184, 187n4,n8,n11
adjudication: and scores 7; setting up for 140; and percussion 145; and feedback 149; and sightreading 154, 157; and portfolios 191, 193; and competition 195; and marching 205; and jazz 215
Aebersold, Jamey 37, 50
aleatoric 10
alternate fingerings: and score study 5, 7; and intonation 93–5; and teaching 182, 198
alternative rehearsal techniques **153–173**
alternative seating: and the band's sound 59, 75, 90–91; and percussion 145; and rehearsals 151, 154–155, 160–161; and auditions 189, 192, 196; in jazz ensemble 211, 217
analogies/metaphors: and the band's sound 59, 60–62, 64–66, 70–71, 75; and intonation 81; and rhythm 111, 121–124; in rehearsals 156; and interpretation 181, 182–183, 187n7
analysis: and score study 1, 5–7, 17, 22–23, 25, 30, 40, 161; self-analysis 133
Anderson, Leroy (*Sleigh Ride*) 30, 48
announcements 152, 159, 196
anonymity/anonymous 196–197
Arban method 43
Archer, Kimberly (*Awakenings*) 32
Armstrong, Louis 206
articulation: and score study 2, 22, 28; during warm-ups 34–35, 39, 43–44, 48; and tone quality 57, 60, 68–74; and rhythm 110, 112, 116, 121–124; and percussion 145; in the rehearsal 157, 161, 164, 166, 168–169, 172; and artistry 174, 183
artistry/artistic interpretation: and teaching xvi, xix, 174–185, 199; and conducting 5, 6; and adjudication 7; and score study 27; and warm-ups 36, 55; and the band's sound 62, 66; and intonation 89; and rhythm 104, 116, 121; and percussion 139, 145; in the rehearsal 149, 153, 155–156, 158–159
assessment 27, 180, 188–190, 207, 211
attendance 60, **152**, 159, 191, 193
attentiveness 1, 111, 126, 128, 138, 144, 157, **159**, 171, 172

audiate/audiation 82, 85, 116, 161, **168**
audition 41, 65, 75, 141–142, 188–189, 195–197
aural concept 1, 35, 57, 60, 155, 161–162
autostereogram 77

balance: and score study 7, 28; in warm-ups 34, 36, 40–41, 44, 46, 53; in the band's sound 57–59, 63–68, 75; intonation and 86, 91–92; and rhythm 102, 123; in percussion 128–129; rehearsal strategies for 156, 164, 166–167, 169, 172; in marching 207; in jazz ensembles 216, 223–225, 227–228, 230
beaming 123, **177**
Beeler, Walter 17, 21, 76, 101, 103, 113, 120–121, 126–127
Bernotas, Chris (*Sound Innovations for Concert Band*) 33, 41
Bernstein, Leonard: *Overture to Candide* 17, 21; *West Side Story* 49
best practice 2
Bierschenk, Donald (*Symphonic Band Technique*) 41
blend: 1; and warm-ups 36, 40–41, 53; and the band's sound 57, 59–60, 62–64, 67, 75; intonation and 91–92; in percussion 144; rehearsal strategies for 156, 169; in jazz ensemble 224
Boomwhackers 51, 102
Boonshaft, Peter (*Sound Innovations for Concert Band*) 33, 41
bopping strategies 101–103, 108, 112–113, 166, 168, 172
Boysen, Andrew Jr. (*Fantasy On A Theme By Sousa*) 29
breathing: in warm-ups 33, 34–36; and the band's sound 59–62; breath control 34, 62; using breath impulses 35, 101; for rhythm 123, 158; for interpretation 158–159, 174, 178, 180, 183; in marching band 206
Bukvich, Dan (*Voodoo*) 12
bulletin board 193, 198, 200; *see also* showcase

cadence: harmonic 28, 91, 174; melodic 39, 81, 174; percussion 41, 143
calendar 1, 200
call-and-response: in warm-ups 39, 49; and rhythm 98, 113; for percussionists 141; in rehearsals 168; in jazz 219
canon 22, 41, 44, 85–86, 90
Chaconne 21
chamber music 60, 80, 92, 154, 171, 192

233

INDEX

Chance, John Barnes *(Incantation and Dance)* 20
Charms Office Assistant 194
Chick Corea and The Elektric Band 226
chorales: "Instant" (impromptu) Chorales 41, **45, 50**, 86; in warm-ups 33, 36, 40–41, 44–47, 50, 54–55; and the band's sound 59, 64, 68, 72, 76; for tuning 83, 86, 90, 92; in rehearsals and concerts 129, 151, 160, 166, 168, 175, 178–180, 185
chord progression 45–46, 50, 87, 94, 169, 215, 226–227
Cichowicz, Vincent 73
Circle of 4ths (Circle of Keys) 36–40, 50, 53–55, 58, 84, 98, 222
clapping: exercises for conductors 6; in warm-ups 35; exercises for rhythm 98–100, 103–105, 110, 116, 119–121; and percussion 139; rehearsal strategies 154, 157–158, 166; for parade music selection 209
collection of papers/forms/music 120, 130, 151–152, 192–194
Colwell, Richard *(The Teaching of Instrumental Music)* 62, 129
communication: in conducting 5, 6, 13; in teaching 6, 28, 36, 94–95; non-verbal 51, 73, 125, 149, 156, 159, 181, 183–184; and salesmanship 68; written 136, 192, 199; in rehearsals 144, 149–150, 152, 155, 158–159, 173, 176, 179, 181; and engaging delivery 1, 68, 72, 95, 144, 150, 182–186, 187; and leadership 152, 193–194, 198–199, 211; *see also* director's delivery
compositional techniques: 12-tone 32; augmentation 22, 28–29, 45; cryptograms 29; diminution 22, 28–29; fragments 10, 20, 22, 28, 30, 41, 50, 105, 111; inversion 22, 28, 75, 87–88; modulation 5, 30; octatonic 32; quotation 22, 29; retrograde 28; serialism 29
comprehensive musicianship 25, 27, 84, 133, 136, 141, 145, 163
conducting: study 1, 6–7; gestures and movement in 5, 6, 14, 46, 67, 73, 86, 100, 104, 111, 124–125, 141, 146, 155–156, 183–184; and score study 10, 14, 17, 22, 28; cueing in 1, 5–8, 14–15, 17, 22, 27, 30, 63, 83, 86, 89–90, 109, 156, 172, 230; and teaching strategies 155–156, 159–160, 162, 230
context clues 177
Cook, Gary D. *(Teaching Percussion)* 128, 131
correspondence 199
countersubject 20
Crain, Richard 61
creativity xviii, 1, 3, 33, 51–52, 54–56, 86, 88, 90, 95, 171, 181–182
culture 1, 138–139, 182, 194–195, 211, 216, 219
curriculum 1, 27–28, 32–33, 60, 112, 117, 133, 137, 140–141, 143, 188–192, 214
Curwen, John (hand signals) 39, 50

Dartboard Challenge 88, 172
diagnosis-repair 152–153, 189
diaphragm 35, 60–62
director's delivery 158–159, 183; *see also* communication
divide and conquer 59, 166
Doyle, James 139
drill (marching) 202–207

drill (practice/rehearsal) 33, 120, 141, 175
drone 41, 44, 51, 78–83, 85–86, 89, 92, 167
Duffy, Thomas 185
DuFour, Richard *(Professional Learning Communities at Work)* 195
dynamics: 5, and conducting 6, 13; in warm-ups 36, 40; and the band's sound 57, 63–69, 75; and intonation 85, 88, 90, 93, 95–96; and rhythm 110, 116, 123–125; in the rehearsal 156–157, 160, 164, 166–167, 172; and artistry 174–175, 183–184; in marching band 205; in jazz ensemble 221, 229, 230; *see also* crescendo-decrescendo
crescendo-decrescendo 36, 76

Eagleman, David 4
ear training 77–78, 82, 84, 87, 112, 161
McBeth, W. Francis *(Effective Performance of Band Literature)* 57, 64–65
elimination game 170
embouchure 33, 35–36, 59–60, 69, 72, 78, 91, 221
emotion/emotional xvi, 69, 75, **156, 174–175**, 181, 184, 186, 195
emphasis (of musical elements) xvii, 121, 124, 166, 172, 175, 178–179, 183, 224, 229
encouragement 8, 36–37, 39, 60, 64, 71, 75, 77, 84, 89, 110, 133, 138, 144, **150–151**, 157, 159, 164, **169–171, 181–187**, 191, **197**, 205–207, 220, 227–229; *see also* motivation
endurance 34, 153, 168, 187
engagement: general xvi, xviii, xix; the engaging teacher 1, 56, 66, 72, 88, 97, 117, 128, 141–142, 150–151, 158–159, 182–184, 186, 194, 198–201, 221; engaging activities 4, 22, 29, 32–33, 63–64, 74, 77, 80, 98, 110, 122–123, 157–159, 163, 166, 168, 170, 173, 179, 181, 193; engaging larger numbers of students 18, 40, 44, 48, 79–80, 92, 100–101, 110, 122, 133–134, 136, 139, 142, 144–145, 154–155, 177–180, 185, 195; engaging the audience 145, 209
enharmonics 37, 39
ensemble (timing, precision) 43, 52, 99–102, 110, 112–114, 209
ensemble-to-director connection 104, 125, **160**
entrances: and the conductor's role 5–8, 19, 22, 27, 66, 206, 230; and precision 34, 104, 112, 120, 123, 168; and musicianship 72, 73, 102, 155, 156, 164, 169, 170
environment 1, 59, 129, 136, 144, 150, 152, 155, 161, 194, 199, 204–205, 213
EQ/equalizer 75
Erickson, Frank: *The Artistry of Fundamentals* 41; *Air for Band* 136
errata list 25
error identification (fault detection) 1, 93, 96, 152, 161
essential questions 140
executive presence 1, 186
exhale/exhaling/exhalation 34, 61–62, 206
expression/expressiveness 104, 116, 149, 156, 158–159, 162, 172, 174, **175–185**, 200

feedback: from score study 7, 22; in warm-ups 40, 48; for the band's sound 59, 64, 68, 70–71, 76; for intonation 79, 82–83, 89, 92, 96; for rhythm 113; for percussion 139, 144; in rehearsals 149–150, 152,

234

154–155, 157–159, 170, 173, 187; for marching band 205, 207; for jazz ensembles 220–221
Feldman, Evan and Contzius, Ari (*Instrumental Music Education*) 68, 77, 114, 118, 120, 150, 152, 168, 175, 191, 197
Feldman, Evan (*The Rehearsal Toolkit*) 77, 168, 175
filing (storage) 132, 192–194
first reading 157
first-in last-out philosophy 67, 70
Firth, Vic 40, 131
flexibility 34, 36, 43, 68, 76
Flippity 171
Floyd, Richard (*The Artistry of Teaching and Making Music*) 34, 66, 70, 75, 89, 175
fluency: and the teacher 2, 15, 115; development of 97, 120–122, 153, 176–177; movement and 103, 105
Fonder, Mark xx, 129, 175
form (compositional technique) 23–25, 30, 45, 158
form (jazz) 221, 226, 230
form (marching) 206–207
form (score study) 5–7, 18, 23, 25, 30
Forque, Charles E. (*Harmonized Rhythms for Concert Band*) 53
fugue 19–20, 66, 84
fundamental (acoustics) 57; *see also* partials (acoustics)
fundamentals (performance skills) 28, 30, 34–35, 41, 55, 59–60, 169, 185–187, 215
funneling strategy 153

Galante, Rossano (*Cry of the Last Unicorn*) 181
Gilbert, Kristen *Centurion* 9; *Via La Acadia* 14; *Jubilation* 17
Gilroy, Gary (*Spitfire!*) 22–23
Girsberger, Russ (*Percussion Assignments for Band & Wind Ensemble*) 131
Gordon, Edwin (*Music Learning Theory*) 115–116
grading policy **191–192**
Grainger, Percy 14–15, 25
Green, Elizabeth A.H. (*The Modern Conductor*) 32n2
Gregson, Edward (*Festivo*) 49
groove (jazz ensemble) 219–220, 222, 229
groove (marching band) 205–206
grooves 32, 47, 49, 104–105, 110, 122, 141, 148
guest artists/performers 59, 169, 172

hand signals and signs 39, 50–51, 83, 86, 156, 167
handbells 52, 102
handbook/band handbook 191–192, 199
handouts 151–152
Hanson, Howard (*Chorale and Alleluia*) 131
harmonic analysis 5–6, 17, 22, 25
harmonics 78, 91
Harmonized Rhythms for Concert Band 53
Hazo, Samuel (*Our Yesterdays Lengthen Like Shadows*) 88
help sheet 137, 156, 190, 193
hemiola 21–22
Hewitt, Michael 62, 129
highlighter tape 6, 22
hissing 34, 206
hocket 52
Holsinger, David (*Havendance*) 13

Holst, Gustav: *First Suite in E-Flat for Military Band* 21–22, 158; *Hammersmith* 130
How to Play Jazz & Improvise 50

imagery 62, 168, 182–183
improvise/improvisation 215, 217, 220–221, 224, 226, 229
IMSLP: the International Music Score Library Project 54
inflection 109, 114, 149, 175–180, 184
inhale/inhaling/inhalation 34, 61–62, 206
instrumentation in jazz ensemble 214–215, 217
instrumentation: incomplete/imbalanced 68, **164**, 199, 203, 209, 214–215, 217
intangible 57, **174–187**
intellectual processes 175–176
internal clock (pulse, rhythm, subdivision) 35, 54, 97–104, 110, 114, 122
interpretation: and score study 5–7, 26; in warm-ups 36, 44, 55; in the band's sound 60, 64, 66, 68–71, 74; and rhythm 97, 114, 116, 124–125; in the rehearsal 155, 157, 159, 167–170, 172; and the Intangibles **174–185**; other 1, 199; in marching 202; in jazz 217, 219, 225, 227
intervals: and playing 22, 33, 36, 39–40, 43, 49; and hearing 55, 78–83, 85, 92–93, 140; in marching 207
intervention 31, 130, 133, 137, 164–165
intonation and tuning xvi, xviii, 1, 30, 34, 36, 54–55, 57, 63–64, 68, **77–96**, 150, 155, 164, 216, 221, 224, 225; *see also* intonation
intonation: and acoustics 85, 91–92; and beats 39, 55, 77–79, 81, 83, 85, 89, 94, 95; "intonation map" 85, 93; markings for 80–81, 90, 94; the tuner 77–79, 82, 84, 88–89, 91, 93–94, 151, 228; tuning strategies xviii, 7, 19, 27–28, 30, 36, 39–40, 55, 64, 75, 77–96, 133, 137, 139–140, 144, 146, 147, 151, 159, 164, 167–169, 171–172, 223, 225; using targets in tuning 40, 77, 81–82, 91, 94; *see also* intonation and tuning
intramural music 170
isolation 46, 52–53, 63, 81–82, 89, 94, 112–113, 120, 153–154, 161, 166, 168, 170
It-Factor 174, 185–186, 194

Jacobs, Arnold 73
Jagow, Shelley (author) 154, 156, 175
Jagow, Shelley (*Tuning for Wind Instruments*) 77
jazz 32, 37, 41, 49–50, 71, 91, 123–124, 192, **214–230**
Jazz Ensemble (chapter) **214–230**
Jazz Ensemble: acoustic bass in 215, 228; adaptable charts for 215; altered chords 220, 223; articulation in 216, 221, 224; auxiliary percussion in 216, 229; ballads 217, 220–221, 229; bass and basslines 214–217, 224, **226–229**; call-and-response in 219; Circle of 4ths in 222; color notes in 223, 229; double-time swing 217; doubling 215, 225, 227; drum set 214, 216, **226–229**; extended harmonies 220, 223; flugelhorn 216, 225; form in 221, 226, 230; grooves 219, **220**, 222, 229; guitar 214, 216, 224, 227, **228**, 229; improvisation 215, 217, **220–221**, 224, 226, 229; instrumentation **214–215**, 217; jamming 226, 227; effects 216, **219**, 224; jazz styles 216, **217–221**, 223–224, 228–229; jazz vocalists 216, **221**; literature selection for 214,

INDEX

215–216, 225; mutes 215, **225**; piano 214, 216, 220, **227–228**, 229; rhythm section 216, 221-2, 224, **226–30**; saxophones 216, **224–225**; setups for 214, **216–217**, 229; soloists 214–6, **220–221**, 224–225, 227, 230; swing 216, **217–220**, 223, 228–229; the role of the jazz conductor **230**; trombones 214, 216, **225**, 226; trumpets 214, 216, 220, **225**; vibraphone in 216, **229**

Jazz Handbook, The 37, 50; see also Aebersold, Jamey

Kabalevsky, Dmitri (*Colas Breugnon, Overture to*) 16
Key Sequences: Warmups for Band 38, 41
key signature 37, 55, 92, 157
Kirchhoff, Craig (*The Plus and Minus Method*) 66, 175
Klangfarbenmelodie 53, 54
Kodály, Zoltán 39, 50, 115

La Fiesta Mexicana (H. Owen Reed) 9
landmarks (aural) 112, 123
landmarks (rehearsal) 7, 158
language (as a teaching tool) 71–72, 97, 105, 113–115, 117, 124, 126, 144–145, 149–150, 176, 178, 181, 221
layering/layers 4, 59, 64, 67, 112, 122, 169, 171
leaders/leadership 65, 78, 104, 139–140, 145, 150–152, 158, 161–162, 171, 180, 191, 193–195, 198, 200, 203, 207–208
Leinsdorf, Erich (*The Composer's Advocate*) 6
Levitin, Daniel 97
linking (strategy) 166
Lisk, Edward 36–38, 44, 50, 53, 58–59, 64, 84, 98, 101, 161
Lisk, Edward (*The Creative Director: Alternative Rehearsal Techniques*) 36–37, 44, 50, 58, 84, 98, 101
listening 5, 25, 28–29, 33, 35–36, 48, 54, 63, 73, 75, 89, 91, 94, 100, 110, 114, 121, 159, 169, 186, 205, 226
listening: and plugging ears 83, 169; audio anchors 168; critical listening 66, 169, 185–6; listening guides 169, 185; record-playback strategies 6, 28, 35, 66, 70–73, 75, 78, 89–90, 98, 101, 109–111, 121–122, 125, 142, 154, 158, 161–162, 169, 171, 175, 180, 184–186, 191, 193, 195–198, 220; the "playing in trios" concept 64, 89, 169
listening (activities for) 25, 29, 41, 48, 63, 66, 70, 73, 83, 85, 89, 92, 110, 154, 157, 160–161, 167–170, 185, 193, 217, 221
listening (skills in) 34, 36, 40, 53, 55, 66, 77, 79, 85, 87–89, 96, 110, 143, 156–157, 169, 216
literature/repertoire selection 71, 129–130, 132, 189, 198, 214–216
Lo Presti, Ronald (*Elegy For A Young American*) 90
long tones: in warm-ups 33, 35, 51; for the band's sound 62, 64, 68, 76; for tuning 82, 87; in rehearsals 168; in Jazz ensembles 221, 222
loop/looping 28, 41, 48, 110, 112, 121
lungs/lung capacity 34, 60–62

macro-micro-macro 152–153, 159
march/marches/marching 25, 41, 45, 52, 74, 97–98, 110–11, 143, 145, 147, 168, 185, 192, 202–213, 217
marching/marching band xix, 143, 197, 202–213

marching band: commands in 208; drill in 202–207; form in 206–207; Groove exercise in 205–206; parades and parading 202, 206–211; pep band 202, 211–212; "Plus One - Minus One" strategy in 206–207; programming in 205, 209; shows and show-design in 202–206, 209; stadium 206, 211–212; storyboard for 204; subdivision of the foot shape for 207; timing in 202, 205–207; triangle in 208; uniforms 205, 212
Marching Percussion 101: Essential Drumline Warmups (Mason, Brian S.) 40
Maslanka, David *(Collected Chorale Settings)* 54
Mason, Brian S. *(Marching Percussion 101: Essential Drumline Warmups)* 40
Mason, Lowell 114, 115
McBeth, W. Francis: *Effective Performance of Band Literature* 57, 64–65, 161; Pyramid balance concepts 57, 59, 64–65
McKee, M. Max 135
measure numbers 5, 8, 120
measure repeat sign 26
mechanics 33, 103
Meeks, Dan (*Technicises for Band*) 41, 53
Melillo, Steven (*Function Chorales*) 54
melody: and score study 6–7, 16–17, 21, 30; in warm-ups 52–53; in the band's tone quality 66, 68; for intonation improvements 81, 83, 92, 94; in rhythmic exercises 101, 122; and percussion 136; and rehearsal strategies 157, 167–169, 171; and marching band 209; and jazz band 221, 223, 226–227
mentoring/mentors 60, 78, 134, 144–145, 195, 197
meter signatures 10, 97, 99, 110, 115, 116, 117, 118, 119, 120, 124, 125
meter signatures: and conducting 1, 5–6, 13–14, 47, 100, 104; and movement 97, 104; and music reading 97, 116–120, 189; markings for 13, 15, 22, 118–119; meter changes 5, 13–14, 125; odd/irregular/asymmetric 15, 39, 44, 48, 101, 104–105, 113, 118, 216, 220
method books 29–30, 53, 103, 120, 150, 188–189, 192, 197
metronome/metronomic 6, 28, 35, 71, 77, 98–99, 105, 109–112, 121, 139, 142, 154, 156, 189, 190, 205, 208, 224
metronomic steps/increments 154, 156
modeling/demonstrations: and conducting 6; call-and-response 48–49; and phrases 17; and breathing 34, 60, 83; and role-models 56, 199; the importance of modeling 59; for tone 59–60; for articulation 68–73; and descriptors 75–76; for intonation 78; for pulse and rhythm 98, 110–111, 113, 115, 119, 123, 125; for percussion 136, 138–139, 142–143, 146; in rehearsals 149, 152, 155–157, 160, 165, 167–168, 172; using language 176, 178–179, 181, 185–187; for jazz performance 219
motif/motive 7, 10, 20, 157, 163
motivation/motivational 2, 30, 60, 71, 129, 141, 144, 149–150, 159, 183, 187, 191, 195, 197
mouthpiece buzzing 35, 68, 73, 83
Murphy's Law 151, 172
muscle memory 41
music history 25, 114, 118, 198

236

INDEX

music theory 7, 25, 32, 37, 41, 46, 54, 119
musicianship 25, 27–28, 36, 50, 84, 127, 144, 163, 169, 174, 186

National Band Association 198
Newell, David (*Teaching Rhythm*) 97, 109, 116, 118, 126
non-harmonic tones 7, 22
note-grouping 36, 70, 121, 125

objectives sheet 190
Occam's Razor 69
oral cavity/shape 59–60, 63, 71–72, 83
orchestration 17, 30, 90
ostinati 20–22, 66
"overlap" strategies 66, 112, 154, 166, 167
overtones 57; *see also* partials (acoustics)

PACE – The Performance Achievement Cumulative Evaluation 190, 197
pacing 1, 154, **159**, 185, 194
page turn 5–8, 25, 28, 131, 161
partials (acoustics) 57, 84, 94–95
Paulson, John (*Epinicion*) 10–11
Pearson, Bruce 135
percussion (general) xvii, xix, 1, 7, 20, 28, 40–41, 48, 51, 101, 109, 126, **128–148**
percussion: and acoustics 78, 92, 145; and notation 7, 12, 27, 130, 146; body percussion 52; cadences and grooves 41, 49, 105, 110; the conductor's perspective 27, **143–148**; curriculum information for **140–143**; ensembles 40, 52, 141, 145; marching percussion 40, 143, 145, 147, **210–211**; number of required players 129, 131, 138, 143; part assignments for 27, **129–136**, 146; repertoire selection and 129–130; rudiments 28, 30, 137, 143, 151, 189–190; section culture and identity 138–140; sticks/mallets/strokes 35, 69, 73; storage 145
percussionists xix, 27, 34–36, 40–41, 51, 56, 60, 63, 66, 80, 92, 105, 128–148
percussion materials: *All-Inclusive Audition Etudes* (Willie, Eric and Hill, Julie) 141; *Alfred's Drum Method* (Feldstein, Sandy) 141; *Audition Etudes* (Whaley, Garwood) 141; *The Drummer's Daily Drill* (DeLucia, Dennis) 141; *Percussion Section Techniques* (Grimo and Snider) 141; *Percussion With Class* (Wallace, Douglas B.) 141; *The Rudiments Inventory* (Linaberry, Robin) 143
"Percussion 21" game strategy 141
Percussion Day 145
phrasing: and artistry 6, 17, 36, 40, 41, 44, 60, 75, 82, 149–150, 157–158, 160, 172, **174–181**, **183–184**; and breathing 34, 40, 60, 62, 75, 82, 157, 160–161, 166, 172, 174, 178, 183; diagramming 15–17; length 6, 8, 15–17, 41; odd/asymmetric length 15–17; and rehearsal strategies 2, 7–8, 15, 75, 149–150, 157–158, 160–161, 166, 172, 174, 178, 181, 183–184, 229; and score study 7–8, 15–17, 21, 158, 161
Pilafian, Sam (*The Breathing Gym*) 62, 205–206
pitch awareness 33, 77–79, 81–83, 90, 93–96, 133, 168; *see also* auditory acuity
pitch bending 78–79, 83
play-through 152–153

pointillism 52
portfolios/portfolio assessment 133, 191
positioning (hand position, play position) 34, 35–36, 59, 61, 69, 71–72, 83, 145, 160, 207–208, 227
posture 33–36, 59–61, 69, 83, 145, 170, 202
"power of the pencil" lesson 180
principal players 40, 79, 85, 89–90, 110, 121, 145, 156, 160, 168–169, 171–172, 193, 198
print-to-speech 176
Prism Concert 140, 185
private study 60, 197
Probasco, Jim (*Technicises for Band*) 41, 53
processing disorder 2
prompts and prompting 61, 66, 73, 77–78, 141, 144, 169, 174, 178–179, 186
punctuation 176–178
pyramid (acoustics for the band's sound) 57–59, 64–65, 68, 75, 172, 183

QR codes 59, 143, 193
Quick-Fix strategies: for breathing 62; for blend 62–64; for dynamics and balance 64–67; for the band's overall sound 75; for intonation 95–96; for pulse 98–99; for precision 112–113; for rhythm 122–124; for tempo and meter 124–127; for percussion 136; in the rehearsal 172; for the *Intangibles* 183–185; for marching band 205–208
quotes 152, 182–183, 198–199

randomness (as a teaching strategy) 66, 88–89, 166, 168, **171–172**, 217
range 34, 66, 71, 90–91, 93, 96, 189–190, 205, 215, 221, 225
reading (as a musical skill): overview 1; and score study 27; during warm-ups 41, 47, 54; "The Need to Read Rhythm" 114, 122, 126; for percussionists 133, 136, 138, 140, 143, 145; sight-reading 154–155, 157, 168, 185, 188–190; score-reading 159, 168, 185; connections to speech and reading 176–177; beaming and fluency 177–179; in jazz instruction 215, 219, 226–228
reading (as a text skill) 176–177
recital day 171
recruitment/retention 68, 198, 202, 203
Reed, Alfred (*Armenian Dances, Part 1*) 48
Reed, H. Owen (*La Fiesta Mexicana*) 9
rehearsal numbers/letters 5, 7–8, 18, 25, 90, 109, 144, 154, 158, 166, 168
rehearsal techniques (general) 22, 67, 83, **149–173**, 205–206, 210, 221
rehearsal techniques: alternative seating arrangements 160–161; customizing strategies 170; error detection and solutions **161–166**; feedback in 149–150, 158–160; methods and strategies **152–158**; promoting student engagement **166–167**; quick-fix tips 172; rehearsal games and diversions **170–172**; the room/setup/environment **150–152**; singing- and listening-based strategies **167–169**
Reineke, Steven: *Sedona* 18; *Fate of the Gods* 165; *River of Life* 29
releases 34, 67–70, 73, 125, 169, 174, 182–183, 206, 224, 230
Remington, Emory (*The "Remington"*) 36, 40, 86

237

INDEX

repetition 4, 22, 33, 71, 161–162, 172, 175, 187, 205, 207–208
resonance 36, 54, 59, 68, 70, 83, 91–92
Rhodes, Tom C. (*Symphonic Band Technique*) 41
rhythm **97–127**
rhythm: books/sheets/exercises 43–50, 52–53, 68, 70–71, 97–127, 139, 155–157, 166–167, 172; counting/count-offs 8, 20, 88, 98–101, 105, 109, 111, 114–117, 120, 123–125, 131, 155, 158, 171, 183, 207–208, 230; dictation 117, 120; fluency 97, 103, 105, 115, 120–122, 127, 176–177; movement/eurhythmics 97–98, 103–105, 109, 114, 116, 121, 124, 154, 167, 174, 176, 185; note-grouping 121, 125; precision 34–35, 37, 43, 52–53, 57, 60, 67–68, 71, 101–102, 104, 108, 110, 112–113, 120, 123, 169; pulse 35, 40, 43–44, 47, 54, 71, 97–100, 102, 104–105, 109–112, 114, 119–120, 123, 125–126, 138, 143, 168, 170, 172, 205, 207, 228–230; reading/learning 1, 33, 37, 47, 97, 105, 109, 113–120, 122–126, 177, 217, 219; rhythmic "homonyms" 117, 120; rhythmic syllable systems 115, 219
rotate parts 130, 166
rote teaching 40, **49–52**, 83, 113–114, 124
rubric 180–181, **189–192**, 195–196
Rudgers, Gregory 175
Rudiments Inventory, The (Linaberry, Robin) 143
Ruler of Time, The (Lisk, Ed) 37, 101
Rush, Scott 190

salesmanship (persuasiveness) 33, 66, 146, 198
scales: and articulation 35, 68; building a scale 43–44; and the Circle of 4ths 37–40, 44, 50; and dynamics 64; and improvising 220; and rhythm 43–44, 48, 100, 105, 125, 190; and tone 59; and transposition 55, 92; and tuning 55, 79–81, 83, 90, 92–93; as fundamental skills 20, 28, 35, 39, 41, 50; during warm-ups 33, 36, 39–44, 51; expanding scales 36, 43–44; scale canons 41–42, 44, 85–86, 90; scale degrees 50, 79–81, 86; scale games and strategies 36, 39, 41, 48, 52–55, 83, 85–87, 89, 92–94, 109, 160, 178, 185, 190
scores and score study: general score study xvi, xvii, xviii, 1, 4, **5–32**, 155, 161, 163, 172, 198; cutaway/open scores 11–12; full/condensed scores 7, 10, 25, 27; marking of 1, 5–17, 20–22, 28, 116, 176; playing from 28, 157
seating plan/arrangement 59, 75, 145, 151, 154–155, 160
section leaders 78, 104, 110, 130, 136, 145, 152, 158, 162, 180, 193, 195, 205, 208
sectional rehearsal 75, 140–141, 154, 195
self-development 7
Selmer Band Manual, The (Hovey, Nilo) 179
Shapiro, Alex: *Lights Out!* 123, 185; *Paper Cut* 170; *Tight Squeeze* 32
Sheridan, Patrick *(The Breathing Gym)* 62, 205–206
showcase 193, 198, 200; *see also* bulletin board
sight reading 41, 47, 54, 114, 140, 154, 157, 168, 185, 188–190
SightReadingFactory, The 189
silent rehearsal 156
"simultaneous rehearsal" strategies 18–20, 22, 39–40, 54, 83–84, 105, 122, 163

singing 35, 48–50, 55, 63, 68, 71, 78, **82–83**, **86–87**, 92, 98, 105, 114, 119–120, 124, 154, 156–157, 166, **167–169**, 205, 219, 221
SMART Goal 190
SmartMusic 28, 90, 190
Smith, Claude T.: *Declaration Overture* 19; *Emperata Overture* 20; *Eternal Father, Strong To Save* 31, 109, 165; *Symphonic Warm-Ups for Band* 41
Solfege 17, 50–51, 83, 86, 161, 167
sorter 152, 192–193
Sound Innovations for Concert Band: Ensemble Development 33, 41
sound-before-symbol (*sound-to-symbol*) philosophy 97, 114, 119
sound-color melody 53
Sousa, John Philip (*The Fairest of the Fair*) 29, 45, 83
Sparke, Phillip (*Yorkshire Overture, A*) 26–27
Spartan Proclamation 46–47
speech 72, 111, 114, 145, 175–178; *see also* language
Starnes, David (*Colors of Sound*) 75
start-stop technique 153, 162
straight-line sound 62, 78, 88
stretches 34
Strommen, Carl 185
structured chaos 156, 158
student-centered philosophy 66, 69, 73, 111, 144, 155, 160, 199
style (in branding) 212
style (in performance) 1, 17, 22, 35, 40, 47–48, 68, 71, 74, 95, 97, 104, 123–125, 150, 158, 163, 167, 175, 183
style (in jazz) 214, 216–217, 219, 221, 223–224, 228–229
style (in learning, cognitive) 2–3, 133
style (of teaching, delivery, management) 95, 114, 126, 150–151, 158, 178, 181–182, 198
subdivision/subdivide 98–104, 110, 112–115, 118–120, 122, 126, 205, 207–208, 217
summer camps 60, 197
Swan Parallel, The 126, 182
Swearingen, James 181
system divider/separator 9–10

Teaching Music Through Band Performance 198
Technicises for Band 41, 53
technique (in performance) 1, 7, 26–27, 30, 35–36, 40, 51, 60, 71, 78, 94, 111–112, 121, 128, 139, 143, 145, 148, 150–151, 156, 164, 168–169, 175, 184, 202–203, 205, 225, 228–229
techniques (in composition) 28, 29, 32, 52, 53
techniques (in rehearsal/teaching) 1–2, 33, 36, 72, 77, 81, 92, 101–103, 113, 125–126, 129, 146, 152, 154, 156, 160, 167–168, 170, 175, 184, 202, 206–207
tempo **97–127**, 154, 156, 169, 172, 175, 205
tetrachords 85
texture 17, 28, 30, 36, 53, 66, 75, 112, 183, 228–229
The Composer's Advocate 6
The Modern Conductor 32n2
Thornton, James 53
Thornton, Paula 59
timpani (tuning of) 27, 91–92, 131, 133, 137–140, 144, 147

INDEX

tonal bass drums 143
TonalEnergy tuner app 94
tone/tone quality (overview) **57–76**
tone/tone quality: and acoustics 57, 59, 68, 75; tone generator 77–78; development of **35**, 57
tracking (visual) 160
transposition/transposing 1, 7, 25, 39, 50, 54–55, 83, 90, 92, 189
Treasury of Scales 40, 53, 90, 185
tremolo 26, 198
tuning and intonation: overview **77–96**; and problems 7, 27, 81, 90, 169; *see also* intonation

Vaughan-Williams, Ralph 167
vertical harmonies 7

vocabulary 27–28, 66, 68, 105, 112, 146, 156, 215, 220
voice-leading 80–81, 227–228
Vollmer, Jamie (*The Blueberry Story*) 200
volunteers/volunteerism 28, 63, 85, 98, 100, 124, 129, 139–140, 150, 170, 177, 192–193, 198

Wagner, Sally 68
warm-ups **33–56**
Watkins–Farnum Performance Scale 189, 197
Wheel of Names 171–172
Why Music Matters (Stamp, Jack) 185
Wong, Harry K. and Rosemary T. 152

Yaus, Grover C. (*101 Rhythmic Rest Patterns*) 47
YouTube 5, 28, 110–111, 143, 181, 185

Taylor & Francis eBooks

www.taylorfrancis.com

A single destination for eBooks from Taylor & Francis with increased functionality and an improved user experience to meet the needs of our customers.

90,000+ eBooks of award-winning academic content in Humanities, Social Science, Science, Technology, Engineering, and Medical written by a global network of editors and authors.

TAYLOR & FRANCIS EBOOKS OFFERS:

- A streamlined experience for our library customers
- A single point of discovery for all of our eBook content
- Improved search and discovery of content at both book and chapter level

REQUEST A FREE TRIAL
support@taylorfrancis.com